Schriften zum Recht der Digitalisierung

Herausgegeben von

Florian Möslein, Sebastian Omlor und Martin Will

44

Control and Ownership of Digital Assets

A Comparative Law Survey

Edited by
Mirjam Eggen, Linda Jeng and Sebastian Omlor

Mohr Siebeck

Mirjam Eggen is a full professor of private law and co-director of the Civil Law Institute at the University of Bern's Faculty of Law.

Linda Jeng is a visiting scholar on financial technology at the Institute of International Economic Law, Georgetown University Law Center, and CEO of Digital Self Labs.

Sebastian Omlor is a full professor of private law, commercial and business law, banking law, and comparative law and the co-director of the Institute for Law and Regulation of Digitalization (IRDi) at Marburg University's Faculty of Law.

ISBN 978-3-16-200134-4 / eISBN 978-3-16-200135-1
DOI 10.1628/978-3-16-200135-1

ISSN 2700-1288 / eISSN 2700-1296 (Schriften zum Recht der Digitalisierung)

The Deutsche Nationalbibliothek lists this publication in the Deutsche Nationalbibliographie; detailed bibliographic data are available at *https://dnb.dnb.de.*

Published by Mohr Siebeck Tübingen 2026.

Printed on non-aging paper.

Mohr Siebeck GmbH & Co. KG, Wilhelmstraße 18, 72074 Tübingen, Germany
www.mohrsiebeck.com, info@mohrsiebeck.com

Foreword

The rise of blockchain-based systems and digital assets has compelled courts, legislators, and regulators to confront foundational questions of private law. Central to these debates is the issue of *control*: who, in legal terms, has the ability to exercise dominion over a digital asset, to exclude others from it, and to transfer it to another? For much of the early history of digital assets, this appeared relatively straightforward. Externally-owned accounts (EOAs) premised on a single private key linked technical control and legal ownership in an apparently seamless way. Many early legal analyses, and even legislative frameworks, implicitly assumed this model, grounding the attribution of ownership in the possession of the key.

Yet this technical landscape has shifted dramatically. In the interest of enhanced security, user experience, and operational resilience, key management systems have evolved. Multi-signature arrangements, threshold signature schemes, multi-party computation (MPC) wallets, and account-abstraction mechanisms now distribute control across multiple actors or embed it within automated processes. These developments sever the simple one-to-one relationship between a single private key and legal ownership, raising complex questions for private commercial law. Frameworks premised on earlier wallet models risk obsolescence unless they adapt to these new realities.

This volume seeks to explore precisely this tension. It brings together leading scholars and practitioners to examine how diverse legal systems – both common law and civil law, national and international – approach the questions of control and ownership of digital assets. The comparative inquiry reveals not only doctrinal differences, but also shared concerns over legal certainty, market efficiency, and the adaptation of traditional legal categories to new technologies.

The chapters traverse a wide range of jurisdictions. Contributions from Germany, France, Switzerland, and Australia illustrate how civil law systems grapple with the limitations of traditional doctrines of tangibility and experiment with electronic securities legislation. The United States chapter analyzes the introduction of Article 12 to the Uniform Commercial Code, with its creation of "controllable electronic records," and its attempt to extend concepts of negotiability and secured transactions to crypto-assets. The United Kingdom and Brazil chapters demonstrate how common law and hybrid systems have sought to adapt flexible doctrines to novel technical architectures. The Hong Kong and Singapore chapters show how Asian common law jurisdictions combine pragmatic judicial reasoning with increasingly granular regulatory oversight, particularly in relation to custody and safekeeping. The Mexico chapter highlights how pioneering statutory definitions – such as those in the 2018 Fintech Act – proved both innovative and unduly narrow, creating gaps in the classification of assets under private law. The Taiwan chapter examines the courts' characterization of virtual assets as "movable things," while suggesting a shift toward a ledger-based model of public notice. Finally, the chapter on UNIDROIT's Digital Assets and Private Law Principles (DAPL) situates these national approaches within an emerging body of international soft law, where the concept of "control" serves as a functional analogue to possession.

Taken together, these contributions illustrate convergence in recognizing that digital assets must be capable of being treated as objects of property rights, while also exposing divergence in the doctrinal and institutional means by which that recognition is achieved. Some systems rely on legislative innovation, others on judicial creativity, and still others on contractual devices that fill the gaps left by statutory law.

This project originated in the recognition that private law frameworks continue to serve as the backbone of global commerce, and that they must now adapt to a technological environment in which control is no longer synonymous with the knowledge of a single private key. The editors were motivated by the conviction that without legal clarity, uncertainty in areas such as insolvency, enforcement, and cross-border disputes will proliferate, to the detriment of both users and institutions. Conversely, with careful doctrinal analysis and comparative engagement, private law can continue to perform its essential functions of structuring ownership, enabling transfer, and protecting legitimate expectations in commerce.

It is our hope that this volume will serve both as a reference for scholars, practitioners, and policymakers, and as a catalyst for further research and reform. The reconciliation of centuries-old concepts of ownership and possession with digital-native assets is among the central legal challenges of our time. By drawing together insights from across jurisdictions, the contributions collected here aim to advance a shared understanding of how private law can evolve to meet this challenge.

This outcome would not have been possible without the invaluable support of our research staff Patricia Sanchez, Michael Toneatti, and Hans Wilke. We also gratefully acknowledge the Ripple Impact Fund for covering the publication costs of this open access book.

Bern, Washington D.C., and Marburg, October 2025

Mirjam Eggen, Linda Jeng and Sebastian Omlor

Table of Contents

Australia

Scott Farrell and Max Allan

I. Introduction

"What is it about cryptocurrency that makes it a kind of property? Most fundamentally, the answer lies in the fact that it is actively bought and sold, and it is therefore sufficiently analogous to things which are already treated as property. And it would not be actively bought and sold unless it was sufficiently definable, identifiable by third parties, capable of assumption by third parties, and permanent and stable. These are all relative concepts and raise questions of degree."[1]

[1] *Justice Jackman*, Is Cryptocurrency Property?, Speech of 21 June 2024, <https://www.fedcourt.gov.au/digital-law-library/judges-speeches/justice-jackman/jackman-j-20240621> (16 September 2025) 14.

Digital assets are becoming more prevalent in Australia's financial services and markets. As in other jurisdictions, their use is progressing from 'digital asset natives' to everyday investors and market participants. This has drawn into focus the need to answer key questions of personal property law. As shown by the above extra-curial quotation from an Australian judge, the first question – how digital assets are treated as property – is being answered. However, more questions of high relevance to commercial practice remain, such as how interests in that property, including security interests, can be established and protected.

This chapter explains the recent Australian judicial decision that answered the question of whether digital assets are property under Australian law, and how that answer differs from some other jurisdictions. Then, it examines the relevance of control in the treatment of interests in digital assets as property under Australia's common law,[2] and its two most relevant legislative security regimes. It touches on how those legislative regimes deal with the unresolved choice of law questions related to digital assets and concludes by identifying areas where Australian law could be developed to provide further certainty to support the use of digital assets in Australia's financial markets and systems.

II. Property in digital assets under Australian law

Although there have been many Australian cases concerning digital assets,[3] Australian courts have taken their time in clarifying that digital assets are property under Australian law. In fact, it wasn't until November 2024 that a superior Australian court determined upon a trial of a proceeding that an interest in a digital asset is property.[4]

In *Re Blockchain Tech Pty Ltd*,[5] the Supreme Court of Victoria decided that an interest in bitcoin was property under Australian law, constituted a chose in action, and could be the subject of a trust. The court also found that an interest

---

[2] In this chapter, the term "common law" is used in contrast with legislation and it includes principles of equity.

[3] E.g., *Australian Securities and Investments Commission (ASIC) v. Web3 Ventures Pty Ltd* [2025] FCAFC 58; *Australian Securities and Investments Commission (ASIC) v. Finder Wallet Pty Ltd* [2024] FCA 228; *Australian Securities and Investments Commission (ASIC) v. BPS Financial Pty Ltd* [2024] FCA 457; *Australian Securities and Investments Commission (ASIC) v. Bit Trade Pty Ltd* [2024] FCA 953.

[4] Some Australian courts have determined or proceeded up to an interlocutory application on the basis that a person's interest in a digital asset is property: *Australian Securities and Investments Commission v. NGS Crypto Pty Ltd* (No. 3) [2024] FCA 822. In others, digital assets were in effect assumed to be property, e.g., *Commissioner of the Australian Federal Police v. Bigatton* [2020] NSWSC 245; *Chen v. Blockchain Global Limited* [2022] 66 VR 30. See also *Jackman*, Property (n. 1).

[5] *Re Blockchain Tech Pty Ltd* [2024] VSC 690.

in bitcoin could not be the subject of a bailment under Australian law because it was not tangible and could not be possessed.

Like decisions in other common law jurisdictions, the Court applied the principles set out by Lord Wilberforce in *National Provincial Bank v. Ainsworth*,[6] namely that the bitcoin was identifiable subject matter, identifiable by third parties, capable of assumption by third parties and had some degree of permanence and stability.[7] In doing so, the Court gave some important clarifications as to how these principles are to be applied to digital assets under Australian law:

- *Digital assets can fall within the broad meaning of property.* Property goes beyond traditional definitions of something that belongs to another or 'a bundle of rights'. It refers to a degree of power exercised over a thing that is permissibly recognised by the law. An interest in bitcoin can fall within that description, as a unique digital address on a network of computers, identifiable by third parties, which has a degree of permanence or stability afforded by the cryptographic keys. Through this, "[a] person has the power to control and deal with the Bitcoin and to exclude third parties from accessing or dealing with it."[8]
- *Digital assets do not need to be alienable to be property.* There are many examples under the Australian law of rights which are not capable of being assigned because of their nature or public policy, which are nevertheless considered to be property. Accordingly, the fact that a transaction in bitcoin results in the creation of a new record on the Bitcoin blockchain and not the actual transfer of the transferee's interest in bitcoin does not affect the characterisation of an interest in bitcoin as property.
- *Digital assets are more than a mere interest in information.* Although Australian law is reluctant to recognise information as constituting property,[9] an interest in bitcoin can be distinguished from a mere interest in information. This is because it includes the power to undertake transactions on a network using a public key and a private key, and to exclude third parties from accessing or dealing with the bitcoin.
- *Digital assets can be choses in action without being enforceable legal rights.* Australian law has already established that choses in action include more than enforceable legal rights against someone.[10] They include different groups of rights which only have in common that "they do not confer the present possession of a tangible object."[11]

---

[6] *National Provincial Bank v. Ainsworth* [1965] AC 1175.

[7] [reference to other chapters of this book that refer to *Ainsworth* to be added].

[8] *Re Blockchain Tech Pty Ltd* (n. 5) 385.

[9] See *Farah Constructions Pty Ltd and Others v. Say-Dee Pty Ltd* [2007] 236 ALR 209, 246.

[10] *Re Blockchain Tech Pty Ltd* (n. 5) 389.

[11] *Re Blockchain Tech Pty Ltd* (n. 5) 389.

This characterisation by the Victorian Court of bitcoin as a chose in action differs conceptually from the position of the United Kingdom Law Commission in its final report on digital assets,[12] and the basis of the United Kingdom's *Property (Digital Assets etc) Bill*.[13] Due to the extent of property recognised as choses in action under Australian law, the Court did not find it necessary to find any "third category of things" beyond choses in possession and choses in action.[14] This also aligns with the recent extra-curial comments of Jackman J:

> "the mental gymnastics involved in creating a third category of personal property made up such diverse subject matter as milk and export quotas, on the one hand, and cryptocurrency, on the other hand, are an unnecessary distraction in the Australian context."[15]

The finding that a digital asset such as bitcoin can constitute property under Australian law is not remarkable in the context of the laws of the other common law jurisdictions analysed in this book. However, the finding that they constitute choses in action, and not choses in possession or a third type of property, is different to some other jurisdictions,[16] and impacts the relevance of control to establishing interests in that property under the Australian common law.

III. Interests and control in digital assets under Australian common law

Control is not a core concept to proprietary interests in choses in action under Australian common law. Australian law does not recognise possession of choses in action, and it has no equivalent to the recognition of relative title in choses in possession. Legal title to choses in action is indivisible. While equitable interests in choses in action can be established, for example through assignments and trusts, and the concept of control can be relevant to the equitable rules which determine priorities between such interests,[17] control does not perform a determinative role in establishing interests in choses in action.

The Court's decision in *Blockchain Tech* demonstrates how these principles apply to digital assets by its finding that a bailment over them was not possible, and that a trust over them, and beneficial interests in them, was established. The Court did not articulate any new principles applicable to choses in action that

[12] *United Kingdom Law Commission*, Digital Assets: Final Report of 27 June 2023, Law Com No. 412.

[13] Property (Digital Assets etc) HL Bill (2024) 31 (UK).

[14] *Re Blockchain Tech Pty Ltd* (n. 5). However, the case for recognising such a third category was given some judicial support in the subsequent decision of *Poulton v Conrad* [2025] TASSC 2.

[15] *Jackman*, Property (n. 1). The Court in *Re Blockchain Tech* referred to comments of *Justice Jackman* in this speech: *Re Blockchain Tech Pty Ltd* (n. 5) 377.

[16] [reference to relevant other chapters of the book to be added].

[17] Cf. section III. 2. below.

are digital assets, nor did the court expressly call out control as a critical factor for any of its conclusions.

Nevertheless, *Blockchain Tech* does, by implication, provide some insights into the relevance of control of the private key relating to a holding of digital assets with respect to ownership, transfer and trusts under Australian law.

1. Relevance of control of private key to ownership of digital assets under common law

As noted above, the Court in Blockchain Tech found that bitcoin constituted a person's property under Australian law. The foundation of this property was the person's power to control and deal with the bitcoin, and to exclude others from doing so, through the private cryptographic key. This power established the rivalrous qualities needed for the bitcoin to have the necessary identifiability, capability of assumption, and degree of permanence and stability to be property.

The Court made no statement as to the level of control over the private key to constitute ownership. Nevertheless, it implied that a level of control over a digital asset's private key sufficient to deal with the digital asset, and prevent others from doing so, was a critical element of the digital asset's ownership. The Court referred to the New Zealand High Court's decision in *Ruscoe v. Cryptopia* at length including, most relevantly, the following:

> "The degree of control necessary for ownership (namely the power to exclude others) is achieved for cryptocurrencies by the computer software allocating to each public key a second set of data made available only to the holder of the account (the private key), and requiring the combination of the two sets of data in order to record a transfer of the cryptocurrency attached to the public key from one account to another."[18]

Similarly, in his extra-curial comments referred to in the Court's decision, Jackman J said that holding the private key "confers practical control" over the digital asset.[19]

The importance of being able to control the private key in establishing property and ownership in digital assets is also conceptually consistent with the principle set out by the Australian High Court decision of *Yanner v. Eaton* (relied on in the *Blockchain Tech* decision).[20] In that case, which concerned "the quintessentially Australian problem of rights over hunting estuarine crocodiles",[21] the Court defined property as a "legally endorsed concentration of power over things and resources".[22] It follows that, if digital assets are property,

---

[18] *Ruscoe v. Cryptopia Ltd (in liq)* [2020] 2 NZLR 809, 112.
[19] *Jackman*, Property (n. 1) 2.
[20] *Yanner v. Eaton* [1999] 201 CLR 351.
[21] *Jackman*, Property (n. 1) 2.
[22] *Yanner v. Eaton* (n. 20).

then that concentration of power is derived from being able to transfer it to another, which is a consequence of holding and controlling the private key.

The importance of controlling the private key to ownership of a digital asset is not new. In its Statement on Cryptoassets and Smart Contracts, the UK Jurisdiction Taskforce noted, "The starting point, in our view, is that a person who has acquired knowledge and control of a private key by some lawful means would generally be treated as the owner of the associated cryptoasset."[23] The UK Law Commission also recognised the significance of controlling the transfer of a digital asset as an integral part of the property comprised in the digital asset,[24] and in its definition of holding a digital asset "as the capacity to exercise, or to coordinate or direct, the exercise of full factual control".[25]

Accordingly, it is safe to conclude that control over the use of the private key relating to an interest in a digital asset is an important factor in determining the legal ownership of that digital asset under Australian law. However, it should be noted that there is nothing in the *Blockchain Tech* decision to indicate that control on its own is determinative of legal title.[26] Other circumstances, such as the presence of intermediated arrangements, can affect the holding of legal title, as noted further below.

2. Relevance of control of private key to transfers of digital assets under common law

As part of its finding that an interest in bitcoin constituted property, the Court in *Blockchain Tech* defined a "Bitcoin transfer transaction", which had the effect of the bitcoin at the address of one person being replaced with bitcoin at the address of another. The transfer transaction depended on the use by the owner of bitcoin of their private key to "digitally sign a hash which records the details of the transaction."[27] The Court did not expressly state that legal title to the digital assets passed with the private key in a manner similar to the US court in *Archer v. Coinbase*,[28] but the description of the transaction by the Court makes it clear that a change in control of a digital asset to a new private key was necessary for a transfer of title to a digital asset to take effect.

---

23 *UK Jurisdiction Taskforce*, Legal Statement on Cryptoassets and Smart Contracts of November 2019, <https://technation.io/wp-content/uploads/2019/11/6.6056_JO_Cryptocurrencies_Statement_FINAL_WEB_111119-1.pdf> (16 September 2025) 13.

24 *United Kingdom Law Commission,* Digital Assets (n. 12) 60.

25 *United Kingdom Law Commission,* Digital Assets (n. 12) ch. 7.

26 This aligns with the statement of the *UK Jurisdiction Taskforce* that "The ledger cannot however be treated as a definitive record of *legal rights* unless statute has given it binding effect": *UK Jurisdiction Taskforce*, Legal Statement (n. 23) 30.

27 *Re Blockchain Tech Pty Ltd* (n. 5) 386.

28 *Archer v. Coinbase Inc.* 267 Cal.Rptr.3d 510, p. 243.

As previously noted, unlike the UK Law Commission, the Australian Court found no need to contemplate that digital assets constituted a third type of property and instead the Court found them to comprise a chose in action. This meant there was no need for the Court to consider special requirements for the transfer of digital assets as a third type of property, such as rules relating to sufficient control and intention.

However, the application of the Australian common law for transfers of, or interests in, choses in action to digital assets is complicated. This is because the law has been established based on an assumption that a chose in action is not independent of the legal system and has an obligor or trustee. In other words, the Australian common law rules for dealings in choses in action do not contemplate things which are established more through process than promise. This complexity can be seen in applying the rules for assignments of choses in action under law, and the priorities of interests in choses in action under equity.

- *Legal assignments of choses in action.* Under the Australian law, debts and "other legal choses in action" can be assigned in accordance with a statutory provision in the property conveyancing legislation of the various Australian states.[29] These provisions depend on the giving of express written notice of the assignment to the "debtor, trustee, or other person from whom the assignor would have been entitled to receive or claim such debt or chose in action".[30] They are not able to operate if there is no such person to whom notice could be given, as would be the case for many digital assets.[31]

  It might be argued that, if a digital asset is a chose in action, then this is an impediment to the legal recognition of its transfer. However, the better view is that it is not. No such concern arose in *Blockchain Tech* where the Court expressly considered the way an interest in bitcoin could be transferred. Also, the statutory process for assigning choses in action at law is not exclusive for all choses in action. Instead, it is better seen as applicable to a "debt or right which the common law looks on as not assignable by reason of its being a chose in action, but which a Court of Equity deals with as being assignable."[32]
- *Priorities of interests in choses in action under equity.* Australian equitable principles provide rules for the priority of interests in choses in action, many

[29] *Federal Commissioner of Taxation v. Everett* [1980] 143 CLR 440; Civil Law (Property) Act (ACT) 2006 s. 205; Conveyancing Act (NSW) 1919 s. 12; Law of Property Act (NT) 2000 s. 182; Property Law Act (Qld) 1974 ss. 199–200; Law of Property Act (SA) 1936 s. 15; Conveyancing and Law of Property Act (TAS) 1884 s. 86; Property Law Act (VIC) 1958 s. 134; Property Law Act (WA) 1969 s. 20.

[30] Conveyancing Act (NSW) 1919 s. 12.

[31] It could be argued that the law relating to assignments is irrelevant where there are no legally enforceable rights being transferred. However, assignment has been given an extended meaning by Australian courts, to be the "immediate transfer of an existing proprietary right": *Norman v. Federal Commissioner of Taxation* [1963] 109 CLR 9, 26.

[32] *Torkington v. Magee* [1902] 2 KB 427 at 434.

of which will also be difficult to apply to digital assets which have no obligor or trustee.[33] For example, there is a general principle that two equitable interests will rank in order of their temporal priority. However, there are three exceptions to this which could be instructive to a court seeking to determine priorities between competing interests in digital assets. They are:

- *Priorities between equitable assignees of personal property:* the holder of a later equitable interest in a chose in action can gain priority if they obtain their interest for value without notice of the existing interest, and they are the first to give notice of their interest to the person they are looking to for performance of the chose in action.[34] Just as with the legal assignment provision described above, this process may be difficult to apply literally for many digital assets as there may be no person who is responsible for performance to whom notice could be given. Nevertheless, it would be possible that a court could apply the principles of this rule to digital assets as choses in action by treating the recording of the transaction on the relevant digital asset system as amounting to notice required for such priority. This would reinforce the importance of control over the private key which would enable the transaction to be recorded.
- *Postponing conduct of holder of prior interest:* the holder of an equitable interest in property can have their priority postponed when their conduct has led someone to acquire a later interest in the belief that the earlier interest did not exist.[35] In some cases, this postponement has occurred because the earlier holder has armed a third party with the indicia of absolute ownership, which arguably could be satisfied by control of the private key. Alternatively, this postponement has occurred because it is reasonably foreseeable that a later interest will be created and that the holder of the later interest will assume that no earlier interest exists. Again, a court may find that failing to control the private key for a holding of digital assets meets the requirement of conduct sufficient to postpone a prior interest.
- *Bona fide purchaser for value without notice:* a subsequent transferee of the legal title to personal property who has given consideration, has acted in good faith and has no notice of the equitable interests of another in that property can take the legal title free of that equitable interest.[36] The most problematic element in practice in the application of this principle is ascertaining what

[33] The leading Australian treatise on these principles is *John D. Heydon/Mark J. Leeming/Peter G. Turner*, Meagher Gummow and Lehane's Equity: Doctrines and Remedies[5] (2015). See in particular ch. 6 and 8.

[34] This equitable principle is often known as the rule in *Dearle v. Hall* [1828] 38 ER 475.

[35] This principle is not limited to personal property. An example of its application can be found in the High Court of Australia's decision in *Heid v. Reliance Finance Corp Pty Ltd* [1983] 154 CLR 326.

[36] The application of this to digital assets appears to have been implicitly accepted by the UK High Court in *Ellis v. Digit Europe Ltd* [2021] CL-2021-000733. See also *Helen Pugh*,

constitutes notice, and what level of enquiry is required on behalf of the receiver of the legal title. In a transaction in digital assets, it may be difficult to establish notice of anything other than the state of the digital asset system, on the basis that this would be the level of investigation usually made in similar transactions. In this context, factual control over the means to transfer the legal title would be a practical way of ensuring that no such legal transferee could arise.

Although the application of these common law principles to choses in action comprised of digital assets is complicated, none of them derogate from the importance of controlling the private key to ensure no change to the relevant digital asset system with respect to the digital assets can take place. In fact, a reasonable application of these principles to digital assets would support taking a high level of control over the private key to protect an interest in those assets.

It could be argued that these principles should not be relevant as there is no actual transfer of the chose in action. Instead, the consequence of the "bitcoin transfer transaction" as referred to by the Court in *Blockchain Tech,* is that "the old asset is replaced by a new one".[37] Arguably, this termination of an existing interest and its replacement with a new one is more analogous to a novation of a contractual right than its assignment. However, even if this were found to be the case, this does not change the importance of controlling the private key to protect an interest in a digital asset so that the "novation" cannot occur.

Of course, it is common for digital assets to be held through intermediaries, such as digital asset exchanges. This has the potential to further complicate the application of common law principles applicable to choses in action. Under Australian law, this raises the need to consider trusts.

3. Relevance of control of private key to trusts over digital assets under common law

Further relevance of control can be inferred from the *Blockchain Tech* decision in relation to the trust over the defendant's interest in bitcoin. The Court found that the bitcoin were subject to a trust because they were provided to the defendant by Blockchain Tech for the purpose of being sold by the defendant and it was a term of that trust that the proceeds were to be remitted to Blockchain Tech. Because the proceeds of sale were not remitted, the Court found that the defendant was liable to pay equitable compensation.

On its face, this finding supports the use of equitable principles to determine different interests in digital assets, rather than concepts of control. However,

---

Crypto fraud and the bona fide purchaser for value defence, Butterworths Journal of International Banking and Financial Law 2023, 5–7.

[37] *Jackman*, Property (n. 1) 12.

the decision does provide greater insight into the relevance of control to ownership of digital assets. This is because the relevant bitcoins were not transferred to the defendant by Blockchain Tech, but instead they were transferred to an address maintained by the defendant's husband. Consequently, the Court found that the husband held "a legal interest" in the bitcoins for the benefit of the defendant, and that the defendant held their interest as trustee for Blockchain Tech. If the assumption is made that the defendant's husband held the private key for the relevant address, which was not made clear in the decision, then this supports the view that practical control over the private key is required to support legal title to digital assets.

However, this is blurred by two further aspects of the case. First, it appears that the bitcoin was in an "account" which the defendant's husband held with a digital asset exchange. No clarification is made in the decision as to the legal nature of the relationship between the husband and the exchange, but it would seem unlikely that the exchange did not retain the private key to the relevant bitcoin. If only the digital asset exchange had access to the private key and the defendant's husband did not, it is hard to see that the defendant's husband did have any sort of legal interest in the relevant bitcoin. Instead, it would appear more likely that the legal title was held by the exchange and that the defendant's husband held a beneficial interest in the bitcoin.[38] Second, the nature of the relationship between the defendant and their husband is also unclear. The Court found that the transfers of the bitcoin from the account were made by the defendant. No clarity is provided as to how this took place given that the account was not in the defendant's name and no statements were made relating to the control of the account. However, as it is likely that the account represented a beneficial rather than legal title in the bitcoin, no inference can be taken from this relating to the relevance of control to legal ownership of digital assets.

Accordingly, it is possible that the case concerned more complex arrangements relating to the holding of the private key of digital assets, but there is insufficient information to determine what they are. Nevertheless, it remains clear that the Court determined the consequences of the arrangements between, and activities of, the parties by reference to equitable principles of trust and equitable compensation, rather than any control-based analogue to possession and relative title for choses in possession. This is consistent with the Court's finding that the interests in bitcoin comprised a chose in action.

[38] There is no analysis in the decision as to whether the "account" is a segregated or omnibus account.

4. Application of control in protecting interests in digital assets under common law

The analysis above shows that the decision in *Blockchain Tech* does not provide comprehensive guidance on obtaining and protecting interests in digital assets through control.

Nevertheless, the application of the existing Australian common law relating to the transfer and priorities of interests in choses in action remains informative. For example, if a person holding an interest in digital assets fails to control the use of the private key applicable to the digital assets, such that another is able to take an interest in them without notice of the person's interest, then it would seem likely that the interest of that other person would prevail. Accordingly, in order to protect an interest in digital assets under Australian common law, it is preferrable to maintain a high level of practical control over the private key to permit dealings in that interest, whilst also preventing any other person from doing so.

Such a focus on factual control would be consistent with another specific application of control to interests in choses in action which had applied under Australian common law before the introduction of Australia's statutory personal property legislation, namely the level of control required over the proceeds of a book debt to ensure that a charge over the book debt is a fixed charge. Whilst Australian courts have not definitively determined what level of control is required for this purpose, primarily because the issue is now addressed by Australia's statutory personal property legislation analysed in the next section, Australian judicial decisions have reinforced the importance of the chargee being able to prevent, as a factual matter, the property from being transferred or otherwise disposed of or dealt with including, in some cases by use or collection.[39]

This approach aligns with the importance given to "full factual control" over a digital asset by the UK Law Commission, which it stated was comprised of two components:

"(1) positive control, which involves the factual ability to use, dispose of or transfer an asset; and
(2) negative control, which involves the factual ability to exclude others from doing so."[40]

However, as noted by the UK Law Commission, what amounts to that level of control is fact specific and can be complicated depending on the systems in-

[39] See *Boulos Holdings Pty Ltd v. Edwin Davey Pty Ltd* [2021] NSWSC 689; *Hamersley Iron Pty Ltd v. Forge Group Power Pty Ltd (in liq) (Recs and Mgrs Apptd)* [2018] 53 WAR 325; *Westpac Banking Corporation v. Bell Group (in liq)* (No. 3) [2012] WASCA 157; *Australian Receivables Ltd v. Tekitu Pty Ltd (Subject to Deed of Company Arrangement) (Deed Administrators Appointed) & ors*; [2012] NSWSC 170; *Australian Securities and Investments Commission (ASIC), Re Richstar Enterprises Pty Ltd v. Carey* (No. 9) [2006] FCA 1242.

[40] *United Kingdom Law Commission,* Digital Assets (n. 12) 152.

volved.[41] We will need to await further decisions of Australian courts for further guidance of the requirements under Australian common law.

As noted in the introduction, in addition to the common law, there are two pieces of legislation under Australian law which apply a statutory regime to interests in personal property which could be relevant to interests in digital assets which are security interests. These are considered in the next two sections.

IV. Interests and control in digital assets under personal property securities legislation

Although Australian law is based on a foundation of English law, it differs from English law in its recognition of interests in personal property. This is because of the Personal Property Securities Act (Cth) 1998 ("PPSA"), which established a personal property regime modelled on the equivalent regimes in New Zealand, Canada and the United States.

The PPSA established a national system for the registration of security interests in personal property, whether given by a company or a natural person, together with rules for the creation, priority and enforcement of security interests in personal property. It replaced certain existing Australian Commonwealth and State based regimes co-ordinated by the Australian Securities and Investments Commission ("ASIC") and other regulators, including the previous regime for registration of charges under the Corporations Act 2001 ("Corporations Act"). It also makes certain transactions registrable as security interests which were previously not registrable at all.

Most of the provisions of the PPSA relate to security interests in personal property. A security interest is defined as an: "interest in personal property provided for by a transaction that, in substance, secures payment or performance of an obligation".[42] The form of the transaction, or the identity of the person who has title, is irrelevant.

1. Characterisation of digital assets as property under the PPSA

The PPSA applies to personal property. Personal property means property other than land or a right, entitlement or authority that is granted under an Australian law and other than property which is declared not to be personal property for the purposes of the PPSA. Based on the principles set out in the *Blockchain Tech* decision, digital assets are personal property under the PPSA.

The PPSA categorises personal property into different collateral classes. The manner of application of the PPSA to digital assets depends on the collateral

41 *United Kingdom Law Commission,* Digital Assets (n. 12) ch. 5.

42 Personal Property Securities Act (Cth) 2009 s. 12.

class that they fall into. This will depend on the structure and features of the digital asset, but the most likely ones are:

- Financial property. This comprises specific assets, meaning chattel paper, currency, documents of title, negotiable instruments and investment instruments (primarily debentures, bonds, derivatives, foreign exchange contracts, managed investments). The definitions of the components of investment instruments have their broad regulatory meaning under Australian law which could include some digital assets which are not included in similar definitions under the laws of other jurisdictions. This can be most easily seen from the recent consultation of the ASIC on the regulatory treatment of digital assets.[43] In addition to the inclusion of tokenised securities and contracts for differences over digital assets as regulated financial products, the paper also demonstrates the breadth of Australian financial services regulation by clarifying that stablecoins and fundraising tokens are likely to be also included. Accordingly, some digital assets could be financial property even if they do not directly relate to financial assets such as shares, bonds, futures and swaps.[44]
- Intermediated securities. This is comprised of the rights of a person in whose name a licensed intermediary maintains a securities account, most relevantly being an account to which interests in financial products (shares, bonds or any other financial instrument or financial asset, other than cash) may be credited or debited.[45]
- Intangibles. This is the collateral class applicable to personal property which is not included in another collateral class.

It can be seen from this that the regulatory treatment of a digital asset under the Corporations Act also influences how interests in it are treated under the PPSA. This is important because control is not relevant to all collateral classes under the PPSA, as discussed below.

2. *Relevance of possession and control of digital assets under the PPSA*

The concepts of possession and control are most relevant under the PPSA to determining if a security interest is enforceable against third parties and is perfected.

The first step is attachment. Attachment requires that the grantor has rights in the property, or the power to transfer rights in the property to the secured

[43] *Australian Securities and Investments Commission (ASIC),* Consultation Paper 381 of 4 December 2024, Updates to INFO 225: Digital Assets: Financial Products and Services.

[44] This characterisation differs from token to token and is heavily fact-based. It can be complicated, and sometimes contentious, in practice.

[45] This requires that the intermediary holds an Australian Financial Services Licence or an Australian Clearing & Settlement Facility Licence, or a licence under the law of a foreign jurisdiction permitting them to maintain securities accounts on behalf of others.

party, and either value is given for the security interest or the grantor does an act by which the security interest arises. Once a security interest is attached to personal property, it is referred to as "collateral" under the PPSA.

To be enforceable against a third party, a security interest must be attached to the collateral and the secured party must either possess the collateral or have perfected the interest by control, or the security interest must be provided for by a written security agreement which complies with the requirements of the PPSA. A security interest in particular collateral can be perfected by registration (in addition to by possession or control), in each case where the security interest is attached to the collateral and is enforceable against a third party. While the PPSA does not require a secured party to "perfect" its security interest in the collateral, if the secured party does not do so, another security interest could take priority, another person may acquire an interest in the collateral free of the secured party's security interest, and the security interest may not be enforceable in the event of the grantor's insolvency.

In most cases, a security interest can only be perfected by possession if physical possession of the collateral is possible, meaning that there is some tangible evidence of the collateral which can be possessed. For example, possession is possible for negotiable instruments that are not evidenced by an electronic record, and investment instruments if they are evidenced by a certificate. Accordingly, perfection of a security interest in a digital asset by possession should not be available under the PPSA.

Security interests in uncertificated negotiable instruments, investment instruments, intermediated securities and accounts with authorised deposit-taking institutions (primarily banks) can be perfected by the secured party taking control of the collateral. Perfection by control is not available for security interests in intangible property (as defined in the PPSA). Perfection by control confers greater priority than perfection by registration.

Assuming that a licensed intermediary is not involved, this means that perfection of a security interest in digital assets by control is relevant for digital assets which are investment instruments.[46] Control could be taken if the secured party has an agreement with the grantor to the effect that the secured party (or a person who has agreed to act on the instructions of the secured party) is able to initiate or control sending instructions by which the investment instrument could be transferred or otherwise dealt with. If the digital asset has an issuer, then control could also be taken if:

- the issuer registers the secured party as the owner of digital asset, or
- the registered owner (not being the grantor or debtor) acknowledges in writing that it holds the digital asset on behalf of the secured party,

[46] As noted above, this requires a regulatory analysis to be conducted.

and in each case, there is an agreement with the secured party under which the secured party (or a person who has agreed to act on the instructions of the secured party) is able to initiate or control sending some or all electronic messages or other electronic communications by which the digital asset could be transferred or otherwise dealt with.[47] This control can persist even if the registered owner of the digital asset retains the right to make substitutions for the digital asset, to originate instructions to the issuer or to otherwise deal with the instrument.

3. Application of control in protecting interests in digital assets under PPSA

The PPSA control requirements described above give rise to two issues of interpretation relevant to the application of those requirements to digital assets that are investment instruments (in addition to the complexity of determining the status of a digital asset under the PPSA). These relate to the instructions to transfer and the registration of ownership.

- *Control of means of giving instructions.* As noted above, control can be obtained over a digital asset that is an investment instrument if the secured party has an agreement with the grantor under which the secured party, or someone who acts on its instructions, is able to initiate or control the sending of instructions by which the digital asset is transferred or dealt with. This means control does not properly contemplate instruments where no agreement is required or feasible, because of the decentralised nature of the system which records transfers of the assets. However, based on the principles set out in the Court's decision in *Blockchain Tech*, it remains possible that this could be satisfied by the combination of an agreement with the grantor of the security interest and a level of practical control by the secured party of the private key applicable to the relevant digital assets in a manner which prevents transfer.
- *Control by issuer registration.* Also, as noted above, control can also be obtained through the registration by the issuer of either the secured party or another person as the registered owner of the digital asset. There is no definition of either issuer or registered owner in the PPSA and they should have their ordinary meanings under Australian law. The availability of this method of taking control for particular digital assets will be fact dependent. Nevertheless, where a digital asset comprises legal obligations performable by someone, and the holding of the asset comprises ownership of that obligation under its terms, then the holding of the digital asset in a person's address could amount to sufficient control.

[47] Other methods of taking control exist for certificated investment instruments. However, these should not be applicable to digital assets.

It can be seen from this that the PPSA does not properly contemplate arrangements which apply to digital assets. As a result, it does not properly contemplate that control will apply in the manner often used by the digital asset market.

However, it is not the only statutory regime which protects the application of security interests and it is important to consider how control could be relevant to interests in digital assets under Australia's financial collateral legislation.

V. Interests and control in digital assets under financial collateral legislation

In addition to the PPSA, Australia has a specific financial collateral regime in its Payment Systems and Netting Act (Cth) 1998 ("PSNA"), which facilitates the enforcement of particular forms of security relating to particular types of obligations. The PSNA provisions perform a similar function to the financial collateral regimes of the European Union and the United Kingdom,[48] and their development was informed by the approach taken by those regimes, and the issues which arose from them.[49]

The protection granted by the PSNA is very strong. Where it applies, security may be enforced in accordance with the written terms of the security, the enforcement is not void or voidable in the external administration of a party, and the protection applies 'despite any other law' other than some very specific provisions relating to stays on taking action against banks and clearing houses in the context of their distress and resolution proceeding.[50]

The types of security contemplated by the PSNA are the traditional forms of security under Australian common law, being the charge, mortgage, pledge and lien and analogous concepts under foreign law, rather than the broader substantive concept of "security interest" as contemplated by the PPSA.[51]

1. Limits on protection of enforcement of security under the PSNA

The PSNA protects enforcement of security for obligations of a party under bilateral financial market contracts, described as "close-out netting contracts".

[48] Directive (EC) No. 47/2002 of the European Parliament and of the Council of 6 June 2002 on financial collateral arrangements, OJ 2002 L168/43 and The Financial Collateral Arrangements (No. 2) Regulations 2003 (UK) as amended by The Financial Collateral Arrangements (No. 2) Regulations 2003 (Amendment) Regulations 2009 (UK) and The Financial Markets and Insolvency (Settlement Finality and Financial Collateral Arrangements) (Amendment) Regulations 2010 (UK).

[49] *House of Representatives*, Explanatory Memorandum, Financial System Legislation Amendment (Resilience and Collateral Protection) Bill 2016, 1.145.

[50] Payment Systems and Netting Act (Cth) 1998 ("PSNA") ss. 14, 14A.

[51] *House of Representatives*, Explanatory Memorandum (n. 49) 1.105.

This has a very specific meaning but is designed to cover the industry master agreements used in the international derivative and treasury markets.

However, the obligations which may be secured and discharged through an enforcement of security which is protected by the PSNA are further limited. One of these limitations is that the protection provided applies only to the extent that the obligations secured are "eligible obligations" in relation to the contract, or related interest, costs and expenses. Those "eligible obligations" only include obligations that relate to a derivative or foreign exchange contract, as defined in the Corporations Act, or an obligation that results from netting two or more of those obligations.[52] It does not include other obligations, such as those under credit facilities, deposit-taking facilities, reciprocal purchase agreements (or "repos"), or securities loan agreements.[53]

The PSNA could be relevant to security interests in digital assets which are to be used as financial collateral for such transactions. However, there is another relevant limitation, namely that the protection only applies to the extent that these obligations are secured by financial property. Accordingly, it is important to determine whether the digital assets are financial property for the purpose of the PSNA.

2. Characterisation of digital assets as financial property under the PSNA

To have the benefit of the protections available under the PSNA, the property over which security is granted must be "financial property". The "financial property" concept is intended to cover property which is commonly provided as collateral in financial markets transactions, and it includes (amongst other things):

- securities and derivatives, as defined under the Corporations Act;
- financial products traded on licensed or exempted Australian markets;
- currency (whether of Australia or of any other country);
- gold, silver or platinum, or documents evidencing ownership of them; and
- "intermediated financial property", being the rights of a person in whose name an intermediary maintains an account to which interests in property or rights to payment or delivery of financial property may be credited or debited, to the extent that those rights relate to the interests in that property or the rights to payment or delivery of that property.

As with the definition of investment instruments and intermediated securities under the PPSA, this meaning of financial property links the protection of

---

52 Regulations include obligations relating to forwards, swaps, options, or combinations of them, that relate to commodities, due to some technical carve-outs of the definition of derivative in Corporations Act (Cth) 2001.

53 This "eligible obligation" concept is significantly narrower than the "relevant obligation" concept used in The Financial Collateral Arrangements (No. 2) Regulations 2003 (UK).

security interests under the PSNA to the regulatory treatment under the Corporations Act. As noted above, these can have a broad regulatory meaning under Australian law which could include some digital assets which are not included in similar definitions under the laws of other jurisdictions. Accordingly, some digital assets could be financial property. However, others will not be and security interests in respect of those will not be protected under the PSNA.[54]

3. Relevance of possession and control of digital assets under the PSNA

The protection provided to the enforcement of security under the PSNA applies only to the extent that, before the enforcement, the financial property is transferred or otherwise dealt with so as to be in the possession or under the control of the secured person, or another person (who is not the grantor) on behalf of the secured person under the terms of an arrangement evidenced in writing.

Possession and control are not comprehensively defined in the PSNA. The terms have their general meaning, and in addition, the PSNA sets out specific circumstances in which they will, and will not, exist.

Where there is an issuer of the financial property, that property is in the possession of the secured person (or relevant person acting on its behalf), if they are registered by, or on behalf of, the issuer as the registered owner of the financial property.[55] In a case where the financial property is intermediated financial property, that property is in the possession of the secured person (or relevant person acting on its behalf), if they are the person in whose name the intermediary maintains the account.[56]

In addition, intermediated financial property would be under the control of the secured person (or relevant person acting on its behalf), if:

(a) the intermediary is not the grantor (but may be the secured person or any other person); and

[54] There would also be some complexity in determining whether any particular digital asset is a "financial product" (within the meaning of the Corporations Act) that is traded on a financial market (within the meaning of Division 3 of Part 7.1 of the Corporations Act) that is: *(i)* operated in accordance with an Australian market licence (within the meaning of the Corporations Act); or *(ii)* exempt from the operation of Part 7.2 of the Corporations Act.

[55] The *House of Representatives*, Explanatory Memorandum (n. 49) 1.153 provides that the "first limb of section 14A(4) is intended to cover the situations where the secured person or third party is registered by, or on behalf of, the issuer as the registered owner of the financial property, including where such registration happens on the Clearing House Electronic Sub register System (CHESS) sub register, maintained by ASX Settlement, or the issuer sponsored sub register, maintained by the issuer or a share registry on the issuer's behalf".

[56] The *House of Representatives*, Explanatory Memorandum (n. 49) 1.153 provides that: "Due to the breadth of the concept of 'intermediary', this would include circumstances where, if the financial property is traded or settled through a clearing house or securities depository, the clearing house or securities depository, as the case may be, records the interest of the person in the financial property".

(b) there is an agreement in force between the intermediary and one or more other persons, one of which is the secured person or the grantor, which has one or more of the following effects:

(i) the person in whose name the intermediary maintains the account is not able to transfer or otherwise deal with the financial property;

(ii) the intermediary must not comply with instructions given by the grantor in relation to the financial property without seeking the consent of the secured person (or relevant person acting on its behalf); and

(iii) the intermediary must comply, or must comply in one or more specified circumstances, with instructions (including instructions to debit the account) given by the secured person in relation to the intermediated financial property without seeking the consent of the grantor (or any person who has agreed to act on the instructions of the grantor).

Financial property is taken to *not* be in the possession or control of a person if, under the security, the grantor is free to deal with the financial property in the ordinary course of business[57] until the secured person's interest in the financial property becomes fixed and enforceable.[58] This applies even if the secured person's interest in the financial property becomes fixed and enforceable before the enforcement of the security over that property.[59]

However, the PSNA also states that the grantor retaining specific rights such as the right to receive and withdraw income in relation to the financial property, the right to substitute other property, the right to withdraw excess financial property or the right to determine the financial property's value, does *not* of itself mean that the secured person (or relevant person acting on its behalf) does not have possession or control.

---

[57] The *House of Representatives*, Explanatory Memorandum (n. 49) 1.147 states that this concept reflects the "ordinary course of business" concept set out in *In re Yorkshire Woolcombers Association Ltd, Houldsworth v. Yorkshire Woolcombers Association Ltd* [1903] 2 Ch 284 in respect of floating charges.

[58] The *House of Representatives*, Explanatory Memorandum (n. 49) 1.147 states that the reference to an interest in the financial property being "fixed and enforceable" means that circumstances arise such that the floating charge attaches to specific property and the grantor ceases to be able to deal with the property and the secured person has a presently exercisable right to take enforcement action in respect of the secured property.

[59] Section 14A(3) of the PSNA has the effect that security under which the grantor was free to deal with the financial property in the ordinary course of business at some time on or after creation of the security is taken not to be in the possession or under the control of a person even if the interest in the financial property becomes fixed and enforceable before the enforcement of the security over financial property which is described in paragraph 14A(1)(b) of the Netting Act: *House of Representatives*, Explanatory Memorandum (n. 49) 1.147.

4. Application of possession or control in protecting interests in digital assets under PSNA

The specific PSNA requirements regarding possession and control described above give rise to some similar issues of interpretation relevant to its application to digital assets as arise under the PPSA.

The clearest is the ability to take possession by registration. The PSNA defines possession to include registration of the secured person by the issuer of the financial property as the registered owner of the financial property. There is no definition of either issuer or registered owner in the PSNA and they should have their ordinary meanings under Australian law. As with the PPSA, the application of this to particular digital assets will be fact dependent and could be problematic. Nevertheless, where a digital asset is financial property with an issuer and under its terms, the recording of the holding of that digital asset constitutes the holder as the registered owner, then the holding of the digital asset in a person's address could amount to possession for the purposes of the PSNA.

Like the PPSA, the PSNA also provides for control in relation to the ability to give instructions relating to dealings in the financial property. However, unlike the PPSA, this is limited to intermediated financial property and should not be applicable to direct holdings of digital assets.

The PSNA is also different from the PPSA in that the PSNA does not seek to prescribe the sole circumstances of control. It also permits control to be taken within the ordinary meaning of that term.[60] Accordingly, the common law analysis of control in relation to digital assets set out in section II. of this chapter could also be relevant to determining control of financial property under the PSNA.

VI. Australian choice of law for interests in digital assets

The complexities of applying conflicts of laws principles to digital assets are well known.[61] These are equally applicable under Australian law and Australian courts have not yet developed any conflicts of law principles for the property law aspects of digital assets, such as the relevant choice of law rules, or the location of digital assets for that purpose. These will be difficult issues to resolve. However, the two statutory security regimes described in the sections above do

---

[60] See the *House of Representatives*, Explanatory Memorandum (n. 49) 1.145. Similar to the concept of control used in section 341 of the PPSA in relation to determining whether a security interest is granted over a circulating asset.

[61] E. g., *United Kingdom Law Commission*, Digital assets and ETDs in private international law: which court, which law? Call for Evidence, 22 February 2024, <https://cloud-platform-e218f50a4812967ba1215eaecede923f.s3.amazonaws.com/uploads/sites/54/2024/11/Digital-assets-and-EDTs_call_for_evidence.pdf> (16 September 2025).

provide some clarity in that they have their own provisions which determine their cross-border application.

1. Cross-border application of the PPSA to digital assets

The PPSA contains jurisdictional provisions which define its application to a security interest by reference to a connection with Australia. These jurisdictional provisions provide that the PPSA applies to a security interest if the grantor is an Australian entity. This includes individuals with their principal place of residence in Australia, Australian companies registered under the Corporations Act and other bodies registrable under that Act. It also applies to investment instruments if Australian law governs the transfer of the investment instrument, intermediated securities if the intermediary is located in Australia, and other intangible property if it is an account that is payable in Australia or if it is created, arises or is provided for by a law of Australia (including the general law).[62]

Whilst the asset-specific rules will not have general application to digital assets which do not fall within the scope of relevant regulatory categories, the general rule of the PPSA's application to any security interest created by an Australian individual or Australian company could be particularly important – especially where there is significant uncertainty as to the choice of law applicable to the proprietary aspects of dealings in digital assets.

2. Cross-border application of the PSNA to digital assets

The PSNA's jurisdictional provisions define its application to a security interest by reference to the relevant close-out netting contract. If that contract is governed by Australian law, then the PSNA applies to the security interest if either one of the parties is subject to an insolvency proceeding, or if one of the parties is a foreign corporation, or a trading or financial corporation formed in Australia.[63] The PSNA also applies to the security interest with respect to a close-out netting contract not governed by Australian law if one of the parties to it is subject to an insolvency proceeding which is governed by Australian law.

---

[62] There is a technical threshold issue to consider in relation to these provisions, being whether they are intended to be exclusive or inclusive. In other words, should these provisions be construed on the basis that the PPSA applies *only* to these security interests, or that it does apply to those security interests and may also apply to others. The drafting of the PPSA is not completely clear on this point. The better view is that the effect of these provisions should be that the PPSA does not apply to security interests which are not described in these provisions. This is because the intention of the section appears to be to define the jurisdictional connection needed for the PPSA to apply, rather than specifying examples of when it does apply.

[63] Or if the contract or arrangement is entered into in circumstances that are otherwise within Commonwealth constitutional reach, as defined in the PSNA.

If digital assets are provided as collateral for the financial market contracts to which the PSNA applies, then these choice of law rules have the benefit of clarity not dependent on the location of the digital assets.

VII. Conclusion

"The tendency to assume that cryptoassets are property is based on the intuitively sound premise that the law follows the economic reality it purports to govern. The market, nationally and internationally, is treating cryptoassets with various characteristics of economic assets. In general, the law should try to serve the needs of society. That should include its economy and financial system. Divergence between the law and the market without a sound basis in policy or principle are probably best avoided."[64]

This chapter has shown that an Australian court has already taken the Australian common law on this path of following economic reality, applying principles of the Australian common law to recognise digital assets as property, and as choses in action. This chapter has also shown where general Australian law needs more development, particularly in how equitable principles relating to dealings and priorities in choses in action apply to digital assets, which are decentralised and independent of the legal system, so that they are based more on process than promise.

Difficulties in applying existing Australian law to digital assets as property also extend to both of Australia's statutory regimes for security interests in personal property. The control and possession concepts used in those regimes for protecting and perfecting security interests, and rules for deeming situations that constitute "possession" or "control" for the purposes of those regimes, do not easily apply to digital assets. However, this chapter has also shown that those two security regimes do provide some clarity in relation to choice of law applicable to security interests which is still lacking in the common law.

The commercial use of, and reliance on the value of, digital assets is increasing. For this, and the digital assets themselves, to develop further, it will be important that the law upholds the certainty expected by businesses and consumers to facilitate effective and efficient commercial transactions. A key element which is required to ensure that the law supports commercial transactions in digital assets will be that the law provides clarity and certainty as to how interests in digital assets, such as security interests, are to be protected and perfected and the role performed by control of the private key. To some extent, this could be provided by statutory intervention. Statutory intervention is likely to be needed for an effective application of the PPSA if digital assets are to become

---

[64] *Geoffrey Vos*, End-to-End Smart Legal Contracts, Moving from Aspiration to Reality, in: Smart Legal Contracts: Computable Law in Theory and Practice, ed. by Jason Allen/Peter Hunn (2022) 54–69.

more commonly involved in financial transactions. By contrast, reform to the PSNA would seem less likely unless the use of digital assets as collateral for financial market exposures of systemically important market participants becomes significant or the Australian Government decides to signal support for ensuring the Australian statutory framework can facilitate digital assets being used as collateral for these types of transactions.

At present, statutory intervention to change the application of the Australian common law to digital assets, in a manner similar to the United Kingdom's *Property (Digital Assets etc) Bill,* seems unlikely.[65] Instead, it is more probable that the necessary clarity needs to be provided by further decisions of Australian courts, in considering the cases that appear before them. This approach of relying on the common law, so that it "fulfils its purpose of embodying in a relatively predictable way the reasonable expectations of ordinary and honest people", is preferred by some commentators,[66] who doubt the ability of statutory intervention to keep pace with technological intervention. Others may also doubt the ability of the common law to match technology's speed. However, whilst aspects of digital assets present new legal challenges, particularly in relation to their foundation in processes rather than promises, it is a mistake to assume that the Australian common law will not be able to adapt. As noted by Professor Sir Roy Goode just before the turn of the century, "Commercial law has evolved from the needs and practises of the mercantile community; from the opportunities to be grasped and problems to be overcome."[67]

---

[65] Property (Digital Assets etc) (n. 13).

[66] *Jackman*, Property (n. 1) 12.

[67] *Roy Goode*, Commercial Law in the Next Millenium (1998), 3.

Brazil

Guilherme Centenaro Hellwig and Marcus Paulus de O. Rosa

I. Introduction

In Brazil, addressing digital assets from a legal standpoint presents multiple challenges. Beyond the rapid pace of technological advancement, which continually reshapes the landscape for legal norms, there are considerable gray areas in Brazilian law regarding this topic, spanning property law, the law of obligations, intellectual property law, and other mandatory regulatory provisions.

Furthermore, although Brazilian legal doctrine already refers generally to "digital assets" (*bens digitais*), the term itself lacks a legal definition. Legal scholars have broadly defined digital assets as anything that exists as a mere sequence of bits and holds human interest.[1] It has also been emphasized that with the progressive virtualization of human relationships, information emerg-

[1] *Augusto Tavares Rosa Marcacini/Nivaldo Sebastião Vícola*, "Os Bens e as Coisas Digitais: tentativa de conceituação e seus contornos jurídicos", in: Bens Digitais: implicações jurídicas contemporâneas, ed. by Lucélia de Sena Alves/Cássio Augusto Barros Brant (2023) 173–200, 189.

es as a vital new asset, necessitating both individual and collective protection.[2] In this sense, digital assets are those assets that, having an IT origin or being initially generated in a material and tangible form, are converted into digital files and preserved as such.[3]

The advancement of digitalization within the Brazilian economy holds significant potential to alleviate poverty, create employment opportunities, foster educational inclusion, and reduce inequalities. An increasing number of Brazilians are embracing digital products and services. However, there remains vast untapped potential in this sector, which can be further developed through both government initiatives and private economic efforts.[4]

Over their lifetimes, businesses and individuals will amass social media posts, electronic correspondence (e-mails), photos, e-books, audiovisual works, and documents, whether self-authored or not. All these items, stored digitally, constitute their belongings, and this unique characteristic defines them as digital assets.[5] The advent of smart contracts and tokens on blockchain-based structures, on the other hand, has brought about changes of institutional significance, suggesting that a new economic paradigm (*tokenomics* or the crypto economy) is emerging, creating new opportunities for organising business and commerce.[6] A comprehensive legal foundation is therefore essential to effectively regulate the digital economy and its circulating assets, addressing both private and public law aspects.

The aim of this article is to address this topic, by examining Brazilian private law treatment of control and ownership of digital assets. It begins by seeking to define how the term "digital asset" should be understood within the context of Brazilian law. Although the digitalization of economy and social interactions has already ignited debates and controversies in various legal domains, a recently enacted law by the Brazilian Congress specifically addresses virtual assets that constitute digital representations of value which can be traded or transferred electronically.[7] The principle-based nature of this legislative act,[8] however, has left many aspects outside its normative scope.

---

[2] *Bruno Zampier*, Bens Digitais (2021) 56.

[3] *Roberta Mauro Medina Maia*, Posse e Propriedade na Era do Metaverso, Revista Brasileira de Direito Civil, v. 32, n. 2 (2023) 301–327, 310.

[4] *Organization for Economic Cooperation and Development (OECD)*, "O Brasil na Transformação Digital: oportunidades e desafios", in: Going Digital in Brazil OECD Publishing (2020) 15–26, 16.

[5] *Medina Maia*, Posse e Propriedade na Era do Metaverso (n. 3) 310.

[6] *Iris H-Y-Chiu*, Regulating the Crypto Economy: business transformations and financialisation (2021).

[7] Federal Law No. 14.478/2022, on guidelines to be observed in the provision of virtual asset services and in the regulation of virtual asset service providers.

[8] Principles-based legislation means shifting the normative approach from a focus on specific, detailed rules to broader, more flexible standards, and the establishing of regulatory competences. Instead of prescribing exact behaviours, it sets out overarching principles and

For this reason, this article investigates how key institutions of Brazilian private law might be utilized to govern digital assets effectively. It includes an analysis of the materialistic conception of property as outlined in the Brazilian Civil Code, the mechanisms for transferring digital assets, the importance of good faith in business transactions, and the legal framework governing negotiable instruments. The article then delves into issues related to the custody and control of digital assets, as well as the legal implications of custody and control by contracted third parties and the legal challenges that arise in the event of a custodian's or other intermediaries insolvency. Finally, it addresses the private international law aspects of digital assets, providing a comprehensive overview of the legal landscape regulating digital assets in Brazil. The conclusion summarizes the findings and suggests potential future developments in this dynamic area of law.

II. Interpreting the Term "Digital Asset" within the Context of Brazilian Law

The ordinary meaning of the term "digital asset" refers to a collection of data stored electronically that holds value or utility.[9] It encompasses anything that has value to a stakeholder and exists solely in digital form or as a digital representation of another asset.[10]

Brazilian law currently lacks a formal legal definition for 'digital asset.' However, this absence has not prevented various legal fields from addressing issues arising from the digitalization of the economy, thereby sparking debates and discussions around this concept.

In the realm of inheritance law, for example, Brazilian legal doctrine strongly supports the notion that an individual's "digital inheritance" can be transferred to their heirs, despite the absence of specific legislation governing this issue.[11] Conversely, in the realm of tax law, there has been considerable debate over the appropriate taxation for software commercialization.[12] Should digital assets be

objectives that guide how firms should operate within the regulatory framework. *Julia Black*, Principles Based Regulation: Risks, Challenges and Opportunities, London School of Economics and Political Science (2007), 3.

[9] *United Nations Commission on International Trade Law (UNCITRAL)*, Taxonomy of legal issues related to the digital economy (2023) 35.

[10] *International Organization for Standardization (ISO)*, Blockchain and Distributed Ledger Technologies: Vocabulary, ISO Standard No. 22739 (2020).

[11] This understanding was adopted in 2022 by the Federal Justice Council (CJF), an entity that is part of the Brazilian Judiciary, through its Statement (*Enunciado*) No. 687, produced at its Ninth Civil Law Conference. Although CJF statements are not binding, they serve as an important interpretative guide in Brazilian law.

[12] *Celso de Barros Correia Neto/José Roberto Rodrigues Afonso/Luciano Felício Fuck*,

classified as services or goods for tax purposes in Brazil? The approach to this subject is continually evolving, with no definitive stance yet from Brazilian courts and tax authorities on various aspects of the so-called crypto economy.[13]

Besides, although the term "digital asset" continues to be broadly used by Brazilian legal doctrine to refer generally to any assets related to the digital economy, it is important to note that a narrower interpretation of the term can also be applied within Brazilian law. Certain types of digital assets, such as cryptocurrencies and asset-backed digital tokens, have received special attention due to their transferability, which distinguishes them from mere collections of data messages or electronic records.

These specific types of digital assets are supported by systems that ensure control over the asset (i. e., the ability to transfer it from one person to another), and they offer guarantees regarding its uniqueness or exclusivity. This means that the digital asset can be controlled,[14] distinctly identified, and protected against replication.[15]

This category of digital asset, often referred to as a token, signifies a profound evolution – if not a true revolution – beyond the traditional concept of digitizing processes or routines within economic organizations in the financial sector. Unlike merely converting a physical asset into digital information or creating and storing data relevant to the exercise of rights exclusively in digital form (e. g., records of ownership of assets or contractual rights), tokens typically integrate such representations into a decentralized system.[16] These systems are

A Tributação na Era Digital e os Desafios do Sistema Tributário no Brasil, Revista Brasileira de Direito, v. 15, n. 1 (2019), 145–167, 162.

[13] In November 2024, for example, the Brazilian Federal Tax Authority released a draft regulation for public consultation that proposes the creation of specific reporting requirements on transactions involving crypto-assets, known as the "Declaração de Criptoativos" (DeCripto). Its aims to facilitate Brazil's future adherence to the OECD's initiative on the exchange of information between tax authorities under the Crypto-Asset Reporting Framework (CARF), while also modernizing the existing regulatory regime established by Normative Instruction RFB No. 1,888/2019, which currently governs the reporting obligations of crypto-asset exchanges and individuals domiciled in Brazil.

[14] The 2023 *UNIDROIT Principles on Digital Assets and Private Law* define a digital asset as "an electronic record which is capable of being subject to exclusive control".

[15] Distributed Ledger Technology (DLT) prevents double spending problem by ensuring that all transactions are recorded on an immutable, transparent, and shared ledger. Transactions are validated by independent participants (nodes in DLT) before being incorporated into the ledger, ensuring that the same digital asset cannot be used more than once. The consensus mechanism ensures that only one version of the transaction history is accepted across the network, effectively eliminating the risk of duplicating or double spending a digital asset. Bank For International Settlements (BIS). "The Future Monetary System", in BIS Annual Economic Report. BIS, June (2022), 80.

[16] A decentralized system, beyond its multifaceted nature, generally refers to a technological and governance infrastructure – typically built on distributed ledger technologies – that enables the representation, storage, and transfer of assets or rights without relying on a centralized trusted authority. In contrast to traditional financial market infrastructures operated

not exclusively controlled or reliant on a single operator, as is common in traditional financial market infrastructures. This decentralization enables the automation of complex economic operations and facilitates the programmable transfer of these digital assets.

The defining characteristics of tokenization are frequently attributed to the adoption of innovative technologies, such as distributed ledger technology (DLT) and smart contracts. Unlike simple digitization, which is often seen as the prevailing paradigm of legacy central banking systems and other centralized financial market infrastructures, decentralization and tokenization have the potential to disrupt traditional value chains in financial services and products.

Tokenization transforms assets into programmable, transferable units within decentralized systems, enabling the automated execution of transactions. Specifically, it can either eliminate long-standing financial intermediaries or fundamentally redefine their roles, particularly those of institutions traditionally responsible for managing ownership registries of financial assets within the financial and capital markets.[17]

This redefinition of roles introduces significant tensions within traditional legal institutions, which have historically served as the foundation for legal certainty in private economic relationships. Established legal concepts such as ownership, possession, and custody are increasingly being challenged and reinterpreted in response to the transformative dynamics of digital assets. The decentralized and relatively immutable nature of DLT records, combined with the possibility of exclusive control over digital assets and their programmability, necessitates a thorough reevaluation of these foundational concepts to accommodate new ways of representing and transferring goods and rights. As these historically established legal constructs are deconstructed and adapted to align with this evolving paradigm, ensuring legal clarity and the effective pro-

---

by intermediaries such as banks, clearinghouses, or central securities depositories, decentralized systems distribute data validation and control across a network of independent nodes. See: *Fabian Schär*, Decentralized Finance: On Blockchain- and Smart Contract-Based Financial Markets, Federal Reserve Bank of St. Louis Review, v. 103, n. 2 (2021), 153–174; *Dirk Zetzsche/Douglas Arner/Ross Buckley*, Decentralized Finance, Journal of Financial Regulation, v. 6, n. 2 (2020), 172–203; *Douglas Jeng/Lauren Stephanian/John Beccia/Christopher Giancarlo*, Key Elements of an Effective DeFi Framework (2023).

[17] One of the features of DLT systems that allows for different roles and arrangements compared to traditional systems is the use of consensus mechanisms to achieve agreement among network participants on the state of the ledger. These mechanisms can reduce the need for a single central party to perform record-keeping. When tokens are issued on a DLT platform, data are stored on the infrastructure (i. e., the ledger) and can include information related to the asset type, ownership details, and asset valuation, among other elements. While such functionality can potentially reduce reliance on or change the roles of intermediaries, some functions associated with tokenized markets still need to be provided by third parties. Services such as the custody and redemption of tokens issued on a DLT may require third-party service providers. *Financial Stability Board (FSB)*, "The Financial Stability Implications of Tokenisation" (2024) 7.

tection of rights becomes essential to fostering trust in private legal relationships among economic agents.

1. The Treatment of "Virtual Assets" by Law No. 14,478/2022

Although Brazilian law does not define the concepts of tokens or digital assets, a narrower and more specific meaning applies to "virtual assets" as defined by Federal Law No. 14,478/2022. This recently-enacted statute defines virtual assets as "digital representations of value that can be traded or transferred electronically and used for payments or investment purposes".[18]

While Federal Law No. 14,478/2022 represents a significant milestone for the legislative framework of crypto assets in Brazil, it is fundamentally principled in nature. Its primary aim is to set forth guidelines for the provision of virtual asset services and the regulation of virtual asset service providers.[19] The key guidelines established by the federal statute include: (i) free enterprise and competition; (ii) good governance practices, operational transparency, and a risk-based approach; (iii) information security and personal data protection; (iv) consumer and user protection; (v) safeguarding popular savings; (vi) operational soundness and efficiency; and (vii) the prevention of money laundering, terrorist financing, and the proliferation of weapons of mass destruction, in line with international standards.[20]

Virtual asset service providers, on the other hand, are defined by law as legal entities that perform, on behalf of third parties, at least one of the following services: (i) exchange between virtual assets and national or foreign currency; (ii) exchange between one or more virtual assets; (iii) transfer of virtual assets; (iv) custody or administration of virtual assets or instruments that enable control over virtual assets; or (v) participation in financial services and the provision of services related to the offer or sale of virtual assets by an issuer.[21] Federal Law No. 14,478/2022 also granted broad regulatory powers to a federal public administration entity – the Central Bank of Brazil, which was designated as responsible for regulating the operation and supervision of virtual asset service providers.[22]

Certain types of digital assets, however, were expressly excluded from the legal definition of "virtual asset" as established by Law No. 14,478/2022 and therefore are not regulated by this statute. Among the types of digital assets excluded from the regulatory scope of Law No. 14,478/2022 are national and foreign currencies, electronic money (regulated by Law No. 12,865/2013), instruments for accessing products, services, and benefits (such as points, rewards,

18 Art. 3 Federal Law No. 14.478/2022.
19 Art 1 Federal Law No. 14.478/2022.
20 Art 4 Federal Law No. 14.478/2022.
21 Art. 5 Federal Law No. 14.478/2022.
22 These powers were assigned to Central Bank of Brazil by Federal Decree 11,563/2023

and loyalty programs), and representations of assets whose issuance, registration, trading, or settlement is governed by specific laws or regulations, such as securities and financial assets.[23] By excluding these categories from the definition of virtual assets, the law ensures that they remain under their existing legal and regulatory regimes.

Having been granted by Law No. 14,478/2022 the authority to regulate the provision of virtual asset services, Central Bank of Brazil conducted a public consultation to address various relevant topics related to the matter.[24] This consultation, held between December 2023 and January 2024, sought to gather insights on issues such as asset segregation in virtual service provision, the types of assets to be traded, cybersecurity, and the provision of information and consumer protection. Drawing on the information collected and subsequent studies on the subject, draft regulations have been formulated to address the issue. These drafts have, in turn, prompted new public consultations, scheduled to take place between late 2024 and early 2025.[25]

An aspect of particular relevance for private law in the draft regulations is addressing issues related to the control of virtual assets, the effective exercise of their economic benefits, and the possible arrangements for their custody. These discussions aim to clarify who has effective ownership of digital assets, especially in the event of a custodian's insolvency. The proposed regulations seek to establish clear rules for these aspects, requiring custodians to distinguish between their own assets and those held on behalf of clients, and include provisions to ensure that the rights of asset holders are respected even in scenarios of financial distress.

2. Other Legislative Initiatives Currently under Consideration in the Brazilian Congress

These same concerns led the Brazilian Chamber of Deputies to approve a bill amending Law No. 14,478/2022 in November 2024.[26] This amendment, which still needs to be approved by the Brazilian Senate to enter into force, introduces a provision stating that assets held by clients of virtual asset service providers constitute a separate estate, distinct from the provider's own assets, and must be returned to the clients in the event of the provider's insolvency.

Additionally, another proposal is currently under consideration in the Brazilian parliament that intends to go beyond the existing legislative framework on this matter. Also in November 2024, the Special Committee on Digital Law of the Chamber of Deputies initiated a public consultation to refine the legal

---

[23] Art. 3, I to IV, Federal Law No. 14.478/2022.

[24] Central Bank of Brazil Public Consultation No. 97/2023.

[25] Central Bank of Brazil Public Consultations No. 109/2024, 110/2024, and 111/2024.

[26] Legislative Proposal (PL) 4932/2023.

framework for digital assets. This special committee, established to modernize Brazilian legal norms related to digital law, unveiled a draft legislative proposal aimed at regulating the digital asset market in Brazil. The topics addressed include cryptographically-based digital assets, distributed ledger technology, decentralized platforms, smart contracts, and asset tokenization.

III. Applying General Principles and Central Institutes of Brazilian Private Law to Digital Assets

Despite the progress made in this area, several topics related to the legal treatment of digital assets, particularly those concerning private law, have yet to receive specific attention from Brazilian legislators. This omission has not prevented economic transactions involving these assets from taking place. Therefore, the resolution of legal issues related to digital assets often needs to be sought in the general principles and central institutes of Brazilian private law.

While traditional principles of financial market and commercial law will typically apply to digital asset intermediaries, distributed ledger technology or similar innovations may introduce new legal and practical challenges. Digital assets based on these technologies depend on consensus mechanisms to manage the current state of the ledger. This ledger, in turn, documents the technological control of the assets it records. Consequently, the technological features of digital assets can complicate the application and interpretation of established legal frameworks, which depend on centralized entities to determine ownership and manage asset transfers.

Moreover, many of the central institutes of Brazilian private law were designed to meet the demands of periods preceding the digitalization of the economy and the emergence of assets issued and traded on decentralized platforms. The novel technological features of digital assets not only influence their legal characterization but also typically require efforts from interpreters to adapt these assets to existing legal categories.

1. The Materialistic Conception of Property Adopted by Brazilian Civil Code

The Brazilian legal system inherited from Roman tradition a materialistic conception of property, according to which only things (*coisas*), as a general rule, deserve proprietary protection. This view was adopted by the current Brazilian Civil Code (Federal Law No. 10.406/2002), which, in its book on property rights (*direito das coisas*), provides in Article 1.228 that the owner (*proprietário*) has the right to use, enjoy, and dispose of the thing owned by him, and the right to reclaim it from anyone who unjustly possesses or holds it.[27]

[27] Article 1.228 of the Brazilian Civil Code: "*O proprietário tem a faculdade de usar, gozar*

Although there is no rule in the Brazilian Civil Code explicitly stating that the term "thing" should be understood as referring only to tangible goods (*res corporales*),[28] this view is implicit in Book III of the Special Part of that statute – which deals with property rights – and was advocated by Ebert Chamoun, the author of the draft code on the subject. For this reason, the current Civil Code has received criticism from Brazilian legal scholars.

It is argued that it would have been preferable to maintain the wording of the previous Civil Code (Federal Law No. 3.071/1916), according to which the owner's right was linked to a good (*bem*), not to a thing.[29] Moreover, the materialistic view adopted in Book III of the Special Part of the current Civil Code seems to be incongruous with Brazilian special legislation, which recognizes proprietary protection for certain intangible goods, such as industrial property,[30] copyright[31] and software.[32] It is important to note, in this regard, that the Brazilian Constitution of 1988 itself provides that the law must ensure proprietary protection for trademarks, considering the technological and economic development of the country.[33]

Therefore, although Brazilian private law acknowledges proprietary interests in intangible assets (i. e., non-material assets) in specific cases,[34] the absence of clear guidelines on this matter in the 2002 Civil Code's section on proprietary rights creates an undesirable state of legal uncertainty in general for parties in relationships involving intangible assets.

---

e dispor da coisa, e o direito de reavê-la do poder de quem quer que injustamente a possua ou detenha".

[28] Such a rule can be found in other civil law legal systems. The German Civil Code, for example, provides in Article 90 that only corporeal objects are considered "things" under the legal definition ("*Sachen im Sinne des Gesetzes sind nur körperliche Gegenstände*").

[29] The Brazilian Civil Code of 1916 granted the owner (*proprietário*), in Article 524, the right to use, enjoy, and dispose of their goods (*bens*), and to reclaim them from anyone who unjustly possessed them.

[30] Federal Law No. 9.279/1996 (Industrial Property Law).

[31] Federal Law No. 9.610/1998 (Copyright Law).

[32] Federal Law No. 9,609/1998 (Software Law). In Brazil, software is protected under Copyright Law, but its primary regulation as an intangible asset is provided by the Software Law.

[33] Article 5°, XXIX of the Brazilian Constitution: "*A lei assegurará aos autores de inventos industriais privilégio temporário para sua utilização, bem como proteção às criações industriais, à propriedade das marcas, aos nomes de empresas e a outros signos distintivos, tendo em vista o interesse social e o desenvolvimento tecnológico e econômico do País*" (The law shall ensure to the authors of industrial inventions a temporary privilege for their use, as well as protection for industrial creations, trademark ownership, company names, and other distinctive signs, considering the social interest and the technological and economic development of the country).

[34] Exceptional situations can also be found in the jurisprudence of Brazilian courts where proprietary protection for certain intangible assets has been acknowledged, even in the absence of specific legislation. A notable example in this context is the judicial recognition of the right of use – classified as a real right – concerning telephone lines in the 1990s.

There is no clear indication in Brazilian law that the holder of a digital asset is entitled to protection equivalent to that granted to the owner of a physical property (proprietary entitlement). However, a systematic interpretation of the legal framework suggests a potential trend towards such recognition, whether through legislative amendments, doctrinal developments, or judicial rulings. Both the draft resolutions from the Central Bank of Brazil, which aim to regulate the activities of virtual asset service providers, and the legislative initiatives currently under consideration in the Brazilian Congress foresee the necessity of segregating clients' virtual assets from the assets of the service providers. Additionally, similar protections are already legally granted to holders of financial assets and securities maintained within traditional financial market infrastructures, such as registrars and central depositories.[35]

2. *Transfer of Digital Assets*

Traditional assets, such as bonds and shares, are typically defined by a set of rights and obligations established by law or contract. Their existence depends on the legal framework that governs their constitution, characteristics, and use. The applicable legislation and the contract between the parties define how the asset can be used and transferred.

Digital assets, however, are based on protocols and technological platforms that govern various aspects of their use, including transfer mechanisms. While these protocols and platforms may reflect common notions of property and asset transfer recognized by legal systems, they can sometimes operate in ways that are inconsistent with the laws and regulations governing traditional assets.

The Unidroit Principles on Digital Assets and Private Law distinguish, for that reason, the change of "control" of a digital asset from one person to another – a factual concept capable of having legal consequences – from the actual transfer of the asset. According to the Principles, "transfer" specifically relates to the change of "proprietary rights" over the asset from one person to another.[36] It is important to note, however, that the Unidroit Principles assume that digital assets can be linked to proprietary rights, an understanding that, as noted above, does not have specific normative recognition in Brazilian law.

In the absence of specific legislation in Brazil regulating the transfer of digital assets, such transfers will be governed by the contractual agreements made between the involved parties.

---

[35] When dealing with the ownership of financial assets and securities held in trade repositories and central depositories, Law No. 12,810, of May 15, 2013, mandates that these assets must be kept in specific accounts in the name of their holders and are distinct from the general assets of the infrastructures where they are registered or deposited.

[36] *International Institute for the Unification of Private Law* (UNIDROIT), UNIDROIT Principles on Digital Assets and Private Law (2023) 53.

3. Good Faith as a Guiding Principle in Business Relations

Brazilian private law enshrines good faith as a fundamental principle guiding business relations. The Civil Code stipulates, for instance, that legal transactions must be interpreted in accordance with good faith and the customs of the place where they are concluded,[37] and that contracting parties are obliged to observe the principles of honesty and good faith both in the conclusion and execution of the contract.[38] Moreover, legal transactions are null and void if they aim to defraud or violate the imperative law[39] or if their object is illicit.[40] Also, according to the Civil Code, legal transactions are voidable due to defects resulting from error, deceit, coercion, state of danger, injury, or fraud against creditors.[41]

Similarly, the good-faith agent is afforded specific legal protection under various provisions. For instance, the Civil Code safeguards the rights of third parties acting in good faith against the parties to a simulated legal transaction.[42] Likewise, the good-faith possessor is entitled, while the possession lasts, to the fruits received.[43] If the transfer of an asset is made by someone who is not the owner, it does not transfer its property, except if the asset, offered to the public at auction or in a commercial establishment, is transferred under circumstances such that, to the good-faith acquirer, as to any person, the transferor appears to be the owner.[44] Finally, a negotiable instrument cannot be taken from the bearer who acquired it in good faith and in accordance with the rules governing its circulation.[45]

These rules, which enshrine the protection of good faith in Brazilian law in both its subjective and objective dimensions, have broad application and can be employed, depending on the specific circumstances, to resolve legal problems or disputes involving digital assets. However, the unique characteristics of these assets may present new issues that warrant a legal response tailored to their peculiarities.

The Unidroit Principles on Digital Assets and Private Law, for example, specifically address the need for legal protection of the innocent acquirer of a digital asset. Nonetheless, they link this protection to the acquisition of "control" over the asset, a concept that has not yet been adopted in Brazilian law.

---

37 Art. 113 Brazilian Civil Code.

38 Art. 422 Brazilian Civil Code.

39 Art. 166, VI, Brazilian Civil Code. The expression used in the Brazilian Civil Code is "lei imperativa" meaning a rule that cannot be modified or disregarded by the will of the parties and that imposes an obligation or prohibition in an absolute manner.

40 Art. 166, II Brazilian Civil Code.

41 Art. 171, II, Brazilian Civil Code.

42 Art. 167, § 2°, Brazilian Civil Code.

43 Art. 1.214 Brazilian Civil Code.

44 Art. 1.268 Brazilian Civil Code.

45 Art. 896 Brazilian Civil Code.

4. The Legal Regime of Negotiable Instruments

In Brazilian Commercial Law, negotiable instruments emerged as innovative documents that diverged from the previous approach to common private law. This is because negotiable instruments embody the very rights they represent, in order to facilitate its circulation through simple transfer of possession to the bearer.[46] They also establish a new, entirely autonomous right that is independent of any personal exceptions that the debtor might raise against the previous holder or the original creditor. Consequently, this new autonomous right linked to the negotiable instrument circulates as a movable asset embedded in the document itself, offering greater certainty and legal security to *bona fide* third-party purchasers.

In Brazil, Article 887 of the Civil Code draws inspiration from Cesare Vivante's traditional concept of a negotiable instrument, defined as a document necessary for the exercise of the literal and autonomous right mentioned therein.[47] Article 889, § 3, of the Civil Code introduced an important innovation by allowing these instruments to be issued from digital characters created by computer or equivalent technical means and recorded in the issuer's books.

Furthermore, several laws have been enacted to explicitly authorize and regulate the issuance and circulation of book-entry negotiable instruments through entries in electronic bookkeeping systems. These systems are managed either by the issuer (in the case of financial institutions) or by a manager authorized by the Central Bank of Brazil to perform this activity. Notable examples include the provisions of Federal Laws No. 13,775/2018[48] and Federal Law No. 13,986/2020.[49]

In this context, Brazilian legal doctrine has proposed a new concept of a negotiable instrument as a record of information that, in accordance with the law, specifies a credit enforceable through compulsory execution, where personal exceptions cannot be invoked against a bona fide third party.[50] Although this

[46] The circulation of the rights incarnated on instrument may occur either by mere transfer of possession (bearer instruments) or by this transfer combined with endorsement (endorsable instruments), which involves a signature placed on the instrument, with or without the designation of a beneficiary. The Brazilian Civil Code (Article 921) also allows for the issuance of nominative instruments, whose beneficiary are recorded in the issuer's books. When physical certificates are issued to represent these instruments, the transfer of it only produces legal effects against the issuer after proper registration.

[47] *Waldiro Bulgarelli*, Títulos de Crédito (1996), p.57.

[48] Law No. 13775/2018 authorizes the issuance of duplicates, a type of negotiable instrument recognized under Brazilian law, through entries in an electronic bookkeeping system managed by authorized entities.

[49] Law No. 13.986/2020 authorizes the issuance of various negotiable instruments – such as the rural real estate note (*cédula imobiliária rural*), the bank deposit certificate (*certificado de depósito bancário*), and the rural product note (*cédula de produto rural*) – through entries in electronic bookkeeping systems.

[50] *Fábio Ulhoa Coelho*, Títulos de crédito: uma nova abordagem. (2021) 29.

new concept was not originally intended to include digital assets among electronic or book-entry negotiable instruments, it aligns with the perspective that a digital asset is a type of "controllable" electronic record. As long as it complies with the relevant governing law, it can individualize an autonomous negotiable right, enforceable through compulsory execution outside the system in which the digital asset exists. In such cases, personal exceptions would not be opposable to a bona fide third-party purchaser.

The fundamental difference between traditional commercial instruments digitally represented in centralized electronic registry systems and tokenized digital assets lies in the technology. For the latter, the use of distributed ledgers and consensus mechanisms can modify or even eliminate the role of traditional intermediaries.

Moreover, as tokenized assets are based on advanced technologies of digitalization and cryptography, there are advantages in its operation over the use of other types of commercial instruments. The contractual relationship underlying digital assets can be coded and automated through the use of smart contracts. Because of their programmability and flexibility, tokenized assets can operate with both less costs and more security than traditional negotiable instruments.[51]

IV. Custody, Control, and Insolvency

1. Custody and the Effects of Control of Digital Assets by Contracted Third Parties

In Brazilian law, as is typical in civil law jurisdictions, patrimonial rights are traditionally divided into property rights (*jus in rem*) and personal rights (*jus in personam*). Property rights are characterized by a direct and immediate legal relationship between individual and thing (*res*), conferring powers that are enforceable against the entire community (*erga omnes*). They are governed by stricter and exhaustive legal criteria (*numerus clausus*), meaning that only a limited number of property rights can be recognised by law. Personal rights, by contrast, create legal obligations between specific parties, whereby the debtor is bound to perform an obligation (to give, to do, or to refrain from doing something) in favor of the creditor under penalty of default. This fundamental legal distinction is crucial for understanding the application of concepts such as property and possession within the civil law tradition.

Technological advancements and the institutional improvement of civil law have enabled certain personal or contractual intangible rights to undergo a pro-

---

[51] *José M. Garrido*, Digital Tokens: A Legal Perspective, International Monetary Fund WP/23/151 (2023) 20.

cess of "thingness"[52] or "appropriation"[53], thereby becoming objects of property law. This includes intellectual creations (such as copyright and industrial property), software, know-how[54], and, according to some scholars, information itself.

On the other hand, the discussion of tokens as objects of property law reveals that they do not fit easily into traditional private law categories. Although tokens are intangible, they possess unique characteristics that enable perfect identification, control (exclusivity), and transferability.[55] Therefore, tokens as digital assets represent a new type of "controllable electronic record" allowing for the exercise of de facto powers (control) similar to those exercised over tangible objects subject to property rights (possession).

The aforementioned Unidroit Principles on Digital Assets and Private Law employ the concept of "control" to describe the power exercised by the "holder" of a digital asset (token). This control grants the holder the ability to: (i) prevent others from obtaining the economic benefits of the token; (ii) obtain for themselves all the economic benefits of the token; and (iii) change control of the token by transferring its ownership. However, the various contractual possibilities for the custody of digital assets highlight the challenges faced by the civil law system in reconciling traditional legal concepts with contemporary technological realities.

In civil law jurisdictions, the legal debate became evident in the judgement of the Mt. Gox Co. case[56] by the Tokyo District Court in 2015. This case involved a customer of the bankrupt Japanese bitcoin exchange who claimed the segregation and return of bitcoins on the basis of property rights, arguing that the bit-

---

[52] *Pablo Stolze Gagliano*, Direitos Reais (2023).

[53] *Daniel Fideles Steinberg*, Navigating Property and Contractual Rights in Digital Assets: Custodial Challenges in Civil Law Revista de Direito e as Novas Tecnologias 24, No. 7 (2024).

[54] In the realm of legal discipline of numerous intangible assets, Brazil has enacted Laws No. 9,279 of May 14, 1996, No. 9,609 of February 19, 1998, and No. 9,610 of February 19, 1998. These laws recognize the ownership of intellectual property assets and rights, including copyrights and computer programs, with the latter being acknowledged even without prior registration.

[55] The discussion is not exclusive to civil law. The Law Commission, an independent UK body made up of renowned jurists and experts, has presented a proposal to create a third category of property in common law. Currently, two categories are recognised: things in possession (tangible goods, such as physical objects) and things in action (legally enforceable rights, such as debts or contracts). However, digital assets, such as crypto-assets and tokens, do not fall into either of these categories, despite having characteristics that make them susceptible to proprietary rights, such as rivalry, exclusivity and technological independence. The draft bill entitled Property (Digital Assets) Bill was presented to the House of Lords on 11 September 2024. The commission proposes expressly recognizing a third thing, which digital assets would fall into. Law Commission. Explanatory Notes: Property (Digital Assets etc.) Bill. 2024. Law Commission.

[56] No. 2014(wa)33320 (Tokyo District Court, 5 August 2015). An unofficial English translation is available at: https://www.law.ox.ac.uk/sites/default/files/migrated/mtgox_judgment_final.pdf. (September 19, 2025)

coins did not belong to the bankruptcy estate of the bankrupt exchange and were owned by the plaintiff under Article 62 of Japan's Bankruptcy Law. The court denied the request, citing Article 85 of the Japanese Civil Code, which defines property as "tangible things" with physical existence. The court concluded that bitcoin was not a "thing" in the legal sense because its existence as an electronic record on a blockchain does not meet the criteria of tangibility and exclusive control. Arguments that control of the private key would confer exclusivity were rejected, with the court emphasizing the role of third parties (miners) in blockchain transfers, thus negating the rationale of exclusive control. This case is often cited as an example of the challenges faced by civil law jurisdictions in addressing the legal nature of digital assets and their implications for insolvencies.[57]

The rationale behind this decision could be applied by a court in Brazil in insolvency cases, where the jurisdiction is subject to similar legal provisions. Tokens and cryptocurrencies lack corporeality and do not have explicit legal recognition as goods subject to property rights.

In an effort to distinguish digital asset custody models, Daniel Steinberg identified three categories, each offering different levels of protection to the actual owners (clients) of digital assets: direct custody, indirect custody, and "shadow" custody. He defines custody as gaining "control of one's assets", which can be broadly defined as "having factual *possession* of an intangible asset and the exclusive ability to prevent others from obtaining substantially all of the benefit from the digital asset".[58]

Under this definition and the proposed taxonomy, custody will not be confused with self-custody services enabled by self-custodial wallet platforms or applications. These services provide clients with the means to directly manage and access their private keys, allowing them to control transaction records directly on the DLT.[59] While this option favors individual autonomy, it also introduces certain inconveniences, risks, and complexities in managing private keys, including the potential for losing private keys or forgetting recovery phrases, which are essential for maintaining access to the assets. In all custody structures

[57] Asian Business Law Institute and Singapore Academy of Law, Cryptoassets and Property Law (Civil Law Edition): China, Indonesia, Japan, Thailand, and Vietnam (Singapore: Asian Business Law Institute and Singapore Academy of Law, 2024). Available at: https://www.lexology.com/library/detail.aspx?g=ab80403e-04cd-4301-afac-d6f50126cbea. (September 19, 2025)

[58] *Daniel Fideles Steinberg*, Navigating Property and Contractual Rights in Digital Assets: Custodial Challenges in Civil Law. Revista de Direito e as Novas Tecnologias, v. 24 (2024), 24, No. 7 (2024) 2–3.

[59] DLT-based networks rely on two cryptographic keys to control transactions involving digital assets: a public key and a private key. The first one can be shared with third parties, allowing assets to be received and associated with transactions, while the second serves as the mechanism that ensures effective control over digital assets, presuming ownership of the asset.

classified by the author, the client authorizes the custodian to act on their behalf, which could include the ability to control and dispose of assets, although in certain models this is strictly for the client's account and order.

In direct custody, while the custodian technically has the ability to change control over the client's digital assets, contractual obligations prevent such actions, allowing the client direct control over their transactions on the DLT network. In this case, the client's ownership rights over the digital asset are functionally preserved, as the client maintains exclusive control over the identifiable digital asset on the DLT network (often through technological mechanisms such as multi-signature wallets).[60]

In indirect custody, there is a legally or contractually established segregation of assets – functionally comparable to trust structures in common law jurisdictions – under which fungible digital assets are held collectively by the custodian, but they are separated from the custodian's own estate.[61] This arrangement allows clients to retain functional or beneficial ownership over specific portions of the pooled fungible digital assets, despite not holding formal legal title or the private keys required for effective control the transactions on network.[62] Moreover, clients typically retain preferential rights to request the return of their assets held collectively by the custodian on demand, including in cases of insolvency.

---

[60] Contractual and technological design ensure that the client maintains exclusive or co-exclusive control over the assets in direct custody. It is structured so that the custodian cannot unilaterally dispose of the asset, reflecting the legal preservation of the client's exclusion rights. See: *Daniel Fideles Steinberg*, Navigating Property and Contractual Rights in Digital Assets: Custodial Challenges in Civil Law (2024), 6–7.

[61] "In the 'indirect' custody, the client has a claim in rem for a specific token because of the legal architecture in place: an artificial non-fungibility, created by law and designed as unique by the parties. In particular, the multiplier of assets is not allowed, and a factual co-ownership is in place. [...] Although blockchain creates a rivalrousness environment ('if I have it, you don't'), uniqueness is something harder: since every token worth the same as any other of the same nature (e.g., one bitcoin worth one bitcoin) and have the same attributes, they are exchangeable. Legally, therefore, they are fungible. [...] The co-ownership characteristic of the indirect custody derives from two facts, [...]. Firstly, although both the client and the custodian have the right to request the assets on demand, the client has always the preference. Secondly, the custodian is not authorized to issue new tokens to extend digital assets credit to a borrower, thus the client maintains, in theory, its claim in rem for a specific token. Note that the latter framework is created by law, because, in fact, the uniqueness is not present." *Daniel Fideles Steinberg*, Navigating Property and Contractual Rights in Digital Assets: Custodial Challenges in Civil Law (2024) 8.

[62] In Brazil, this kind of segregation is recognised under different legal frameworks. For example, Law No. 12,810/2013 establishes a type of fiduciary ownership (*titularidade fiduciária*) in favor of investors in the context of central securities depositories, creating a legal separation between the custodian's and the clients' assets. Similarly, Law No. 12,865/2013 imposes a legal segregation regime on funds held in payment accounts by e-money issuers. In both cases, the structure creates a separate pool of fungible assets – commonly referred to in Brazilian legal scholarship as *patrimônio de afetação* – which is shielded from the custodian's or issuer's general estate and serves to protect the rights of clients or account holders.

Finally, the client only has a contractual claim (*jus in personam*) against the custodian in shadow custody, and not a property right (*jus in rem*). The tokens, similarly other fungible goods, are absorbed into custodian's estate, thus exposing the client to the custodian´s credit risk in the event of insolvency.[63]

The Brazilian Civil Code does not specifically regulate fiduciary custody services provided by intermediaries in the financial and capital markets, or in other sectors. Consequently, in accordance with the principle of private autonomy that allows parties to negotiate the terms and conditions of their contract, the rules applicable to deposit contracts under Chapter IX of the Civil Code should apply to digital assets held under third-party custody. This encompasses all the legal challenges associated with classifying digital assets as things subject to property and the implications of their functional fungibility.

Under a deposit contract in Brazilian law, the depositary receives a movable asset to keep until the depositor claims it (Article 627). The depositary is obliged to take the same care and diligence in the custody and conservation of the deposited asset as he would exercise over his own property and must return it "with all its fruits and additions, when required by the depositor" (Article 629).

Since the deposit of fungible items (such as currency) is legally treated as a loan contract (Article 645), the depositary is obliged to return to the lender an item of the same kind, quality, and quantity (Article 586), thus transferring control of the deposited asset to the custodian.

Under this contractual foundation of private law, banks are permitted to maintain only fractional reserves of the total value of their liability obligations arising from bank deposits. This allows them to appropriate the remaining funds raised from the public for investment in credit operations (financial intermediation), thereby creating deposit money (book money) in the economy through the banking multiplier. This contractual structure is very similar to what is referred by Daniel Steinberg as shadow custody.

Regarding payment accounts used to hold electronic money issued by nonbank payment service providers in Brazil, the asset segregation regime explicitly provided for in Articles 12 and 12-A of Law No. 12,865/2013, applies. Al-

[63] "In the 'shadow' custody, however, the client does not have a claim in rem for a specific token, only a personal right. Because of the multiplier capability of the custodian (enabling the custodian to issue more tokens of, in theory, the same quality and quantity), both the rivalrousness and uniqueness characteristics are not present. [...] In both 'indirect' and 'shadow' types of custody the underlying legal methodology is similar, but it is not the same. Although the dual availability is present in both, the client preference is only a rule in the indirect type, whereas in shadow custody the client only generally has the preference, i.e. not a rule. In addition, there is a very salient distinction: in the indirect custody the client does not bare the creditworthiness risk of the custodian, while in the shadow custody the custodian's creditworthiness is the central element for the client to re-claim its assets." *Daniel Fideles Steinberg*, Navigating Property and Contractual Rights in Digital Assets: Custodial Challenges in Civil Law. (2024) 8.

though these providers receive fungible assets transferred to their ownership under "deposit" structure (either money transferred from other account or physical cash deposits), such funds are segregated from their general state and must be allocated to the fulfillment of contractual payment obligations. They cannot engage in financial intermediation activities with these funds (leverage), which is a privilege reserved for financial institutions (Article 6, § 2 of Law nº 12,865/2013). To ensure the effectiveness of this legal segregation, regulatory requirements issued by the Central Bank require the maintenance of 100 percent reserves on the amounts held on deposit in electronic money. This is achieved through the preservation of liquid and safe assets maintained in accounts held at the Central Bank or invested in federal government bonds, which must be available to meet transfer or redemption requests on demand.

This type of legal segregation closely resembles the concept of indirect custody, where the digital assets segregated from the custodian´s estate can be freely managed and sold by the custodian, since equivalent asset of the same type, quality, and quantity are held and could be return on the client demands. An example of this structure is found in collective portfolios for exchange clients' digital asset, which allow greater freedom in the management and disposal of the assets under collective custody.

A bill recently approved by the Chamber of Deputies and pending approval by the Federal Senate seeks to amend Law nº 14.478/2022[64] to establish a legal segregation regime for financial resources held in client accounts and virtual assets held by clients that are on deposit or in direct or indirect custody by virtual asset service providers in Brazil.

However, Article 3 of Law No. 14.478/2022 excludes from its definition of virtual assets certain digital assets, such as utility tokens and digital assets that represent other assets whose issuance, bookkeeping, trading, or settlement is provided for by law or regulation, such as securities and other financial assets. Depending on the restrictive or broad interpretation of this legal segregation, this may create gaps or overlapping legal regimes applicable to virtual assets or virtual asset service providers.

Additionally, the draft regulation submitted for public consultation by the Central Bank of Brazil[65] aims to outline the main characteristics of the contractual arrangement for the custody of virtual assets. This includes the safekeeping and effective control of the virtual asset and the instruments, such as private keys in a blockchain, that influence ownership rights. The regulation requires the maintenance of accurate and continually updated records of client's assets, the reconciliation of these records with distributed ledger systems, and the execution of client instructions related to asset transfers, encumbrances, or other

[64] Legislative Proposal (PL) 4932/2023.
[65] Central Bank of Brazil Public Consultations No. 109/2024.

transactions. Custodians must ensure that the rights, utility, and economic benefits linked to the asset remain exclusively accessible to the client and are available in a timely manner. They are also responsible for preserving the asset's inherent characteristics and addressing incidents that may affect its value, quantity, or ownership.

The exercise of custody serves as a legal translation of the factual "control" over virtual assets by providing mechanisms that protect the client's ability to assert their rights and enjoy the asset's economic and utility benefits. These measures include ensuring exclusivity and prompt accessibility, as well as mitigating risks of unauthorized access or misuse. By defining these operational and legal standards, the draft regulation strengthens legal certainty and aligns the technological management of digital asset ownership with regulatory requirements, fostering trust and clarity in the separation between ownership and custody (control) of virtual assets.

2. Legal Challenges in the Event of the Custodian's Insolvency

In the Brazilian context, the absence of legal provisions ensuring the segregation of digital assets or recognizing tokens as subject to property right within legislation (*numerus clausus*) could leave clients under custody contract more vulnerable to legal and financial risks, especially in insolvency scenarios.

Article 85 of Law nº 11.101/2005 (the Brazilian Bankruptcy Law) allows for the restitution of assets unduly seized in bankruptcy proceedings. This rule seeks to ensure that third-party assets, which for contractual, legal, or circumstantial reasons were in the bankruptee's possession, are not unduly included in the bankruptcy state for satisfaction of creditors. The law draws no distinction regarding the nature of the assets eligible for restitution; however, the application of this right faces limitations from the very notion of an "asset" under civil law. It depends on clear criteria for segregation and on the ability to establish that the bankrupt party did not have legal or contractual control or ownership over the asset (availability) seized in the judicial bankruptcy process. A long-standing judgment by the Brazilian Supreme Court[66] reinforces the possibility of restitution (recovery) of funds (credit rights) under specific conditions, but the lack of effective segregation remains a practical and legal barrier to its unrestricted application. This context highlights the need for both contractual mechanisms and legal provisions to ensure the segregation of assets, protecting third parties and enhancing legal certainty in bankruptcy proceedings.

Therefore, the restitution of digital assets under bankruptcy law remains controversial due to the absence of legal recognition of tokens as identifiable assets or of express segregation mechanism. Custody models that recognize property

[66] Súmula No. 417/1964 of the Brazilian Supreme Court. Journal of Justice. Section 1. 06/07/1964. p. 2182.

rights over tokens offer stronger legal protection in insolvency scenarios, underscoring the need to adapt traditional legal concepts to emerging technologies. The challenges inherent to custody structures demonstrate the need for regulatory and legislative development to guarantee both legal certainty and the economic functionality of digital asset market.[67]

More effective legal protection in insolvency proceedings seems to require legal or regulatory improvements that address the following issues: (i) the legal and factual segregation of digital assets held in custody, to avoid the commingling of assets between those of the custodian and those of clients, and, where applicable, between assets of clients with different rights; (ii) the legal recognition of tokens as intangible movable good (asset) that can be subject of property rights, thus addressing the *numerus clausus* limitation; and (iii) the legal definition of direct or indirect control over private keys as a functional equivalent to possession in civil law.

V. Private International Law Aspects

Digital assets based on distributed ledger technology present complex issues in private international law, especially due to the geographic distribution of nodes that maintain the ledger recording the data constituting or representing these assets.[68] The varying legal treatments of digital assets across different jurisdictions mean that choice of law rules can significantly influence the rights and obligations of parties involved in transactions with these assets.

In the realm of cross-border distributed ledger technology, two crucial questions arise: which legal framework governs the digital asset, and how can ownership claims be enforced within the appropriate jurisdiction. The use of decentralized, permissionless blockchains can therefore present challenges, particu-

[67] The ability to promptly return custodied digital assets in the context of an intermediary's insolvency depends on the custodian's records enabling the insolvency administrator to identify and trace the specific digital assets held on behalf of each client. In arrangements involving shared control, such as shared-signature mechanisms (e.g., multisignature arrangements), the client retains partial control over the digital asset, which helps preserve ownership and ensures that the assets remain segregated from the custodian's estate. In contrast, indirect custody refers to structures in which the intermediary retains exclusive control over the private keys and holds digital assets collectively on behalf of multiple clients. In such cases, the custodian must maintain accurate, individualized records linking each client to their specific custodied assets. Proper individualization and traceability – whether through DLT and through internal books and records – are critical. When the custodied digital assets are properly identified, they are not considered part of the insolvent custodian's estate and are shielded from general creditors. Conversely, if the custodian fails to maintain adequate records that allow for the traceability, clients can be treated as unsecured creditors, without priority in the recovery of their digital assets.

[68] *United Nations Commission on International Trade Law (UNCITRAL).* Taxonomy of Legal Issues related to the Digital Economy (2023) 46.

larly when there is no identifiable legal entity to address claims related to disputed on-chain assets. In such cases, it may be unclear which governing law applies to the platform or which courts have jurisdiction to resolve disputes and enforce claims. Addressing these issues may necessitate the development of new conventions for resolving conflict-of-laws matters.[69]

The resolution of private international law problems is less challenging when a legal entity responsible for the custody or safekeeping of digital assets can be identified. Under current Brazilian legislation, both financial intermediaries and virtual asset services providers are permitted to operate within the country only with prior authorization from the regulatory authorities,[70] and must comply with Brazilian laws.[71] From a regulatory standpoint, therefore, companies engaged in asset tokenization activities must comply with Brazilian laws and obtain authorization to operate in the country, particularly if they are classified by law as financial institutions or virtual asset services providers. These companies will be under the supervision of the regulatory authorities and must adhere to Brazilian constitutional, legal, and regulatory norms. This includes their interactions with national public entities (such as financial regulatory authorities) and the contractual relationships they establish with end users of their services and products.

There is, however, concern about the challenges of applying traditional rules and connecting factors to digital assets within distributed ledger systems, particularly when these systems are highly decentralized.[72] Since these assets can be classified as intangible and lack a physical location, applying the existing Brazilian legal rule – which requires the law of the country where the assets are located to govern their qualification and regulation[73] – becomes a difficult task.

---

[69] *International Swaps and Derivatives Association (ISDA).* Navigating Bankruptcy in Digital Asset Markets: Digital Asset Intermediaries and Customer Asset Protection (2023) 24

[70] For financial institutions, the requirement for authorization from the Central Bank of Brazil is established in Article 18 of Law No. 4,595/1964. For providers of virtual asset services, this requirement is specified in Article 2 of Law No. 14,478/2022, and further regulated by Decree No. 11,563/2023, which, in its Article 1, assigns this authority to the Central Bank of Brazil. Engaging in capital market activities, on the other hand, including the issuance, brokerage, and settlement of securities transactions, requires authorization from the Securities and Exchange Commission, as mandated by Law No. 6385/1976.

[71] The *Law of Introduction to the Brazilian Legal Rules* (Decree-Law No. 4,657/1942), the main Brazilian statute on private international law, mandates that legal entities "must comply with the law of the state in which they are constituted" (Article 11). Additionally, foreign legal entities are prohibited from establishing 'branches, agencies, or establishments' in Brazil "until their constitutive acts are approved by the Brazilian government, and they are subject to Brazilian law" (Article 11, § 1).

[72] *José M. Garrido*, Digital Tokens: A Legal Perspective, IMF WP/23/151 (2023) 40.

[73] Article 8 of Decree-Law n° 4,657/1942 enshrines the principle of "*lex rei sitae*", stating that "the law of the country where the assets are located shall apply to qualify them and regulate the relations concerning them".

VI. Conclusion

Brazilian private law provides legal protection to holders of digital assets but faces significant challenges in integrating some of the characteristics of DLT technology into traditional civil law institutions, which have historically ensured legal certainty in private economic relationships. As we have concluded in this article, established legal concepts such as ownership, possession and custody are increasingly being challenged and reinterpreted in response to the transformative dynamics of digital assets.

The decentralized and relatively immutable nature of DLT records, combined with the possibility of exclusive control over digital assets and their programmability, demands a reevaluation of these fundamental legal concepts to accommodate new ways of constituting, representing and transferring assets and rights under private law.

Law nº 14,478/2022, which defines "virtual assets" as digital representations of value that can be traded or transferred electronically and used for payment or investment purposes, establishes guidelines for the provision of services related to "virtual assets". However, the principle-based nature of this law leaves many issues outside its normative scope, requiring the application of general principles and central institutes of private law to digital tokens.

An example was the need to clarify, in the draft regulation submitted for public consultation by the Central Bank of Brazil based on the authority of the Law No. 14.478/2022, the main characteristics of the contractual arrangement for the custody of virtual assets. This included incorporating into the regulatory proposal the effective custody and control of a virtual asset and the associated instruments (e.g. private keys) that influence their property rights.

The Brazilian Civil Code adopts a materialist conception of property, protecting mainly tangible assets. Although private law in Brazil recognizes the protection of intangible assets in specific cases, such as industrial property and copyright – including, notably, software – the lack of clear guidelines on digital property can create situations subject to legal uncertainty. The segregation of virtual assets from the assets of service providers, as envisaged in legislative proposals under consideration in Congress, suggests a legislative trend towards recognizing these digital assets as capable of being subject to property rights, including in cases of dispute between different types of creditors in insolvency proceedings.

The exclusion of certain digital assets from the definition of virtual assets in Law No. 14.478/2022 – such as utility tokens and digital assets that represent other assets whose issuance, bookkeeping, trading or settlement is provided for by law or regulation, such as securities and other financial assets – highlights the need for a broader approach in Brazilian private law. Tokens can be classified as intangible assets subject to control and ownership by an owner, which does not exclude then from being considered a new type of digital instrument that evidences (e.g. a ticket, a digital identity or a copyright) or constitutes rights over other tangible or intangible assets (e.g. negotiable instrument with an unconditional promise or order to pay, deliver a good or perform a service).

This approach would prevent relevant legal issues with a transversal application to economic relations from being confined to the functional approach typical of regulatory law (e.g, payment tokens, security tokens, cryptoassets, etc.). Such an approach to digital assets within private law does not necessarily require implementation of a general digital assets act, rather, it could be achieved through specific legal amendments, aligned with demands and development of economic relations.

For example, the absence of specific legislation in Brazil on the transfer of digital assets means that these transfers are currently governed by contractual agreements between the parties involved. However, the reliance on on-chain transfer records as proof of ownership requires legislative clarification to align digital practices with traditional property law (*jus in rem*).

The distinction between control and transfer of property rights, according to the UNIDROIT Principles, highlights the need to adapt legal rules to accommodate the unique characteristics of digital assets. Good faith is a fundamental principle of Brazilian private law, which guides the interpretation and execution of legal transactions. Although the protection of good faith in the digital assets environment has not yet been fully incorporated in Brazilian practice, the application of this principle, consistent with the UNIDROIT Principles, could help resolve disputes involving digital assets and ensure legal certainty in token-based transactions.

Negotiable instruments (either in physical or book-entry form), which incorporate autonomous rights and circulate like a movable good, offer an interesting parallel for the regulation of digital assets. The possibility of issuing negotiable instruments in digital form, recognized by the Brazilian Civil Code and some specific legislations of negotiable instruments in Brazil, suggests that digital-assets could be treated in a similar way, provided they meet the relevant legal requirements.

Finally, to improve the legal treatment of digital assets in Brazilian private law, it seems necessary to introduce some specific improvements to explicitly recognize tokens as: (i) intangible movable asset that can be the subject of property rights (thus expanding *numerus clausus*); and (ii) controllable, movable and transferable digital instrument (controllable electronic records), which may either merely evidence a right or actually incorporate and constitute autonomous rights over goods or contractual obligations, exercisable on-chain or off-chain, similar to traditional negotiable instruments.

Such an approach would allow tokens to "encapsulate" rights over goods or contractual rights with the same legal certainty, thereby facilitating their circulation and use in commercial transactions. In addition, it is essential to create clear rules on the fiduciary custody of tokens and the rights or goods attached to them. In the same way that the fiduciary ownership structures are provided for the operators of traditional financial market infrastructures under Brazilian law for the exclusive purposes of safekeeping and controlling beneficial owners' assets, it is crucial to specify the duties of custodians and the rights of token holders in the event of custodian's insolvency, ensuring the protection of clients' assets and the proper segregation of the assets under custody. These are examples of measures that may be adopted in private law to promote greater trust, enhance legal certainty in digital assets, and further encourage the development of the token economics in Brazil.

France

Etienne Farnoux

I. Introduction

For more than a decade, legal practitioners, academics, judges and legislators in France and elsewhere have been grappling with the issues raised by the legal apprehension of digital assets.

In the French legal system, the expression "digital asset" ("*les actifs numériques*") did not, until very recently, designate a legal category to which a specific homogenous legal regime would correspond. For one thing even the terminology remained unsettled for a long time. The term "crypto currency" ("*crypto-monnaie*") has been in use in the public discussion, no doubt because of the evocative power of the term currency ("*monnaie*"), which designates a well-defined legal category.[1] This term can however, and for that very reason, be the source of unfortunate misunderstandings, or at least shortcuts. The terms "digital asset" ("*actif numérique*") or "crypto-asset" ("*crypto-actif*") both have the advantage of being more legally neutral, as the term "asset" ("*actif*") does not itself constitute an identified pre-existing legal category. "Digital asset" is the term used by the recent UNIDROIT Principles on Digital Assets and Private Law ("UNIDROIT Principles") (and by the French legislator in 2019) while the term "crypto-asset" is preferred in the recent European Regulation

[1] *Caroline Kleiner*, La monnaie dans les relations privées internationales (2010) 15–88; Rémy Libchaber, Recherches sur la monnaie en droit privé (1992) 19–71.

MiCA ("MiCA Regulation"[2]), as well as, even more recently, by the French legislator (in 2024).

The French legal framework on crypto-assets mainly consists of three successive texts. The first one is domestic law, *Loi Pacte* of the 22 May 2019 (*"Loi Pacte"*[3]) which sought to regulate, among other things, token issuers and digital asset service providers ("DASPs" or *Prestataires de services sur actifs numériques, "PSAN"*). The *Loi Pacte* proposed an initial definition of crypto-assets, referred to as "digital assets". This definition, contained in article ("art.") L. 54-10-1 of the French Monetary and Financial Code, distinguished between tokens representing a value and those conferring a right. A third category concerned tokens that qualified as financial instruments and were subject to the regime of this latter category of assets. A regime covering transactions and service providers was established. However, no regime covering the transfer of ownership had been included in 2019.

Then came the MiCA Regulation of the 31 May 2023 which aims to establish a harmonized European regulatory framework for crypto-assets, while protecting European citizens from the risks inherent in their use. This text governs, among other things, the offering and admission to trading of crypto-assets, as well as crypto-asset service providers ("CASSPs", *Prestataires de service sur crypto-actifs, "PSCA"*). Art. 3 para. 1 subpara. (5) of the MiCA Regulation defines "crypto-asset" as "a digital representation of a value or of a right that is able to be transferred and stored electronically using distributed ledger technology or similar technology". Where the French *Loi Pacte* referred to "digital assets", the European regulation prefers to use the notion of "crypto-assets". This is essentially a semantic difference.[4] Indeed, the French and European definitions are similarly based on the notions of representation of rights and value. However, the two concepts do not completely overlap. As will be explained later, the French definitions will remain in force for the transitional period, i.e. until the end June 2026. After the 1 July 2026 French law will align itself with the notion of crypto-asset within the meaning of the MiCA Regulation.[5]

The Regulation applies to the various categories of crypto-assets defined by the European regulation[6], while those that do not fall into these categories, such as NFTs, are not affected. It sets out the terms and conditions of transactions

---

[2] Regulation (EU) No. 2023/1114 of the European Parliament and of the Council of 31 May 2023 on markets in crypto-assets and amending Regulations (EU) No. 1093/2010 and (EU) No. 1095/2010 and Directives 2013/36/EU and (EU) 2019/1937, OJ 2023 L150/40.

[3] Loi n° 2019-486 relative à la croissance et la transformation des entreprises, J.O. No. 0119 of 23 May 2019.

[4] On this dicussion see the Haut Comité Juridique de la Place Financière de Paris (HCJP), Rapport sur le règlement MiCA, 27 January 2024, <https://hcjp.fr/fr/nouvelles-technologies-financieres> (16 September 2025) 14.

[5] *HCJP*, Rapport MiCA (n. 4) 14.

[6] Art. 3 para. 1 subpara. (5) MiCA Regulation.

involving these crypto-assets, and the issue of their transfer is taken into account.[7] Exchanges of these crypto-assets or against legal tender are defined within the framework of market platforms,[8] and service providers responsible for their transfer have even been set up.[9] The circulation of these goods is therefore secure. Additionally, art. 70 para. 1 of the MiCA Regulation provides that "Crypto-asset service providers that hold crypto-assets belonging to clients or the means of access to such crypto-assets shall make adequate arrangements to safeguard the ownership rights of clients, especially in the event of the crypto-asset service provider's insolvency, and to prevent the use of clients' crypto-assets for their own account". If the Regulation envisages transfers of crypto-assets and makes a reference to ownership rights, it calls for a more detailed examination of the property status of crypto-assets, especially as certain questions have a non-negligible practical impact. For example, what triggers the transfer of ownership of crypto-assets? Does the handing over of private keys entail the transfer of ownership, or does the transfer only result from a change of registration on the blockchain? Will a bona fide purchaser of a crypto-asset be able to rely on possession as a basis for title against a claim by the true owner? These questions are not answered by the MiCA Regulation.

Last, came an Ordinance n°2024-936 of the 15 october 2024 ("2024 Ordinance"[10]) amending the French legislation to bring it in line with the MiCA Regulation. It should be noted that another Ordinance of the same day includes money laundering provisions concerning crypto-asset transfers, but will not envisaged here.[11] The 2024 Ordinance was influenced by a report, directed by H. de Vauplane and P. Barban, for the Haut Comité Juridique de la Place financière de Paris and published on the 27 January 2024 ("HCJP Report"[12]).

Certain innovations of the 2024 Ordinance are directly linked to the MiCA Regulation. For instance, the provisions of the regulation put an end to the national regime of PSANs and replace it with that of PSCAs, and modified the regime of companies authorized to provide services in crypto-assets. However, following the proposals of HCJP Report, the 2024 Ordinance went further than

---

[7] Art. 70 to 74 MiCA Regulation.

[8] Art. 77 MiCA Regulation: "Exchange of crypto-assets for funds or other crypto-assets".

[9] Title V MiCA Regulation: "Authorization and operating conditions for crypto-asset service providers".

[10] Ordonnance n° 2024-936 relative aux marchés de crypto-actifs, J.O. No. 0247 of 17 October 2019. The ordinance was adopted on a parliementary authorization Loi n° 2024-364 portant diverses dispositions d'adaptation au droit de l'Union européenne en matière d'économie, de finances, de transition écologique, de droit pénal, de droit social et en matière agricole, J.O. No. 0095 of 23 April 2024, art. 6, III.

[11] Ordonnance n° 2024-937 relative au renforcement des obligations de lutte contre le blanchiment de capitaux et le financement du terrorisme en matière de transfert de crypto-actifs, J.O. No. 0247 of 17 October 2024; Ordonnance n° 2024-936 relative aux marchés de crypto-actifs (rectificatif), J.O. No. 0266 of 6 November 2024.

[12] *HCJP*, Rapport MiCA (n. 4).

the MiCA Regulation, which mostly concerns the regulation of crypto-assets. Indeed, as the HCJP Report pointed out, the Regulation "raises questions about the private law aspects of crypto-assets, and especially their patrimonial aspects".[13]

Before spelling out the rules clarifying the legal nature of digital assets and their ownership transfer regime (see section III. below), it is necessary to identify the relevant provisions (see section II. below). Some miscellaneous issues, which have so far been left open in the French legislation, will briefly be outlined at the end (see section IV. below).

II. Identification of the relevant texts applicable to "digital assets"/"crypto-assets"

The 2024 Ordinance introduced a new title – Title II bis "Digital assets" (Les actifs numériques) – into the Book II of the French Monetary and Financial Code, entitled "Products" ("*Les Produits*") and which includes two other titles, "Title I – Financial instruments" ("*Les instruments Financiers*") and "Title II – Savings products" ("*Les produits d'épargne*"). The new Title II bis has come into force on the 30 December 2024 and, as of the 1 July 2026, will be entitled "Crypto-assets" ("*Les crypto-actifs*"). It contains four provisions (art. L. 226-1 to L. 226-4).

These provisions are not the only ones dealing with digital assets. Art. L. 54-10-1 of the French Monetary and Financial Code was introduced by the *Loi Pacte*, as part of a Chapter dedicated to digital assets and crypto-assets service providers. This provision was also amended by the 2024 Ordinance. As a consequence, two successive versions will be applicable. The first one applicable from the 18 October 2024 to the 1 July 2026 and the second one will come into force on the 1 July 2026.

As a result of this temporal distinction two different terminologies must be distinguished: one temporary, until the 1 July 2026 and one supposedly definitive, after.

Between the 18 October 2024 and the 1 July 2026, art. L. 54-10-1 of the French Monetary and Financial Code provides, temporarily, that "digital assets" encompass three categories of assets: *(i)* the "crypto-assets" subject to MiCA Regulation ; *(ii)* "tokens" which are defined as "as intangible assets representing, in digital form, one or more rights that can be issued, registered, retained or transferred by means of distributed registry technology enabling the owner of said asset to be identified, directly or indirectly" and *(iii)* "any digital representation of value that is not issued or guaranteed by a central bank or public authority,

[13] *HCJP*, Rapport MiCA (n. 4) 23.

that is not necessarily attached to a legal tender and that does not have the legal status of a currency, but that is accepted by natural or legal persons as a means of exchange and that can be transferred, stored or exchanged electronically".

The relevance and legitimacy of such an approach has been questioned, as the tokens covered by art. L. 54-10-1 are crypto-assets subject to MiCA Regulation. The temporary retention of the notion of "digital assets", formally in use in the French legislation, alongside that of "crypto-assets", preferred by the MiCA Regulation, is due to the existence of a transitional period for the application of the MiCA Regulation. Fortunately, after the 1 July 2026, the framework will be simplified. Art. L. 54-10-1 of the French Monetary and Financial Code will apply to "crypto-assets" subject to MiCA Regulation. Title II bis will accordingly be renamed "crypto-assets".

As of the 1 July 2026, the new art. L. 226-1, L. 226-2 and L. 226-3 of the French Monetary and Financial Code, introduced by the 2024 Ordinance, will also apply to "crypto-assets", and no longer to "digital assets". It should be noted that art. L. 226-1 states that, for the purposes of Title II bis, crypto-assets are those subject to MiCA Regulation. However, it cannot be inferred from this statement that only such crypto-assets exist. Indeed there are other types which are not subject to MiCA Regulation, such as financial instruments represented using distributed ledger technology.

III. Nature and legal regime of digital assets/crypto-assets

It was argued for some time that several private law or proprietary issues regarding digital assets needed to be tackled in the French legislation, notably the exact nature of incorporeal assets, the regime of transfer of ownership, the protection of *bona fide* purchasers, as well as the seizure of crypto-assets.[14] Before spelling out the proposals of the HCJP Report on these pressing issues (see section 2. below), as well as the solutions set out in the 2024 Ordinance (see section 3. below), it is necessary to set the scene by outlining the general elements of the discussion (see section 1. below).

1. General elements of discussion

As crypto-assets are "representations of value or of a right", in the expression of the MiCA Regulation,[15] the wording suggests that all crypto-assets do not confer the same rights, and are therefore not of the same nature: some represent a claim against an issuer, while others represent value. This difference in nature potentially gave rise to the application of different patrimonial regimes in do-

[14] *HCJP*, Rapport MiCA (n. 4).
[15] Art. 3 para. 1 subpara. (5) MiCA Regulation.

mestic French law, especially in the absence of specific provisions. It was argued that crypto-assets representing rights or claims (notably stable-coins) should be subject to the French rules governing the transfer of claims,[16] which should not be the case for crypto-assets representing values, which allegedly constitute *sui generis* intangible assets.

Under French law, the right of ownership is defined by art. 544 of the French Civil Code, which states that "ownership is the right to enjoy and dispose of things in the most absolute manner, provided that one does not make use of them in a way prohibited by laws or regulations". The right of ownership is divided into three components: *usus*, the right to use the thing one owns; *abusus*, the right to dispose of the thing one owns; and *fructus*, the right to receive the fruits or products of the thing one owns. Before the MiCA Regulation came into force, French law did not strongly affirm (in a striking difference with the provisions on financial securities) that digital assets could be subject to a right of ownership. However, this did not seem to be a matter of debate. The debate, rather, concerned the legal nature of the asset, along the lines of the distinction traditional in the French law (and admittedly most civil law countries) between, real rights and personal rights. It seems, in this respect, that the legal qualification of digital assets could be similar to that of financial securities: the asset itself (financial security or digital asset) is not a real right as such, but the holder has a real right of ownership over it. The asset itself constitutes a complex claim, namely a personal right against the issuer covering the repayment of the asset. However, some crypto-assets do not have issuers and hence do not confer any rights "against" a person.

In any case, the starting point is that if digital assets are susceptible of appropriation, the question then arises as to how ownership of a digital asset is assigned. Two key concepts must be discussed in this respect, that of "possession" and its relations with the concept of "control", as well as that of ownership and its transfer.

a) Possession and control

In the French context, the question of appropriation naturally raises the issue of whether the traditional concept of "possession" applies to digital assets, which exist solely as code within a computer protocol. From this perspective, the debate closely parallels those surrounding digital financial securities, which are no longer recorded through book entries but instead represented by code on a blockchain or distributed ledger technology (DLT). French law generally recognizes the effects of possession of movable property. Art. 2276 of the French civil Code famously provides that "in the case of movable property, possession is the equivalent of title". However, the Cour de cassation refused to apply

[16] Art. 1321 to 1326 French Civil Code.

art. 2276 of the French Civil Code to intangible property[17] and an art. L. 211-16 was inserted into the French Monetary and Financial Code in 2009, giving the same effects as possession in good faith first to the entry of financial securities in a registry, and then to the registration in a blockchain or DLT of digital financial securities in the name of the person identified by the blockchain or DLT.[18]

As an element of comparison, the UNIDROIT Principles are based on the notion of control. According to the Principles, the notion of control is intended to protect the *bona fide* acquirer of a digital asset, even though control is not the exclusive element necessary to benefit from such protection.[19] The notion of control also serves the purpose of ensuring third-party effectiveness of a security right in a digital asset[20] as well as to organize the priority of its beneficiaries.[21]

In the French context, it is generally argued that the notion of control is used as a substitute for the traditional concept of possession.[22] Indeed, the UNIDROIT Principles confer a dual effect on control. The first, which can be described as the "positive side", refers to the ability to use an asset (for example, by exercising a voting right attached to it), or to dispose of it (for example, by transferring it on the blockchain); and the second effect, which can be described as the "negative side", relates to the power to block. When it comes to settling disputes between successive purchasers of the same asset, the first meaning is a priori the most appropriate, but when it comes to ensuring the third-party enforceability of a guarantee, the second effect is pertinent. Understood in this way, control makes it possible to attribute to the holder of a digital asset prerogatives similar to those of possession.[23]

In technical terms, the notion of "control" is closely linked, in the UNIDROIT Principles, to the ability to transfer digital assets onto the blockchain (or DLT). It is this ability to move and transfer that characterizes control, which implies an element of exclusivity. That element of exclusivity is also present in the concept of possession: possession only characterizes the situation of a single person, to the exclusion of all others. This is obvious when possession relates to a tangi-

---

17 Cass.civ. 1e 2 March 1960, n° 141, Bull.civ. 1960, I, n° 141; Cass.com. 7 March 2006, n° 04-13.569, Bull. civ. 2006, IV, n° 62.

18 Art. L. 211-16 French Monetary and Financial Code: "Nul ne peut revendiquer pour quelque cause que ce soit un titre financier dont la propriété a été acquise de bonne foi par le titulaire du compte-titres dans lequel ces titres sont inscrits ou par la personne identifiée au moyen d'une technologie des registres distribués mentionnée à l'article L. 211-3".

19 *UNIDROIT*, UNIDROIT Principles on Digital Assets and Private Law: Draft for Consultation (2023), no. 8: "Innocent Acquisition".

20 *UNIDROIT*, Principles (n. 19) no. 15: "Control as a method of achieving third-party effectiveness".

21 *UNIDROIT*, Principles (n. 19) no. 16: "Priority of security rights".

22 *Hubert de Vauplane/Patrick Barban/Thiery Granier*, Le transfert de propriété des crypto-actifs, Revue de droit bancaire et financier N° 1 (2025) 66–70, 66.

23 *De Vauplane/Barban/Granier*, Le transfert (n. 22) 69.

ble asset, as in art. 2276 para. 1 of the French Civil Code. This idea of exclusivity is also clear in the case of intangible movable property that are registered in an official register (e.g., certain intellectual property rights) or recorded in a single account. Less so when the intangible movable property is not registered or recorded.

b) Ownership applied to crypto-assets, and transfer of ownership

Prior to the 2024 Ordinance, the French law regime applicable to ownership and transfer of ownership of crypto-assets was not unified but differentiated depending on the specific nature of the asset. The general issue was that traditionally in French civil law, the existence of a transfer of ownership depends on the individualization of the object of transaction. With the advent of blockchain technology, the field became marred with hesitations, as the legal nature of crypto-assets appeared not to be unitary, but falling in different alternative categories.

A first category was that of so-called "crypto-currencies", characterized by the absence of any right conferred on the holder, which were classified as a "*bien*" ("property"), and more precisely intangible movables ("*meubles incorporels*") which are fungible ("*choses de genre*"). This is the case for the best-known crypto-assets such as bitcoin and ether. This characterization was adopted in a remarkable but isolated decision by the Nanterre Commercial Court.

In this case, the dispute arose in the context of a bitcoin loan contract between companies specializing in the trading of digital assets.[24] The loan was repaid, but only in principle (in bitcoin), with interest still due (also in bitcoin). Furthermore, a so-called "hard fork" had occurred during the operation, affecting the Bitcoin blockchain[25] and resulting in the creation of a new cryptocurrency, bitcoin cash ("BCH"). Who was to receive these new crypto-assets, the lender or the borrower? At stake in the dispute was the characterization under French law of the bitcoin loan, between a "loan for use" ("*prêt à usage*") and a so-called "consumption loan" ("*prêt de consommation*"), meaning that the goods are to be consumed then replaced by the borrower. That characterization was itself dependent in turn on the legal characterization of the bitcoin. Did it constitute a "*corps certain*" (thing susceptible of individualization) or a fungible object ("*chose de genre*")? The court ruled that the bitcoins were fungible objects.[26] As a result, it was the object of a "consumption loan", and the bitcoin cash consti-

[24] T. com. Nanterre 26 February 2020, JurisData n° 2020-002798 (*BitSpread v. Paymium*); *Maxime Julienne*, Le régime civil des actifs numériques : l'exemple du prêt de bitcoins, Semaine juridique Entreprises et Affaires N° 19 (2020) 41–44; *Hubert de Vauplane*, Fongibilité du Bitcoin: l'exemple du "Bitcoin Fork" et des contrats de prêt de Bitcoin, RTDF N° 2/3 (2018) 89–92, 89.

[25] For details of this operation, see the commentaries above.

[26] On the debate, see comments above. *Nicolas Barbaroux, Richard Baron and Amélie*

tuted fruits to be enjoyed by the borrower. A necessary implication of this characterization was that the transfer of ownership of these crypto-assets was governed by the ordinary rules applicable to intangible property, namely the exchange of consents and transfer of property *solo consensus.*[27] It should be noted that in French sales law, transfer of ownership is a legal effect of the contract, but the seller's obligations relate to delivery of the item sold and a specific warranty ("*garantie d'éviction*" or warranty of quiet possession) to the benefit of the new owner.

For all other tokens, those conferring rights on the holder, it was necessary to analyze the nature of these rights. These tokens could fall in two different categories: financial securities or claims. In the first case, the transfer would be governed by the rules relating to the transfer of financial securities. In the second case, the rules applicable would be those provided for the transfer of claims.

As a result, a crypto-asset could receive three possible characterizations: that of a fungible object ("*chose de genre*"), that of a claim ("*créance*") and that of a financial security ("*titre financier*"). These three characterizations have consequences for the system of transfer of ownership.

The first category, that of "fungible objects", requires reference to French general sales law. As a rule, it generally provides for the principle of a *solo consensu* transfer of ownership once agreement has been reached on the thing and the price.[28] However, in the case of movable property, a distinction must be made as to whether the thing sold is fungible or not, as illustrated by the case decided by the Nanterre Commercial Court. For a "*corps certain*" (non fungible) such as an NFT, the transfer will take place *solo consensu* on the date of the agreement, unless otherwise stipulated. For other types of crypto-assets, which are fungible ("*chose de genre*"), usually issued as part of a mass, the transfer of ownership is delayed until the date of their individualization.[29] This could take place at the time of registration on the blockchain, i.e. at the time of delivery. However, the law excludes the case of goods sold *en bloc* (block sale) – an entire stock, for example – which can be immediately identified and for which the transfer of ownership will be immediate. As a result, the transfer of all crypto-assets attached to an address can be carried out *en bloc*, following the same rules as for the sale of certain objects.[30]

Favreau, Blockchain et finance – approche pluridisciplinaire, Répertoire IP/IT et Communication 2020, 125, no. 61.

[27] Art. 1196 para. 1 French Code civil: "Dans les contrats ayant pour objet l'aliénation de la propriété ou la cession d'un autre droit, le transfert s'opère lors de la conclusion du contrat"; art. 1583 French Code civil: "[La vente] est parfaite entre les parties, et la propriété est acquise de droit à l'acheteur à l'égard du vendeur, dès qu'on est convenu de la chose et du prix, quoique la chose n'ait pas encore été livrée ni le prix payé".

[28] Art. 1196 para. 1 and art. 1583 French Code civil.

[29] Art. 1585 French Civil Code.

[30] Art. 1586 French Civil Code.

The second category, that of crypto-assets characterized as claims, calls for the application of specific rules governing the transfer of claims, rules that differ from the ordinary law of sale. Thus, prior to the 2024 Ordinance, tokens representing claims against an issuer were treated as claims. The assignments of claims have to be made in writing[31] and ownership is transferred on the date of the deed, unless otherwise stipulated.

Finally, for financial tokens classified as financial securities a specific regime is applicable, that of art. L. 211-17 of the French Monetary and Financial Code: the formation of the contract is consensual but the transfer of ownership will result from registration in the decentralized securities register in the name of the new owner.

This differentiated approach to transfers of ownership, depending on the exact nature of the assets or rights transferred was not completely unworkable but it was not without difficulties either. Even though these are all digital assets relying on a similar computerized transaction process, they received widely diverging legal treatments. These difficulties of classification hampered the determination of the regime or regimes applicable to crypto-assets and called for legislative intervention. The 2024 Ordinance, taking its cues from the HCJP Report, took the opposite view and created a unified system of transfer of ownership for crypto-assets.

2. The proposals of the HCJP Report

Published on the 27 January 2024, the HCJP Report[32] recommended the creation of a specific regime for the transfer of ownership of crypto-assets, making no distinction between crypto-assets representing rights or values. The underlying justification is that all crypto-assets are negotiable in practice, by virtue of the unity of their digital medium, and that it is therefore appropriate to set aside the system of assignment of claim, including for the crypto-assets that only represent rights or claims. The proposed regime is largely based on the existing regime for financial securities. The HCJP Report suggested extending the existing regime for the registration of financial securities in an account as a framework for the legal regime of crypto-assets and making the distributed ledger (the blockchain) the basis of ownership, following the example of securities credited to an account. Thus, according to the HCJP Report, and using the existing formulation for financial securities, the transfer of ownership would result from the entry in the register.

---

[31] Art. 1322 French Civil Code: "La cession de créance doit être constatée par écrit, à peine de nullité".

[32] The HCJP was tasked by the Direction générale du Trésor (a service of the Ministry of the economy and finance), the Autorité des Marchés Financiers and the Autorité de Contrôle Prudentiel et de Résolution in order to assess the need for changes to French legilsation on digital assets, in anticipation of the entry into application of the MiCA regulation.

The HCJP Report then distinguished between two situations. First, a general principle, according to which the registry in question is a DLT on which the crypto-assets in question are backed. In this case, it is this inscription in the blockchain that constitutes the transfer of ownership. The second situation is seen as an exception to the first, and concerns only "intermediated" crypto-assets, i.e. crypto-assets that are held in the custody of a crypto-asset service provider mentioned in para. 1 of art. 75 of the MiCA Regulation, providing custody and administration of crypto-assets on behalf of clients. In this case, it is not the DLT register that constitutes the medium of the transfer of ownership, but the register of positions held by the intermediary mentioned in art. 75 para.2 of the MiCA Regulation. Apart from these two cases, the ordinary law regime for intangible movable property would apply, notably to the case of off-chain transfers. Lastly, the HCJP Report recommended the inclusion in positive law of a specific provision on the protection of *bona fide* purchasers, along the lines of the existing regime for financial securities.

3. The contribution of the 2024 Ordinance

The 2024 Ordinance echoed these proposals by addressing some of these issues in the new Title II bis introduced into the French Monetary and Financial Code, which comprises 4 new texts, including art. L. 226-1, L. 226-2 and L. 226-3. A stand is finally taken on the nature and regime of "digital assets", soon to be renamed "crypto-assets".

Here again it is necessary to distinguish between the two successive versions of art. L. 226-1 (again due to the transitional period of application of the MiCA Regulation). At present, art. L. 226-1 of the French Monetary and Financial Code defines "distributed registry technology", "consensus mechanism", "DLT network node" and "distributed registry". In so doing, it echoes the definitions set out in art. 3 para.1 subparas. (1)–(4) of the MiCA Regulation.[33] From the 1 July 2026 on, a last paragraph will be added, stating that "For the purposes of this title, crypto-assets are those subject to Regulation (EU) 2023/1114 of the European Parliament and of the Council of May 31, 2023 on crypto-asset markets". The definitions will however remain, even though they have been made useless. In the following provisions (L. 226-2 and L. 226-3), the terms "digital

[33] Art. L. 226-1 French Monetary and Financial Code: "Aux fins du présent titre : 1° La 'technologie des registres distribués' ou 'DLT' désigne une technologie qui permet l›exploitation et l›utilisation de registres distribués ; 2° Le 'mécanisme de consensus' désigne les règles et les procédures par lesquelles les nœuds d›un réseau DLT parviennent à un accord sur le fait qu›une transaction est validée ; 3° Le 'nœud de réseau DLT', désigne un dispositif ou un processus qui fait partie d'un réseau et qui détient une copie complète ou partielle des enregistrements de toutes les transactions dans un registre distribué ; 4° Le 'registre distribué' désigne un répertoire d›informations qui conserve un enregistrement des transactions et qui est partagé et synchronisé au sein d›un ensemble de nœuds de réseau DLT, au moyen d›un mécanisme de consensus".

assets" will be replaced by "crypto-assets" at the same date. It is generally argued that by the 1 July 2026 French Law will effectively be in tune with MiCA Regulation.

The new art. L. 226-2, I of the French Monetary and Financial Code states quite simply that "digital assets are negotiable intangible assets" ("*des biens incorporels négociables*"). This specific characterization also appears in the definitions of the tokens in art. L. 54-10-1, 1°, of the French Monetary and Financial Code (see above) and is consistent with art. 3 para. 1 subpara. (5) of the MiCA Regulation, which defines crypto-assets.

The characterization as a "*bien*" ("asset") implies that the digital asset may be the object of ownership right ("*appropriation*"). French law is open to the idea of a right of ownership on intangible assets but usually provides for specific regimes relating to the ownership of such assets. The negotiability of the asset implies that it will be able to circulate (and be transferred) according to the simplified formalities of commercial law, without having to comply with the formality required of transfers of claims in order to be effective against third parties. This characterization implies that crypto-assets, like financial securities, may be transferred in a simplified way, without having to apply the formalities of art. 1690 of the French Civil Code.[34] This, by the way, is clearly specified in the new art. L. 226-2, II of the French Monetary and Financial Code, which sets out the regime for the transfer of ownership of digital assets. The characterization set out in L. 226-2, I of the French Monetary and Financial Code is widely accepted in the literature.[35]

In the second part of art. L. 226-2 para. 1 lays down a rule of principle: "the transfer of ownership of digital assets results from the registration of these digital assets for the benefit of the acquirer in the DLT". This formulation clearly mirrors the provision applicable to financial securities, art. L. 221-17 of the French Financial and Monetary Code.[36] This method of transfer is the most obvious in the sense that it relies on the operation of a blockchain register, preceded by a transaction.[37]

However, this is not the only way to transfer a crypto-asset. Indeed, following again the HCJP Report, para. 2 of the second part of art. L. 226-2 provides

---

[34] Art. 1690 French Civil Code: "Le cessionnaire n'est saisi à l'égard des tiers que par la signification du transport faite au débiteur. Néanmoins, le cessionnaire peut être également saisi par l'acceptation du transport faite par le débiteur dans un acte authentique".

[35] *De Vauplane/Barban/Granier*, Le transfert (n. 22) 69; *Thierry Bonneau*, L'ordonnance n° 2024-936 du 15 octobre 2024 relative aux marchés de crypto-actifs, Revue de droit bancaire et financier N° 6 (2024) 44–50, 46.

[36] Art. L. 211-17 French Financial and Monetary Code: "I. – Le transfert de propriété de titres financiers résulte de l'inscription de ces titres au compte-titres de l'acquéreur ou de l'inscription de ces titres au bénéfice de l'acquéreur au moyen d'une technologie des registres distribués [...]".

[37] *HCJP*, Rapport MiCA (n. 4) 24.

that "by exception, when digital assets are held by a crypto-asset service provider mentioned in para. 1 of art. 75 of Regulation (EU) 2023/1114 [...] on crypto-asset markets, the transfer of ownership of digital assets results from the registration of the acquirer's position in the register mentioned in para. 2 of art. 75 of the same regulation". In short, "the transfer takes place by change of registration in a position register held by a crypto-asset custodian".[38] This specific regime is explained by the specific circumstances in which crypto-assets are held in practice. Indeed, custodians do not typically register a transaction on the distributed ledger for each crypto-asset movement request. The financial cost and time consumption of each transaction means that more conventional registry movements are preferred. Nevertheless, the duties imposed on these custodians highlights the decisive role they play in the transfer of ownership of crypto-assets. The 2024 Ordinance therefore distinguishes between crypto-assets held by an intermediary system and those held independently. This is an appropriate choice, as it leaves it up to the owner to decide whether to hold the crypto-asset in his or her own custody or to have it held by a professional.[39] An interesting point is that this regime would seem to preclude any transfer of ownership of a cryptographic key directly to the new owner. In the views of French law, possession of this key does not confirm transfer of ownership. At most, it confers control over crypto-assets, but without any translative effect on ownership.

Finally, art. L. 226-3 of the French Monetary and Financial Code provides for the protection of bona fide purchasers: "no one may claim, for any reason whatsoever, a digital asset whose ownership has been acquired in good faith by the owner of such digital assets". This text reproduces the rule laid down in art. L. 211-16 of the French Monetary and Financial Code for financial securities.

IV. Miscellaneous issues

The analysis developed above only applies to transfers of ownership *inter vivos*. The solution is different in the case of inheritance or bequest.[40] In the case of inheritance, the transfer takes place by operation of law – subject to the rules governing acceptance. A priori, the transfer is not based on the blockchain transaction. In practice, the main difficulty for heirs is to identify the *de cujus*' assets and find the keys to access them.[41] In the case of bequests, practice also

[38] *HCJP*, Rapport MiCA (n. 4) 25.

[39] *De Vauplane/Barban/Granier*, Le transfert (n. 22) 69.

[40] *HCJP*, Rapport MiCA (n. 4) 28.

[41] *Olivier Boudeville/Christophe Vernière*, La transmission, in : L'hérédité numérique, ed. by Sara Godechot-Patris/Nicolas Laurent-Bonne (2023) 37–45, nos. 18 s.

tends to ensure that the legatee can be given the keys themselves. It should be noted, however, that in this case, handing over the key is not so much a condition for transferring ownership as a means of entering into possession.[42]

As movable property, crypto-assets can be seized by a creditor under its general right of lien. However, there is currently no regime under French Law for seizing crypto-assets.[43] Art. L. 231-1 of the French Code des procédures civiles d'exécution ("*CPCE*")[44] nonetheless regulates the seizure of intangible rights other than money claims. While the associated regime currently covers the seizure of shares and securities, the wording of art. L. 231-1 *CPCE* seems sufficiently broad to encompass crypto-assets representing rights or claims. Nevertheless, the system put in place relies on the presence of a third party (issuer, agent, authorized intermediary) who is involved in the seizure operations. It is this third party who is responsible for declaring the assets held on behalf of the debtor, and for transferring the assets involved in the seizure. When crypto-assets are held *via* a service provider, this scheme can be transposed without too much difficulty: the service provider will play much the same role as the authorized intermediary for shares and securities. On the other hand, when the debtor holds his crypto-assets in his own name, they cannot be seized without knowledge of the private key. There are specific provisions punishing the failure to disclose cryptographic keys but these are specific to criminal law (art. 434-15-2 Penal Code) and are not applicable in the context of art. L. 231-1 *CPCE*. Overall, the issue with the seizure of crypto-asset is not really a legal one, but rather a technical one: the risk is that digital assets held in their own right without a third-party custodian or service-provider are *de facto* exempt from any seizure.

Lastly, the patrimonial regime of crypto-assets also influences the rules applicable to their restitution in the event of default by a custodian or service provider.

The first paragraph of art. 70 of the MiCA Regulation provides that "Crypto-asset service providers that hold crypto-assets belonging to clients or the means of access to such crypto-assets shall make adequate arrangements to safeguard the ownership rights of clients, especially in the event of the crypto-asset service provider's insolvency, and to prevent the use of clients' crypto-assets for their own account". Such an obligation imposed on crypto-assets service providers is of course welcome, but it does not mean that they will always perform it adequately, and the consequences of failure are not provided for in the MiCA Regulation. Here, a distinction should be made between different situations: the intermediary is placed under an insolvency regime; the intermediary commits a

---

[42] *HCJP*, Rapport MiCA (n. 4) 28.

[43] *HCJP*, Rapport MiCA (n. 4) 28.

[44] Art. L. 231-1 *CPCE*: "Tout créancier muni d'un titre exécutoire constatant une créance liquide et exigible peut faire procéder à la saisie et à la vente des droits incorporels, autres que les créances de sommes d'argent, dont son débiteur est titulaire".

fault or error in his or her crypto-asset custody mission; the intermediary is involved in fraud; the intermediary participates in fraud.

In the first case, that of the insolvency of the intermediary, French law does not provide for any particular and specific regime derogating from the ordinary regime applicable to intermediaries, whether regulated or not, who are custodians of their customers' digital assets. There is a debate on the question of whether the owner of a digital asset held through an intermediary is entitled to the recovery of the digital assets he owns, or whether he merely has a claim for restitution in equivalent terms. In the French legal context, the outcome depends on the characterization of the deposit or of the loan if the digital assets are the subject of a loan.[45] According to an opinion, the owner of the digital assets is entitled to the recovery of the assets, provided that assets of the same kind are held by the custodian, as is the case with financial securities. According to others, and due to the fungible and sometimes consumable nature of these digital assets, digital asset holders have merely a personal claim against the intermediary. Their situation may be even less protected if they have authorized their intermediary to dispose of their digital assets (e. g., through "staking" operations) in the contract they have signed with the intermediary, insofar as this is permitted under national law, which would be tantamount to the intermediary becoming the actual owner of the digital assets.

In the second hypothesis, that of the fraud committed by the intermediary, the intermediary may be held contractually liable in the event of non-compliance with its obligation to hold crypto-assets under the custody agreement. French case law imposes an absolute obligation on the custodian of financial securities to return the securities, even in the event of fraud, taking the view that the role of the custodian[46] and the obligations incumbent on it are a matter of public policy.[47] On this point, the applicable French law for digital assets differs from the solution applicable to financial securities. Under French law (and more precisely the General Regulation of the AMF, the French Financial Markets Authority), a custodian of digital assets is not strictly obliged to return the digital assets, but merely to ensure "that the necessary procedures are in place to return to customers the digital assets it holds on behalf of customers, or the means of access, as quickly as possible".[48] The provision used to reserve the case where the disappearance of the digital assets could not be attributed to the cus-

---

[45] T. com. Nanterre 26 February 2020 (n. 24).

[46] Cass.com. 10 March 2015, n° 14-11.046.

[47] Cass.com. 4 May 2010, n° 09-14.187, Bull. civ. 2010, IV, n° 83 (*Société Générale*); Cass. com. 4 May 2010, n° 09-14.975, Bull. civ. 2010, IV, n° 82 (*Société RBC Dexia Investor services bank France*); Cass.com. 4 May 2010, n° 09-14.976.

[48] Art. 722-1 no. 6 General Regulation of the French Financial Markets Authority (*Règlement général de l'AMF*): "[Le conservateur des actifs numériques] veille à ce que les procédures nécessaires soient en place pour restituer le plus rapidement possible aux clients les actifs numériques qu'ils détiennent pour le compte des clients ou les moyens d'accès".

todian.[49] It is no longer the case, even though the definition of "events not attributable to the digital asset custodian" remains in place.[50] The outcome is not entirely clear: do "events not attributable to the digital asset custodian" still constitute an excuse for the custodian? In which case is the custodian under an obligation to return to customers the digital assets itself rather than the means of access to it? In which case is the customer entitled to indemnification? In the third case, if the intermediary has been hacked or defrauded by a third party in relation to the digital assets in its custody, the intermediary's liability will be that of a custodian of fungible intangible assets, and will depend on the proper performance of its custodial obligation. Here again, the classic case law on deposit contracts will apply. Finally, if the intermediary has participated in the fraud, either as a perpetrator or as an accomplice, he may be prosecuted for breach of trust or fraud.[51]

[49] Art. 722-1 no. 6 General Regulation of the French Financial Markets Authority (version before the 29 July 2023): "[...] Sauf en cas d'événements non imputables, directement ou indirectement, au prestataire de services sur actifs numériques, il effectue la restitution de la maîtrise des moyens d'accès aux actifs numériques au client dans les meilleurs délais. En cas d'impossibilité de restitution de la maîtrise de ces moyens d'accès, le conservateur d'actifs numériques indemnise son client".

[50] Art. 722-1 no. 6 General Regulation of the French Financial Markets Authority: "Les événements non imputables au conservateur d'actifs numériques comprennent notamment tout événement dont il pourra démontrer qu'il est indépendant de son fonctionnement, notamment un problème inhérent au fonctionnement du dispositif d'enregistrement électronique partagé ou à un programme informatique automatisé ('smart contract') pouvant reposer sur un dispositif électronique d'enregistrement partagé qu'il ne maîtrise pas".

[51] Cass.crim. 30 May 1996, n° 95-82.487, Bull. crim. 1996, n°224 (*Société de bourse Tuffier, Ravier, Py); Bernard Bouloc*, Abus de confiance et valeurs mobilières dématérialisées, Revue des sociétés 1996, 806–806, 806.

Germany and the EU

Sebastian Omlor

I. Introduction

German private law, like many other continental European private law systems, faces the challenge that its property law is limited to tangible objects. However, data sets such as crypto-assets in particular are not physically tangible, which causes difficulties in the applicability of property law, if not even ruling it out entirely. This narrow definition results in numerous consequential problems with regard to the absolute protection of crypto-assets and their transfer. Against this background, this article ends with legal policy statements on a new private law of crypto-assets in the German Civil Code (*Bürgerliches Gesetzbuch*, BGB). However, electronic securities represent a special area which permits the in rem tokenisation of fund units, shares and bearer bonds on the basis of a special law.

In contrast, there is no comprehensive codification of private law at EU level. The EU lacks the corresponding legislative competence, as the principle of limited individual authorisation applies to the member states. According to this principle, the EU may only take action to the extent that the member states have assigned it corresponding legislative powers in the treaties. As a result, the EU can only make use of its legislative competence in specific areas, including legal harmonisation in the internal market, consumer protection and the single currency. For this reason, the following section will focus on crypto-regulation, currency law, payment services law and EU money laundering law.

II. German Private Law

1. Lack of Definition and Concept

The German Civil Code, the central codification of German private law, still lacks a cross-sectoral legal definition of tokens or crypto-assets. This applies not only to German private law, but also to the entire German legal system. Elements of a transnational soft law definition (e.g. in UNIDROIT Principles) can be established in order to increase the global coherence of regulatory concepts. However, such concepts, especially if they originate exclusively from the academic sphere and have not been legitimised by the legislator, do not replace subsumable facts with sharpened edges that lead to practical application results in the respective legal systems. Only the specific case of electronic securities finds a legislative statement in the form of the German "Electronic Securities Act" (eWpG). However, there is also no fully formulated legal definition of electronic securities or tokens in general.

In contrast, both EU law and the derived German banking supervisory law provide a legal definition of crypto-assets, which could potentially be transferred to private law in the future. This definition is rooted in the concept of "crypto-assets" as outlined in the Markets in Crypto-Assets Regulation (MiCAR), which has since been adopted by the German Banking Act (KWG). The MiCAR definition of crypto-assets is broad and designed to be adaptable to future developments, thereby encompassing various types of crypto-assets. It does not differentiate based on the function or legal nature of the crypto-asset, and it is not limited to a specific technology; it also acknowledges technologies similar to Distributed Ledger Technology (DLT).

2. *Legal Nature under Property Law*

German private law limits the scope of its property law to tangible objects[1], as laid out in § 90 BGB, which, owing to the intention of the authors of the law, is not to subject incorporeal objects to the third book of the BGB.

Accordingly, the motives state that 'real power cannot be exercised over things that exist only in the imagination, namely over aggregated assets and rights'[2]. The requirement of physicality is intended to functionally ensure spatial delimitation and controllability of the object.[3] In order to ensure the latter, the object must be perceptible to the senses. Accordingly, electricity,[4] sound waves[5] and heat[6] are excluded as objects. Software[7] and other digital content[8] cannot be categorised as objects either; only their storage media[9] have physicality and therefore material quality. However, storing software on a physical storage medium does not make it a physical object; both objects – storage medium and software – must be considered separately.

Consequently, tokens do not constitute objects within the meaning of § 90 BGB[10] unless a special statutory provision for electronic securities (§ 2 (3) eWpG) applies. As with other data, it is not sufficient for a physical data carrier to exist.

---

[1] *Jörg Fritzsche*, in: Beck-Online, Kommentar zum BGB (2024) § 90 no. 4.

[2] Mot. III S. 2: "(ü)ber Dinge, welche nur in der Vorstellung bestehen, namentlich über Sachgesamtheiten und Rechte, ... sich eine reale Macht nicht üben (läßt)".

[3] *Malte Stieper*, in: Staudinger, Kommentar zum BGB (2021) § 90 no. 1.

[4] Reichsgericht in Zivilsachen 5 February 1904 – VII 424/03, RGZ 56, 403, 404; *Christina Stresemann*, in: Münchener Kommentar zum BGB (2025) § 90 no. 24.

[5] *Jörg Mössner*, in: Beck-Online, Großkommentar zum Zivilrecht (Stand: 15.03.2024) § 90 no. 71.

[6] BeckOK BGB/*Fritzsche* (n. 1) § 90 no. 7.

[7] *Helmut Redeker*, IT-Recht (2023) nos. 278 ss.

[8] Differentiating *Marietta Auer*, Digitale Leistungen, ZfPW 2019, 130–147, 137 ss.

[9] *Redeker*, IT-Recht (n. 7), no. 281; *Thorsten Ammann*, in: Computerrechts-Handbuch, ed. by Jürgen Thager/Jan Pohle (looseleave, April 2024) chapter 32.2 no. 14; *Georg Borges*, Kann ein Gegenstand nicht Sache und doch Sache sein? Computerprogramme im Privatrecht, in: FS Martinek (2020) 45–59, 47.

[10] *Franziska Boehm/Paulina Pesch*, Bitcoins: Rechtliche Herausforderungen einer virtuellen Währung: Eine erste juristische Einordung, MMR 2014, 75–79, 77; *Christian Engelhardt/Sascha Klein*, Bitcoins – Geschäfte mit Geld, das keines ist Technische Grundlagen und zivil-

It would not do justice to the nature of a decentralised database to link it to a data carrier that can be distributed geographically at will. The private key also only grants technical access to individual tokens, but does not represent the token as such.[11] The sectoral insertion of a material fiction exclusively for electronic securities also argues in favour of the private law legislator being aware of the lack of material quality of tokens and therefore ordering a fiction and not a presumption. The legislative materials to the electronic securities act (eWpG) explicitly state the following about tokens in general: 'There is no physical reference object, a thing.'[12]

Tokens cannot be owned within the meaning of § 903 BGB; electronic securities are once again an exception. As tort law only protects property within the meaning of §§ 90 ss. and 903 BGB,[13] the only potential classification for tokens under § 823 (1) BGB is as *'sonstiges Recht'*. In material terms, this requires the object of protection to be similar to property.[14] However, tokens do not have an exclusion and utilisation function comparable to property under German law.[15] There is also no comparability with property, especially as only authorised possession is recognised as an *'sonstiges Recht'*.[16] In contrast, electronic securities can be considered property within the meaning of § 903 BGB due to § 2 (3) eWpG, so that they are subject to the scope of protection of property in § 823 (1) BGB.[17]

---

rechtliche Betrachtung, MMR 2014, 355–360, 357; *Benjamin Beck/Dominik König*, Bitcoin: Der Versuch einer vertragstypologischen Einordnung von kryptographischem Geld, JZ 2015, 130–139, 132; *Paulina Pesch*, Crypto-Schulden (2017) 101 ss.; *Sebastian Omlor*, Kryptowährungen im Geldrecht, ZHR 183 (2019), 294–345, 308; *Andreas Walter*, Bitcoin, Libra und sonstige Kryptowährungen aus zivilrechtlicher Sicht, NJW 2019, 3609–3614, 3611 ss. (arguing in favour of a partial analogy in this context); to the contrary *David John*, Zur Sachqualität und Eigentumsfähigkeit von Kryptotoken, BKR 2020, 76–81, 76 ss.

[11] *Leonid Shmatenko/Stefan Möllenkamp*, Digitale Zahlungsmittel in einer analog geprägten Rechtsordnung, MMR 2018, 495–501, 497.

[12] *Deutscher Bundesrat*, Entwurf eines Gesetzes zur Einführung von elektronischen Wertpapieren, BR-Drs. 8/21 of 1 February 2021, p. 39.

[13] *Gerhard Wagner*, in: Münchener Kommentar zum BGB (2024) § 823 no. 285

[14] *Alexander Peukert*, Güterzuordnung als Rechtsprinzip (2008) 249; *Herbert Zech*, Information als Schutzgegenstand (2012) 86.

[15] *Gerald Spindler/Martin Bille*, Rechtsprobleme von Bitcoins als virtuelle Währung, WM 2014, 1357–1369, 1359 ss.; *Markus Kaulartz*, Die Blockchain-Technologie, CR 2016, 474–480, 478; to the contrary *Shmatenko/Möllenkamp*, Digitale Zahlungsmittel in einer analog geprägten Rechtsordnung (n. 11) 498; *David Paulus/Robin Matzke*, Smart Contracts und das BGB – Viel Lärm um nichts?, ZfPW 2018, 431–465, 453.

[16] BGH 4 September 1997 – VI ZR 348/96, NJW 1998, 377; *Claus-Wilhelm Canaris*, Die Verdinglichung obligatorischer Rechte, in: FS Flume, vol. I (1978) 371–427, 401; MüKoBGB/*Wagner* (n. 13) § 823 no. 370; BeckOK BGB/*Förster* (n. 1) § 823 no. 156.

[17] *Sebastian Omlor*, Allgemeines Privatrecht, in: Handbuch Kryptowährungen und Token, ed. by Sebastian Omlor/Mathias Link (2023) chapter 6 no. 38.

3. Transfer

Beyond the eWpG, there are no specific rules governing the transfer of tokens. As a result, the rules for transferring tokens differ depending on the type of token in question. The process of identifying the relevant transfer regime is divided into two stages:[18]

a) Form

The first step is to determine whether the transfer is carried out through a legal transaction or as a factual act. The German Civil Code (BGB) does not contain any exclusivity rule requiring that assets must always be transferred through legal transactions. Rather, if tokens do not qualify as crypto securities, they do not fall under any of the existing legal provisions for the transfer of goods (§§ 873, 929 ss. BGB), claims (§§ 398 ss. BGB), or other rights (§ 413 BGB). Tokens are neither objects under § 90 BGB nor claims or rights within the meaning of § 413 BGB, as they lack the necessary subjective legal position.[19] Consequently, the determination of whether the transfer constitutes a simple factual act or a legal transaction depends on whether the parties involved have the intention to be legally bound.

The presence of a binding legal intention can generally be determined for each blockchain network. The underlying program code and the whitepaper play a decisive role in this assessment. For instance, the Bitcoin whitepaper assumes the irreversibility of transactions and the replacement of interpersonal trust with cryptographically-based system trust. As a result, Bitcoins are transferred through a factual act. In contrast, the transfer of crypto securities is carried out through legal transactions, as stipulated by the eWpG (see §§ 9, 25 ss. eWpG).

b) Contractual Transactions

In the case of a legal transfer, various opinions have emerged in the legal literature. Some advocate for an analogy to the rules on movable property under §§ 929 ss. BGB[20] or real property under §§ 873, 892 BGB[21]. Others favor the application of the rules on the assignment of claims and rights under §§ 398 ss., 413 BGB.[22]

---

[18] To the following already *Omlor*, Allgemeines Privatrecht (n. 17) chapter 6 no. 76 ss.

[19] *Jan Busche*, in: Staudinger, Kommentar zum BGB (2022) § 413 no. 3.

[20] *Philipp Koch*, Die "Tokenisierung" von Rechtspositionen als digitale Verbriefung, ZBB 2018 359–368, 362 ss.; *Andreas Walter*, NJW 2019, 3609–3614, 3611 ss.; *Rüdiger Veil*, Token-Emissionen im europäischen Kapitalmarktrecht, ZHR 183 (2019) 346–387, 350; for security tokens *Maurice Ribak*, Wertpapierrecht der Security Token Offerings (2023) p. 315.

[21] *Thorsten Ammann*, Bitcoin als Zahlungsmittel im Internet, CR 2018, 379–386, 382 ss.; for an analogy to both §§ 929 ss. and §§ 873 ss. see *Johannes Arndt*, Bitcoin-Eigentum (2022) p. 113 ss.

[22] *Jan Lieder*, in: Beck-Online, Großkommentar zum Zivilrecht (Stand: 01.08.2024) § 413

Proponents of a property law-based solution already consider tokens to be quasi-proprietary rights de lege lata, relying on the comparable legal interests. Tokens are separable and distinguishable from one another, cannot be arbitrarily duplicated, and are accessible for exclusive use. Thus, transfer is achieved through agreement and registration on the blockchain. In the context of movable property law, this registration is viewed as a substitute for delivery in the public ledger of the blockchain. If a comparison to real property law is drawn, the blockchain serves as a private registry, functioning as a substitute for a land registry.

In contrast, those who support the application of §§ 413, 398 ss. BGB argue that property law does not require "dematerialization" but rather "rematerialization." Property law is not coincidentally linked to the concept of an object under § 90 BGB, which requires physicality. Possession law, in particular, is based on the physical nature of objects. On the other hand, the law governing the assignment of claims and rights provides a separate transfer regime that is inherently tailored to intangible assets. However, this approach faces the challenge that privately uncategorized tokens do not constitute other rights under § 413 BGB, making a direct application of these provisions infeasible.

c) Bona Fide Acquisition

The good faith acquisition of tokens constitutes a distinct doctrinal area. This issue is not only rooted in private law dogmatics concerning a suitable apparent authority and the attribution of such appearance to the rightful owner, but also involves a constitutional law perspective. Good faith acquisition provisions in private law are considered to be content and limit determinations of property rights under Article 14 (1) sentence 2 of the German Basic Law (GG). As a result, constitutional law requires a statutory basis for intervention that sufficiently defines the guidelines and limits.

These constitutional boundaries and the methodological prerequisites for applying analogies complicate the good faith acquisition of ownership by analogy to §§ 932 ss., 892 BGB, as the legally recognized holder of apparent authority would need to be substituted by an entity that is not regulated by law – namely, the public ledger of the blockchain. Nevertheless, proponents of a property law-based approach also consider the possibility of acquiring tokens in good faith from an unauthorized party.

If, however, the legal transfer of tokens is analogized to §§ 413, 398 ss. BGB, good faith acquisition is not permissible under current law. § 405 BGB can

no. 31; *Marc d'Avoine/Phil Hamacher*, Kryptowerte in der Insolvenz (Teil II), WM 2024, 525–535, 530; for utility and investment tokens *Thomas Eckhold/Frank A. Schäfer*, Kryptowerte, Kryptowährungen und Kryptowertpapiere, in: Handbuch des Kapitalanlagerechts, ed. by Heinz-Dieter Assmann/Rolf A. Schütze/Petra Buck-Heeb (2024) § 17 no. 33, 44; for an analogous application see *Omlor*, Allgemeines Privatrecht (n. 17) chapter 6 no. 85.

neither be applied directly nor by analogy, as the rightful owner has not issued a certificate (or its equivalent, if applied analogously).

4. Protection

The German Civil Code offers protection for assets against third parties, i.e., absolute protection, not only through property law but also through statutory obligations related to unjust enrichment and tort law. The level of protection that the current private law framework provides for tokens needs to be examined.

a) Property law

Since tokens cannot be classified as objects under § 90 BGB – unless they are crypto securities under the eWpG – property ownership cannot be established for them. Consequently, property law protection does not apply to tokens. Specifically, claims such as vindication under § 985 BGB[23] or claims arising from possession-related issues (EBV) cannot be asserted. Similarly, the provisions governing possessions can neither be applied to tokens directly nor by analogy, as confirmed by § 1029 BGB. An exception exists only for the quasi-negative protection under § 1004 BGB by analogy. If there is protection under § 823 (2) BGB,[24] then injunctive relief and removal claims may also be asserted by analogy to § 1004 BGB.

b) Tort Law

Tort law provides only partial protection against interference with tokens. The main issue arises from the fact that tokens, due to their lack of physicality and classification as objects, cannot be considered protected property under § 823 (1) BGB.[25] Moreover, tokens do not qualify as "other rights" under § 823 (1) BGB because they lack the necessary property-like characteristics. Exceptions apply only to electronic securities, which are considered property under § 823 (1) BGB due to the legal fiction established in § 2 (3) eWpG. Additionally, § 823 (2) BGB can give rise to claims for damages if there are relevant protective laws

---

[23] *Christian Baldus*, Münchener Kommentar zum BGB (2023) § 985 no. 62; *Alexander Wilhelm*, Initial Coin Offerings (ICOs), in: Unternehmensfinanzierung am Kapitalmarkt, ed. by Mathias Habersack/Peter O. Mülbert/Michael Schlitt (2025) § 20 no. 20.60 ss.; *Florian Möslein/Sebastian Omlor/Nils Urbach*, Grundfragen eines Blockchain-Kapitalgesellschaftsrechts, ZIP 2020, 2149–2164, 2151.

[24] For details cf. *Alexander Koch*, Strafrecht (n. 17) chapter 18 no. 42 ss., 89 ss.

[25] *Andreas Walter*, Bitcoin, Libra und sonstige Kryptowährungen aus zivilrechtlicher Sicht, NJW 2019, 3609–3614, 3611; *Philipp Maume*, Die Rechtsnatur von Kryptotoken, in: Rechtshandbuch Kryptowerte, ed. by Philipp Maume/Lena Maute/Mathias Fromberger (2020) § 4 no. 39 ss.; *Alexander Weiss*, Die Rückabwicklung einer Blockchain-Transaktion, NJW 2022, 1343–1348 no. 10.

(e.g., §§ 202a, 303a StGB). Due to the requirement of intent, § 826 BGB plays only a minor role in tort law related to tokens.

c) Law of Unjust Enrichment

For absolute protection of legal interests, the general claim for restitution based on interference under § 812 (1) sentence 1, alternative 2 BGB is particularly relevant.[26] Its partial resemblance to tort law is evident in that no special relationship (e.g., contractual) is required between the debtor and creditor – unlike the performance-based restitution claims, which require such a relationship, albeit with a defect in validity. The aim is to protect legal interests by granting a claim for the continuation of rights. This is contingent on an interference ("at the expense of") with the allocation content of another's right. A key factor in determining such allocation content is whether the legal order provides a marketable exploitation opportunity.

III. German Electronic Securities Law

The eWpG created a material-free security in Germany for the first time: a security without paper.[27] This was also associated with the ground-breaking innovation of tokenisation in rem[28], although this remains limited to the scope of application of the eWpG. A first step has thus been taken with an 'experimental law'[29] to modernise German securities law and ensure its international competitiveness.

1. Scope

The material scope of application of the eWpG is defined in § 1, according to which bearer bonds are the subject matter of the Act. In addition to traditional bonds, bearer bonds also include participation certificates, warrants, certain commercial papers, investment certificates, asset-backed securities (ABS), collateralised debt obligations (CDOs) as well as convertible bonds and income bonds.[30] Shares of funds are also covered by the scope of application (§ 95 (1) KAGB). They can only be issued as bearer share certificates (*Inhaberanteils-*

---

[26] *Omlor*, Allgemeines Privatrecht (n. 17) chapter 6 no. 73 ss.

[27] To the following already *Sebastian Omlor*, Elektronische Wertpapiere nach dem eWpG, RDi 2021, 371–377.

[28] for definition of the term see *Omlor*, Allgemeines Privatrecht (n. 17) chapter 6 no. 93 ss.

[29] *Anne-Christin Mittwoch*, Der Entwurf eines Gesetzes zur Einführung elektronischer Wertpapiere – ein Quantensprung für das Zivil- und Finanzmarktrecht?, WM 2021, 375–390, 378.

[30] *Matthias Lehmann*, Wertpapierarten, in: Elektronische Wertpapiere, ed. by Sebastian Omlor/Florian Möslein/Stefan Grundmann (2021) 62.

scheine), but not as registered share certificates (*Namensanteilsscheine*). Since December 2023, shares have also been subject to the scope of application of the eWpG.

2. *Typology and Subtypes*

a) *Type of Registration*

Electronic securities can be held in individual or collective registration. According to § 8 (1) eWpG, these alternatives apply to both central register and crypto securities.[31] Collective registration is administered by a central securities depository or a custodian, without this entity becoming the authorised party (§ 9 (2) sentence 1 eWpG). Instead, the authorisation within the meaning of § 3 (2) eWpG lies with the individual co-owners. Only the ownership as a formal register allocation (§ 3 para. 1 eWpG) is assigned to the central securities depository or the custodian. Pursuant to § 9b (1) sentence 1 DepotG, electronic securities in collective registration are largely subject to the same regulations as securities held in collective custody. Depending on the registration model, the eWpG thus opens the door to two different regulatory complexes for a transfer: the link to the standard for collective safe custody under securities deposit law and the new model between eWpG special rules and BGB substantive law as a result of the fiction of fact.

b) *Type of Register*

The eWpG recognises two subtypes of registers in which electronic securities can be recorded. These are the central register and the crypto securities register. While the central register is regulated in §§ 12–15 eWpG, the legal framework for the crypto securities register can be found in §§ 16–23 eWpG. Specific details for both subtypes can be found in the Ordinance on Requirements for Electronic Securities Registers ("*Verordnung* über *Anforderungen an elektronische Wertpapierregister*" – eWpRV).

The crypto securities register is not managed centrally, but is modelled on distributed ledger technology (DLT).[32] Although the requirements for the register are formulated in a technology-neutral manner, blockchain technology, currently the most important application of DLT, fulfils the legal requirements perfectly. Despite its decentralised nature, a crypto securities register also requires a register-keeping body. If no such entity is appointed, the issuer assumes this role on a subsidiary basis (§ 16(2) eWpG).

---

[31] *Matthias Casper*, Digitaler Effektenhandel, in: FinTech-Handbuch, ed. by Sebastian Omlor/Florian Möslein (2024), § 28 no. 22.

[32] *Matthias Casper*, in eWpG-Kommentar, ed. by Ulrich Segna/Sebastian Omlor/Florian Möslein/Julia von Buttlar (2024) § 4 no. 12.

3. Private Law of Electronic Securities

a) Legal Fiction

The legal fiction in § 2 (3) eWpG forms the basis for the typological categorization of electronic securities under German private law and consequently the associated legal framework. [33] Accordingly, an electronic security is deemed to be an object within the meaning of § 90 BGB. This fiction is subject to legal policy concerns, as it refers without exception to the entire BGB property law without reflecting its customisation to physical objects in any way. In response to the criticism expressed in the expert hearing, the lead Finance Committee of the Bundestag clarified in its report that 'the legal fiction does not preclude the non-application or corresponding application of the provisions of property law in this individual case.'[34] The application of the provisions of property law can be adapted to the special features of electronic securities on a provision-specific basis.[35] In this respect, the historical interpretation argues in favour of a 'soft' application of the fiction.

b) Ownership and Possession

Due to dogmatic links to both the law of movable and immovable property in the BGB, it is not possible to clearly categorise electronic securities.[36] The legal fiction of § 2(3) eWpG is deliberately linked to § 90 BGB from the General Part of the BGB, but not to individual provisions of the Third Book of the BGB (i.e. property law). The legislative materials[37] indicate that, despite the fictitious order, all standards of property law are not to be applied across the board. Rather, a differentiated approach is required, which is dogmatically compatible with the more specialised eWpG concept. Therefore, electronic securities fit best into a separate category of property, without generally establishing an exclusive connection to BGB property law; they are electronic property sui generis.[38] Which rules of the BGB serve to fill gaps and as a model for regulation, depends on the nature of the individual issue concerned. The eWpG provisions always serve as a starting point and framework.

---

[33] To the following already *Omlor*, Elektronische Wertpapiere nach dem eWpG (n. 27) 371 no. 7.

[34] *Deutscher Bundestag*, Gesetz zur Einführung von elektronischen Wertpapieren, BT-Drucks. 19/29372 of 5 June 2021, p. 53: "die gesetzlich angeordnete Sachfiktion einer Nichtanwendung oder entsprechenden Anwendung der sachenrechtlichen Vorschriften in diesem Einzelfall nicht entgegen[stehe]".

[35] *Deutscher Bundestag*, BT-Drucks. 19/29372 (n. 34) 53.

[36] SMOB/*Omlor* (n. 32) § 25 no. 11; similar *J. Meier*, Elektronische Wertpapiere in der Zwangsvollstreckung, MMR 2021, 381–385, 384.

[37] Deutscher Bundestag, BT-Drucks. 19/29372 (n. 34) 53.

[38] *Sebastian Omlor*, Re- statt Dematerialisierung des Sachenrechts, RDi 2021, 236–241, 236 no. 4.

Neither the eWpG nor German property law contain specific provisions on ownership and possession of electronic securities. The fiction in § 2 (3) eWpG ensures that full ownership of electronic securities exists. The protection of this ownership position against interference by third parties is equivalent under private law to the protection of ownership of physical objects. Whether and how the rules of the German Civil Code on ownership and its protection apply to electronic securities, however, is often unclear. In the case of electronic securities, ownership could be represented by the entry in the register. Ownership of electronic securities would thus be a possession mediated by the entry in the register.

c) *Transfer of Title*

The transfer of title fundamentally differs depending on the type of entry in the register. While the legal framework in the eWpG is detailed in the case of an individual registration (§§ 24–27 eWpG), the provisions of deposit law apply in the case of a collective registration (§ 9 (1) sentence 1 eWpG). § 25 (1) eWpG applies to the transfer of ownership for electronic securities in individual registration. Only the transfer of ownership by the authorised party is covered. Firstly, § 25(1) sentence 1 eWpG sets out the substantive legal elements for a legal singular succession in electronic securities. Contractual agreement ("*Einigung*"), instruction ("*Weisung*"), registration ("*Eintragung*") and authorisation ("*Berechtigung*") of the disposing party are required. A lack of authorisation can be overcome in accordance with § 26 eWpG in the case of a bona fide purchase. If all the requirements of § 25 (1) sentence 1 eWpG are met, the acquirer immediately acquires ownership together with the transferor's loss of ownership.

There must be a legal agreement between the transferor and the transferee that ownership of an electronic security is to be transferred.[39] In terms of content, the declarations of intent only extend to the persons of the parties, the identity of the security to be transferred and the legal consequences of the transfer of ownership. In principle, the agreement is not subject to any special form. As in German property law,[40] it is a contract in rem.

According to the eWpG publicity concept for electronic securities in individual registration, there should be no disposal outside the electronic securities register. Accordingly, § 25 (1) sentence 1 eWpG requires a constitutive register entry for the transfer of electronic securities. The transfer typically, but not necessarily, represents the chronologically last act of the acquisition of rights.[41]

The further required instruction of the authorised party, which is aimed at the registration of the new owner, constitutes a declaration of intent ("*Willens-*

[39] SMOB/*Omlor* (n. 32) § 25 no. 15.
[40] MüKoBGB/*Oechsler* (n. 13) § 929 no. 5; MüKoBGB/*Lettmaier* (n. 13) § 873 no. 50.
[41] SMOB/*Omlor* (n. 32) § 25 no. 20.

erklärung").[42] It is therefore also subject to the general requirements of the BGB for declarations of intent, such as the relevance of defects of intent (§§ 104 ss. BGB) and the possibility of avoidance due to error or deception (§§ 119 ss. BGB).

Finally, a transfer of ownership pursuant to § 25 (1) sentence 1 eWpG requires that the entitled party disposes of the property; otherwise, a supplementary recourse to § 26 eWpG for a bona fide purchase is required. The power of disposal is originally vested in the owner as a consequence of the positive rights of intervention pursuant to § 903 sentence 1 BGB. By way of derogation, the law may assign the power of disposal to a third party who is not the owner. The executor of a will (§ 2205 BGB) and the insolvency administrator (§ 80 InsO) are of particular relevance in this respect. In addition, the power of disposal can also be transferred to third parties derivatively by the owner.[43]

d) Bona Fide Acquisition

Pursuant to § 26 eWpG, electronic securities can also be acquired by unauthorised persons. The publicity concept of the eWpG for electronic securities in individual registration is based on the legal appearance of the electronic securities register. In this way, it is strikingly linked to the market protection concept of BGB property law, which is also based on the land register as an artificial legal document.[44] A bona fide acquisition pursuant to § 26 eWpG requires: the legitimisation of the disposing party by the register, a contractual agreement ("*Verkehrsgeschäft*"), an entry of the acquirer in the register and his lack of bad faith. Good faith is lacking in the case of positive knowledge or grossly negligent ignorance of the register inaccuracy.

IV. EU (Secondary) Law

The European Union does not have a self-contained private law that would be comparable to the member states' civil law codes, which is another reason why there is currently no EU private law of tokens. Central areas of regulation remain at Member State level due to a lack of harmonisation: property law, the absolute (*erga omnes*) protection of tokens and their transfer. At EU level, a distinction must be made between individual legal acts in the EU secondary law.[45]

---

[42] SMOB/*Omlor* (n. 32) § 14 no. 4; MüKoBGB/*Schäfer* (n. 13) § 665 no. 7.

[43] *J. Meier*, in: Conreder/J. Meier, eWpG (2023) § 25 no. 11.

[44] *Omlor*, Verfügungen über Elektronische Wertpapiere (n. 30) 147; to the contrary Conreder/*J. Meier* (n. 43) § 26 no. 14.

[45] To the following already *Sebastian Omlor*, Stablecoins unter MiCAR: EU-Zahlungsverkehrsrecht für vermögenswertereferenzierte und E-Geld-Token, ZHR 187 (2023) 635–671, 641 ss.

1. MiCAR

MiCAR only creates a frequently fragmented Union private law of tokens in some areas. Furthermore, MiCAR does not deal with the private law status and protection of e-money tokens, but is limited to the contractual relationships of the actors who transfer e-money tokens. Therefore, MiCAR brings only partial changes to the private law of payment tokens. In particular, the legal relationships for the issue and transfer of e-money tokens will be reorganised under private law. In contrast, the legal relationships in transactions with asset-referenced tokens remain subject to the national legal systems via conflict-of-law references. MiCAR also does not harmonise the fundamental preliminary question of the legal nature of payment tokens, their transfer in rem and their absolute protection; in this respect, too, the competence of the Member States remains with the Union.

Outside of MiCAR, there are numerous legal and non-legal terms for forms of payment tokens. So far, the codification density is lowest in civil law, while regulatory and anti-money laundering law has already partially completed a legal categorisation. MiCAR continues to pursue some of these lines of regulation; this affects e-money with its new special form of e-money tokens. Other phenomena such as stablecoins, on the other hand, require an empirical case-by-case examination based on the MiCAR typology of crypto-assets.

2. EU Currency Law

Private payment tokens are not a currency in the legal sense and therefore not within the meaning of the Union's monetary constitution. Therefore, they are not subject to any legal obligation to accept them in the euro area, as stipulated in Art. 10 sentence 2, 11 sentence 2 of the euro introduction regulation only for euro cash. A private-law acceptance obligation is only conceivable on the basis of a legal agreement. Such an obligation already exists for traditional book money in numerous constellations (e.g. distance selling, amounts greater than € 10,000).[46] In the case of private payment tokens, however, this can only be assumed in rare exceptional cases, as there is still a lack of sufficient legal validity.

With the introduction of digital central bank money (CBDC) by the ECB, however, sovereign payment tokens will also be recognised as having currency status. Whether the secondary legal acceptance requirement is extended to the digital euro, is subject to the decision of the Union legislator. The draft regulation on the introduction of the digital euro provides for such equalisation with cash.

---

[46] *Sebastian Omlor*, in: Staudinger Kommentar zum BGB (2024), Vorb. A75 zu §§ 244–248.

3. EU Payment Services Law

The harmonised payment services law does not apply to private (payment) tokens if – as is currently the empirical rule – they do not represent an amount of money within the meaning of Art. 4 No. 25 PSD2.[47] Both the acceptance of scriptural money[48] and e-money[49] within the meaning of the legal definition would require an underlying claim against an issuer with legal capacity. In the case of private blockchain networks, such an issuer is regularly absent, meaning that no claim relationship can arise due to the lack of a suitable debtor.[50] E-money tokens, which MiCAR declares to be e-money and thus subject to payment services law, are a significant exception. The absence of such a claim therefore does not imply a structural necessity for blockchain networks with private payment tokens,[51] as is also shown by the exemption provision for e-money in § 1 (11) sentence 5 no. 1 German Banking Act (*Kreditwesengesetz* – KWG). The failed Diem project, i. e. the initiative originally named 'Libra' by Meta Platforms (formerly: Facebook) for a private stablecoin payment system, would have had a potentially suitable legal entity and central issuer in the Diem Association.[52] The open and non-restricted (public, permissionless) blockchain network as such cannot typically be categorised as a debtor due to the participants' lack of sufficient willingness to be legally bound.[53]

---

[47] *Sebastian Omlor*, Kryptowährungen im Geldrecht, ZHR 183 (2019) 294–345, 308; cf. *Jörg Mimberg*, in: ZAG-Kommentar, ed. by Frank Schäfer/Sebastian Omlor/Jörg Mimberg (2022) § 1 no. 219; BeckOGK/*Köndgen* (n. 5) § 675c no. 137; *Shmatenko/Möllenkamp*, Digitale Zahlungsmittel in einer analog geprägten Rechtsordnung (n. 11) 495; *Lutz Auffenberg*, E-Geld auf Blockchain-Basis, BKR 2019, 341–345, 342 ss.

[48] *Christof Münch*, Das Giralgeld in der Rechtsordnung der Bundesrepublik Deutschland (1990) 26, 190; *Omlor*, Elektronische Wertpapiere nach dem eWpG (n. 27) 131.

[49] *Sebastian Omlor*, E-Geld, in: Bankrecht, ed. by. Sebastian Schwintowski (2022) chapter 11 no. 3; *Matthias Casper*, in ZAG-Kommentar, ed. by Matthias Casper/ Matthias Terlau (2023) § 1 ZAG nos. 207 ss.; BeckOGK/*Köndgen* (n. 5) § 675c no. 7.

[50] VG Frankfurt am Main 25 June 2022 – 5 L 1307/22.F, NVwZ-RR 2022, 377 no. 25; *Spindler/Bille*, Rechtsprobleme von Bitcoins als virtuelle Währung (n. 15) 1360; *Katja Langenbucher*, Digitales Finanzwesen, AcP 218 (2018) 385–429, 406; *Thomas Eckhold*, Crowdlending und Crowdinvesting, in: Handbuch des Kapitalanlagerechts, ed. by Heinz-Dieter Assmann/ Rolf Schütze/Petra Buck-Heeb (2024) § 17 no. 18.

[51] VG Frankfurt am Main (n. 50) 377 Rdn. 26; *Lutz Auffenberg*, E-Geld auf Blockchain-Basis, BKR 2019, 341–346, 341 ss.

[52] *Matthias Terlau*, Elektronisches Geld, virtuelle Währungen (Bitcoins, Ether Coins etc.), in: Bankrechts-Handbuch, ed. by Jürgen Ellenberger/ Hermann-Josef Bunte (2022) § 35 no. 202 ss.; on how the coin was supposed to work: *Sebastian Omlor*, 3.1 Stanford Journal of Blockchain Law/Policy 83, 85–86 (2020).

[53] *Eduard Hofert*, Blockchain-Profiling – Verarbeitung von Blockchain-Daten innerhalb und außerhalb der Netzwerke, ZD 2017, 161–166, 165; *Stefan Möllenkamp*, Blockchain, Kryptowährungen und Token, in: Handbuch Multimedia-Recht, ed. by Thomas Hoeren/ Ulrich Sieber/Bernd Holznagel (looseleaf, June 2024) chapter 13.6 no. 96; *Dominik Skauradszun*, Kryptowerte im Bürgerlichen Recht, AcP 221 (2022) 353–398, 365 ss.; *Alexander*

Furthermore, private payment tokens that are not also e-money tokens are generally not issued against payment of a sum of money, as is required for e-money in accordance with § 1 (2) sentence 3 German Payment Services Supervisory Act (*Zahlungsdiensteaufsichtsgesetz* – ZAG). If tokens are created by mining themselves, such as in the Bitcoin network, this requirement is not met.[54] Furthermore, e-money also requires sufficient market recognition as a neutral universal medium of exchange.[55] Such recognition is currently still lacking for standard market payment tokens,[56] unless they have been recognised by law as e-money tokens by way of exception.

4. EU Anti Money Laundering Law

The so-called 5th Anti-Money Laundering Directive (AMLD5)[57] was the first time that 'virtual currencies' were covered separately under money laundering law.[58] The legal definition of virtual currencies contained in Art. 3 No. 18 AMLD5 since then is primarily aimed at private payment tokens, but is nevertheless formulated in a technology-neutral manner. The legislative motivation to (also) regulate cryptocurrencies only becomes clear in the systematic interaction with the requirements for an electronic wallet. Accordingly, the holding, storage and transfer of virtual currencies requires a private cryptographic key (Art. 3 No. 19 AMLD5); such a key is a characteristic feature of blockchain technology.[59]

According to the wording, however, digital central bank money is excluded because it is issued and guaranteed by a central bank.[60] The digital euro would therefore not fall under the special area of virtual currencies, but would be sub-

Weiss, Zivilrechtliche Grundlagenprobleme von Blockchain und Kryptowährungen, JuS 2019, 1050–1057, 1053.

[54] *Auffenberg*, E-Geld auf Blockchain-Basis (n. 51) 342; *Terlau*, Elektronisches Geld, virtuelle Währungen (Bitcoins, Ether Coins etc.) (n. 52), § 35 no. 201.

[55] *Omlor*, E-Geld (n. 49) chapter 11 no. 15.

[56] With respect to Bitcoins *Langenbucher*, Digitales Finanzwesen (n. 50) 396 et seq; *Stefan Behringer/Marco Passardi/Daniel Noto*, Ausweis von Kryptowährungen nach den IFRS-Bilanzierung dem Grunde und der Höhe nach, IRZ 2022, 225–229, 226; *Shmatenko/Möllenkamp*, Digitale Zahlungsmittel in einer analog geprägten Rechtsordnung (n. 11) 496; *Möllenkamp*, Blockchain, Kryptowährungen und Token (n. 53) 59; to the contrary BeckOGK/*Freitag* (n. 5) § 244 BGB no. 31; also in the decided individual case VG Frankfurt am Main (n. 50) 377 no. 31 ss.

[57] Directive (EU) 2018/843 of the European Parliament and of the Council of 30 May 2018 amending Directive (EU) 2015/849 on the prevention of the use of the financial system for the purposes of money laundering or terrorist financing, and amending Directives 2009/138/EC and 2013/36/EU, OJ L 156, 19.6.2018, p. 43–74.

[58] About the prehistory *Auffenberg*, Geldwäschepräventionsrecht (n. 17) chapter. 17 no. 28.

[59] *Siegel*, Technische Grundlagen (n. 17) chapter 3 no. 20 ss.

[60] Cf. *Mathias Fromberger/Lars Haffke/Patrick Zimmermann*, Kryptowerte und Geldwäsche- Eine Analyse der 5. Geldwäscherichtlinie sowie des Gesetzesentwurfs der Bundesregierung, BKR 2019, 377–386, 379.

ject to traditional money laundering regulation for money transactions. Due diligence obligations would therefore arise in particular when executing transactions in accordance with Art. 11 lit. b AMLD5. De lege ferenda, however, the European legislator could also introduce special rules for digital central bank money, such as those that apply to e-money transactions (Art. 12 AMLD5). In contrast, the new EU Anti Money Laundering Regulation (AMLR)[61] has adopted MiCAR terminology and therefore only refers to crypto-assets.

V. Legal Policy

Using the example of German private law, an overview of the specific steps that the legislator could take to close the gaps identified will be presented below.[62]

1. Uniform Definition of Crypto-Assets

Remedying the deficits and far-reaching gaps in the German and EU legal framework, requires a standardized understanding of the term crypto-assets, which at the same time distinguishes itself from alternative terms. The established and codified concept of crypto-assets offers a reliable and legally secure framework for a BGB regulation in the light of the unity of the legal system and optimal regulatory coherence. Adopting the Union law understanding of the term from MiCAR would also serve the internal market concept. The fragmentation of Union private law for crypto-assets could thus be mitigated. It is true that there is no self-contained Union private law for crypto-assets, partly because the Union's competences in this area are limited. The MiCAR does not establish a private law substructure for its crypto-assets, but is limited to partial aspects of banking contract law and references (e.g. for e-money tokens in Art. 48(2–3) MiCAR). A link to the MiCAR crypto value by the private law systems of the Member States led to partial harmonisation at the decentralised level below Union law.

The MiCAR definition of a crypto-asset is also a broad definition that is open to development and thus to the future and encompasses different types of crypto-assets. The definition does not differentiate according to the function or legal content of the crypto-asset; it is not limited to a specific technology, but also accepts technologies similar to DLT.

---

[61] Regulation (EU) 2024/1624 of the European Parliament and of the Council of 31 May 2024 on the prevention of the use of the financial system for the purposes of money laundering or terrorist financing.

[62] In detail to the following already *Sebastian Omlor*, in: Blockchain und Recht, ed. by Sebastian Omlor/Florian Möslein (2024) § 1.

However, the implementation of the MiCAR crypto-asset definition should not extend to the exceptions to the scope of application in Art. 2 MiCAR. Rather, it would be desirable to be able to fall back on a general private law foundation for all secondary legislation. It should be possible to resolve any conflicts of law in individual cases using the hierarchy of norms and the lex specialis principle.

2. Types of Crypto-Assets

For the purposes of private law, the generic term crypto-asset should be divided into two subcategories: the charged crypto-asset and the autonomous crypto asset.[63] The UNIDROIT Principles on Digital Assets and Private Law speak of 'linked assets' (Principle 4) for charged crypto-assets without any difference in content. This categorisation according to content contrasts with categorisation according to function. According to this, a classic distinction is made between investment tokens, utilisation tokens and payment tokens. The MiCAR also takes up this triad with the legal definition of the utility token (Art. 3 para. 1 no. 9 MiCAR). However, this demarcation criterion has its origins in capital market and supervisory law, not in private law dogmatics. At least the current version of the German Civil Code is not linked to the function of crypto-assets. Any applicable consumer protection regulations are also based on the persons acting and the purposes pursued by them (§§ 13, 14 BGB) and in this way form a special private law for consumers.

3. Proprietary Rights

If crypto-assets are to function as accepted carriers of assets in commercial transactions, they require an absolute assignment and protection equivalent to property ownership. The broad constitutional concept of property under Art. 14 (1) sentence 1 of the German Basic Law ('*Grundgesetz*')[64] provides sufficient leeway for this. In the General Part of the German Civil Code, an arrangement should therefore be made in the systematic connection to the definition and typification of crypto-assets regarding their eligibility for ownership. Principle 3 (1) UNIDROIT Principles on Digital Assets and Private Law also recommends such a provision. Such a provision would have a constitutive and not merely declaratory and clarifying character. This would provide a legally certain solution to the absolute protection of crypto-assets under tort and unjust

---

[63] *Omlor*, Allgemeines Privatrecht (n. 17) chapter 6 no. 24 ss.; *Sebastian Omlor*, Digitales Eigentum an Blockchain-Token – rechtsvergleichende Entwicklungslinien, ZVglRWiss 119 (2020) 41–58, 44 ss.; *Lion Fritsche*, Die Zwangsvollstreckung in Token (2023), 53 ss.

[64] In detail *Hans-Jürgen Papier/Foroud Shirvani*, in: Grundgesetz, ed. by Theodor Maunz/Günter Dürig/Roman Herzog/Rupert Scholz (looseleaf, January 2024) Art. 14 no. 160 ss. with further references.

enrichment law. Crypto-assets would thus be subject to the protection of property in § 823 (1) BGB and would therefore be treated in the same way as electronic securities.

4. Control

Possession, which is tailored to things as physical objects, cannot be exercised over incorporeal crypto-assets. For this reason, the UNIDROIT Principles on Digital Assets and Private Law propose introducing control as the functional equivalent of ownership for digital assets.[65] This is intended to cover de facto power relationships to which legal consequences are then linked. The functions of possession can also be partially transferred to control. To this end, it is necessary to at least functionally relate the possessory protection of ownership to the control of crypto-assets. It is true that the empirical-technical forms of interference with or deprivation of control of incorporeal objects are different from those of possession of things. Nevertheless, a technologically mediated power of domination also arises in the case of incorporeal crypto-assets, which can be interfered with by IT-based measures, among other things. The factual requirements for control are essentially derived from Principle 6 of the UNIDROIT Principles on Digital Assets and Private Law. According to this, control requires a positive ability to use and a negative ability to exclude. A purely factual approach is to be applied, which is not based on legally granted authorisations to use and exclude others.[66]

5. Transfer of Title

The transfer of crypto-assets is to take place through contractual agreement and entry in the public ledger of the blockchain.[67] The public ledger acts as a private register that also ensures the publicity of the allocation relationships.[68] Insofar as control replaces possession and the entry in the public ledger is associated with a corresponding presumption of control, there is also a systematic connection with § 929 sentence 1 BGB. The transfer is replaced by the entry in the register, which is typically categorised as the basis for control. In addition, acquisition in good faith should be permitted, which should be based on the content of the public ledger of the blockchain.

---

[65] *UNIDROIT,* UNIDROIT Digital Assets and Private Law Principle 2(2), Comment 6.2.

[66] *UNIDROIT,* UNIDROIT Digital Assets and Private Law Principle 2(2), Comment 6.3.

[67] To the following already *Sebastian Omlor,* in: Blockchain und Recht, ed. by Sebastian Omlor/Florian Möslein (2024) 4, 20.

[68] *Skauradszun*, Kryptowerte im Bürgerlichen Recht (n. 53) 353, 380 ss.

VI. Outlook

The market success of DLT, blockchain and crypto-assets depends largely on whether a secure and functional legal framework is available. In the early days, the initial focus worldwide was mostly on financial market, tax and money laundering law. The upstream fundamental issues of private law were often misjudged in terms of their importance and therefore not addressed by legislation. As DLT and blockchain networks are transnational phenomena, we ideally also need transnational solutions. Crypto-assets appear to be a prime example of international legal harmonisation. This is why the projects currently underway within UNCITRAL, UNIDROIT and HCCH, among others, deserve strong support at all levels. However, national and supranational legislators will then be called upon to implement any soft law instruments in their legal systems.

Hong Kong

Urszula McCormack[1]

[1] The author wishes to thank Nikita Ajwani, Jessie Chong, Shannon Hatheier, Vince Lee, Jocelyn Pang and Grace Qiu for their research assistance.

I. Introduction

The statutory, judicial and regulatory approach in Hong Kong[2] to the control and safekeeping of virtual assets[3] is characterised by a high degree of flexibility and adaptability, with pragmatism shown by the Courts and an increasingly sharp lens applied by financial regulators to this burgeoning class of assets.

Hong Kong's statutory and judicial treatment of virtual assets illustrates the ease with which they are given passage as the *object* of control and safekeeping, with uncomplicated judicial recognition of virtual assets as "property", capable of forming the subject matter of a trust and deserving of various other protections and interventions. Part II describes several of the landmark judgments and statutory foundations relevant to this topic, demonstrating the capacity of both Hong Kong law and jurisprudence to sensibly address fraud and other criminal activities, large corporate insolvencies, contractual breaches and other disputes that involve virtual assets.

In turn, Hong Kong's regulators play an unequivocally proactive role in shaping the precise manner in which safekeeping occurs (and by whom), through multi-layered and increasingly granular regulatory frameworks. This is exemplified by the considerable body of regulation devoted to virtual asset custody, summarised in Part III, which supports legal certainty and robust investor protection. Overall, it is evidently designed to be flexible and principles-based to accommodate the exigencies of different custodial models – but not necessarily all.

At the heart of regulatory approaches to custody is the vital importance of any ledger being capable to serve as the *source of truth* (safekeeping relevant interests both from a legal and operational standpoint), with *maximum incorruptibility* (ensuring appropriate technological architecture, legal structures and practical control).

Hong Kong's regulatory approach also illustrates a movement toward ensuring investors and their virtual assets are generally retained within a highly regulated ecosystem. This is achieved in several ways, including the ongoing expansion of regulated activities, as well as rules that require interactions by a regulated entity (such as client referrals or omnibus arrangements) to be with other regulated entities, or which limit investor access to certain types of virtual assets to regulated routes. In turn, the expanding pool of regulated entities

---

[2] Hong Kong Special Administrative Region of the People's Republic of China.

[3] The term "virtual asset" is used throughout this Chapter to refer to the general class of distributed ledger technology-based tokens. In certain cases, this term has a specific meaning, such as in statute. However, save for a small number of exceptions, it is not necessary to differentiate between various virtual asset types for the purpose of this topic given the overall scope and findings of this review. A closer inspection is always recommended for any contextual analysis.

controlling virtual assets are subject to a highly structured legal and regulatory custody framework. For many, this involves detailed rules on the identity of the custodian, the capacity in which they must act (generally as trustee), the technology, cybersecurity and resilience parameters that must be met, the individuals who must be involved, the governance arrangements that must be established, where private keys and other material arrangements must be located (generally in Hong Kong), the insurance or compensation arrangements that must support obligations where relevant, the audits and accreditations that must be obtained, and so on. These are onerous, but arguably provide the clarity that the virtual asset industry requires to confidently conduct business and build relationships with banks and other counterparties, and the protection that investors now expect.

An ongoing challenge for regulators internationally is the dynamic nature of the virtual asset industry generally, and custodial models specifically. As Parts III to V illustrate, the further development of Hong Kong's legal and regulatory frameworks relevant to the control and safekeeping of virtual assets is presently a strong area of focus, with several initiatives underway, including a proposed regime more specifically targeting virtual asset custody services. Based on historical trend lines, investor protection, market integrity, preventing criminal activity and meeting international standards are likely to be some of the key driving forces for further reforms.

Balancing the enduring aims of risk-mitigation, Hong Kong's policy objectives and broader digital economy development will likely continue to play a significant role in the precise measures adopted and their implementation.[4] In this respect, the overall positive stance in Hong Kong toward digital innovation and virtual assets is noteworthy. Regulatory rules themselves can have dramatic impacts on technology development, adoption and profitability if they are created to remove risk altogether, as they can render innovation and reasonable commercial outcomes impossible. The same applies if regulatory rules inexorably point to one model or technology over another, either on paper or in practice, which can create a negative feedback loop in the technology development cycle, concentrate solutions in specific custody architectures, impede principles such as technological neutrality and ultimately stall opportunities for further innovation and risk reduction in the safekeeping of virtual assets. In this respect, innovation benefits from non-static regulation and the considerable ongoing change to Hong Kong's regulatory environment for virtual assets signals a sophisticated recognition of this reality. The recent expansion of rules to enable network staking of client assets controlled by regulated exchanges and banks

[4] Policy and economic considerations have played a material role in Hong Kong's digital economy development, and continue to shape the virtual asset industry. However, they are outside the scope of this Chapter, except as expressly addressed for contextual reference only. The author expresses no view on these matters.

is one example of how regulation can forge disciplined safekeeping behaviour by contracting permitted activities, then progressively opening up measured pathways. Part V also describes some of the additional practical ways in which this equilibrium between safety and innovation is being discovered and refined, including collaborative experimentation and piloting.

Looking ahead, several opportunities for further legal and regulatory development and clarification remain. This includes how concepts such as bailment may be leveraged and applied, how complex cross-border questions are adjudicated, what further statutory steps may be taken to support settlement finality for novel financial market infrastructures, how the new proposed virtual custody framework will unfold, how technology requirements may accommodate more novel custodial models, what precise monitoring and intervention standards will be required of stablecoin issuers in relation to the control of their stablecoins by unknown persons, and how the control of multi-stakeholder governance structures such as decentralised autonomous organisations (*DAOs*) will be dissected, appraised and legally characterised. What is clear is that virtual assets will continue to serve as a catalyst for the evolution of venerable old concepts relevant to possession, safekeeping and control, and provide fertile ground to interrogate *why* we regulate, *what* we should regulate, and *how*.

Note. *In this Chapter, the term "control" is used as a deliberately broad term to refer to the technical capability to effect the transfer of a virtual asset, whether alone or with other persons. In certain cases, this term has a statutory meaning, which is addressed accordingly. "Safekeeping" is also used broadly and inclusively, to refer to any combination of legal and/or technical measures to prevent virtual assets from misappropriation or impairment: that is, to prevent the exercise of control of a virtual asset in breach of relevant legal, regulatory or contractual boundaries, or other actions prejudicing relevant rights and interests in relation to it.*

II. Virtual assets as the object of control and safekeeping

1. Overview

Foundationally, Hong Kong law supports the notion that virtual assets can be the object of control and safekeeping. This is primarily because the concept of "property" is broadly construed in statute and as a matter of case law. Further, case law supports the ability of virtual assets to form the subject matter of a trust. This, in turn, has a direct impact on the application of burgeoning regulatory frameworks relevant to virtual assets, the heart of many of which are trusts.

This Part II describes the key Hong Kong statutory provisions and cases relevant to this area. Part III then describes the key Hong Kong regulatory frameworks relevant to the control and safekeeping of virtual assets, with further developments and considerations in Parts IV and V.

2. *Statutory definition of "property"*

As a starting point, the Interpretation and General Clauses Ordinance (Cap. 1) (Interpretation and General Clauses Ordinance) contains a very broad and non-exhaustive definition of "property". Specifically, it states that property:

"includes –
(a) money, goods, choses in action and land; and
(b) obligations, easements and every description of estate, interest and profit, present or future, vested or contingent, arising out of or incident to property as defined in paragraph (a) of this definition;[5]

Even without further judicial consideration, it is evident that this definition carries material import for virtual assets, which can have (or evidence) innumerable features and attributes. This includes virtual assets that indeed represent choses in action, for example. However, Hong Kong case law now strongly supports the position that virtual assets can be "property", as more fully described in paragraph 3 of this Part II.

This position has several downstream implications that therefore necessarily imply that virtual assets can be the object of a person's control. Some illustrative examples include the following:

(a) *Financial services regulation.* A virtual asset can be the "property" the subject of arrangements that involve a "collective investment scheme" under the Securities and Futures Ordinance (Cap. 571) (SFO),[6] which has a direct impact on the development of the virtual asset exchange traded fund (*ETF*) market as well as the regulation of certain staking and profit-sharing arrangements. Similarly, a "regulated investment agreement" (essentially, a contract for difference) is predicated upon the existence of property, being defined as:

"an agreement the purpose or effect, or pretended purpose or effect, of which is to provide, whether conditionally or unconditionally, to any party to the agreement a profit, income or other returns calculated by reference to changes in the value of any property, but does not include an interest in a collective investment scheme".[7]

(b) *Financial crime.* The characterisation of virtual assets to be "property" also means that virtual assets may be the proceeds of crime and the subject of various financial crime-related controls, pursuant to a range of Hong Kong money laun-

---

[5] Interpretation and General Clauses Ordinance (Cap. 1, Laws of Hong Kong) s. 3.

[6] . Securities and Futures Ordinance (Cap. 571, Laws of Hong Kong) pt. 1 sch. 1, definition of "collective investment scheme".

[7] Securities and Futures Ordinance (Cap. 571, Laws of Hong Kong) pt. 1 sch. 1, definition of "regulated investment agreement".

dering, terrorist financing, sanctions, non-proliferation and other statutes. For example, the Organized and Serious Crimes Ordinance (Cap. 455) (*OSCO*) prohibits dealing in any property where a person knows or has reasonable grounds to believe that it in whole or part directly or indirectly represents any person's proceeds of an indictable offence, subject to limited exceptions.[8] A mandatory report to the Joint Financial Intelligence Unit is also required in such cases.[9] The concept of "property" is also relevant to confiscation orders in Part III, restraint orders in Part IV and a range of other matters, under the OSCO.[10]

(c) *Corporations law, insolvency and winding up*. "Property" is central to matters relevant to winding-up orders and various other matters under the Companies (Winding Up and Miscellaneous Provisions) Ordinance (Cap. 32) (*CWUMPO*). This is especially pertinent to Hong Kong's leading case in this area, as described in paragraph 3 of this Part II.

For clarity, the Interpretation and General Clauses Ordinance does not have universal application. Specifically, section 2(1) makes clear that it applies to all Ordinances in force, as well as related instruments,[11] unless the contrary intention appears. For this reason, contextual analysis remains a valuable endeavour to ensure any technical analysis is accurate. For example, the Trustee Ordinance (Cap. 29) (*Trustee Ordinance*) defines property to include movable and immovable property (which together cover the "property" definition in the Interpretation and General Clauses Ordinance), but goes a step further to refer to specify:

"...and any estate, share and interest in any property, movable or immovable, and any debt, and any thing in action, and any other right or interest, whether in possession or not".[12]

Furthermore, the non-exhaustive nature of the definition of "property" in the Interpretation and General Clauses Ordinance, the Trustee Ordinance and other statutes, also makes judicial consideration of the question of "property" of enduring consequence.

The following paragraph 3 of this Part II explores the approach taken by Hong Kong Courts on this topic, among others relevant to the control and safekeeping of virtual assets. A key practical distillation of several of these statutory

[8] Organized and Serious Crimes Ordinance (Cap. 455, Laws of Hong Kong) s. 25.

[9] s. 25A OSCO.

[10] s. 2 of the OSCO expressly states that it includes both movable and immovable property as defined in s. 3 of the Interpretation and General Clauses Ordinance, which collectively capturing the full scope of the "property" definition in that Ordinance.

[11] This includes Ordinances commencing before or after the Interpretation and General Clauses Ordinance itself (being 31 December 1966). "Ordinance" itself is very broadly defined to capture a range of statutory instruments: see s. 3 Interpretation and General Clauses Ordinance.

[12] Trustee Ordinance (Cap. 29, Laws of Hong Kong) s. 3.

and judicial components (to date) is that a virtual asset should generally be expected to be "property" under Hong Kong law, except as the unique fact pattern relevant to a particular scenario requires

3. Judicial consideration of questions relevant to property, control and safekeeping

Overall, Hong Kong Courts have taken a generous and pragmatic approach to applying legal and procedural principles to scenarios involving virtual assets.

The following key principles and observations can be gleaned from the approximately 90 cases identified as part of this present review.

(a) *Virtual assets are "property"*. The leading case in this area is Re Gatecoin Ltd (In Liquidation)[13] (Gatecoin Case), in which the Court of First Instance found that "cryptocurrency is property".[14] In reaching this decision, the Court applied the indicia stated by Lord Wilberforce in *National Provincial Bank v Ainsworth*,[15] and in doing so followed the reasoning in other jurisdictional sources.[16] Importantly, the particular issue was not contested, and the Court did not differentiate between the 45 virtual assets involved in that case, nor did it appear to conduct an asset-by-asset analysis to differentiate between the attributes and characterisation of each. This leaves open the possibility that the issue could be litigated again with a different result in the context of a specific virtual asset, particularly if its features diverge from the attributes ascribed to "cryptocurrencies" in the expert testimony before the Court[17] in this case. For example, a virtual asset on a blockchain that is merely a "mirror" to a separate traditional ledger that has legal precedence in relation to a bundle of rights, may be conceptually very different to a virtual asset on a blockchain that is the *definitive ledger* in relation to those rights, depending on all the facts and any applicable contractual terms. The position established by the Gatecoin case could also change if higher Court takes a different approach. However, for now, it can be said "the preponderance of jurisprudence [in Hong Kong] recognises the proprietary nature of cryptocurrencies," [18] as the following paragraphs illustrate.

---

13 *Re Gatecoin Ltd (In Liquidation)* [2023] HKCU 1456 (*Gatecoin Case*).

14 See *Gatecoin Case* (n.13) at nos. 45 to 59.

15 *National Provincial Bank v Ainsworth* [1965] AC 1175, nos. 1247 to 1248.

16 Namely, *Ruscoe v Cryptopia* [2020] NZHC 728 and the *UK Jurisdiction Taskforce*, Legal Statement on the Status of Cryptoassets and Smart Contracts (November 2019), <https://lawtechuk.io/static/UKJT-Legal-Statement-Cryptoassets-Smart-Contracts-6dd9725753118e61e20330355c2b35c9.pdf> (1 May 2025). The Court also took into account other earlier Hong Kong cases where courts had granted interlocutory proprietary injunctions in relation to virtual assets, including *Nico Constantijn Antonius Samara v Stive Jean-Paul Dan, also known as Steve Jean-Paul Dan, Stive Jean Paul Dan and Steve Jean Paul Dan* [2019] HKCU 4128 and *Yan Yu Ying v Leung Wing Hei* [2022] HKCU 2620 (*Yan Yu Ying 2022*).

17 As attributed to counsel for the Liquidators in relation to their international case law research. See *Gatecoin Case* (n. 13) at nos. 11 to 20.

18 See *Gatecoin Case* (n. 13) at no. 48.

(b) *Virtual assets are capable of being the subject matter of a trust.* This was also confirmed in the Gatecoin Case,[19] with variable outcomes for creditors following liquidation, depending on the contractual terms and other facts applicable to each.[20] A trust may be an express trust or a constructive trust, depending on the facts, with multiple factors underpinning the assessment, including (for example) the contractual arrangements between relevant parties, segregation of assets and retention of profits (following forks or airdrops, for example).[21]

(c) *Virtual assets are capable of being the subject of injunctions.* Courts are willing to grant proprietary injunctions, as against particular virtual assets,[22] and Mareva injunctions, as against the assets of a person more generally,[23] depending on the facts.

(d) *Courts wish to see sufficient specificity in the description of wallets.*[24] They may also be willing to form a view on how virtual asset wallets and holdings should be adequately described.[25]

(e) *Courts can make an "intelligent estimate" of the value of virtual assets as part of a dispute.*[26]

(f) *Courts are willing to assist in recovery efforts.* This includes uncovering information on the whereabouts of assets through a disclosure order, although a proprietary claim against that asset may be necessary.[27] Courts may also grant declaratory relief that certain assets are held on trust for another person.[28]

---

[19] See *Gatecoin Case* (n. 13) at nos. 45 to 59.

[20] See *Re Gatecoin Ltd* [2025] HKCFI 493 (*Gatecoin 2*).

[21] Several Hong Kong cases examine the existence, nature and implications of a trust. For example, see *Gatecoin Case* (n. 13), *Gatecoin 2* (n. 20), *Feng Bo, and Chan Wing Yan and Another v JP-Ex Crypto Asset Platform Pty Ltd and Others* [HKCU] 4485. As to the interests of beneficial interest holders upon liquidation, see *Gatecoin 2* (n. 20).

[22] See *Yan Yu Ying v Leung Wing Hei* [2022] HKCU 2620 (*Yan Yu Ying 2022*).

[23] See *Yan Yu Ying v Leung Wing Hei* [2021] HKCU 5024; *Nico Constantijn Antonius Samara v Stive Jean-Paul Dan, also known as Steve Jean-Paul Dan, Stive Jean Paul Dan and Steve Jean Paul Dan* [2019] HKCU 4128.

[24] *Yan Yu Ying 2022* (n. 22) no. 119, which stated that "I add that this case is a useful illustration that in future applications of similar natures, when it comes to the scope of discovery in aid concerning the whereabouts of digital assets, cryptocurrency in particular, it may be necessary to specify with more technical accuracy the information that has to be disclosed. Whilst discovery is not a game of words, it is only fair that the discovery duty, backed up by pain of sanction, should be clear and unambiguous. Such clear delineation will also avoid disputes, save costs, resources, and court time."

[25] For example, see *BC v MSH Also Known As H, MSO and Others* [2023] HKCU 4800.

[26] *Yan Yu Ying 2022* (n. 22) no. 100.

[27] For example, see *Huobi Asia Ltd and Another v Chen Boliang (陳栢良) and Another* [2020] HKCU 3859.

[28] For example, see *Feng Bo, and Chan Wing Yan and Another v JP-Ex Crypto Asset Platform Pty Ltd and Others* (n. 21).

(g) *Courts are also willing to compel others to assist with recovery efforts.* This includes compelling a person to trace, recover and repay virtual assets, as well as traceable substitutes and assets or monies derived from them.[29]

(h) *Control of virtual assets may also be highly relevant to the control of decentralised autonomous organisations (DAOs).* While not yet settled, the position of DAO-related governance token holders and other persons has been considered by the Court of First Instance as part of preliminary proceedings.[30]

(i) *Technical control and legal authority can both be relevant to civil and criminal matters.* For example, matters beyond the technical control of a wallet, such as the authority of a person to direct transactions, can be relevant to the adjudication of a dispute.[31] Further, being the designated owner of a virtual asset wallet (account) with an exchange can also imply knowledge of fraud in relation to activity in that wallet.[32]

(j) *Courts wish to examine virtual asset-related matters carefully and in depth.* In general, Courts have been reluctant to reach their decisions on substantive matters involving virtual assets as part of preliminary or expedient applications, including requests for summary judgment.[33] They are still grappling with evidentiary matters, such as determining what records are sufficient to demonstrate that a particular transaction occurred.[34]

(k) *Courts may adopt creative solutions to address issues specific to virtual assets.* For example, enabling substituted service to persons unknown, by sending messages through a blockchain transaction or airdropping a non-fungible token, for example.[35]

This snapshot of judicial decisions illustrates a high level of engagement by Hong Kong Courts on matters relevant to the control and safekeeping of virtual assets, as well as significant pragmatism to assist in the resolution of disputes, the adjudication of relevant interests, and the pursuit and recovery of misappropriated virtual assets. However, it is important to emphasise that this snapshot is neither exhaustive, nor is it definitive. Novel fact patterns may well arise that

---

[29] For example, see *Feng Bo, and Chan Wing Yan and Another v JP-Ex Crypto Asset Platform Pty Ltd and Others* o (n. 21) no. 17.

[30] *Mantra Dao Inc and Another v John Patrick Mullin and others* [2024] HKCFI 2099.

[31] For example, *Mantra Dao Inc and Another v John Patrick Mullin and others* (n. 30) involved allegations of misappropriation from a particular virtual asset account and an argument that the defendant in fact had authority to authorise withdrawals for legitimate business purposes.

[32] As seen in *Feng Bo,* and *Chan Wing Yan and Another v JP-Ex Crypto Asset Platform Pty Ltd and Others* (n. 21) at no. 12.

[33] For example, see *Cheung Him Shing v Lui Ho Cheung* [2024] HKCU 1247.

[34] For example, see *Cheung Him Shing v Lui Ho Cheung* (n. 33).

[35] HCA 553/2025.

challenge the notions summarised above, particularly given the exceptionally broad spectrum of virtual assets, and the wide variety of legal contexts, that may arise.

4. Bailment

Finally, it is noteworthy that the concept of bailment has not been expressly extended to apply to virtual assets or other intangible property in Hong Kong. Overall, there is little Hong Kong case law on the subject of bailment generally, nor is the concept defined in the Interpretation and General Clauses Ordinance. That said, the case of *Hong Kong Hua Guang Industrial Co v Midway International Ltd* [2000] 2 HKC 348 makes clear that a bailor must have either physical possession or the immediate right to physical possession.

This condition can easily be misinterpreted as precluding the application of bailment to virtual assets. However, even with a narrow reading of this condition, it is reasonable to infer the following:

(a) a virtual asset itself, as a digital record, may not be the object of a bailment arrangement, as it is not itself capable of *physical* possession in a literal sense;

however:

(b) a physical device or other object that is used to safekeep and/or control the virtual asset may well be the object of a bailment arrangement. For example, this could be a hardware wallet or even a piece of paper used to record the relevant public and private key. Similarly, hardware used to validate virtual asset transactions could be the object of a bailment arrangement. For clarity, the bailment in such case would generally relate to that physical object – any further entitlements, such as to the virtual asset itself, would be highly fact-dependent – for example, there may be contractual terms expressly addressing that question; and

(c) the virtual asset could *represent* an immediate right to physical possession of something in physical form. That is, the virtual asset may be pertinent to the bailment arrangement not as its *object*, but as evidence of its existence and relevant entitlements, how it is created and terminated and how relevant interests may be transferred to others. This means, for example, that bailment can play a valuable role in real-world asset tokenisation involving physical objects such as precious metals, fine art and real estate, depending on the precise nature of interests represented by the virtual asset and other structural components.

Accordingly, despite the ostensible limitations of bailment in the context of intangible phenomena such as virtual assets, there are several ways in which bailment may be relevant to the control and safekeeping of virtual assets, given the opulence of circumstances in which virtual assets can interact with the physical world. The examples above also demonstrate the importance of interrogating *what* can be physically possessed in a given factual scenario, and examine carefully what follows legally and practically from its physical possession, or the right to its possession. It is also possible that Hong Kong statutory intervention occurs to support a bailment framework for virtual assets to enhance the legal architecture for their safekeeping: that is, improving the interests of the rightful owner beyond the beneficial interest created under trust law. Further, a Court may adopt a more expansive interpretation of physical possession or bailment more generally in the context of virtual assets.[36] To this end, as the reasoning in the *Gatecoin Case* demonstrates, it may be valuable to monitor local case law, international jurisprudence and academic commentary to help predict the direction that Hong Kong Courts may take.

III. Statutory and regulatory frameworks for control and safekeeping

1. *Overview*

Hong Kong has a multi-layered and elastic statutory and regulatory framework that bolsters and shapes the control and safekeeping of virtual assets. The ongoing evolution of that framework is characterised by a fundamental (implicit and explicit) expectation of technological change, in the sense that statutory provisions are flexibly drafted, principles-based standards and technological neutrality are regularly espoused by relevant regulators such as the Hong Kong Securities and Futures Commission (*SFC*) and the Hong Kong Monetary Authority (*HKMA*),[37] and market developments are kept under close review.

36 As to which, see for example, Jiabin Lai, *Possession of cryptoassets* [2023] Journal of Business Law 41, < https://papers.ssrn.com/sol3/papers.cfm?abstract_id=4860851> (19 September 2025). See also the discussion of the statutory concept of "possession" in relation to the regulatory regime for virtual asset exchanges in paragraph 3 of Part III.

37 For example, in the SFC's keynote speech regarding Hong Kong's virtual asset licensing regime, the SFC notes "we adopt a technology-neutral regulatory approach. We believe the use of innovative technology can help make the delivery of financial services more efficient, robust and cost-effective. To facilitate the use of technology whilst maintaining resilience, the SFC strives to ensure that our rules – designed for investor protection, and orderly and fair markets – also apply in digital environments", *Julia Leung*, Embracing Change: Enhancing Regulatory Cooperation and Building Trust in the Virtual Asset Ecosystem (19 June 2023), <https://www.sfc.hk/-/media/EN/files/COM/Speech/Bangkok-VA-speech_Eng_20230613.pdf?rev=449886ac2fba43dc99096d5fb5a205d0&hash=A75C3F4AF9EBFDBFC261A830669BE03D> (19 September 2025). The HKMA has also made similar statements regarding technology neutrality. For example, in the HKMA's "Circular regarding risk management considerations related to the use of distributed ledger technology", the HKMA notes that it adopts a "risk-based and technology-neutral approach to supervision", *Hong Kong Monetary Authority*, Risk Management Considerations Related to the Use of Distributed Ledger Technology

That said, financial regulatory standards can have the effect of championing particular models for the control and safekeeping of virtual assets through regulators' powers of licensing, standard-setting and supervision. This should not be interpreted as suggesting that regulators favour any particular model (including related technology) *for its own sake*. Rather, it is the coalescence of crucial elements relating to investor protection, market integrity and effective supervision that propels perceptions of "good practice" toward a certain model over another. As the span of Hong Kong's regulatory licensing regimes and the ecosystem of regulated market participants grows, so too does the impact of such preferences on the virtual asset industry.

In particular, some key areas of regulatory focus that are relevant to the control and safekeeping of virtual assets include the following:

(a) *Licensing for trust services*, which can apply to numerous virtual asset custodial arrangements.

(b) *Highly granular safekeeping obligations* imposed upon regulated entities such as banks, exchanges and tokenised securities issuers, with standards that operate as de facto (or indirect) regulation of underlying custodians and technology providers.

(c) *Mandatory back-up compensation mechanisms* for certain entities to address safekeeping failures, fraud and other misappropriation or loss.

(d) *Proof of ownership/control requirements and risk controls* in relation to client's wallets, as part of anti-fraud and anti-money laundering and counter-terrorist financing (AML/CFT) controls.

(e) *A focus on settlement finality*, amongst other technical and governance safeguards.

(f) *Multiple areas of further regulatory expansion*, including a dedicated virtual asset custody regime.

The following paragraphs and Part IV provide further detail, with a short "at a glance" summary provided in Table 1: Regulatory Regimes on the Control and Safekeeping of Virtual Assets.

(16 April 2024), <https://www.hkma.gov.hk/media/eng/doc/key-information/guidelines-and-circular/2024/20240416e1.pdf> (19 September 2025).

Table 1: Regulatory Regimes on the Control and Safekeeping of Virtual Assets

<table>
<tr><th>Regulatory regime</th><th>Short synopsis</th><th>Detailed standards for control and safekeeping of virtual assets?</th></tr>
<tr><td colspan="3">Regimes in force at the time of writing</td></tr>
<tr><td>Trust or company service provider (TCSP) regime</td><td>Licensing regime for trustees and other company service providers</td><td>No.
However, TCSPs are indirectly required to comply with other regulators' standards if they support their regulated entities – eg see next row.</td></tr>
<tr><td>Securities and futures regime</td><td>Licensing regime and related conduct standards for those who conduct a range of activities in respect of securities, futures contracts and other financial products</td><td rowspan="2">Yes.
Detailed requirements in multiple scenarios including:
– VATPs (exchanges)
– Network staking arrangements by VATPs.
– Dealing and introducing arrangements.
– Retail funds.</td></tr>
<tr><td>Virtual asset trading platform (VATP) regime</td><td>Licensing regime and related conduct standards for custodial virtual asset exchanges</td></tr>
<tr><td>Banking regime</td><td>Licensing regime and related conduct standards for banks and money brokers</td><td>Yes.
Detailed requirements largely aligned with the SFC, in scenarios including:
– Digital asset custodial services
– Network staking arrangements.</td></tr>
<tr><td colspan="3">Incoming regimes</td></tr>
<tr><td>Stablecoin regime</td><td>Licensing and related conduct standards for issuers of specified stablecoins. Minimum requirements for the offer / marketing of stablecoins by intermediaries.</td><td>Yes.</td></tr>
<tr><td>Future virtual asset custody regime</td><td>Proposed regime for virtual asset custodians.</td><td>Anticipated.
Further detail pending.</td></tr>
<tr><td>Future virtual asset dealing regime</td><td>Proposed regime for virtual asset dealers</td><td>Anticipated.
Further detail pending.</td></tr>
</table>

2. *TCSP Regime*

A key catalyst for the evolution of Hong Kong's regulatory framework for the control and safekeeping of virtual assets, perhaps not intentionally, was the introduction of the licensing and conduct framework for "trust and company service providers" (*TCSPs*) on 1 March 2018, under the Anti-Money Laundering and Counter-Terrorist Financing Ordinance (Cap. 615) (*AMLO*).

Specifically, a person carrying on a trust or company service business requires a licence from the Registrar of Companies; a failure to do so is a criminal offence.[38] Licences are valid for up to 3 years,[39] subject to renewal. Applicants and their ultimate owners and directors (where applicable) must be "fit and proper".[40] A range of general duties flow from licensing, arguably the most critical of which is compliance with the customer due diligence, ongoing monitoring and record-keeping standards in Schedule 2 to the AMLO.

A *"trust or company service"* is defined in section 1 of Part 1 of Schedule 1 to the AMLO to include, of most pertinence to this Chapter:

> "the provision, in Hong Kong, by a person, by way of business, of one or more of the following services to other persons –
>
> ...
>
> (d) acting, or arranging for another person to act –
>
> (i) as a trustee of an express trust or a similar legal arrangement;...

This definition largely tracks the equivalent concept in the Financial Action Task Force (*FATF*) Recommendations (*FATF Recommendations*). More specifically, FATF Recommendation 22(e) defines "trust or company service providers" as including, among others, persons:

> "acting as (or arranging for another person to act as) a trustee of an express trust or performing the equivalent function for another form of legal arrangement;"

This is no accident. The FATF Recommendations and related Mutual Evaluation Review process plays a material role in the ongoing development of Hong Kong's regulatory framework from at least[41] an AML/CFT standpoint. Hong Kong has been a member of FATF since 1991 and continues to participate in periodic Mutual Evaluation Reviews, most recently in 2018–19.[42] The Legislative Council Brief explaining the relevant bill to implement the AML/CFT re-

---

[38] Anti-Money Laundering and Counter-Terrorist Financing Ordinance (Cap. 615, Laws of Hong Kong) s. 53F.

[39] s. 53O AMLO.

[40] s. 53H and 53I AMLO.

[41] The term "at least" is used here because of the trajectory of standards imposed on regulated sectors (whether directly or indirectly via controls on their regulated users) that tends to exceed AML/CFT controls alone. A key example is the regime described in paragraph 3 of this Part III.

[42] See *Financial Action Task Force*, Mutual Evaluation Report of Hong Kong, China (Sep-

gime for TCSPs (and other designated non-financial businesses and professions)[43] expressly referenced the FATF Recommendations and Mutual Evaluation Review as the evident precursor to this new regime.[44]

While the FATF definition is drafted more flexibly than the AMLO definition, it is reasonable to expect that this was important to accommodate jurisdictions that do not recognise trusts at law,[45] rather than any narrowing of scope for Hong Kong.

Indeed, the flexibility of the Hong Kong TSCP regime is such that it is the *capacity* of the relevant person that is important, less so the nature of the underlying interests in question. This is of material significance to virtual assets. This is because it allows the TCSP regime to bend to accommodate various custodial models – whether they involve a person controlling a private key itself, or something that contains it (say, a safe deposit box or even a piece of paper). The crux is that the person acts as trustee of a relevant trust or similar arrangement.

The terms "trustee", "express trust" and "similar arrangement" are not defined in the AMLO, nor in the Interpretation and General Clauses Ordinance. Paragraph 3 of Part II summarises judicial consideration of trust concepts as they pertain to virtual assets. At a high level, it is clear that a trust can arise in multiple scenarios and need not be express. The upshot is that the TCSP regime can rise to the challenge posed by a lack of strong clear legal documentation, which remains common in the virtual asset industry, albeit rapidly changing.

There are, however, limitations to the TCSP regime's coverage of virtual asset control and safekeeping arrangements. For example, the provision of software tools that enable a person to control their own virtual assets would not general-

tember 2019), <https://www.fatf-gafi.org/en/publications/Mutualevaluations/Mutualevaluationofhongkongchina.html> (19 September 2025).

[43] Namely, the Anti-Money Laundering and Counter-Terrorist Financing (Amendment) Bill 2017.

[44] See *Financial Services and the Treasury Bureau*, Legislative Counsel Brief, Anti-Money Laundering and Counter-Terrorist Financing (Financial Institutions) Ordinance (Cap. 615), Anti-Money Laundering and Counter-Terrorist Financing (Amendment) Bill 2017" File Ref.: B&M/4/1/41C, <https://www.fstb.gov.hk/fsb/aml/en/info-pub-press/doc/b23062017a_e.pdf> (19 September 2025).

[45] Support for this proposition can be found in *FATF*'s discussion on trusts and similar arrangements in paragraphs 14 to 18 of its Guidance for a Risk-Based Approach, Beneficial Ownership and Transparency of Legal Arrangements (March 2023), < https://www.fatf-gafi.org/content/dam/fatf-gafi/recommendations/Guidance-Beneficial-Ownership-Transparency-Legal-Arrangements.pdf.coredownload.inline.pdf> (19 September 2025). The FATF Recommendations define "trust" and "trustee" by reference to Article 2 of the Hague Convention on the Law Applicable to Trusts and their Recognition (Hague Convention), citing the foundational characteristics of a trust in footnote 98 to the FATF Recommendations. Of interest is that the Hague Convention refers to "assets" and recognises that neither the reservation by the settlor of certain rights and powers, nor the trustee having rights as a beneficiary, are inconsistent with the existing of a trust. This Chapter does not delve into these issues further, but they are also relevant to a holistic assessment of the conceptualisation of trusts and TCSPs with respect to the myriad existing and potential virtual assets and models for safekeeping.

ly itself require the software provider to become a licensed TCSP. There are exceptions of course, where the software provider can also access and control the private keys: these are far more nuanced situations that require deeper review. The same is true of administrators or other persons whose involvement in virtual asset transactions is limited, but still important, in relation to multi-signature (*multi-sig*) or other custodial models. Their role may not properly be construed as a "trustee" at all, depending on all the facts. For this reason, as well as the related evolution of the FATF Recommendations, Hong Kong is likely to pursue a further expansion to its regime in relation to virtual asset control and safekeeping. Please refer to Part IV.

The primary conduct duties of a TCSP as a licensee relate to AML/CFT controls, as more fully set out in Schedule 2 to the AMLO and related guidelines. There are currently no virtual asset-specific control or safekeeping rules directly imposed on TCSPs under that regime. However, a TCSP's conduct in relation to virtual assets is likely to be shaped by:

(a) the general duties of a trustee under Hong Kong law, including applicable statutory duties as set out in the Trustee Ordinance. These are principles-based, making them highly adaptable to almost any context, noting the very broad definition of "property" as observed in paragraph 2 of Part II;

(b) if it is also registered as a "trust company" with the Registrar of Companies, its additional duties under Part 8 of the Trustee Ordinance, which add structural, financial, governance, transaction-related and other duties; and

(c) if it performs functions in a broader regulatory context, the relevant rules that apply. This is where virtual asset-specific requirements are of most relevance. For example, a TCSP that performs the role of an "Associated Entity" under the AMLO regime for a virtual asset exchange will need to meet very stringent standards: see paragraph 3 of this Part III.

Notably, certain institutions, such as banks licensed by the Hong Kong Monetary Authority, are exempt from the TCSP regime.[46] This lacuna is both explainable by, and (in principle) materially addressed by, the controls imposed on such entities by their respective regulators, with increasing specificity in relation to virtual assets: see paragraph 4 of this Part III.

Bringing this together, the TCSP regime is one of the lynchpins of Hong Kong's framework for the control and safekeeping of virtual assets, spanning multiple arrangements and being highly adaptable to different custodial mod-

[46] See s. 53B, AMLO. More specifically, the following are exempt (in addition to the Government itself): an "authorized institution" regulated by the HKMA under the Banking Ordinance Cap. 155, a "licensed corporation" regulated by the SFC under the SFO where the trust or company service business is ancillary to the corporation's principal business, certain accounting and legal professionals, and others by statutory designation.

els. However, its effectiveness in relation to virtual assets depends on the layering of additional controls imposed by other regulators as described in the following paragraphs of this Part III, and its reach will require bolstering as explained further in Part IV.

3. AMLO VATP regime

The AMLO also contains a regime for virtual asset exchanges that has become highly relevant to the control and safekeeping of virtual assets in Hong Kong. This regime came into effect on 1 June 2023, as a further evolution of Hong Kong's AML/CFT framework in step with concomitant updates to the FATF Recommendations.[47]

The SFC administers this regime, under a harmonised framework for "virtual asset service platforms" (*VATPs*) under its Guidelines for Virtual Asset Trading Platform Operators (*VATP Guidelines*).[48] In essence, this framework enables a consistent approach to regulating exchanges that provide their services in relation to virtual assets, irrespective of whether they are simply "virtual assets" as defined under the AMLO[49] or "securities" under the SFO.[50] Licensees are generally expected to have a licence under Part X of the AMLO, as well as for Type 1 (dealing in securities) and Type 7 (providing automated trading services) under the SFO.[51]

The control and safekeeping of virtual assets is relevant to the VATP regime in two key ways, described as follows.

---

[47] As explained in the *Legislative Council of Hong Kong Special Administrative Region of the People's Republic of China*, Legislative Council Brief, Anti-Money Laundering and Counter-Terrorist Financing Ordinance (Chapter 615), Anti-Money Laundering and Counter-Terrorist Financing (Amendment) Bill 2022, File Ref.: B&M/4/1/41C https://www.legco.gov.hk/yr2022/english/brief/bm4141c_20220622-e.pdf (19 September 2025).

[48] *Securities and Futures Commission*, Guidelines for Virtual Asset Trading Platform Operators (June 2023), < https://www.sfc.hk/-/media/EN/assets/components/codes/files-current/web/guidelines/Guidelines-for-Virtual-Asset-Trading-Platform-Operators/Guidelines-for-Virtual-Asset-Trading-Platform-Operators.pdf> (19 September 2025).

[49] s. 53ZRA, AMLO, definition of "virtual asset".

[50] s. 1 of pt.1 of sch.1, SFO, definition of "securities".

[51] This expectation was articulated in the *Securities and Futures Commission*, Circular on Transitional Arrangements of the New Regime for Virtual Asset Trading Platforms (31 May 2023), <https://apps.sfc.hk/edistributionWeb/gateway/EN/circular/doc?refNo=23EC27> (19 September 2025), no. 31, "Given that the terms and features of virtual assets may evolve over time, a virtual asset's classification may change from a non-security token to a security token (or vice versa). To avoid contravening any of the licensing regimes and ensure business continuity, it would be appropriate for VATPs (together with their proposed [responsible officers] and [licensed representatives]) to apply for approvals under both the SFO and the AMLO and become dually-licensed.". The SFC also makes substantially the same statement on its VATP webpage <https://www.sfc.hk/en/Welcome-to-the-Fintech-Contact-Point/Virtual-assets/Virtual-asset-trading-platforms-operators> (19 September 2025).

a) Control of virtual assets as a threshold regulatory trigger

First, the AMLO licensing requirements only apply to centralised custodial exchanges. More specifically, a licence is required by a person who carries on a business of providing a "VA service", or holds themselves out as doing so.[52] There are several important concepts to unpack here.

(a) A "*VA service*" is further defined as "*operating a VA exchange*", which requires a custodial component. It means:

"providing services through means of electronic facilities –
(a) whereby –
   (i) offers to sell or purchase virtual assets are regularly made or accepted in a way that forms or results in a binding transaction; or
   (ii) persons are regularly introduced, or identified to other persons in order that they may negotiate or conclude, or with the reasonable expectation that they will negotiate or conclude sales or purchases of virtual assets in a way that forms or results in a binding transaction; and
(b) where client money or *client virtual assets* comes into *direct or indirect possession* of the person providing such service."[53] [emphasis added]

(b) The term "*possession*" is defined broadly and non-exhaustively:

"...in relation to any matter, includes custody, control and power of or over the matter"[54]

The reference to "direct or indirect" possession in the definition of operating a VA exchange further expands the potential scope of arrangements caught.

(c) The term "*client virtual asset*" is defined as:

"any virtual asset received or held by or on behalf of a licensed provider or an associated entity of a licensed provider..."[55] [emphasis added]

(d) The term "*hold*" is defined by reference to section 1 of Part 1 of Schedule 1 to the SFO.[56] Similar to the AMLO definition of "possession", this SFO definition is inclusive and expansive and is extracted as follows:

"in relation to any property, includes –
(a) possession of the property;
(b) being registered or otherwise recorded, as having title to or being entitled to receive the property, in any register or other record (however compiled or stored) which is established or created for the purpose of identifying persons having title to or being entitled to receive any property; and

---

52 s. 53ZRD, AMLO.

53 pt. 1 of sch. 3B, AMLO.

54 s. 53ZR, AMLO. This applies to sch. 3B by virtue of s. 1 of pt. 2 of sch.3B, AMLO. The breadth of the word "matter" in this definition supports the multiple ways in which the term "possession" is used, not only in relation to virtual assets.

55 s. 53ZR, AMLO.

56 s. 53ZR, AMLO.

(c) in the case of a person carrying on business, the person being in a position to transfer the property to [themselves] or otherwise receive the benefit of the property –
    (i) where another person has a legal or equitable interest in the property;
    (ii) where there is a connection between the property and the business which is carried on by the person; and
    (iii) regardless of whether it would be lawful or unlawful for the person to transfer the property to [themselves] or otherwise receive the benefit of the property,

    but does not include, in the case of a cheque or other order made payable to any person, the possession of the cheque or other order during the course of dispatching or delivering it to that person or any other person on behalf of that person;" –

The term "receive" is not defined in the SFO, the Interpretation and General Clauses Ordinance or the AMLO.

There is a degree of circularity in these concepts, particularly as possession is defined by reference to the concept of holding, which in turn also includes a reference to possession. However, paragraph (c) of the definition of "hold" is perhaps the most instructive that is, being in a position to transfer property to oneself or otherwise receive the benefit of it.

Further, inherent in the concept of "hold" is the concept of "property". However, this is not a barrier to the term being applied to virtual assets by virtue of Hong Kong's broad conceptualisation of "property" both in statute and by the Courts, as more fully explained in Part II.

Viewing these points in totality, the key implications are that the AMLO regime is focussed on custodial exchanges, and therefore not all virtual asset exchanges are captured, but it is inherently flexible such that various types of custody can be sufficient to trigger its application.

b) Safekeeping measures

As noted in paragraph 1 of this Part III, Hong Kong's overall framework in relation to the control and safekeeping of virtual assets is heavily shaped by regulatory frameworks.

In the case of the VATP regime, the requirements are significant and highly granular.

Part X of the VATP Guidelines includes a range of minimum standards in relation to virtual assets, some of which also apply to client money (which is subject to further expectations). Key standards are briefly summarised as follows:

(a) Segregating and holding virtual assets on trust through its Associated Entity, which cannot conduct any other business. The Associated Entity must be a TCSP and a wholly owned subsidiary of the VATP,[57] among other requirements.

[57] *SFC*, Guidelines for Virtual Asset Trading Platform Operators (n. 48) no. 1.1.

(b) Procedures to protect the virtual assets from theft, fraud and other acts of misappropriation.

(c) Maintaining a minimum 98 % of client virtual assets in cold storage,[58] unless otherwise approved (see below on the type of storage preferred), with hot <> cold transfer mechanisms.

(d) Detailed specifications on authorising and validating access to cryptographic devices or applications, covering key generation, distribution, storage, use and destruction.

(e) Documented measures to dealing with events such as voting, hard forks or airdrops, with related client disclosures.

(g) Whitelisting of client addresses and related controls on deposits and withdrawals. See also paragraph 5 of this Part III in relation to clients proving ownership or control.

(h) Private key management controls to ensure secure seed and private key generation, storage and back-up, including:
- (i) generation offline, in a non-deterministic manner;
- (ii) "offline" storage in Hong Kong, using Hardware Security Module (HSM)-based storage or another secure environment with appropriate certification;
- (iii) personnel , anti-collusion and key person risk controls; and
- (iv) distributed backups.

(i) Ongoing risk assessment, upgrades and testing.

(j) Measures to address key or seed compromise.

(k) Fair and transparent approach to suspending withdrawals.

(m) Appropriate standing authorities to deal with client assets.

Alone, these are material obligations. However, they are supplemented by multiple additional requirements relevant to the control and safekeeping of virtual assets, as summarised below.

---

[58] *Securities and Futures Commission*, Position Paper on Regulation of Virtual Asset Trading Platforms (6 November 2019), <https://www.sfc.hk/-/media/EN/files/ER/PDF/20191106-Position-Paper-and-Appendix-1-to-Position-Paper-Eng.pdf?rev=3458562e036845879879b6a8649e6c40> (19 September 2025), p. 50, ""hot wallet" describes the practice where the private keys to virtual assets are kept online and are therefore highly vulnerable to external threats, such as hacking and social engineering (for example, phishing). Storage in a "cold wallet" refers to the private keys which are kept offline, ie, without access to the internet, and therefore provide more security". This is supported by the Joint Circular (defined in paragraph 0) in which footnote 19 states "A "hot wallet" or "hot storage" describes the practice where the private keys to virtual assets are kept in an online environment. As "hot wallet" or "hot storage" is connected to the internet, it is more susceptible to cyberattacks. In contrast, a "cold wallet" or "cold storage" describes the practice where the private keys to virtual assets are kept in an offline environment.

c) Client engagement, cybersecurity and other key controls

The client asset protection requirements in Part X of the VATP Guidelines are bolstered by multiple other rules relevant to the control and safekeeping of virtual assets. These include the following:

(a) Client disclosure requirements relevant to custodial arrangements, including the rights and obligations of each party and how client assets are stored.[59]

(b) Minimum client disclosures and client agreement content. This includes the following duty which would *contractually* preclude the VATP from defeating the mandatory regulatory custody requirements:

"A [VATP] should not incorporate any clause, provision, or term in the client agreement or in any other document signed or statement made by the client at the request of the [VATP] which is inconsistent with its obligations under [the VATP Guidelines]."[60]

(c) Mandatory contract notes, statements of account and receipts.[61]

(d) Mandatory trading and operational rules, including coverage of custodial arrangements.[62]

(e) Detailed cybersecurity requirements in Part XII of the VATP Guidelines.

(f) Significant custody-related guidance in additional materials such as the SFC's FAQs on conduct and licensing,[63] its Licensing Handbook for Virtual Asset Trading Platforms (*VATP Licensing Handbook*)[64] and the SFC's more recent findings of its inspections of licensing applicants (*SFC Thematic Review Findings*).[65]

---

[59] *SFC*, Guidelines for Virtual Asset Trading Platform Operators (n. 48) no. 10.17.

[60] *SFC*, Guidelines for Virtual Asset Trading Platform Operators (n. 48) no. 9.16.

[61] *SFC*, Guidelines for Virtual Asset Trading Platform Operators (n. 48) no. 9.33.

[62] See *SFC*, Guidelines for Virtual Asset Trading Platform Operators (n. 48) no. 7.27(m).

[63] *Securities and Futures Commission,* FAQs on Conduct Related Matters, <https://www.sfc.hk/en/Welcome-to-the-Fintech-Contact-Point/Virtual-assets/Virtual-asset-trading-platforms-operators/Regulatory-requirements/FAQs-on-conduct-related-matters> (19 September 2025) and *Securities and Futures Commission*, FAQs on Licensing Related Matters <https://www.sfc.hk/en/Welcome-to-the-Fintech-Contact-Point/Virtual-assets/Virtual-asset-trading-platforms-operators/Regulatory-requirements/FAQs-on-licensing-related-matters> (19 September 2025).

[64] *Securities and Futures Commission*, Licensing Handbook for Virtual Asset Trading Platform Operators <https://www.sfc.hk/-/media/EN/assets/components/Guidelines/File-current/Licensing-Handbook-for-VATPs-31-05-2023.pdf> (19 September 2025).

[65] *Securities and Futures Commission*, FAQs on Conduct Related Matters, Circular to Licensed Corporations, SFC-licensed Virtual Asset Service Providers and Associated Entities – Findings from inspections on deemed-to-be-licensed virtual asset trading platform applicants and expected standards of conduct for virtual asset trading platform operators (16 January 2025), <https://apps.sfc.hk/edistributionWeb/gateway/EN/circular/intermediaries/supervision/doc?refNo=25EC3> (19 September 2025).

Of particular note are the following additional expectations set out in the SFC Thematic Review Findings:

(i) *Real-time monitoring* of client virtual assets in hot storage, and real-time automatic sweep into cold storage upon receipt.[66]

(ii) *Personnel limitations*, with only responsible officers, managers-in-charge and their delegates permitted to handle and access client virtual assets.[67]

(iii) *Robust algorithms*. Ensuring encryption technology is up-to-date, and cryptographic algorithms reviewed before deployment, and on an ongoing basis.[68]

(iv) *Around-the-clock continuity of resources* to ensure continuous and uninterrupted security monitoring and incident handling, noting the 24/7 operation of platforms.[69]

(g) External assessment under a tripartite arrangement between the VATP, the SFC and the assessor, with in-depth requirements in relation to the eligibility of the assessor, as well as their scope and methodology.[70]

(h) Network staking control measures, if applicable.[71] These relatively newer control measures are particularly interesting as they pave the way for deploying client virtual assets to generate yield. However, both regulatory consent and additional conditions apply.

d) Compensation when custody controls fail

On top of the stringent controls above, VATPs are also required to have an insurance or compensation arrangement in place that meets the following key requirements:[72]

(a) *Coverage:* Potential loss of 50 % of client virtual assets in cold storage plus 100 % of client virtual assets in hot / other storage.

---

[66] Expected standard K of app. 2 to the *SFC*, Thematic Review Findings (n. 65).

[67] Expected standard G of app. 2 to the *SFC*, Thematic Review Findings (n. 65).

[68] Expected standard C of app. 2 to the *SFC*, Thematic Review Findings (n. 65).

[69] Expected standard D of app. 2 to the *SFC*, Thematic Review Findings (n. 65). A range of other standards and observations in the SFC Thematic Review Findings elaborate upon other controls described earlier in this Chapter.

[70] *VATP*, Licensing Handbook (n. 64) no. 3.2.23; the *SFC*, VATP Licensing FAQs (n. 63) under "External assessment reports for licensing applications" and *Securities and Futures Commission*, Circular to New Virtual Asset Trading Platforms Seeking to be Licensed – Enhanced Licensing Process and Revamped External Assessments (16 January 2025) <https://apps.sfc.hk/edistributionWeb/gateway/EN/circular/doc?refNo=25EC2> (19 September 2025).

[71] *Securities and Futures Commission,* Circular on staking services provided by virtual asset trading platforms <https://apps.sfc.hk/edistributionWeb/gateway/EN/circular/doc?refNo=25EC22> (19 September 2025).

[72] *SFC*, Guidelines for Virtual Asset Trading Platform Operators (n. 48) nos. 10.22–10.26.

(b) *Form*: One or a combination of the following:
   (i) Third-party insurance.
   (ii) Funds or virtual assets set aside on trust.
   (iii) Bank guarantee by an HKMA-regulated licensed bank or other "authorized financial institution" (*HKMA Authorised Institution*).

(c) *Ongoing monitoring.*

(d) *SFC engagement:* To approve the arrangement and any variations to it, as well as in relation to any breach.[73]

e) The "travel rule" and its relevance to custody

As part of the suite of AML/CFT controls that apply to VATPs under the AMLO, the SFC also imposes the "travel rule" on VATPs and other regulated entities under Chapter 12 of its Guideline on Anti-Money Laundering and Counter-Financing of Terrorism (for Licensed Corporations and SFC-licensed Virtual Asset Services Providers) (*SFC AMLO Guideline*). In essence, this requires certain information to move alongside virtual asset transactions.

Of particular relevance to this Chapter is the differentiated treatment of "hosted" and "unhosted" wallets in relation to the controls that are to be applied by the relevant regulated entity, with the latter requiring the most robust controls. An "unhosted wallet" in this context is defined in footnote 116 to the SFC AMLO Guideline as:

"software or hardware that enables a person to store and transfer virtual assets on [their] own behalf, and in relation to which the private key is controlled or held by that person".

It is beyond the scope of this Chapter to delve into the specific rules that apply to each scenario. However, one key impact of this differentiation is that Hong Kong's AML/CFT regime (and others that impose the travel rule) makes it more onerous for institutions to interact with unhosted wallets. This could well have flow-on impacts to market development over time. For example, it may reduce institutional tolerance of clients' self-custody of virtual assets (that is, clients using unhosted wallets as the origin or destination of assets), although arguably, sophisticated on-chain analytics that are required as part of transaction monitoring, and which can be used as part of pre- and post-transaction screening, should provide a material degree of comfort, and (at least) make institutions more tolerant of unhosted wallets than they are of clients depositing or withdrawing physical cash.

The travel rule is also relevant to proof of control expectations. See paragraph 5 of this Part III.

---

[73] For example, under *SFC*, Guidelines for Virtual Asset Trading Platform Operators (n. 48) no. 16.7.

f) Application to Associated Entities

Associated Entities play a pivotal role in the control and safekeeping of virtual assets. However, they are not directly regulated by the SFC. As noted above, they are regulated under the TCSP regime described in paragraph 2 of this Part III. This is addressed through indirect regulation. Specifically, relevant expectations on the VATP are extended to the Associated Entity throughout the VATP Guidelines: that is, the VATP is obliged to ensure the Associated Entity complies with relevant requirements. In practice, this is effected through the combination of the trust arrangements mandated by the VATP Guidelines, a service agreement, the controls implemented by each entity (including audit) and the sole shareholding structure: that is, the VATP owns the Associated Entity, so it has the power to compel it as necessary.

g) Ongoing relevance of other regimes

Virtual assets can evidence a plethora of interests, many of which are regulated under other regimes. For example, a tokenised interest in a portion of a gold bar could be a "collective investment scheme", "OTC derivative" or "structured product" under the SFO, among other things; it could also involve dealing in precious metals as contemplated by the AMLO. For this reason, other regulatory regimes designed before tokenisation, and which must have an enduring broader application, may well be relevant to the custody and safekeeping of virtual assets. Hong Kong regulators have rapidly sought to apply those regimes to the novel features and risks of tokenisation, with a significant focus on custody controls. The following paragraphs provide some key examples.

4. Regulatory standards for other regulated entities

The SFC and the HKMA have issued a range of rules relating to the activities of their regulated entities in relation to virtual assets, even where the virtual asset in question, or a service in relation to it, would not alone constitute a regulated activity. While some of these activities may exceed the scope of the regulatory perimeter administered by these regulators, these standards evidently intend to support the overarching rubric of supervision, to ensure entities remain fit and proper to be licensed. The following paragraphs summarise some of the key developments in this area.

a) Dealing and introducing arrangements

First, the SFC and the HKMA jointly issued the "Joint circular on intermediaries' virtual asset-related activities" on December 2023 (*Joint Circular*). Of particular relevance to the control and safekeeping of virtual assets, the Joint Circular requires relevant intermediaries:[74]

(i) to partner only with SFC-licensed platforms in relation to any virtual asset dealing services, whether through an introduction to, or in establishing an omnibus account with, the relevant platform. This partnering rule inexorably leads to the creation of a controlled ecosystem involving highly regulated market participants, where the bar to entry is regulation itself. Paragraph 3 of this Part III describes the exceptionally high standards imposed upon VATPs in relation to the control and safekeeping of virtual assets, while paragraph 4(d) of this Part III describes the standards also imposed on HKMA Authorised Institutions and the subsidiaries of locally incorporated HKMA Authorised Institutions;

(ii) only to offer virtual asset dealing services to clients who are also their securities dealing clients: that is, under a licence or registration for Type 1 (dealing in securities) regulated activities under the SFO; and

(iii) to comply with a range of obligations when providing virtual asset dealing services under an omnibus account arrangement. This includes, for example, meeting minimum liquid capital, operational, market integrity and client protection obligations, including custody-specific standards. Particularly restrictive rules apply when dealing with retail clients, including mandatory pre-funding, a prohibition on financial accommodation or return-generation (through staking or otherwise), limitations on which virtual assets are eligible for trading and various disclosure obligations. As a general observation, many requirements track intermediaries' existing statutory and regulatory obligations.[75] However, even where there is a close match, they are necessary for two key reasons: first, to ensure that those obligations "bite", as virtual asset dealing may not strictly be caught by the language used in existing rules (if, say, a virtual asset is not a "security" or some other regulated product); and secondly, to calibrate the obligations appropriately to this special context; and

(iv) to notify the SFC and HKMA, as appropriate.

[74] See *Securities and Futures Commission / Hong Kong Monetary Authority*, Joint Circular on Intermediaries' Virtual Asset-Related Activities (22 December 2023), <https://www.hkma.gov.hk/media/eng/doc/key-information/guidelines-and-circular/2023/20231222e1.pdf> (19 September 2025), nos. 17–19 and app. 6 that sets out key terms and conditions.

[75] For example, under *Securities and Futures Commission*, Code of Conduct for Persons Licensing be or Registered with the Securities and Futures Commission (October 2024), <https://www.sfc.hk/-/media/EN/assets/components/codes/files-current/web/codes/code-of-conduct-for-persons-licensed-by-or-registered-with-the-securities-and-futures-commission/Code_of_conduct-Oct-2024_Eng-with-Bookmark-Final.pdf?rev=0d85942581714ea183634112e8e9d474> (19 September 2025).

In sum, there is highly focussed oversight of regulated entities' virtual asset and virtual asset-related products, and restrictions that help prevent regulatory arbitrage.

Another clear message from the Joint Circular – and other regulatory instruments relating to virtual assets – is that the "same activity, same risk, same regulation" adage is generally applied in Hong Kong, though it tends to *increase* the regulatory standards by an appreciable measure.

b) Retail funds

The SFC has also supplemented its guidance for dealers generally with a further set of expectations in relation to SFC-authorised virtual asset-related funds in its "Circular on SFC-authorised funds with exposure to virtual assets" dated 22 December 2023 (*SFC Funds Circular*).

The SFC Funds Circular contains requirements in two key areas relevant to the control and safekeeping of virtual assets, summarised as follows:

(i) Transactions. All transactions and direct acquisitions of virtual assets must be conducted through SFC-licensed VATPs or HKMA Authorised Institutions (or subsidiaries of locally incorporated HKMA Authorised Institutions) that meet the HKMA's requirements[76] (*Permitted Regulated Entities*). There is a further breakdown of expectations depending on whether in-kind and/or in-cash subscriptions and redemptions are involved.

(ii) Custody. Several rules apply to virtual asset holdings by the trustee/custodian of the SFC-authorised fund, including delegation being limited to a Permitted Regulated Entity, mandatory segregation, cold and hot wallet storage requirements and local storage of seeds and private keys, with restricted personnel access and appropriate back-up, key generation and transaction signing arrangements.[77]

Again, the SFC Funds Circular illustrates the observations noted in paragraph 4(a) of this Part III in relation to Hong Kong's financial regulators advancing a highly regulated ecosystem for virtual asset activities, with an elevated focus on the quality of the control and safekeeping of virtual assets.

c) Tokenised securities

Custodial arrangements are also a key area of focus for the SFC in connection with tokenised securities,[78] particularly where the tokenised securities are in

---

[76] See paragraph 4(d) of this Part III for further detail.

[77] *SFC*, ETF Circular (n. 74) nos. 16–20.

[78] For these purposes, the SFC defines tokenised securities as "traditional financial instruments (eg, bonds or funds) that are "securities" as defined in section 1 of Part 1 of Schedule 1

bearer form. In November 2023, the SFC published detailed requirements in its "Circular on intermediaries engaging in tokenised securities-related activities" (*SFC Tokenised Securities Circular*).[79]

The SFC Tokenised Securities Circular provides high-level guidance on the topic of custody selection, stating that:

"intermediaries should take into account the features and risks of the Tokenised Securities in considering the most appropriate custodial arrangement for the Tokenised Securities to manage ownership and technology risks."[80]

It then goes on to provide very specific expectations for "bearer form" tokenised securities "which use permissionless tokens on public-permissionless networks" in Part B of the Appendix. This contains 10 non-exhaustive principles relating to the selection of custodial arrangements, covering various matters such as security, track record, private key controls, segregation, financial resources, managing conflicts of interest, operational capabilities and so on. One particular point of interest is the expectation of the "immobilisation of the [tokenised securities] with central custody". The SFC explains this as follows:

"Generally, financial instruments are "immobilised" by being safekept with a custodian in such way that it is not possible for them to enter into circulation and by having the entitlement to them recorded with account-entry records and transferred with book entries."[81]

This speaks to the vital importance of any ledger being capable to serve as the source of truth (safekeeping relevant interests), with maximum incorruptibility (ensuring appropriate control).

---

to the [SFO] which utilise [distributed ledger technology] (such as blockchain technology) or similar technology in their security lifecycle." It also notes these are "fundamentally traditional securities with a tokenisation wrapper". The SFC then articulates these as a subclass of a broader concept of "digital securities", which are still "securities" under the SFO, but which "may be structured in more bespoke, novel or complicated forms", such as a fractionalised interest in a real-world asset in a manner different from a traditional fund. It is beyond the scope of this Chapter to explore the merits and complexities of this distinction, save as to note that in many scenarios, it would appear difficult to justify (and potentially even apply), as would a purely technical reading of the application of the SFC's custodial expectations (namely, in practice, the principles would merit being applied more broadly). For reference, the SFC's VATP Guidelines cover "security tokens", which appear to relate to the broader class of "digital securities" in the SFC Tokenised Securities Circular.

[79] *Securities and Futures Commission*, Circular on intermediaries engaging in tokenised securities-related activities (2 November 2023), < https://apps.sfc.hk/15edistributionWeb/gateway/EN/circular/doc?refNo=23EC52 > (19 September 2025).

[80] *SFC*, Tokenised Securities Circular (n. 79) nos. 16–20.

[81] *SFC*, Tokenised Securities Circular (n. 79) pt. B, Appendix, footnote 2.

d) Custody standards for banks

For its part, the HKMA issued extensive and granular standards on the "Provision of Custodial Services for Digital Assets" on 20 February 2024 applicable to HKMA Authorised Institutions (*HKMA Custody Rules*).[82]

These apply when HKMA Authorised Institutions engage in custodial activities while acting as an intermediary, distributing tokenised products or providing standalone custodial services. They also apply to locally incorporated HKMA Authorised Institutions' subsidiaries. In-scope "digital assets" for the purposes of these HKMA Custody Rules include the reasonably narrow class of "virtual assets" as defined in the AMLO, but also extend to tokenised securities and other tokenised assets. They exclude certain assets such as limited purpose digital tokens (per the AMLO), proprietary assets of the relevant institution or its group companies or central bank digital currencies (CBDCs).

In summary, the HKMA Custody Rules substantively track other standards imposed under the AMLO VATP regime and the Joint Circular. They cover a very broad range of areas including:

(i) Governance and risk management.
(ii) Segregation of client digital assets.
(iii) Safeguarding of client digital assets.
(iv) Delegation and outsourcing rules.
(v) Disclosure.
(vi) Record-keeping.
(vii) Reconciliation of client digital assets.
(viii) AML/CFT.
(ix) Ongoing monitoring.[83]

The HKMA has also published guidance on network staking, generally commensurate with the SFC's requirements for VATPs.[84] As we allude to above, this provides an extremely valuable pathway to a more expansive deployment of client virtual assets to access yield, albeit with high conduct standards.

---

[82] *Hong Kong Monetary Authority*, Provision of Custodia Services for Digital Assets (20 February 2024), < https://www.hkma.gov.hk/media/eng/doc/key-information/guidelines-and-circular/2024/20240220e4.pdf> (19 September 2025).

[83] A synopsis of the requirements is available at *King & Wood Mallesons*, HKMA Issues Digital Asset Custody Rules for Banks (22 February 2024), <https://www.kwm.com/hk/en/insights/latest-thinking/hkma-issues-digital-asset-custody-rules-for-banks.html> (19 September 2025).

[84] *Hong Kong Monetary Authority*, Provision of Staking Services for Virtual Assets from Custodial Services (7 April 2025), < https://www.hkma.gov.hk/media/eng/doc/key-information/guidelines-and-circular/2024/20240220e4.pdf> (19 September 2025).

5. Other key considerations – proving control, settlement finality, capital, conflict of laws and CBDCs

There are multiple other areas of law and regulation relevant to the control and safekeeping of virtual assets. The balance of this paragraph addresses four areas: proving control, settlement finality, capital, conflicts of law and CBDCs.

a) Proving control

The pseudonymity of virtual asset wallet addresses and the uneven implementation of AML/CTF controls internationally poses an inherent challenge to institutional financial crime and anti-fraud controls. This is because name matching is not possible from a virtual asset transfer alone (as it might be from a bank account transfer), its digital nature precludes in-person verification (which can support cash transfers, for example), and sometimes information from providers of hosted wallets may not be trustworthy. Something more is required, as exemplified by on-chain analytics processes and the travel rule described earlier in this Chapter.

To help attenuate the residual risks, the SFC and the HKMA require their regulated entities to ensure that incoming virtual asset deposits from, and outgoing transfers to, their clients are supported by control measures to ensure that the relevant wallet is indeed controlled by the client concerned, or that the virtual asset transfer otherwise originates from the client.

For example, in any situation involving higher ML/TF risk or an unhosted wallet, the SFC requires its regulated entities to:

"ascertain the customer's ownership or control of the account (or wallet address as appropriate) maintained with the ordering or beneficiary institution, or the unhosted wallet, by taking appropriate measures, for example:

(a) using appropriate confirmation methods[141]; and
(b) obtaining evidence from the customer such as statement of account issued by the [virtual asset] counterparty.

[141]Examples of confirmation methods may include requesting the customer to perform the micropayment test (i. e. by effecting a virtual asset transfer with an (typically small) amount specified by the [financial institution]) or message signing test (i. e. by signing a message specified by the [financial institution] which is then verified by the [financial institution]."[85]

[85] *Securities and Futures Commission*, Guideline on Anti-Money Laundering and Counter-Financing of Terrorism (For Licensed Corporations and SFC-licensed Virtual Asset Service Providers), Chapter 12 (1 June 2023), <https://www.sfc.hk/-/media/EN/assets/components/codes/files-current/web/guidelines/guideline-on-anti-money-laundering-and-counter-financing-of-terrorism-for-licensed-corporations/AML-Guideline-for-LCs-and-SFC-licensed-VASPs_Eng_1-Jun-2023.pdf> (19 September 2025), no. 12.10.6.

This is also reflected in the SFC's whitelisting requirements in the VATP Guidelines.[86] The HKMA has a similar expectation in the HKMA Custody Rules.[87]

Importantly, while there are mixed references to "ownership" and "control" in these regulatory sources, there is no specific duty for these regulated institutions to ask clients to prove entitlement to the relevant virtual assets. As a practical observation, this is often addressed in relevant representations and warranties, and concomitant undertakings and other provisions, in client agreements.

b) Settlement finality

Material to the control and safekeeping of virtual assets is settlement finality. That is, to engender trust and legal certainty that virtual assets have (or indeed have not) moved from A to B.[88]

Hong Kong has a limited statutory settlement finality regime under the Payment Systems and Stored Value Facilities Ordinance (Cap. 584) (*PSSVFO*) that currently applies to payments and securities only. More specifically, it pertains to certain systems established for either the clearing and settlement of *payment obligations*, or for *obligations for the transfer of book-entry securities* (or their actual transfer).[89] The HKMA has the power to designated certain clearing and settlement systems and issue a certificate of finality,[90] among other powers. To date, the HKMA has issued certificates of finality in relation to six systems, being:

(i) HKD CHATS (including the HKD FPS).
(ii) US Dollar CHATS.
(iii) Euro CHATS.
(iv) RMB CHATS (including the RMB FPS).

---

[86] *SFC*, Guidelines for Virtual Asset Trading Platform Operators (n. 48) no. 10.10(c).

[87] *HKMA*, Custody Rules (n. 82) no. 11.

[88] The *HKMA*'s report on Bond Tokenisation in Hong Kong in relation to Project Evergreen in 2023, Bond Tokenisation in Hong Kong (August 2023), <https://www.hkma.gov.hk/media/eng/doc/key-information/press-release/2023/20230824e3a1.pdf> (19 September 2025) describes "settlement finality" in the context of payments and securities as "the discharge of an obligation by a transfer of funds and a transfer of securities that have become irrevocable and unconditional. Specifically, "finality" refers to the abrogation of all rights otherwise existing at law that would allow the setting aside of a transfer order effected through, or proceedings within, a clearing and settlement system."

[89] See the definition of "clearing and settlement system" in s 2, the designation provisions in Part 2, and the finality provisions in Part 3, of the Payment Systems and Stored Value Facilities Ordinance (Cap. 584, Laws of Hong Kong).

[90] Further details are set out in *Hong Kong Monetary Authority*, Explanatory Note on Designation and Issuance of Certificate of Finality of Clearing and Settlement Systems under the Payment Systems and Stored Value Facilities Ordinance (Cap. 584), <https://www.hkma.gov.hk/media/eng/doc/key-functions/banking-stability/oversight/explanatory_note.pdf> (19 September 2025).

(v) Central Moneymarkets Unit (*CMU*).
(vi) Continuous Linked Settlement System.[91]

No virtual asset-specific platform is the subject of a certificate of finality, although the CMU has been involved in two major tokenised bond projects as part of "Project Evergreen", for example.[92]

To effectively broaden the reach of the existing finality regime to address the virtual assets, two key things would need to occur. First, the PSSVO would need to expand beyond payments and securities, or other applicable laws implemented. Second, off-platform finality would need to be addressed. After all, it is one thing to address on-platform virtual asset transfers (which may be off-chain book entry transfers), and another to address on-chain finality, which must tackle the specifics of each underpinning distributed ledger technology and related consensus algorithm.

Absent statutory clarity, comfort in relation to settlement finality can only therefore realistically be found through a proper understanding of the technology itself, and contractual agreement. Regulators have called attention to the former. For example, the SFC provides the following guidance to its VATPs:

> "[VATPs] are generally expected to consider the following factors (where applicable) when conducting due diligence on virtual assets:...
>
> (d) the technical aspects of a virtual asset, for example, the security infrastructure of its blockchain protocol, the size of the blockchain and network, and especially how resistant it is to common attacks (eg, a 51% attack1 or similar attacks with an impact on transaction finality)".[93]

Similarly, the HKMA drew attention to the issue in its circular on "Risk management considerations related to the use of distributed ledger technology", noting:

> "... with respect to the issuing and trading of tokenised products, while settlement finality under traditional financial systems is a clear and well-defined point in time that is underpinned by a strong legal foundation, the point at which settlement finality is reached under DLT arrangements may be less clear-cut given the use of consensus-based

---

[91] As reported on the HKMA's website relating to the PSSVFO, available at <https://www.hkma.gov.hk/eng/key-functions/international-financial-centre/financial-market-infrastructure/oversight-of-financial-market-infrastructure-fmi/oversight-framework/> (19 September 2025).

[92] See *Hong Kong Monetary Authority*, "EvergreenHub: Navigating Bond Tokenisation, Digital Bond Knowledge Repository", <https://www.hkma.gov.hk/eng/key-functions/international-financial-centre/bond-market-development/digital-bond-knowledge-repository//> (19 September 2025).

[93] *Securities and Futures Commission*, "Trading of virtual assets" (31 May 2023), < https://www.sfc.hk/en/Welcome-to-the-Fintech-Contact-Point/Virtual-assets/Virtual-asset-trading-platforms-operators/Regulatory-requirements/FAQs-on-conduct-related-matters/Trading-of-virtual-assets/31-May-2023-Trading-of-virtual-assets> (19 September 2025).

validation mechanisms. Subject to how a traditional product is "tokenised", there may also be changes to its legal standing and subsequent regulatory treatment. AIs should be aware of these possible legal grey areas, seek professional advice where necessary and put in place measures during the design process to mitigate the ensuing legal risks."[94]

The topic of settlement finality also appears in far more specific terms in the HKMA's materials implementing the Bank for International Settlements Basel Committee on Banking Supervision standard on the "Prudential treatment of cryptoasset exposures" (*Basel Cryptoassets Prudential Standard*), with several references in its proposed Supervisory Policy Module, CRP-1 "Classification of Cryptoassets".FOOTNOTE In particular, settlement finality is relevant to meeting certain classification conditions that can lead to more favourable capital treatment, with the expectation that this be addressed both at primary and secondary market levels with proper documentation.[95]

The practical consequence of this focus on settlement finality across multiple sources remains to be seen. It is possible that a further wave of regulatory standards and statutory clarity will follow the current swell of reform to address this far more technical, yet systemically significant, area of law. If so, it may be reasonable to expect this will involve the combination of platform-specific finality designation to cover major platforms operating in Hong Kong (akin to past practice), plus additional guidance for regulated entities to support their adjudication of finality in relation to other platforms, including relevant blockchains themselves. It may also be reasonable to expect that this legal and regulatory development would be hastened (and standards tightened) if a platform suffered a settlement-related incident, causing loss.

c) Financial resources

Capital and liquidity are squarely relevant to regulated entities' involvement in virtual assets, and both their decision to, and actual assumption, of custodial activities. Several of these are addressed in the discussion in the VATP and other regimes above. Financial resources must also support mandatory compensation arrangements when they apply. A corollary of these requirements, especially when coupled with the mandatory trust arrangements, other significant mandatory human, technical and third-party resource expenditures, and business model restrictions, can make regulated virtual asset activities very difficult to justify commercially, particularly if a prospective client can access any number of offshore service providers at the click of a button, or use an OTC virtual asset

[94] Available at *Hong Kong Monetary Authority*, Risk Management Considerations Related to the Use of Distributed Ledger Technology (16 April 2024), <https://brdr.hkma.gov.hk/eng/doc-ldg/docId/20240416-1-EN> (19 September).

[95] See, *Hong Kong Monetary Authority*, Cryptoassets standard: consultation on new and revised SPM modules and code of practice, <https://brdr.hkma.gov.hk/eng/doc-ldg/docId/20250905-5-EN> (19 September 2025).

broker that is not regulated at all, to access tighter spreads made possible by lower levels of regulation, lower costs and/or more varied business models. However, some of the restrictions and regulatory gaps are under review, as described in Part IV.

As noted above, Hong Kong is also working to implement the Basel Cryptoassets Prudential Standard, which is likely to influence Hong Kong banks' approach to the custody and safekeeping of virtual assets.

d) Conflict of laws

Conflict of laws principles and challenges are highly relevant to the control and safekeeping of virtual assets and related disputes. This Chapter does not address these, as they merit far deeper treatment.

However, it is worth pointing out the trendlines that can be observed in the regulatory requirements described in this Chapter, including the general expectation of local private key storage, the restriction on partnerships to those with other locally regulated entities, and significant other localisation requirements including in relation to certain data, personnel, premises, technology and other areas. These measures can have a material impact on both the exercise of regulatory supervisory and enforcement powers, as well as asset recovery efforts where necessary – assuming dissipation has not already occurred.

Furthermore, the SFC requires its VATPs and other regulated entities, at least when dealing with individuals and/or retail clients, to avoid any terms that are inconsistent with their obligations under regulatory requirements.[96] This can preclude a choice of governing law that imperils a client's rights in relation to their assets. For example, if a particular jurisdiction's law cannot give effect to the SFC's mandated trust arrangements because there is no concept of a trust, this would be problematic.

e) CBDCs

Finally, CBDCs are generally expressly excluded from the virtual asset-specific regulatory regimes cited above. Certain other regimes, such as the stored value facility regime under the PSSVO, can arguably accommodate CBDCs given the flexibility of their drafting, particularly when broad and non-exhaustively defined concepts of "money", "value of an amount of money", "money's worth" or similar are used. However, more work is likely to be required to provide legal certainty as to the proper construction of legal and regulatory frameworks as they apply to the control and safekeeping of central bank claims represented in digital form. Hong Kong has several initiatives in this area, including those

---

[96] *SFC*, Guidelines for Virtual Asset Trading Platform Operators (n. 48) no 9.16 and *SFC*, Code of Conduct (n. 75) no 6.5.

referenced in Part V. The evolution of CBDCs can also be expected to play an important role in stablecoin development, through the technological capabilities a programmable form of money can play in reserve asset management and the issuance and redemption lifecycle. At the heart of this are sound control and safekeeping mechanisms.

IV. Upcoming developments

Multiple virtual asset-related consultations are currently underway in Hong Kong, or earmarked for the near future.

For example, in the SFC ASPIRE Roadmap,[97] the SFC has outlined 12 major initiatives to enhance the security, innovation and growth of Hong Kong's virtual asset market. This includes new frameworks for regulating virtual asset dealing and virtual asset custodian services, and the expansion of virtual asset product and service offerings, including the scope of services that might be offered by existing regulated entities such as VATPs. Other measures encompass optimisation of operational requirements for VA trading platforms, combatting illicit activities, investor education and proactive stakeholder engagement.

In relation to custody specifically, the SFC hints that there may be greater flexibility in certain control areas, noting the following:

> "The SFC recognises the rapid evolution of custody technologies and the need for a forward-looking regulatory approach. Instead of mandating specific hardware solutions, the SFC will explore transitioning to more technology-neutral, outcome-based standards that prioritise the overall custody control environment".

Of further direct relevance to this Chapter is the proposal to create a specific custody regime for virtual assets.[98] For now, the details remain at an early stage. However, the following are noteworthy:

(a) In relation to *scope*, the Hong Kong proposals adopt the following broad scope:

> "by way of business, the safekeeping of (i) VAs on behalf of clients; or (ii) instruments enabling transfer of VAs of clients (including but not limited to private keys) on behalf of clients."

---

[97] *Securities and Futures Commission*, SFC Sets Out New Roadmap to Develop Hong Kong as a Global Virtual Asset Hub (19 February 2025), <https://apps.sfc.hk/edistributionWeb/gateway/EN/news-and-announcements/news/doc?refNo=25PR20> (19 September 2025).

[98] The relevant consultation paper is available at *Financial Services and the Treasury Bureau and Securities and Futures Commission*, Public Consultation on Legislative Proposals to Regulate Virtual Asset Custodian Services (June 2025), <https://apps.sfc.hk/edistributionWeb/api/consultation/openFile?lang=EN&refNo=25CP7> (19 September 2025).

This is broadly in line with the scope of the custodial services contemplated by the FATF definition of "virtual asset service provider".[99] The Hong Kong proposals also make clear that bank security vaults or security companies merely storing encrypted or de-activated back-up private keys (or a part thereof), as well as technical service providers that support a custodian service but do not safekeep the private keys or similar instruments (eg communication or information technology networks) would not be caught. Of course, there is a vast spectrum of technologies that support custody in relation to which a highly nuanced regulatory analysis will be required to determine their proper characterisation, should these proposals proceed.

(b) In relation to *relevance*, the relevant regulatory regime that is introduced in due course should facilitate a broader range of third-party custodians participating in the Hong Kong regulated virtual asset ecosystem, as described in paragraph 2 of Part III. Support for this can also be found in the SFC ASPIRE Roadmap, which refers to enabling a "two-tier mark#

et structure segregating trading and custodians."[100]

(c) In relation to *approach*, it is reasonable to expect that largely the same standards as applied to other safekeeping scenarios will be applied, although some flexibility and potentially also relaxation of standards may take place across the industry.[101]

The Stablecoins Ordinance[102] that came into effect on 1 August 2025 involves several of the "travel rule" and detailed custody-related controls enumerated above in other contexts. In addition, proposals to regulated virtual asset dealing services,[103] and Hong Kong's implementation of the Basel Cryptoassets Prudential Standard are also highly relevant to the development, control and safekeeping of virtual assets (including who may be disposed to do so, and how).

---

[99] This definition also refers to the transfer of virtual assets, with "transfer" defined in footnote 99 to cover "conduct[ing] a transaction on behalf of another". This may also have a bearing on the direction that Hong Kong takes in relation to the regulatory framework for the control and safekeeping of virtual assets, as well as adjacent regulatory areas such as OTC virtual asset dealing services.

[100] *SFC*, ASPIRE Roadmap (n. 97) at no. 35.

[101] See paragraphs 41 and 42 of the *SFC*, ASPIRE Roadmap (n. 97), as well as paragraph 52 in relation to staking services.

[102] *Legislative Council of the Hong Kong Special Administrative Region of the People's Republic of China*, Stablecoins Ordinance, <https://www.elegislation.gov.hk/hk/cap656> (19 September 2025).

[103] The relevant consultation paper is available at *Financial Services and the Treasury Bureau and Securities and Futures Commission*, Public Consultation on Legislative Proposals to Regulate Dealing in Virtual Assets (June 2025), <https://apps.sfc.hk/edistributionWeb/api/consultation/openFile?lang=EN&refNo=25CP6> (19 September 2025).

Further, Hong Kong is a member of IOSCO, which has issued several virtual asset-related publications relevant to the regulation of relevant service providers, conduct matters (including custody), investor protection, risk management and cross-border co-operation,[104] and investor education.[105] These, together with existing standards and principles for financial market infrastructures,[106] can also reasonably be expected to have an impact on these further developments.

Finally, from a taxation and reporting standpoint, Hong Kong has also committed to implementing the Organisation for Economic Co-operation and Development (OECD) Crypto-Asset Reporting Framework,[107] which will also undoubtedly shape the precise approach adopted by industry participants to the control and safekeeping of virtual assets (and related technology development), because of the transparency and reporting obligations involved.

V. Concluding remarks

The next 2–5 years are likely to continue Hong Kong's trajectory of transformative standard-setting in relation to the control and safekeeping of virtual assets. The precise nature of statutory, judicial and regulatory approaches is likely to be informed by the confluence of multiple factors, including the following:

(a) Regulatory developments already earmarked, as noted in Parts III and IV.

(b) Ongoing international developments, particularly in connection with standards and recommendations by bodies of which Hong Kong is a member or in which it otherwise participates, such as FATF, IOSCO, the BIS and the OECD.

(c) Proliferation of technology developments relevant to custody.

(d) Growth of third-party accreditations, which may bolster the flexibility of safekeeping models beyond the current coalescence of regulatory viewpoints

---

[104] The *Board of the International Organization of Securities Commissions*, Policy Recommendations for Crypto and Digital Asset Markets, Final Report (16 November 2023), <https://www.iosco.org/library/pubdocs/pdf/IOSCOPD747.pdf> (19 September 2025).

[105] The *Board of the International Organization of Securities Commissions,* Investor Education on Crypto-Assets, Final Report (October 2024), <https://www.iosco.org/library/pubdocs/pdf/IOSCOPD747.pdf> (19 September 2025).

[106] See *Bank for International Settlements and International Organization of Securities Commissions*, Committee on Payment and Settlement Systems Technical Committee of the International Organization of Securities Commissions, "Principles for financial market infrastructures (April 2012), <https://www.iosco.org/library/pubdocs/pdf/IOSCOPD377-PFMI.pdf> (19 September 2025).

[107] *The Government of the Hong Kong Special Administrative Region*, Hong Kong Commits to Implementing Crypto-Asset Reporting Framework (13 December 2024), <https://www.info.gov.hk/gia/general/202412/13/P2024121300491.htm> (19 September 2025).

supporting HSM, for example, to consider other mechanisms such as multi-party computation (MPC) or otherwise.

(e) Regulators' experience of licensing and supervising the sector, which is likely to deepen the content of technology and governance-specific requirements. This occurs through ongoing regulated entity assessment (as illustrated by the SFC Thematic Review Findings) as well as vulnerability identification from large-scale incidents involving the misappropriation of client assets[108] or broader business continuity problems.

(f) Regulatory and Central Bank experimentation. In this respect, Hong Kong:
- (i) has itself launched major digital asset projects, such as Project Evergreen, involving a sovereign digital green bond with digital cash leg, and further pilots completed or underway;[109]
- (ii) been an active participant in BIS Innovation Hub and other cross-border initiatives, including Project mBridge, involving a multi-jurisdictional CBDC platform;[110] and
- (iii) supported third party pilots and projects, through initiatives such as the HKMA's "Stablecoin issuer sandbox",[111] as well through the approval of innovative tokenised instruments, such as a bank-issued tokenised gold product approved by the SFC.[112]

(g) Government and regulatory policy positions, which have recently tended toward a highly favourable attitude toward virtual asset sector development, subject to appropriate control measures to protect investors and the market. For example, the Chief Executive Officer of the SFC made the following remark in a speech in April 2024:

---

[108] For example, investigations following the recent incident involving Bybit and Safe infrastructure may well offer valuable insights, although such investigations would not occur through the SFC's direct supervisory framework over its regulated entities, as Bybit is not currently regulated by the SFC as a VATP or otherwise. For now, it features on the SFC's Alert List for "suspicious virtual asset trading platforms" on suspicion of conducting unlicensed activities. See *Securities and Futures Commission*, Alerts (14 March 2024) <https://www.sfc.hk/en/alert-list/3015> (19 September 2025) and the *SFC*, public online register of regulated entities <https://www.sfc.hk> (19 September 2025).

[109] *Hong Kong Monetary Authority*, Project Evergreen: From Concept to Application (28 November 2024), <https://www.hkma.gov.hk/eng/news-and-media/insight/2024/11/20241128/> (19 September 2025).

[110] See the HKMA's landing page for CBDCs for further details of various projects <https://www.hkma.gov.hk/eng/key-functions/international-financial-centre/fintech/central-bank-digital-currency/> (19 September 2025).

[111] *Hong Kong Monetary Authority*, HKMA Announces Stablecoin Issuer Sandbox Participants (18 July 2024), <https://www.hkma.gov.hk/eng/news-and-media/press-releases/2024/07/20240718-4/> (19 September 2025).

[112] See the relevant Principal Brochure for further details, *HSBC*, HSBC Gold Token (27 March 2024), <https://www.hsbc.com.hk/content/dam/hsbc/hk/docs/investments/gold-token/principal-brochure.pdf> (19 September 2025).

"We support the responsible use of innovative technologies such as distributed ledger technology to drive efficiency gains for the financial industry and foster a Web3 ecosystem in Hong Kong, provided that investor protection is safeguarded."[113]

The overall positive and proactive disposition of Hong Kong regulators and Government in relation to the virtual asset sector was also echoed in the Hong Kong Chief Executive's 2024 Policy Address,[114] and the SFC ASPIRE Roadmap.

(h) Ongoing market developments, particularly in relation to decentralised finance.[115]

(i) Case law development, particularly in relation to novel areas including DAOs and the resolution of more complex disputes that may test, for example, settlement finality.

Finally, any analysis of Hong Kong's approach to the control and safekeeping of virtual assets must take into account relevant adjacencies. For example, multiple custodial solutions provide additional features and benefits, such as application programming interface (API) connectivity to third party solutions, as well as staking and blockchain validation opportunities. Similarly, token smart contract standards and blockchain protocols have their own unique attributes, with particularly exciting opportunities for highly regulated entities that may fear financial crime risks often associated with permissionless networks but welcome technical features that permit higher levels of transparency, customisation and control, including intervention in third party transactions. These adjacencies are all relevant to any assessment of the legal and regulatory treatment and implications of any arrangement, and the correct approach to virtual asset control and safekeeping.

---

[113] *Securities and Futures Commission*, Unravelling Myths and Forging Ahead on New Pathway for Hong Kong as International Financial Centre, Keynote Speech at HSBC Global Investment Summit (9 April 2024), <https://www.sfc.hk/-/media/EN/files/COM/Speech/Keynote-at-HSBC-summit-20240409-Eng-FINAL.pdf?rev=4e4f2511438a4d739139c6c34d9440ee&hash=72BDECCB9CC4A33E09375BA0AFB1320D> (19 September 2025).

[114] *The Hong Kong Special Administrative Region of the People's Republic of China*, The Chief Executive's 2024 Policy Address (16 October 2024), <https://www.policyaddress.gov.hk/2024/public/pdf/policy/policy-full_en.pdf> (19 September 2025).

[115] See, for example, *Hong Kong Institute for Monetary and Financial Research*, Decentralised Finance Current Landscape and Regulatory Developments (June 2024), < https://www.aof.org.hk/docs/default-source/hkimr/applied-research-report/defirep.pdf> (19 September 2025).

Mexico

Miguel Gallardo Guerra, Javier Pérez Moreno, and Gustavo Salaiz Gabriel

I. Introduction

The classification of digital and virtual assets as property under Mexican law remains an evolving and unresolved legal issue. Under the Federal Civil Code (*Código Civil Federal*), property is generally categorized as either movable or immovable, and the legal framework does recognize the existence of intangible rights. However, it does not yet expressly regulate or define digital assets within its traditional property classifications.

The global evolution in technology has significantly influenced the evolution of payment methods. This was evident with the introduction of debit and credit cards; not too long ago, it was challenging to envision using a piece of plastic to pay for goods or services. A contemporary regulatory challenge arises in the form of virtual assets, as defined in Chapter Three of the Law to Regulate Financial Technology Institutions, commonly referred to as the Fintech Act (*Ley para Reular las Instituciones de Tecnología Financiera*):

A virtual asset is defined as *"a representation of value registered electronically and used by the public as a means of payment for various legal acts, with transfers conducted exclusively through electronic means"*. Virtual assets explicitly exclude legal tender within national territory, foreign currencies, or any asset denominated in legal tender or currency.

Virtual assets have the following characteristics:

- They are security.
- They exist electronically.
- They serve as payment methods used by individuals.
- Transactions involving them must be executed electronically.
- They explicitly exclude national currency, foreign currencies, and any asset denominated in legal tender.
- They are subject to value volatility, often influenced by market speculation and regulatory evolution.

While the 2018 Fintech Act was pioneering in including a legal definition of virtual assets, its framing is overly restrictive, limiting virtual assets to their function as a 'means of payment.' This leaves out a wide range of crypto assets now used for investment, governance, and decentralized finance. The result is regulatory ambiguity that inhibits innovation and complicates compliance efforts across the digital asset ecosystem

This „means of payment" criterion creates a significant regulatory vacuum. It provides no clear legal classification for assets that are not primarily used for payment, such as:

- Utility Tokens: which grant access to a service or platform.
- Governance Tokens: which confer voting rights in a Decentralized Autonomous Organization (DAO).
- Non-Fungible Tokens (NFTs): which represent ownership of a unique digital or physical asset.
- Staked or Lent Assets in DeFi Protocols: where the primary function is generating yield, not payment.

For these tokens, the absence of precise legal treatment results in uncertainty for practitioners and market participants. They are not explicitly „virtual assets" under the Fintech Act[1]. This uncertainty chills innovation and invites regulatory risk.

---

[1] Mexico's Fintech Act was published in the Diario Oficial de la Federación on March 9, 2018. It establishes a comprehensive legal framework for regulating financial technology institutions (FTIs). The Fintech Act regulates two main FTIs: the collective financing institutions (crowdfunding) and electronic payment fund institutions. The Fintech Act also introduced a novel regulatory mechanism – the "Novel Model" regime – which allows temporary authorization of companies developing new and innovative financial models within a controlled environment. Complemented by various regulatory circulars, including Circular

II. Key Elements of the Definition of Virtual Assets

From a legal perspective, this definition presents several components that merit detailed analysis.

1. Representation of value that is electronically registered

The law adopts a technologically neutral formulation without direct reference to blockchain or distributed ledger technologies (DLT). The term "representation of value" allows for a broad range of digital assets, without classifying them as currency, foreign exchange, or traditional financial instruments. This approach encompasses cryptocurrencies, such as Bitcoin or Ether, as well as tokens used in closed systems, depending on the context.

2. Used among the public as a means of payment

The use as a means of payment is the central criterion to exclude purely speculative assets or those with solely utilitarian functions, such as certain governance tokens or NFTs, unless they are effectively used in transactions.

3. Transferable only through electronic means

This element confirms the digital-native nature of virtual assets, excluding physical or bearer instruments. Under this criterion, cryptocurrencies transferred via smart contracts could fall within the definition.

Virtual assets represent one of the most significant revolutions experienced by the financial sector in recent years, generating considerable interest among financial institutions, users, and customers. This growing interest has led to increased market demand, alongside a rise in their value and volatility. Virtual assets have emerged as an innovative payment method that minimizes the need for third-party involvement.

Although the inclusion of a legal definition for virtual assets in the 2018 Fintech Law was, at the time, an innovative step – placing Mexico among the early adopters of crypto-related regulation in Latin America – the scope and precision of the definition have proven insufficient in light of the rapid evolution of technology and market applications. The definition is narrowly framed around virtual assets used as a means of payment, excluding a wide range of digital assets now commonly used for investment, governance, staking, and other decentralized finance (DeFi) functions. Furthermore, the law offers limited granularity regarding the classification of emerging asset types, leaving significant gaps in regulatory clarity. This narrow legal framing, while forward-looking at its

4/2019 on virtual assets, the Fintech Act represents a foundational – though still evolving – effort to balance innovation and oversight in Mexico's digital financial ecosystem.

inception, has not evolved in tandem with technological innovation, resulting in interpretive challenges for regulators, legal practitioners, and market participants alike.

Bank of Mexico (Banxico), as a member of the Interinstitutional Committee,[2] is the competent authority for authorizing the use of permitted virtual assets and entering into agreements with third parties within the scope of these activities.

III. Taxonomy of Digital Assets: Legal Implications and Classifications

By contrast, international standards – such as those of the Financial Action Task Force (FATF) – adopt a broader and more technology-neutral definition. According to the FATF's 2019 Guidance, a virtual asset is defined as a "*digital representation of value that can be digitally traded or transferred and can be used for payment or investment purposes*"[3]. Similarly, the European Union's Markets in Crypto-Assets Regulation (MiCA) defines crypto-assets as "*a digital representation of value or rights which may be transferred and stored electronically, using distributed ledger or similar technology*"[4], creating a broader legal framework that categorizes tokens into asset-referenced tokens (ARTs), e-money tokens, and other crypto-assets, depending on their function.

The Mexican approach, while pragmatic for its time, has not evolved in tandem with technological innovation and market developments. As a result, it lacks the granularity to address new classes of tokens and business models emerging from Web3 ecosystems. This legal rigidity has generated uncertainty for legal practitioners, fintech companies, and regulators alike, and has limited the country's capacity to provide legal clarity in areas such as tokenization, decentralized applications, and cross-border virtual asset services. Please refer to Table 1.

---

[2] Article 11 of the Fintech Act provides that authorization to operate as a financial technology institution (ITF) must be granted by the CNBV with the prior favorable consent of the Inter-institutional Committee, which is composed of two representatives each from the Secretaría de Hacienda y Crédito Público, Banco de México, and the CNBV, appointed by their respective heads. Resolutions to authorize an ITF require at least one affirmative vote from each authority, and a further approval by Banco de México is mandatory for institutions dealing in virtual assets or foreign currency.

[3] *Financial Action Task Force (FATF)*, „Guidance for a Risk-Based Approach to Virtual Assets and Virtual Asset Service Providers", June 2019. <https://www.fatf-gafi.org/media/fatf/documents/recommendations/RBA-VA-VASPs.pdf> (September 19, 2025).

[4] Regulation (EU) 2023/1114 on Markets in Crypto-assets (MiCA), European Parliament and Council, 31 May 2023. <https://eur-lex.europa.eu/eli/reg/2023/1114> (September 19, 2025).

Element	Mexico (Fintech Act)	FATF (Recommendation 15)	EU (MiCA)
Core definition	Digital value used as a means of payment	Digital representation of value that can be exchanged	Digital representation of value or rights
Scope	Limited to payments	Includes payment, investment, and utility	Categorized into e-money tokens, ARTs, crypto-assets
Exclusions	National currency, peso-denominated instruments	Legal tender, traditional securities	Legal tender, central bank money

Table 1 – Taxonomy of Digital Assets

The evolution of digital assets has led to increasingly complex forms of classification that challenge traditional legal categories such as currency, securities, and commodities. While early regulatory frameworks – such as Mexico's Fintech Act – focused primarily on virtual assets used as a means of payment, international best practices and the progression of technology have given rise to a more granular and function-based taxonomy. According to both technological architecture and regulatory significance, digital assets can be classified as:

1. Blockchain Native Tokens

These digital assets are considered native because they are created by and exist intrinsically within their own blockchain networks. Their foundational role typically includes incentivizing validators or miners who support and maintain the network by securing transactions and adding new blocks. These tokens are often used to pay transaction fees and to reward participants for providing computational power and maintaining consensus across the distributed ledger.

- Bitcoin and Ethereum. Bitcoin (BTC) is the original and most widely recognized cryptocurrency. It functions as a decentralized store of value and medium of exchange, governed by a fixed monetary policy embedded in its protocol. Bitcoin is neither issued nor backed by any central authority, which challenges its classification under traditional monetary or financial law. Ether (ETH) – native currency of the Ethereum network, used to pay transaction fees and execute smart contracts.
- Altcoins. This category includes most cryptocurrencies other than Bitcoin and Ether These cryptocurrencies can differ in terms of features or intended use cases. Examples include:
  - Litecoin (LTC) – a Bitcoin derivative with faster transaction processing.
  - XRP – designed for real-time gross settlement and cross-border payment facilitation.

These assets often resist categorization under existing financial legislation, though some jurisdictions consider them commodities or intangible assets for tax purposes.

2. Smart Contract-Based Digital Assets

Created on programmable blockchain platforms, these assets rely on smart contracts for issuance, governance, and functionality.

- Stablecoins. Stablecoins are digital representations of value designed to maintain price stability, typically by being pegged to fiat currencies such as the US dollar.
  - Fiat-backed Stablecoins: Backed by fiat reserves, crypto collateral, or other assets. Examples: USDC (fiat-backed), USDT (Tether), BUSD.
  - Non-Collateralized or Algorithmic Stablecoins: Employ mechanisms such as algorithmic supply adjustments. Examples: DAI (overcollateralized), AMPL, and formerly UST.

Stablecoins pose a direct challenge to the Mexican framework. If a stablecoin is 1:1 backed by fiat currency, it closely resembles the ‚Electronic Payment Funds' regulated by the Fintech Act for Electronic Payment Fund Institutions (IFPEs). However, Banxico's restrictions in Circular 4/2019 prevent IFPEs from issuing peso-backed stablecoins. This creates a conflict: the entities most suited to issue regulated stablecoins are effectively prohibited from doing so, pushing this activity to unregulated offshore entities.

- Utility and Governance Tokens.
  - Utility Tokens provide access to a digital platform or service but do not confer ownership or financial rights.
  - Governance Tokens grant holders voting rights within decentralized autonomous organizations (DAOs) or DeFi protocols.
    Examples: UNI (Uniswap), MKR (MakerDAO).

  Depending on their design, these tokens may escape traditional financial regulation, though some may fall within consumer protection, anti-money laundering (AML), or securities law frameworks.
- Security Tokens. These represent traditional financial instruments (e.g., shares, bonds) in tokenized form and are generally subject to existing securities regulation.

  While these are tokenized traditional instruments, it's crucial to mention that Mexico's Securities Market Law (*Ley del Mercado de Valores*)[5] does not yet contain a clear framework for the issuance, custody, and trading of securities on a blockchain. The existing infrastructure for registration and transfer

[5] Ley del Mercado de Valores, Diario Oficial de la Federación, 30 de diciembre de 2005. <https://www.diputados.gob.mx/LeyesBiblio/pdf/LMV.pdf> (September 19, 2025).

(e.g., with INDEVAL) is not adapted, creating a significant barrier to a domestic security token market. In jurisdictions with a functional or principles-based approach (e.g., Howey Test in the U.S. or EU MiFID), security tokens may trigger full prospectus, licensing, and disclosure obligations.
- Non-Fungible Tokens (NFTs). NFTs are cryptographic assets that represent unique items, often used in digital art, collectibles, intellectual property licensing, or even real-world asset tokenization.
  Although not fungible or generally considered financial instruments, NFTs may raise issues of copyright, consumer law, and taxation.

3. Central Bank Digital Currencies (CBDCs)

CBDCs are digital representations of sovereign currency, issued and backed by a central bank. They represent a direct liability of the issuing authority and are distinct from decentralized crypto-assets.
- Retail CBDCs: Designed for use by the general public (e.g., e-CNY, Sand Dollar).
- Wholesale CBDCs: Intended for interbank settlements and institutional use (e.g., Project Jura, Project Helvetia).
  CBDCs necessitate a bespoke regulatory framework, involving monetary law, data privacy, financial inclusion, and constitutional considerations regarding central bank mandates.

A robust legal taxonomy of digital assets is essential not only for regulatory clarity but also for ensuring proportional supervision across asset types with different risk profiles. Mexico's current legal framework, particularly the definition of "virtual assets" under the Fintech Law, does not yet reflect the full breadth of digital asset classes outlined above. As the ecosystem evolves, legislators and regulators must adopt a technology-neutral, function-based approach – as exemplified by the EU's MiCA regulation and FATF recommendations – to address gaps in investor protection, financial stability, and legal enforceability.

IV. The Bank of Mexico and its Position

Banxico is an autonomous constitutional entity responsible for issuing currency, formulating economic policies to safeguard the purchasing power of the Mexican peso, promoting the stability of the national financial system, and ensuring the effective operation of payment systems.

In this context, Banco de México (Banxico) has issued clear opinions and regulatory instruments concerning virtual assets, imposing specific limitations on their use within the financial system. According to Banxico, virtual assets pose a number of risks when considered as potential substitutes for the Mexican peso, primarily because they lack essential monetary attributes, such as a stable store of value, a reliable medium of exchange, and a standard unit of account. It is important to note that these concerns apply most directly to blockchain native tokens, such as Bitcoin and various altcoins, which were the most prominent and widely adopted forms of virtual assets at the time of the enactment of the Fintech Law in 2018. These assets operate independently of any centralized issuer and are subject to high levels of price volatility. Banxico's restrictive stance notably articulated in Circular 4/2019 – reflects a cautious approach that seeks to insulate the formal financial sector from the speculative and unregulated nature of this first category of digital assets, establishing a clear policy of regulatory ring-fencing.

The objective is to insulate the regulated financial system (banks and Fintech Institutions) from the risks of virtual assets. The core prohibitions – preventing regulated entities from offering direct public sales of crypto and from passing on price risk to customers – mean that these institutions can only use virtual assets for internal operations (e.g., facilitating cross-border payments), subject to Banxico's prior authorization. This effectively severs the link between the traditional financial world and the public crypto market in Mexico.

Consequently, in Circular 4/2019, Banxico explicitly identifies information asymmetry concerns arising from two primary factors (Circular 4/2019 addressed to Credit Institutions and Financial Technology Institutions concerning General Provisions Applicable to Credit Institutions and Financial Technology Institutions in Transactions with Virtual Assets, 2019):

The inherent complexity of the mathematical and cryptographic processes underlying virtual assets, which creates challenges for users attempting to understand these mechanisms.

The difficulty in comprehending the intricate factors influencing virtual asset pricing, including uncertainty about elements determining supply and demand, and the absence of reliable price-reference benchmarks.

Additionally, Banxico highlights significant risks related to virtual assets, particularly concerning anti-money laundering (AML) and counter-terrorism financing (CTF). These risks are exacerbated by the ease and speed of transferring virtual assets across borders, combined with a lack of unified global regulatory oversight and protection measures.

Marcos Cohen, co-founder of Naos Blockchain Capital – an investment fund focused on startups and companies operating with cryptocurrencies – believes that the Fintech Act supports existing companies and sees a potential for new ventures to emerge from current market players, likely as a response to the anticipated entry of international competitors. Since cryptocurrency businesses operate digitally and do not require a physical presence in Mexico, the legal and operational costs are significantly lower. Given that the platforms function in a standardized manner across markets, established players in Mexico are expected to consolidate, expand, and strengthen their position to face increasing competition. However, at the same time, international players will enter the market, creating their real competitive challenge. Cohen highlights this issue by stating: "The moment a company like Bitso competes against Coinbase, which has access to capital hundreds of times greater, it will become extremely difficult for Mexican companies to survive. This is a major flaw in the Fintech Act, as it may hinder the growth of local companies in the country.[6]

Therefore, Provision Three, second paragraph of Circular 4/2019 explicitly mandates that institutions authorized to engage in virtual asset transactions must ensure that risks associated with these operations are not transferred, directly or indirectly, to their customers.

Institutions intending to operate with virtual assets must: (i) Submit an authorization request to Banxico; (ii) provide a detailed description of the operational model for the virtual assets they intend to use; (iii) explain the benefits associated with operating virtual assets; (iv) describe the characteristics and protocols of the virtual asset they plan to operate, as well as the operational rules of the technological infrastructure (i. e., operational manuals for the cryptocurrency must be developed); (vi) Outline the characteristics of the virtual asset market; and (vii) Detail the measures the institution will implement to prevent its clients from facing risks associated with virtual asset operations. This includes submitting a risk assessment protocol, outlining risk control procedures, allocated resources for risk management, and recovery plans.[7]

V. Anti-Money Laundering provisions applicable to Virtual Assets in Mexico

Under Mexican law, non-financial entities providing services involving virtual assets are not required to obtain prior regulatory authorization to operate. However, they remain subject to the anti-money laundering framework applicable to "vulnerable activities" (*actividades vulnerables*) under the Federal Law for the Prevention and Identification of Operations with Illicit Proceeds (LFPIORPI).

Pursuant to Article 17, Section XVI of the LFPIORPI, the Tax Administration Service (SAT) classifies as a vulnerable activity:

„The regular and professional offering of virtual asset exchange services conducted by entities other than financial institutions through electronic platforms, which facilitate or execute purchase or sale transactions of such assets on behalf of their customers, or pro-

---

[6] *Endeavor Mexico*, Termómetro Fintech: Los retos de la regulación (2019), https://mexico.endeavor.org/fintech2019/, p.88. (September 19, 2025)

[7] *Endeavor Mexico*, Termómetro Fintech (2019), p.81. (September 19, 2025)

vide mechanisms to hold, store, or transfer virtual assets different from those recognized by the Bank of Mexico under the Fintech Act."

Since February 3, 2020, registration with the SAT as a provider of a vulnerable activity is mandatory via its Anti-Money Laundering Portal. Entities are also required, since September 9, 2019, to maintain customer identification records (KYC) for all transactions involving virtual assets.

Additionally, effective April 2, 2020, entities must submit Notices (*Avisos*) to the Financial Intelligence Unit (UIF), via the SAT platform, when a customer's aggregated transactions equal or exceed 645 UMA within a calendar month. If no such transactions occur, a zero-activity notice (*Aviso en ceros*) must be filed.

All information and documentation supporting the vulnerable activity, including customer identification files, must be securely retained for a period of five years and protected against loss, destruction, or concealment.

Entities engaging in this activity must implement and document:
- A Compliance Policy;
- Client risk classification protocols;
- Internal KYC and due diligence procedures;
- Appointment of a Compliance Officer;
- Procedures for the submission and retention of Notices; and
- Protocols to cooperate with verification visits by the SAT.

Mexico's AML regime reflects its obligations under international treaties and recommendations issued by the Financial Action Task Force (FATF). Its classification of virtual asset activities as "vulnerable" forms part of a broader framework designed to detect and deter the use of these technologies for money laundering and terrorist financing.

To comply with Article 18, Section VI of the LFPIORPI, all individuals and entities engaged in vulnerable activities – including virtual asset service providers – must:

i. Register on the SAT portal for AML compliance: SAT Anti-Money Laundering Portal
ii. Submit Notices for any client transactions exceeding the legal threshold of 645 UMAs;
iii. Maintain an up-to-date compliance manual that includes:
   - KYC procedures and documentation;
   - Identification of beneficial owners;
   - Description of clients' occupation or economic activity;
   - Retention of transaction records and submission receipts for at least five years (physically or electronically, per Article 20 of the LFPIORPI Regulations).

Entities must also retain acknowledgment receipts issued by the SAT for each Notice filed.

Additionally, in line with the Financial Action Task Force (FATF) Recommendation 16 – known as the "Travel Rule" – Mexico has taken preliminary steps to align its legal framework with international AML standards for virtual asset transactions.

Currently, the Federal Law for the Prevention and Identification of Operations with Illicit Proceeds (LFPIORPI) does not explicitly impose obligations on Virtual Asset Service Providers (VASPs) to collect and transmit originator and beneficiary data for transactions, as required under the Travel Rule. However, this gap may be addressed through a pending legislative reform.

In 2024, a bill was introduced in the Mexican Senate to amend the LFPIORPI and formally incorporate the Travel Rule. This proposal aims to:

- Require VASPs to collect, store, and transmit identifying information of both the originator and recipient of virtual asset transfers that exceed specified thresholds;
- Extend the definition of vulnerable activities to include cross-border transactions involving Mexican clients by foreign VASPs;
- Impose enhanced compliance obligations on VASPs, including automated transaction monitoring systems, internal and external audits, and comprehensive customer due diligence policies.

If enacted, this reform would enable Mexico to meet key FATF expectations ahead of its upcoming mutual evaluation in 2025 and close a critical regulatory gap in the current AML regime.

VASPs operating in Mexico should begin preparing to comply with the Travel Rule by implementing appropriate technological systems, updating internal policies, and assessing risk exposure across their platforms..

VI. Accounting Implications of Virtual Assets

In recent years, virtual assets – particularly cryptocurrencies – have gained traction as a form of payment and store of value in various economic transactions. In the Mexican regulatory context, Banxico defines virtual assets as units of electronically registered information that do not represent rights over an underlying asset, are uniquely identifiable, divisible, and governed by issuance protocols that prevent duplication and third-party interference.

Although often used interchangeably, the terms "cryptocurrency," "crypto asset," and "virtual asset" are not synonymous. A cryptocurrency is a subtype of crypto asset, primarily used as a medium of exchange and based on encrypted code. Conversely, not all crypto-assets function as currencies, especially those designed for governance, utility, or investment purposes.

1. Legal and Accounting Recognition under Mexican Standards

In Mexico, the Mexican Council for Financial Reporting Standards (CINIF) issued Financial Reporting Standard (NIF) C-22: Cryptocurrencies, effective January 2021. This standard establishes the criteria for recognizing and valuing cryptocurrencies from an accounting perspective.

According to NIF C-22, a cryptocurrency is a unique digital asset that can only be transferred electronically and is used as a means of payment or exchange of goods. It can be sold and is designed for encrypted transactions (cryptography); due to its structure not being backed or centralized, it is referred to as a cryptocurrency. Cryptocurrency may be recognized as an asset if the following four conditions are met:

- Economic Resource: The entity must have control of the cryptographic keys or systems that allow for transactional use.
- Future Economic Benefits: The cryptocurrency must have potential utility for payment or sale.
- Control by the Entity: The benefits and access to the asset must be restricted to the entity.
- Past Event: The asset must have been acquired through mining, exchange, or as consideration for goods or services.

Importantly, while cryptocurrencies are treated as assets with economic value, they do not qualify under traditional asset classifications. Specifically, they are not considered:

- Cash or cash equivalents;
- Inventories;
- Financial instruments;
- Investment properties;
- Tangible assets.

Additionally, an entity should recognize an investment in cryptocurrencies only when the following characteristics of an asset are met:

- Control over an economic resource (e.g., having the private keys and system access).
- Potential to generate future economic benefits, such as their use for transactions.
- Resulting from past events, such as mining or purchase of the cryptocurrency.

This unique treatment creates challenges of accounting and disclosure, particularly for entities that actively trade or hold crypto assets as part of their business models.

2. *Mining Costs of Cryptocurrencies*

Cryptocurrency mining involves the deployment of computational power to validate transactions and secure blockchain networks. This process entails substantial capital and operational expenditures, including:
- Personnel costs (internal teams or outsourced specialists);
- Direct costs such as electricity and cooling systems;
- Depreciation of hardware and infrastructure used in the mining process.

Under NIF C-22, entities engaged in mining must analyze whether the cost structure results in capitalizable assets or operating expenses, depending on whether the output meets the recognition criteria described above.

VII. Virtual assets under Mexican Private Law: Ownership, Transferability, and Classification

Despite regulatory efforts in Mexico through the 2018 Fintech Act, the private law classification of cryptocurrencies remains ambiguous, particularly under the Federal Civil Code in Mexico (*Código Civil Federal*)[8] for private property and civil transaction goals, such as ownership and possession, inheritance and succession, civil labilities and donations, leasing contracts, an others, and the Commercial Code (*Código de Comercio*),[9] for commercial transactions and merchant use, including topics as merchant-to-merchant payments, commercial contracts, pledge of crypt assets as collateral, electronic commerce using crypto assets and business registration, as others.

This regulatory structure in Mexico raises complex legal questions regarding ownership, control, transferability, inheritance, enforceability, liability and protection of rights related to digital assets, especially outside the scope of fintech institutions.

Under articles 752 to 763 of the Federal Civil Code in Mexico, property (*bienes*) is classified as movable or immovable (*bienes muebles o inmuebles*). Cryptocurrencies could be classified as intangible movable assets due to their lack of physical form and their capacity to be controlled and transferred. However, this is not expressly recognized in law, creating legal uncertainty, especially in civil actions involving these assets (e.g., inheritance, asset division, seizure).

---

[8] Federal Civil Code (*Código Civil Federal*), last amended 17 January 2024, <https://www.diputados.gob.mx/LeyesBiblio/pdf/CCF.pdf> (September 19, 2025).

[9] Commercial Code (*Código de Comercio*), last amended 28 March 2018, <https://www.diputados.gob.mx/LeyesBiblio/pdf_mov/Codigo_de_Comercio.pdf> (September 19, 2025).

Under articles 830 to 853 of the Federal Civil Code of Mexico, ownership in civil law is defined as the right to use, enjoy, and dispose of a thing. In the case of cryptocurrencies, ownership is defined by control over private keys. Therefore, the person holding the cryptographic key is effectively the "owner", though this control-based paradigm is not yet recognized by Mexican private law. However, this limited approach has practical implications, in case of inheritance, if the heirs do not possess the private keys, the asset may be unrecoverable and in civil liability or bankruptcy, it is unclear how cryptocurrencies should be identified, seized, or transferred by courts or trustees.

Under articles 1792 to 1811 of the Federal Civil Code of Mexico, from a private law standpoint, the transfer of cryptocurrencies is not explicitly regulated, making it difficult to determine: (i) whether a transfer constitutes a sale, a donation, or an exchange; as well as how the intention to transfer and acceptance are expressed, including how to legally document or prove a cryptocurrency transfer in court.

Finally, although the law provides compensation for damages, without express recognition of cryptocurrencies, holders may lack effective legal remedies in the case of fraud, theft, or unauthorized transfers. Difficulty in proving ownership or rightful control, particularly where pseudonymous wallets are involved. Moreover, issues like usufruct, pledges, inheritance, marital property regimes, and succession planning remain legally undefined when the assets in question are digital.

While Mexican legislation does not yet provide a comprehensive legal framework for the classification and protection of cryptocurrencies under civil and commercial law, many of the associated legal uncertainties, are currently addressed in practice through contractual mechanisms and terms and conditions. Market participants commonly rely on private agreements or platform terms of use to define the rights and obligations of users, including provisions for custody, access, and dispute resolution. These contractual frameworks serve as the primary source of legal certainty in the absence of express statutory regulation, enabling parties to establish enforceable relationships under the general principles of freedom of contract and consensual obligations recognized in Mexico. However, while this contractual approach mitigates certain risks, it does not replace the need for statutory recognition and uniform treatment of digital assets within Mexico's private law system.

VIII. Conclusions

Mexican authorities have made meaningful progress in regulating virtual assets. However, a persistently cautious stance, most evident in the restrictive interpretation of the 2018 Fintech Act and Banxico's supervisory framework, continues to limit innovation in the sector. This approach has placed Mexico closer to jurisdictions that effectively exclude cryptocurrencies from their formal financial systems, rather than those enabling responsible adoption.

Despite these constraints, the Mexican market has evolved organically. Non-financial commercial entities have stepped in to offer virtual asset services under the AML framework, driven by rising consumer demand for digital payments and investment tools. This dynamic underscore a key reality: market forces are advancing faster than the law.

However, these advances, crypto-asset regulation in Mexico still faces challenges. The lack of clarity in certain areas and the absence of a specific tax framework for cryptocurrencies generate uncertainty for companies operating in this sector. Experts highlight the need for a more comprehensive regulatory framework that provides legal certainty and fosters innovation in the industry. While virtual assets are beginning to find a place in the Mexican legal system through financial regulation, their status as property remains undefined under civil law. This ambiguity underscores the need for legislative and judicial clarification to ensure legal certainty in the rapidly evolving digital economy.

Mexico was once a regional pioneer in fintech regulation, but the original framework has become incomplete and outdated. The narrow "means of payment" definition and the blanket restrictions on financial institutions have had unintended consequences, driving users, capital, and innovation offshore.

In order to improve regulation in Mexico and align with the realities of the digital economy and international best practices, Mexican civil and commercial legislation must evolve in a coordinated manner, by explicitly recognizing cryptocurrencies as intangible movable property; clarifying legal principles surrounding ownership, possession, and transfer; establishing judicial criteria for proof of ownership and validity of transactions; enabling notarial and registry practices to accommodate digital asset transactions; including crypto-assets in estate planning, secured lending, and family law regimes, among others.

Such reforms would allow Mexican courts and notaries to protect private rights involving cryptocurrencies and foster legal certainty in civil and commercial relationships.

To realign with international best practices and restore leadership in fintech innovation, Mexico should consider:

1. A "Fintech Act 2.0" with a functional taxonomy similar to the EU's MiCA, establishing differentiated rules for payment tokens, utility tokens, and asset-referenced tokens;
2. Regulatory frameworks for peso-backed stablecoins and permissioned blockchain models;
3. Implementation of FATF's Travel Rule and interoperability standards to ensure AML compliance;

4. A shift in Banxico's approach toward controlled experimentation, enabling regulatory sandboxes for virtual asset use cases within a safeguarded environment.

Without such reform, Mexico risks falling further behind jurisdictions that are actively fostering legal certainty to attract investment, protect consumers, and enable responsible innovation in the digital asset economy.

Singapore

Christian Hofmann and Ryan Chan-Wei

I. Introduction

In this chapter, we attempt to shed light on the question of what role the concept of 'control' plays in Singapore's crypto-asset regime. We start by providing an overview of the regulation of crypto-assets in Singapore (at I) to contextualise where Singapore stands among its international peers. Broadly speaking, Singapore tries to implement a balanced approach that strives to combat money laundering risks and protect consumers, while still providing crypto-asset service providers with the space needed to innovate and experiment. This contrasts with some jurisdictions where crypto-assets are entirely banned, or others where the crypto-asset sector remains largely unregulated.

The second part of this chapter (at II) then provides an overview of how the concept of 'control' is reflected in the regulation of crypto-assets in Singapore and highlights how this notion of 'control' might be applied to real-world business models of crypto-asset service providers. The definition of 'control' is relevant because it shapes the contours of the regulatory perimeter for crypto-assets in Singapore; however, this chapter will also explain that the concept of 'control' is necessary but insufficient for gaining a full understanding of the regulatory framework governing crypto-assets in Singapore.

II. Singapore's approach to crypto-asset regulation

1. Overview

Singapore's legislation does not specifically define what 'cryptocurrencies' or 'crypto-assets' are; instead, it uses more general terms such as 'digital token' and 'digital payment token'.[1] According to the explicit legislative definition, a token does not need to use distributed ledger technology (DLT) to come within the definition of a 'digital token' or 'digital payment token'; to fall under the regulatory purview of Singapore's regime, it is sufficient that the token can be "transferred, stored, or traded electronically".[2]

As digital tokens, crypto-assets in Singapore may fall under one of three legislative frameworks, depending on their characteristics. The Securities and Futures Act (SFA) applies when a crypto-asset functions similarly to a capital markets product, like securities. This aligns with the Monetary Authority of Singapore's (MAS) technology-neutral approach to regulating crypto-assets.[3] The Payment Services Act (PS Act) applies when a crypto-asset displays the traits of a digital payment token, which is typical for most cryptocurrencies.[4] Lastly, the Commodity Trading Act (CTA) may apply when a crypto-asset is backed by commodities.[5] The majority of crypto-assets in Singapore will be regulated under either the PS Act or the SFA. MAS is responsible for monitoring and enforcing compliance with the PS Act and SFA, while compliance with the CTA is overseen by Enterprise Singapore, a statutory board under the Ministry of Trade and Industry.

The PS Act is the primary regulatory framework for crypto-assets in Singapore, as most cryptocurrencies meet the definition of a "digital payment token". According to the PS Act, a "digital payment token" is defined as any digital representation of value that: (a) is expressed as a unit; (b) is not denominated in any currency and is not pegged to any currency by its issuer; (c) is or is intended to be a medium of exchange accepted by the public, or a segment of the public,

---

[1] s2 Payment Services Act 2019 (PS Act), Cap. 222, 2020 Rev Ed, at "digital payment token"; s. 136 Financial Services and Markets Act 2022, Cap. 1101, 2023 Rev Ed, at "digital token".

[2] PS Act s2 at 'digital payment token' at (d); Financial Services and Markets Act s136 at 'digital token' at (b).

[3] *MAS*, Reply to Parliamentary Question on Crypto Asset Market, Question No. 869, Notice Paper No. 348 of 2021 (5 April 2021), <https://www.mas.gov.sg/news/parliamentary-replies/2021/reply-to-parliamentary-question-on-crypto-asset-market> (19 September 2025), p. 6.

[4] PS Act s2 at 'digital payment token'.

[5] Legal definition of a commodity within the meaning of the CTA, see s2 Commodity Trading Act, Cap. 48A, 2009 Rev Ed; See in more detail in regard to the qualification of asset-backed cryptocurrencies: *Jonas Koh*, Crypto Conundrum Part I: Navigating Singapore's Regulatory Regime, 3 SAL Prac. 17–29, 18 (2020).

for goods, services, or debt payment; and (d) can be transferred, stored, or traded electronically.[6]

Courts and government authorities in Singapore have taken positions which suggest that cryptocurrencies are included within the statutory definition of digital payment tokens. For instance, the Inland Revenue Authority of Singapore (IRAS) has indicated that although payment tokens are not equivalent to fiat currency or legal tender,[7] in practice they are accepted as a form of payment in Singapore.[8] The High Court has stated that "(w)hile the word 'currency' connotes a medium of exchange, a cryptocurrency is not associated with any physical object (unlike how a currency such as the US Dollar is)",[9] but still categorised digital tokens such as Bitcoin and Ethereum as virtual currencies;[10] in a similar vein, the Court of Appeal has characterised the usage of cryptocurrencies as 'computer-generated, high-frequency transactions in digital quasi-currencies'.[11] Lastly, MAS has explicitly clarified in the Frequently Asked Questions (FAQs) on the PS Act that digital payment tokens correspond to "what we commonly call cryptocurrencies".[12]

The PS Act may play an indispensable role as the primary regulatory framework governing crypto-assets in Singapore, but it is key to remember that its scope also encompasses the broader payments sector. The PS Act also regulates a variety of other payment services, including cross-border money transfers and merchant acquisition, primarily from a licensing perspective and without addressing private law aspects, such as liability issues arising from the various contractual relationships involved in the initiation and execution of payment services. When the PS Act came into effect in early 2020, it replaced previous legislation governing payment services,[13] expanding the range of regulated services to keep up with technological advancements, including the introduction of the new category of "digital payment token services". Among the principal concerns that the Payment Services Act addresses are risks involving consumer protection, technological vulnerabilities, and compliance with anti-money

---

[6] PS Act s2 at 'digital payment token'.

[7] Which is in line with the interpretation in the Currency Act s13(1) and the PS Act s2(1).

[8] *IRAS*, Income Tax Treatment of Digital Tokens (2020), <https://www.iras.gov.sg/media/docs/default-source/e-tax/etaxguide_cit_income-tax-treatment-of-digital-tokens_091020.pdf> (19 September 2025), no. 5.1.

[9] *CLM v CLN and others* [2022] SGHC 46, at 10.

[10] Ibid.; see also *B2C2 Ltd v Quoine Pte Ltd* [2019] SGHC(I) 03-1.

[11] *Quoine Pte Ltd v B2C2 Ltd* [2020] SGCA(I) 02-1.

[12] *MAS*, FAQs on Payment Services Act 2019 (19 April 2024), <https://www.mas.gov.sg/-/media/mas-media-library/regulation/faqs/pd/faqs-on-payment-services-act-2019/payment-services-act-faq--19-april-2024.pdf> (19 September 2025), no. 12.1.

[13] The PS Act consolidates pre-existing legislation for payment services in a new Act with a wider regulatory scope. This pre-existing legislation is the Payment Systems (Oversight) Act, Cap 222A, 2007 Rev Ed, and the Money-changing and Remittance Businesses Act, Cap 187, 2008 Rev Ed.

laundering and countering the financing of terrorism (AML/CFT) requirements.[14]

At the heart of the PS Act lies a licensing framework for payment service providers that requires them to secure approval from MAS before commencing operations. This enables MAS to impose specific standards upon payment service providers and wield effective supervisory control.[15] Typically, payment service providers receive either a Standard Payment Institution (SPI) or a Major Payment Institution (MPI) licence, with transaction volume serving as the principal differentiating factor between the two.[16] Specifically, an MPI licence becomes necessary when the average monthly aggregate payment transaction amount surpasses SGD 3 million for a single payment service or SGD 6 million for multiple services.[17] Additionally, payment service providers must obtain an MPI licence if they provide e-money accounts[18] where substantial balances are maintained[19] or if they issue significant amounts of e-money.[20]

A notable aspect of the PS Act is that it does not explicitly regulate the issuance of digital payment tokens; rather, it targets the underlying services and activities involved in facilitating the transfer of these tokens, particularly those that function as "gateways to the regulated financial system and nodes through which value may be moved".[21] Furthermore, the PS Act stands out because it regulates crypto-assets only when these tokens are designed or suited for use as a method of payment – there may exist a regulatory lacuna concerning the issuance of digital payment tokens, and the PS Act's implicit treatment of digital payment token transfers as being equivalent to conventional payments using fiat currency may raise further questions due to the fundamental differences between both types of transactions.

---

14 *MAS*, Explanatory Brief on the Payment Services Bill (19 November 2018), <https://www.mas.gov.sg/news/speeches/2018/explanatory-brief-on-the-payment-services-bill> (19 September 2025).

15 Unless one of the narrow exemptions apply, see PS Act s5(1)(a), (b).

16 PS Act s6(4)(a)(vi). The PS Act also covers a third licence, the money changer licence which covers an entirely different area of financial services and is of no relevance for payment transactions. See for all three licences PS Act s6(2)(a)-(c).

17 PS Act s 6(5)(a)(ii)(A) and (B). See also *Paul Yuen*, Payment Systems, in: Financial Services Law & Regulation, ed. by Dora Neo/Hans Tjio/Luh Luh Lan (2019).

18 A service provider engages in an 'e-money account issuance service' when 'each payment account issued stores e-money', PS Act s 6(17).

19 For the detailed list of criteria see PS Act s6(5)(b)(i) and (ii) (A) or (B).

20 PS Act s6(5)(c)(i) and (ii).

21 Based on Singapore's explicit policy decision, see *Ravi Menon*, Singapore FinTech: Innovation, Inclusion, Inspiration (12 November 2018), <https://www.mas.gov.sg/news/speeches/2018/singapore-fintech> (19 September 2025); *MAS*, Consultation Paper on Proposed Payment Services Bill (21 August 2017), <https://www.mas.gov.sg/publications/consultations/2017/consultation-paper-on-proposed-payment-services-bill> (19 September 2025), no. 3.19.

2. *Consumer protection measures*

MAS takes an adaptive approach to crypto-asset regulation, and this is well reflected in the evolution of Singapore's crypto-asset policies since the enactment of the PS Act, which includes the development of consumer protection measures. One of the first measures that MAS introduced was to prohibit digital payment token service providers from promoting their services (e.g. through advertisements) to the public in Singapore. Nevertheless, these providers retained the ability to engage in promotional activities through their own official channels, including corporate websites, mobile applications, and social media accounts, provided they refrained from minimising or downplaying the risks inherent in trading digital payment tokens.[22] Practically speaking, this limitation meant that digital payment token service providers were effectively restricted to promoting themselves primarily to potential customers who were already aware of their services.

While this was a good start, the turmoil in the crypto-asset sector – particularly during the 'crypto winter' of 2022, exemplified by incidents such as the collapse of FTX – highlighted the need for stronger protections against misconduct and consumer harm. It was therefore opportune that MAS had acted decisively in October 2022 by proposing to implement substantially stricter rules regarding business conduct and consumer access.[23] Following a public consultation, MAS published its finalised policy positions through response papers released in July 2023 and November 2023.[24] The measures, detailed further below, began to take effect incrementally from October 2024, with MAS issuing a first set of guidelines in April 2024 to clarify expectations around implementation.[25]

---

22 *MAS*, Guidelines on Provision of Digital Payment Token Services to the Public (17 January 2022), <https://www.mas.gov.sg/regulation/guidelines/ps-g02-guidelines-on-provision-of-digital-payment-token-services-to-the-public> (19 September 2025), p. 2.

23 *MAS*, Consultation Paper P008–2022, Consultation Paper on Proposed Regulatory Measures for Digital Payment Token Services (26 October 2022), <https://www.mas.gov.sg/publications/consultations/2022/consultation-paper-on-proposed-regulatory-measures-for-digital-payment-token-services> (19 September 2025).

24 *MAS*, Response to Public Consultation on Proposed Regulatory Measures for Digital Payment Token Services (Part 1) (3 June 2023), <https://www.mas.gov.sg/-/media/mas/news-and-publications/consultation-papers/2022-proposed-regulatory-measures-for-dpt-services/response-to-public-consultation-on-proposed-regulatory-measures-for-dpt-services-part-1.pdf> (19 September 2025); *MAS*, Response to Public Consultation on Proposed Regulatory Measures for Digital Payment Token Services (Part 2) (23 November 2023), <https://www.mas.gov.sg/-/media/mas/news-and-publications/consultation-papers/2022-proposed-regulatory-measures-for-dpt-services/response-to-public-consultation-on-proposed-regulatory-measures-for-dpt-services-part-2.pdf> (19 September 2025).

25 *MAS*, MAS Expands Scope of Regulated Payment Services; Introduces User Protection Requirements for Digital Payment Token Service Providers (02 April 2024), <https://www.mas.gov.sg/news/media-releases/2024/mas-expands-scope-of-regulated-payment-services> (19 September 2025); *MAS*, Guidelines on Consumer Protection Measures by DPT Service

The business conduct measures, which were designed to ensure that digital payment token service providers treat customers "fairly and properly",[26] introduce stringent requirements relating to segregation and custody.[27] Service providers must clearly separate customer assets from their own assets and hold these assets on trust for the benefit of their customers.[28] The goal is to ensure that customers' funds are safeguarded and can be recovered should the digital payment token service provider become insolvent.[29]

Digital payment token service providers must also keep proper records, carry out daily reconciliation of customers' assets,[30] and establish rigorous risk management controls, such as placing at least 90 % of customers' digital payment tokens in cold wallets.[31]

Additionally, digital payment token service providers must establish custody functions that are operationally independent, to minimise risks arising from internal fraud which could lead to the loss of customer assets.[32] Providers are further prohibited from facilitating lending or staking activities involving retail customers' digital tokens,[33] in recognition of the elevated risks associated with such practices.[34]

Providers (2 April 2024), <https://www.mas.gov.sg/regulation/guidelines/ps-g03-guidelines-on-consumer-protection-measures-by-dpt-service-providers> (19 September 2025).

[26] *MAS*, Consultation Paper P008–2022 (n. 23) no. 4.1.

[27] Ibid., nos. 4.5–4.14.

[28] *MAS*, Response to Public Consultation on Proposed Regulatory Measures for Digital Payment Token Services (Part 1) (n. 24) nos. 2.1–2.6.

[29] Ibid.

[30] Ibid., nos. 2.12–2.14.

[31] Ibid., nos. 2.22–2.28.

[32] Ibid., nos. 2.33–2.37. This change is likely prompted by a case decided by the Singapore Court of Appeal *ByBit Fintech Ltd v Ho Kai Xin and others* [2023] SGHC 199 in which an employee of digital token services provider ByBit embezzled Tether tokens (USDT).

[33] Staking refers to a consensus mechanism that serves as an alternative to the traditional 'proof-of-work' mining system. Under a 'proof-of-stake' model, participants (also known as 'validators') in a network lock up (or 'stake') their cryptocurrency holdings as collateral in a network's protocol to help secure and validate transactions on the blockchain network. This process is broadly analogous to putting up funds to serve as a security deposit, and validators are typically selected to create new blocks and verify transactions in proportion to the amount of cryptocurrency they have staked, though the selection process can vary depending on the specific 'proof-of-stake' protocol. Validators who stake their assets generally receive rewards in the form of additional cryptocurrency tokens, which serves to incentivise network participation and compensate validators for their role in maintaining network security. However, staking also carries inherent risks, such as 'slashing' penalties where staked assets could be partially or completely forfeited due to violations of network rules and liquidity risk arising from staked assets potentially being subject to 'unbonding' periods which prevent them from being withdrawn (or transferred) for a designated timeframe. The latter may be a particular cause for concern given the volatility of cryptocurrency markets.

[34] *MAS*, Response to Public Consultation on Proposed Regulatory Measures for Digital Payment Token Services (Part 1) (n. 24), nos. 3.8–3.15.

Service providers are also required to implement robust procedures for addressing customer complaints effectively[35] and managing conflicts of interest.[36] On the latter, the MAS proposals closely reflect the recommendations presented in the Final Report on Policy Recommendations for Crypto and Digital Asset Markets published by the International Organisation of Securities Commissions (IOSCO).[37] For instance, in alignment with IOSCO's recommendations, if a service provider engages in multiple roles that could potentially create conflicts of interest, it must rigorously segregate these functions and provide adequate disclosures to its customers.[38]

Measures introduced to protect retail customers aim predominantly at increasing understanding about the risks of trading in crypto-assets and discouraging them from engaging in reckless speculation.[39] These include an obligation for digital payment token service providers to carefully assess whether prospective customers are fully cognisant of the relevant risks before onboarding them.[40]

Digital payment token service providers are also barred from offering financial incentives (e.g. referral rewards) to retail customers, to avoid influencing their decision-making regarding whether to trade in crypto-assets.[41] MAS additionally prohibits digital payment token service providers from receiving payments for digital payment token services that may be funded by debt and from providing margin trading services to retail customers.[42]

III. How should 'control' be understood from a regulatory perspective?

1. *Expansion of the scope of regulated digital payment token services*

Before delving into a detailed discussion of how 'control' is defined from a regulatory perspective, it is crucial to appreciate the context that the regulatory ambit of the PS Act has expanded due to developments in the payments space, such as heightened AML/CFT risks. The PS (Amendment) Act, which took

[35] *MAS*, Response to Public Consultation on Proposed Regulatory Measures for Digital Payment Token Services (Part 2) (n. 24) nos. 3.27–3.28.

[36] Ibid., nos. 3.7–3.14.

[37] *IOSCO*, Policy Recommendations for Crypto and Digital Asset Markets: Final Report (16 November 2023), <https://www.iosco.org/library/pubdocs/pdf/IOSCOPD747.pdf> (19 September 2025).

[38] *MAS*, Response to Public Consultation on Proposed Regulatory Measures for Digital Payment Token Services (Part 2) (n. 24) no. 3.10.

[39] Ibid., nos. 2.16–2.20 and nos. 2.23–2.25.

[40] Ibid., nos. 2.16–2.20.

[41] Ibid., nos. 2.23–2.25.

[42] Ibid., nos. 2.29–2.31.

effect on 4 April 2024,[43] broadened the definition of a regulated digital payment token service, and this expansion of MAS' regulatory perimeter appears to be consistent with the Financial Action Task Force's (FATF) guidance on AML/CFT risks in the crypto-asset sector.[44]

Before the amendments came into force, providing a digital payment token service comprised the activities of "dealing in digital payment tokens" and "facilitating the exchange of digital payment tokens",[45] both of which implicitly involved a service provider coming into possession of the relevant digital payment tokens. This has not changed, as further explained below. 'Possession' is still a concept that is relied on by the PS Act and, by extension, the regulatory framework applicable to digital payment tokens in Singapore.[46]

However, 'possession' may not be the most appropriate criterion, because digital tokens are intangible by nature[47] and therefore cannot be possessed, in the sense of requiring actual physical control over a corporeal item.[48] MAS has recognised the shortcomings of 'possession', and this is manifested in the expanded regulatory scope of the PS (Amendment) Act, with the provision of digital payment token services now also encompassing "service providers of [digital payment tokens (DPTs)] that facilitate the use of DPTs for payments, and may not possess the moneys or DPTs involved".[49]

As a result of this expansion, the statutory definition of a digital payment token service now incorporates seven additional services aimed at addressing the heightened AML/CFT risks posed by crypto-assets.[50] This brings the total number of digital payment token services defined under "digital payment token service" in Part 3 of the First Schedule to the PS Act to nine.

---

43 *MAS*, MAS Expands Scope of Regulated Payment Services; Introduces User Protection Requirements for Digital Payment Token Service Providers (n. 25).

44 *FATF*, Updated Guidance for a Risk-Based Approach to Virtual Assets and Virtual Asset Service Providers (28 October 2021), <https://www.fatf-gafi.org/en/publications/Fatfrecommendations/Guidance-rba-virtual-assets-2021.html> (19 September 2025).

45 PS Act, Part 3 of First Schedule.

46 PS Act, Part 3 of First Schedule, definitions of "dealing in" and "facilitating the exchange of" digital payment tokens; *Ong Ye Kung*, Payment Services (Amendment) Bill (4 April 2021), <https://www.mas.gov.sg/news/speeches/2021/payment-services-amendment-bill> (19 September 2025), p. 7.

47 *UK Jurisdiction Taskforce*, Legal Statement on the Status of Cryptoassets and Smart Contracts (November 2019), <https://lawtechuk.io/static/UKJT-Legal-Statement-Cryptoassets-Smart-Contracts-6dd9725753118e61e20330355c2b35c9.pdf> (19 September 2025), at no. 31.

48 Ibid., no. 67; analysing the property aspect of crypto-assets in common law in detail: *Kelvin F.K. Low*, Trusts of Cryptoassets, in: Trusts and Private Wealth Management: Developments and Directions, ed. by Richard C. Nolan/Man Yip/Tang Hang Wu (2021) 153–177.

49 *Ong*, Payment Services (Amendment) Bill (n. 46).

50 PS (Amendment) Act s7; *MAS*, Explanatory Brief for Payment Services (Amendment) Bill (2 November 2020), <https://www.mas.gov.sg/news/speeches/2020/explanatory-brief-for-payment-services-amendment-bill> (19 September 2025), at no. 3.

Four of these nine services pertain to custody activities and are premised on the concept of 'control' rather than 'possession'.[51] For example, one service is defined as "safeguarding a digital payment token, where the service provider has control over the digital payment token" while another is described as "any service of carrying out for a customer an instruction relating to a digital payment token, where the service provider has control over the digital payment token".[52]

The upshot of these recent legislative amendments is that a key determinant of whether a service provider comes within the scope of the PS Act now appears to be whether it exercises some form of 'control' (as opposed to having 'possession') over the digital tokens in question. We welcome this development and suggest that the term 'control' may be more legally precise, as it does not rely on the notion of physical control over a tangible item.[53]

However, the concept of 'possession' is still a feature of the regulatory landscape, and further details about how to interpret it in a regulatory context will be provided in a subsequent section.

Additionally, two of the newly introduced digital payment token services adopt a significantly more expansive approach: they do not require any 'control' or 'possession' to be made out and consider it sufficient that a service provider merely performs a facilitative role in a digital payment token transaction. These are the so-called 'arrangement' and 'inducement' services. The 'arrangement' service is defined as "arranging (whether as principal or agent) for the transmission of digital payment tokens from one digital payment token account (whether in Singapore or elsewhere) to another digital payment token account (whether in Singapore or elsewhere)". An 'inducement' service is understood as "inducing or attempting to induce any person to enter into or to offer to enter into any agreement for or with a view to buying or selling any digital payment token in exchange for any money or any other digital payment token (whether of the same or a different type)".[54]

Only one of these services appears to necessitate the presence of 'possession', and that is the 'acceptance' service, which is understood as the process of "accepting (whether as principal or agent) digital payment tokens from one digital payment token account (whether in Singapore or elsewhere), for the purposes of transmitting, or arranging for the transmission of, the digital payment tokens to another digital payment token account (whether in Singapore or elsewhere)".[55] Interpretive guidance provided in the FAQs on the PS Act state specifically that

---

[51] PS Act, Part 3 of First Schedule, definition of "digital payment token service", at (f)–(i).

[52] Ibid, at (f) and (g).

[53] *UK Jurisdictional Taskforce*, Legal Statement on Crypto-assets and Smart Contracts (n. 47) no. 67.

[54] PS Act, Part 3 of First Schedule, definition of "digital payment token service", (d)–(e).

[55] Ibid., at (c).

this service involves "coming into possession" of digital payment tokens.[56] Although it was previously established that relying solely on the notion of 'possession' may be problematic when attempting to establish whether a service provider is engaging in a regulated activity, these references to 'possession' in legislation and MAS guidance make it essential to evaluate this criterion in the broader context of the expanded list of digital payment token services. Notably, references to 'possession' appear in only three of the nine enumerated activities, with the remaining six relying on either 'control' or forms of facilitation such as 'inducement' or 'arrangement'. Furthermore, these activities are not mutually exclusive; a service provider may be simultaneously caught under multiple categories – for instance, by offering custodial services (which require only 'control') while also facilitating transfers of digital payment tokens between accounts (which may require 'possession'). Given the breadth of the regulatory perimeter, it is plausible that the scope of regulated digital payment token activities is currently wide enough to mitigate any shortcomings arising from reliance on 'possession' as the principal determinant of whether an activity should trigger a licensing requirement.

2. Understanding the concept of "control"

To explain how 'control' should be understood from a regulatory perspective, it is instructive to begin by examining MAS' policy intent as communicated in its response to a public consultation on the proposed amendments to the PS Act. As mentioned above, those proposals included provisions broadening the scope of a regulated digital payment token service and culminated in the enactment of the PS (Amendment) Act. As four of the newly introduced digital payment token services contained references to the concept of 'control',[57] the draft amendments sought to clarify the meaning of 'control' by stating that "a person has control over a digital payment token whether the person has control over the digital payment token solely or jointly with one or more other persons".[58] However, beyond acknowledging the possibility that 'control' may or may not be exercised by one person alone, the proposed amendments did not offer a concrete definition of 'control'. It was therefore unsurprising that some respondents to MAS' consultation paper requested for "clarity on how 'control' of a DPT would be determined".[59]

---

[56] *MAS*, FAQs on Payment Services Act 2019 (19 April 2024), <https://www.mas.gov.sg/regulation/faqs/faqs-on-payment-services-act-2019> (19 September 2025), no. 24.1.

[57] PS (Amendment) Act s7(e).

[58] Ibid., s7(h).

[59] *MAS*, Response to Feedback Received on Proposed Amendments to the Payment Services Act 2019 (4 November 2020), <https://www.mas.gov.sg/publications/consultations/2020/response-to-feedback-received-on-proposed-amendments-to-the-payment-services-act-2019> (19 September 2025), no. 2.16.

In its response to the consultation feedback, MAS clarified that a digital payment token service provider would be deemed to have 'control' of a digital payment token "if it has the ability to control access to any digital payment token or to execute transactions involving the DPT".[60] Such 'control' did not have to be "absolute or exclusive". It also extended to any authority that a digital payment token service provider might possess over a "digital payment token instrument" associated with a digital payment token, such as a private key, because such instruments enable a service provider to "control access" and "execute transactions".[61]

This interpretation was subsequently reaffirmed in the FAQs on the PS Act. There, MAS stated that 'control' would necessitate a service provider having the capability to manage "access to", or "execute transactions" involving digital payment tokens stored in its custodial wallets.[62] Consistent with the position set out in the earlier consultation response concerning proposed amendments to the PS Act,[63] the FAQs also confirmed that such 'control' did not need to be "absolute or exclusive" and that the span of 'control' would encompass digital payment token instruments such as private keys.[64]

3. *Necessary but insufficient*

Before delving deeper into the concept of 'control', it is important to reiterate that only four of the nine digital payment token services, all of which pertain to custody services, rely on the notion of 'control' to determine whether a service provider is caught under the PS Act.[65] Three of the nine digital payment token services still turn on the unsatisfactory criterion of 'possession',[66] but as described above, the scope of the regulatory perimeter for digital payment token services is now so broad that service providers are more likely to be caught by one (or more) of the other six digital payment token services that do not rely on the idea of 'possession'. As mentioned earlier, the remaining two digital payment token services that do not turn on 'control' or 'possession' instead only necessitate the presence of some form of facilitation (i.e. 'inducement' or 'arrangement').[67]

---

60 Ibid., no. 2.19.

61 Ibid.; section 7(d) of the PS (Amendment) Act defines a 'digital payment token instrument' as comprising an instrument, such as a private key, that would allow a person to "control access to one or more digital payment tokens" or "execute a transaction involving one or more digital payment tokens".

62 *MAS*, Frequently Asked Questions on the Payment Services Act (n. 56) no 26.1.

63 *MAS*, Response to Feedback Received on Proposed Amendments to the Payment Services Act 2019 (n. 59) no. 2.19.

64 Ibid.

65 PS Act, Part 3 of First Schedule, definition of "digital payment token service", (f)–(i).

66 Ibid., (a)–(c).

67 Ibid., (d)–(e).

It is therefore necessary for understanding Singapore's crypto-asset regulatory regime to unpack the meaning of 'control', seeing as nearly half of the digital payment token services require some form of 'control'; but it is also insufficient for understanding the full slate of digital payment token services, as the concepts of 'inducement' and 'arrangement' are just as important. Relying on the concept of 'control' works best in the context of digital token service providers offering custody services, because that activity by its very nature often requires a service provider to exercise authority over digital payment tokens or digital payment token instruments. However, as custody services are only a subset of the broader slate of potential activities that digital payment token service providers could engage in, 'control' may not be an appropriate indicium in all contexts. It is instructive to consider the clarification provided by MAS in the FAQs on the PS Act regarding the interpretation of the terms 'inducement' and 'arrangement'.[68]

With respect to 'inducement', the FAQs explain that a service provider would be regarded as engaging in this activity if it induces "[…] any person to enter into […] any agreement for or with a view to buying or selling any digital payment token in exchange for any money or any other digital payment token […]". This would even be the case where the service provider merely served as a "conduit through which a customer may enter into an agreement to buy or sell [digital payment tokens] in exchange for money or any other [digital payment tokens]".[69]

To demonstrate how this interpretation might apply practically, the FAQs include a case study involving a service provider (Company X) that offers an option on its mobile application for customers to use digital payment tokens to add value to their e-wallets.

According to the example, 'inducement' would be made out even if the actual process of converting the digital payment tokens into fiat currency is carried out by a separate service provider (Company Y), and even if Company X never comes into 'possession' of any digital payment tokens throughout the entire transaction.[70]

In line with our general scepticism regarding the suitability of the term 'possession' in the digital context, we suggest that the term 'control' would better capture the legal and functional reality of such cases. In this example, Company X at no point had access to the digital payment tokens in a manner that would have enabled it to execute transactions that would affect any rights or interests, whether legal or economic, attached to the tokens.

---

68 *MAS*, Frequently Asked Questions on the Payment Services Act (n. 56) no. 2.

69 Ibid., no. 25.2.

70 Ibid., no. 25. 3 (Case Study 2).

With regard to 'arrangement', the FAQs state that the intent is to capture digital payment token service providers that arrange for transfers of digital payment tokens from one account/address to another as a service, even if the service provider "does not come into possession of the digital payment tokens".[71] The FAQs illustrate this using a multi-faceted case study which demonstrates that an 'arrangement' would be deemed to occur if a service provider establishes a digital platform that facilitates the transfer of digital payment tokens from its customers to third parties for the purposes of a loan.[72] In the case study, the service provider in question does in fact come into possession of digital payment tokens (and therefore also comes within the regulatory scope of one or more of the other regulated digital payment token services), but the FAQs make it clear that 'possession' is not a required condition for the 'arrangement' option to apply.

This example is problematic insofar as it does not explain what kind of scenario would constitute 'arrangement' without any simultaneous 'possession' in the sense understood by MAS. One may speculate that MAS would regard even any type of facilitator that enables transfers executed on platforms operated by other providers, and involving wallets provided by other licensed digital payment service providers, as falling within the meaning of 'arrangement'. In such a scenario, the facilitator would not 'possess' the digital tokens but would still be caught by the licensing requirement due to its role in facilitating the transaction flow.

Considering how loosely 'inducement' and 'arrangement' are defined and exemplified by MAS (with digital payment token service providers only required to play a facilitative role), it might appear plausible that a significant proportion of facilitators of services would be caught for licensing on the basis of providing either the 'inducement' service or the 'arrangement' service, even if they played only a thoroughly peripheral role in the overall transaction. However, as the following section will demonstrate, that is unlikely to be the case.

4. Applying the concept of 'control'

A close examination of the statutory provisions pertaining to 'control' and related interpretive guidance from MAS suggests that there are three key considerations at play when applying the concept of 'control' to determine whether an activity falls within the regulatory ambit of the PS Act. First, 'control' is assessed against an entity's ability to "control access to any digital payment token or to execute transactions involving the digital payment token".[73] Second, that ability is often derived by holding a "digital payment token instrument", in

[71] Ibid., no. 24.2.

[72] Ibid., no. 24.3 (Case Study 1).

[73] *MAS*, Response to Feedback Received on Proposed Amendments to the Payment Ser-

particular a private key or share thereof.[74] Third, 'control' does not need to be "absolute or exclusive" and can be exercised "solely or jointly with one or more other persons".[75] Viewed collectively, the upshot appears to be that any entity that holds a private key (or a share of a private key) in the context of a custody service will be deemed to have 'control' for the purposes of the PS Act, as that would confer the ability to "control access" to a digital payment token and "execute transactions" involving that digital payment token.

This is an expansive definition of 'control', and it is broader than how 'control' has been described in case law thus far. Singapore courts have yet to pronounce definitively on how 'control' should be understood, but recent cases from the High Court and Court of Appeal indicate that courts are cognisant that private keys "provide control over … cryptocurrency"[76] and take the position that the property right relating to cryptocurrency is that of "exclusive control to the holder in the form of universal exigibility".[77] In particular, *Janesh s/o Rajkumar v Unknown Person ("CHEFPIERRE")*, which was decided by the High Court in 2022, demonstrated that the court viewed 'control' as the exclusive ability to transfer tokens between different digital asset wallets, and subsequently utilised that as the central criterion upon which it based further analysis of whether rights in digital assets could exist and whether a specific individual held such rights.[78]

Notwithstanding the narrower approach that has been borne out in the limited Singaporean jurisprudence concerning crypto-assets, the more flexible definition adopted by the MAS is in fact closely aligned with international guidance from standard-setting bodies. For example, in the FATF's guidance on AML/CFT risks in the crypto-asset sector, it stated that 'control' in the context of custody services should be understood as the ability to change the "disposition" of a digital asset and that such 'control' did not necessarily have to be "unilateral".[79] The rationale behind this appears to be to ensure that custody models involving multiple private keys (e.g. multi-signature wallets[80]) or differ-

vices Act 2019 (n. 59) no. 2.19; *MAS*, Frequently Asked Questions on the Payment Services Act (n. 56) no. 26.1.

[74] Ibid.; PS (Amendment) Act s7(d).

[75] Ibid.; PS (Amendment) Act s7(h).

[76] *ByBit Fintech Ltd v Ho Kai Xin and others* [2023] SGHC 199, 8.

[77] *Quoine Pte Ltd v B2C2 Ltd* [2020] SGCA(I) 02, 142.

[78] *Janesh s/o Rajkumar v Unknown Person ("CHEFPIERRE")* [2022] SGHC 264, 58 and 71.

[79] *FATF*, Updated Guidance for a Risk-Based Approach to Virtual Assets and Virtual Asset Service Providers (28 October 2021), <https://www.fatf-gafi.org/en/publications/Fatfrecommendations/Guidance-rba-virtual-assets-2021.html> (19 September 2025), p. 29.

[80] Multi-signature wallets implement distributed control over digital payment tokens by requiring multiple parties to approve transactions. They operate by establishing a predetermined threshold of required approvals in the form of an "*m*-of-*n*" framework, in which '*m*' signatures from a total of '*n*' authorised parties must be provided to execute any transaction.

ent shares of a private key (e.g. multi-party computation[81]) to authorise transactions are also brought within the regulatory perimeter, even though under such models no single entity wields exclusive control. This has been acknowledged by MAS in both the FAQs to the PS Act and its response to feedback received on the consultation concerning proposed amendments to the PS Act, with the latter stating specifically that "a service provider will be caught within scope as long as it has control over one of the private keys of a multi-signature wallet".[82]

To illustrate how this understanding of 'control' should be applied, it is helpful to consider the case studies provided by MAS in the FAQs to the PS Act. According to MAS, if a service provider that provides custodial wallets holds one of two private keys needed to authorise transactions concerning the digital payment tokens custodied in its wallets (the other key being held by its customer), that would suffice to constitute 'control' for the purposes of the PS Act.[83] This interpretation of 'control' is centred on the notion of authority over the private keys – for example, customers would be deemed to have 'control' over their private keys even if they were stored with the service provider as part of the custodial arrangement, as long as the service provider is contractually bound to only utilise those private keys in accordance with customers' instructions.[84] Additionally, an important nuance is that it is not necessary for the holder of a private key or key share to be an indispensable party to the execution of a transaction for 'control' to be made out. Even if a person holds only one of several keys or key shares in a multi-signature wallet or multi-party computation arrangement, and transactions could technically proceed without their active involvement (e.g. because only three out of five key shares are needed), they would

---

For instance, in a "2-of-3" arrangement, any two participants from a group of three must approve each transaction. The underlying technology relies on cryptographic protocols where each authorised participant maintains their own private key and, prior to transaction execution, the wallet validates that the required number of legitimate signatures has been provided in accordance with the stipulated threshold.

[81] Multi-party computation systems also enable distributed control, by employing advanced cryptographic protocols to distribute shares of a single private key among multiple parties in a way that allows for the collective management of that private key despite no single party ever having access to the complete private key. Unlike multi-signature wallets where each party maintains their own discrete private key, multi-party computation systems allow parties to execute transactions using distributed shares of a single private key without needing to reconstruct the complete private key at any point. However, transactions that have been collectively authorised via multi-party computation systems will nonetheless be reflected on-chain as standard single-signature operations, even though the underlying signing process involved multiple parties.

[82] *MAS*, Response to Feedback Received on Proposed Amendments to the Payment Services Act 2019 (n. 59) no. 2.19; *MAS*, Frequently Asked Questions on the Payment Services Act (n. 56) Case Study 3.

[83] *MAS*, Frequently Asked Questions on the Payment Services Act (n. 56), Case Study 3.

[84] Ibid.

still be regarded as having 'control' because they retain the ability to jointly authorise transactions should their participation be required.[85]

Intuitive as this framework may seem, significant ambiguity remains. The 'arrangement' and 'inducement' examples discussed above are problematic in that their seemingly boundless breadth threatens to undermine efforts to define 'control' meaningfully or to distinguish between relevant and irrelevant fact patterns involving 'control'. The examples provided by MAS to illustrate what constitutes 'arrangement' and 'inducement' could easily be interpreted as encompassing any form of facilitation of digital payment token transactions. If so, any meaningful analysis of 'control' – or indeed 'possession' – would become redundant.

However, MAS provides helpful guidance to mitigate this interpretive overreach. Having examined what qualifies as the presence of 'control', it is also instructive to consider a contrasting case in which 'control' is absent, and thus no licensing obligation arises. MAS highlights the example of a service provider offering "non-custodial digital payment token wallet technology". In such a model, the service provider's core offering is a software solution enabling users to manage their private keys and digital tokens independently. The provider "does not hold on to any private cryptographic keys" and has no role in transaction authorisation.[86] As a result, the provider does not have 'control' within the meaning of the PS Act and is not required to obtain a licence for custody services.[87] This approach aligns with FATF guidance, which affirms that "software developers or providers of unhosted wallets" would generally not be deemed to exercise 'control'.[88]

Importantly, this example offers valuable interpretive guidance on the scope of the 'arrangement' and 'inducement' limbs. If these provisions were intended to cover any form of facilitation, then even software developers ought to fall within the regulatory perimeter. Yet, MAS explicitly exempts such actors from licensing requirements, which is a clear indicator that it does not consider enablement or indirect facilitation by technological means as being generally sufficient to constitute 'arrangement' or 'inducement'.

The implication is that both 'arrangement' and 'inducement' should be interpreted narrowly. The 'inducement' example provided by MAS is particularly illuminating: in that case, the inducing party is contractually involved with the service user, by offering a mobile application that forms a necessary component of the transaction. In contrast, a developer of software that enables the mobile application to function, but who has no direct contractual connection with end

[85] Ibid.

[86] Ibid., Case Study 4.

[87] Ibid.

[88] *FATF*, Updated Guidance for a Risk-Based Approach to Virtual Assets and Virtual Asset Service Providers (n. 78) no. 29.

users, would not fall within the regulatory perimeter. This principle likely applies more broadly: to fall within the scope of 'arrangement' or 'inducement', the entity in question that is facilitating transactions must provide an identifiable service based on a contractual or similarly direct relationship with the service user. That entity must play a clearly defined role in the transaction flow and not merely support the existence of the general technological ecosystem within which transactions are taking place. We suggest that it is only by delimiting the interpretation of 'arrangement' and 'inducement' in this way that Singapore's regulatory framework can preserve internal coherence. Without such a calibrated approach, concepts like 'control' and 'possession' would be rendered meaningless, as overly broad constructions of 'arrangement' and 'inducement' would effectively subsume virtually all forms of transaction facilitation within their scope.

5. Unpacking the meaning of 'possession'

It is crucial to preface this section by clarifying that the preceding explanation of 'control' and the following discussion about 'possession' relate only to how both terms should be understood in a regulatory context, for the purposes of identifying whether an activity falls inside the regulatory perimeter of the PS Act. This is distinct from how both terms are typically construed in a legal sense for the purposes of ascertaining and establishing ownership rights. Notwithstanding this difference, there is still value to analysing how 'control' and 'possession' are intended to be applied in a regulatory setting, because they have a significant practical impact on digital payment token service providers in Singapore. Viewed collectively, the concepts of 'control' and 'possession' underpin the majority of digital payment token services in the PS Act and serve as a key determinant of whether a service provider is required to apply for a regulatory licence.

Turning now to 'possession', it may be helpful to begin by revisiting the three digital payment token services that turn on the presence of 'possession'. The first two are the activities of "dealing in digital payment tokens" and "facilitating the exchange of digital payment tokens",[89] with the former referring to the "buying or selling" of digital payment tokens and the latter defined as "establishing or operating a digital payment token exchange" where the service provider "comes into possession of any money or any digital payment token".[90] Even though 'possession' is not explicitly mentioned with respect to the activity of "dealing in digital payment tokens", it is clear that legislative intent requires the presence of 'possession'. This is evidenced by the Second Reading of the

---

[89] PS Act, Part 3 of First Schedule, definition of "digital payment token service", (a)–(b).

[90] Ibid., definitions of "dealing in" and "facilitating the exchange of" digital payment tokens.

Payment Services (Amendment) Bill, in which a speech delivered on behalf of the Minister-in-charge of MAS stated that the activity of "dealing in digital payment tokens" occurs in situations where the service provider "comes into possession of moneys or digital payment tokens".[91] The third (and final) service involving 'possession' is that of "accepting (whether as principal or agent) digital payment tokens from one digital payment token account (whether in Singapore or elsewhere), for the purposes of transmitting, or arranging for the transmission of, the digital payment tokens to another digital payment token account (whether in Singapore or elsewhere)".[92] Interpretive guidance provided by MAS in its FAQs on the PS Act makes clear that this service involves "coming into possession" of digital payment tokens.[93]

Even though the PS Act does not define 'possession' and MAS has not offered any guidance in the FAQs on the PS Act regarding how to interpret 'possession', it is possible to arrive at a working understanding of how it should be applied by reasoning inductively from the contexts in which 'possession' is referenced. Specifically, 'possession' occurs against the backdrop of "buying and selling digital payment tokens", "establishing or operating a digital payment token exchange", and accepting digital payment tokens "for the purposes of transmitting, or arranging for the transmission of, the digital payment tokens to another digital payment token account".[94] This suggests that 'possession' should be understood as a precondition to a service provider's execution of a transaction involving digital payment tokens (e.g. "buying and selling", "exchange", "transmission").

In light of this, it seems reasonable to conclude that 'possession' has largely the same meaning as 'control'; as established in the previous section, it is necessary for a service provider to hold private keys in order to execute transactions concerning digital payment tokens. Seeing as the execution of some kind of transaction involving digital payment tokens is a common thread connecting the three services that rely on the notion of 'possession', it would appear that 'possession' and 'control' should be understood as having the same meaning to the extent that both are made out when an entity is able to execute transactions concerning a digital payment token by virtue of holding the private key or key share(s) associated with that digital payment token.

However, there is an important definitional nuance: unlike 'control', which can be exercised "jointly with one or more other persons",[95] for practical reasons it seems highly unlikely that 'possession' would permit shared authority to ex-

---

[91] PS Act, Part 3 of First Schedule; *Ong*, Payment Services (Amendment) Bill (n. 46) 7.

[92] PS Act, Part 3 of First Schedule, definition of "digital payment token service", (c).

[93] *MAS*, Frequently Asked Questions on the Payment Services Act (n 56) no. 24.1.

[94] PS Act, Part 3 of First Schedule, definitions of "dealing in" and "facilitating the exchange of" digital payment tokens, and definition of "digital payment token service, (c).

[95] Ibid.; PS (Amendment) Act s7(h).

ecute transactions. This means that a service provider in 'possession' of digital payment tokens would also need to have full authority over the private keys and key shares associated with those tokens. This is because it would be operationally infeasible for a service provider to engage in any of the 'possession'-related services if it lacked the untrammelled authority to execute transactions. To illustrate, consider the service of "operating a digital payment token exchange", where customers would ordinarily send their digital payment tokens to wallets that are wholly owned by the service provider operating the exchange. The digital payment tokens sent to the service provider's wallets will only be disposed of in accordance with instructions from the customers that had deposited them, pursuant to a contractual agreement between the customer and the service provider; however, the service provider holds the entirety of the private keys or key shares required to authorise transactions concerning the digital payment tokens stored in its wallets. This approach is necessary because the alternative – involving customers in the transaction authorisation process (e.g. via multi-signature wallets or multi-party computation systems) would make it extremely cumbersome and impractical to operate an exchange. Much like traditional securities exchanges, a digital payment token exchange would typically execute large numbers of transactions daily in accordance with their customers' trading instructions and may also engage in legitimate internal transactions such as transferring digital payment tokens across different types of wallets to meet liquidity needs. It is not hard to imagine that a digital payment token exchange would quickly grind to a halt if it had to seek additional authorisation via its customers' private keys or key shares every time it sought to engage in a transaction involving a digital payment token. Therefore, unlike 'control', which can be shared between service provider and customer because that is a defining feature of some custody models, for reasons of practicality it seems plausible to assume that 'possession' requires the service provider to have full authority of the private keys and key shares so that it can swiftly execute transactions pursuant to customer instructions. If in the future replaced by different terminology, it would seem reasonable to substitute 'possession' with 'exclusive control'.

IV. Conclusion

Singapore's digital payment token regime distinguishes between regulated and unregulated activities mostly based on the concept of 'control'. We support this conceptual approach and have interpreted 'control' as referring to situations in which a payment token service provider holds the private key necessary to execute transactions involving the relevant tokens.

We have argued that the traditional legal notion of 'possession' is less suitable in the context of digital tokens. 'Possession' typically implies the existence of a corporeal object and the ability to exercise physical control over it. In contrast, non-corporeal digital assets such as payment tokens do not lend themselves to such an interpretation. Accordingly, in the context of digital assets, the term 'possession' must be understood as functionally equivalent to 'control', entailing that the service provider holds the private key enabling token transfers.

Nonetheless, we recognise a nuanced distinction between the concepts of 'possession' and 'control' under Singapore's current regulatory framework. 'Possession' appears to denote a situation in which the service provider is imminently responsible for executing token transfers, implying that it must have exclusive and immediate authority over the private key. This notion of 'possession' is therefore incompatible with models of key sharing, where the execution of transactions requires joint action by multiple key holders.

'Control', by contrast, is a broader concept. It encompasses scenarios in which the ability to initiate transfers exists, even if no transaction is immediately pending. In such cases, the private key may be shared among multiple parties, provided that the service provider retains the capability to authorise or facilitate transactions.

Given the overlapping nature of these concepts in the current framework, we suggest that the concept of 'possession' be abandoned in favour of the broader and more functional notion of 'control'. 'Possession' does not add meaningful regulatory value to the distinction between permitted and unregulated activities. If regulation wishes to differentiate between scenarios involving imminent execution of token transfers and those involving mere transfer enablement, it should clarify this intention – potentially by introducing two levels of 'control'. However, at present, there is no indication that regulation in Singapore envisaged such a distinction. All circumstances in which 'possession' would be relevant are already captured under the existing definition of 'control', rendering the 'possession' concept redundant within the current regulatory architecture.

In addition to the concepts of 'control' and 'possession', Singapore's payment token regime also refers to the notions of 'arrangement' and 'inducement'. We interpret these terms as requiring the presence of an identifiable service grounded in a contractual or similarly direct relationship with the user. Under this interpretation, the service provider engaged in arranging or inducing is assigned a clearly defined role in the transaction process, rather than merely fulfilling a peripheral or supportive function within the broader technological infrastructure in which transactions occur.

Switzerland

Mirjam Eggen and Dominic Wyss[1]

I. Introduction

Switzerland took an early lead in recognizing the importance of digital assets and incorporating them into its legal framework. Its starting point was the understanding that digital assets serve a similar function in trade and financial markets as physical assets. The emergence of Distributed Ledger Technology ("DLT")[2] also made it possible to transfer digital assets directly between parties. Lawmakers were quick to respond, laying the groundwork for peer-to-peer digital asset transfer.

[1] We thank Michael Toneatti, MLaw, Attorney-at-Law, Research Assistant and Doctoral Candidate, University of Bern, for the careful review of the footnotes.

[2] Blockchain is a form of DLT.

A key requirement for secure peer-to-peer transfer of digital assets is individual control over the transfer process, which can be direct or indirect. This article discusses the concept of control under current Swiss law in the context of the transfer of digital assets. It also relates the concept of control to the ownership of digital assets. To what extent is control of the asset not only a prerequisite for its transfer but also for its ownership? How is ownership in the digital space conceived and implemented in legal terms? These questions will be examined and answered in the final part of the article by referring to use cases.

II. Digital Assets under Swiss Law

1. Definition

The term "digital assets" is not defined in Swiss law.[3] However, it has long been possible to record and transfer assets in digital form. This is particularly true for intangible assets that, by definition, do not exist in physical form, such as receivables or intellectual property rights.[4] For example, digitally managed bank accounts are classified as customer receivables from the bank.[5] The transfer of these funds to third parties follows the rules of the law of payment instructions.[6] Stocks or bonds, on the other hand, can be digitized as intermediated securities and transferred to third parties based on the rules of the Intermediated Securities Act.[7] Even the digitization of the transfer of physical assets such as gold or real estate is already possible under current law.[8] The representa-

[3] For an understanding of the term, cf. *Dominic Wyss*, Digitale Vermögenswerte, in: Beiträge zum Schweizer Finanzmarktrecht, ed. by Ueli Studer/Markus Feller (2024) 69–97, 71 ss.

[4] *Wyss*, Digitale Vermögenswerte (n. 3) 70.

[5] *Mirjam Eggen*, Tokenisiertes Buchgeld: Programmierbar? Aber sicher!, AJP 2024, 293–303, 294; *Peter Gauch/Walter R. Schluep/Jörg Schmid/Susan Emmenegger*, Schweizerisches Obligationenrecht Allgemeiner Teil[11] (2020) no. 2312; *Thomas J. Jordan*, Wie Geld durch die Zentralbank und das Bankensystem geschaffen wird, Speech of 16 January 2018, 4; *Corinne Zellweger-Gutknecht*, Digitale Landeswährung – Ein Überblick, Jusletter 31 October 2016, no. 16; cf. *Stefan Kramer*, Rechtsprobleme des Interbanken-Zahlungsverkehrs, Diss. Zurich (2005) 8.

[6] *Eggen*, Tokenisiertes Buchgeld (n. 5) 294; *Gauch/Schluep/Schmid/Emmenegger*, Schweizerisches Obligationenrecht (n. 5) no. 2313.

[7] On the concept of intermediated securities see art. 3, 6 Federal Act on Intermediated Securities (Federal Intermediated Securities Act, FISA) of 3 October 2008, SR 957.1; *Mirjam Eggen*, Chain of Contracts, AJP 2017, 3–15, 12 s. For the transfer of intermediated securities cf. art. 24 FISA; *Patrick Hünerwadel/Roland Fischer*, in: Basler Kommentar zum Wertpapierrecht, Art. 965–1186 OR, Bucheffektengesetz, Haager Wertpapier-Übereinkommen, Art. 108a–108d IPRG, ed. by Heinrich Honsell/Nedim Peter Vogt/Rolf Watter (2012) art. 24 FISA no. 35; *Peter V. Kunz*, in: Basler Kommentar zum Wertpapierrecht, Art. 965–1186 OR, Bucheffektengesetz, Haager Wertpapier-Übereinkommen, Art. 108a–108d IPRG, ed. by Heinrich Honsell/Nedim Peter Vogt/Rolf Watter (2012) art. 3 FISA no. 4.

[8] *Wyss*, Digitale Vermögenswerte (n. 3) no. 42; cf. Dispatch on the adaptation of federal law

tion of real or financial assets on DLT networks is often referred to as "tokenization".[9]

In the following, the term "digital assets" refers to assets that can be represented and transferred digitally. The focus remains on assets that do not exist in physical form and that are to be transferred on a peer-to-peer basis. In technical terms, DLT networks are regularly used for this purpose.[10] Therefore, this technology is implicit in the following discussion. However, future technological developments may result in digital assets being represented and transferred to other networks. Where possible, our paper includes such future developments.

2. *Legal Framework*

The Swiss legal system promotes and supports the digitization of assets in various ways. For example, since 2005, it has been possible to replace a handwritten signature with a qualified electronic signature in accordance with the Federal Act on Electronic Signatures. This means that the written form requirement for the digital transfer of receivables can be met digitally.[11] Further, stocks or bonds can be issued as intermediated securities on a purely digital basis and without any physical representation.[12]

For technological reasons, the trading of digital assets has long been conducted using an intermediary.[13] With the introduction of DLT networks, however, peer-to-peer transactions are now readily available.[14] Swiss law has taken this into account and introduced new rules for digital assets on DLT networks. For example, under debt enforcement and bankruptcy law, crypto-based assets can be segregated by the holders in the event of the custodian's bankruptcy.[15] According to the Dispatch on the DLT Mantle Act, crypto-based assets are any assets "for which the power of disposal is conveyed exclusively via a crypto-based access procedure."[16] The term crypto-based assets is also used in banking

---

to developments in distributed ledger technology of 27 November 2019, BBl 2020, 233–328, 277.

[9] *Mirjam Eggen*, Was ist ein Token?, AJP 2018, 558–567, 561; *Stefan Kramer/Urs Meier*, Tokenisierung von Finanzinstrumenten, GesKR 2020, 60–77, 74; *Yves Mauchle*, Tokens als Effekten, GesKR 2022, 183–194, 187 s.; *Cédric Remund/Dominic Wyss*, Insider Trading im digitalen Zeitalter: Neue Herausforderungen und Risiken, SZW 2023, 24–43, 33 s.; *Rolf H. Weber/Rainer Baisch*, DLT-basierte Finanzprodukte, SZW 2021, 683–697, 684–686.

[10] *Eggen*, Tokenisiertes Buchgeld (n. 5) 296.

[11] See art. 14 para. 2bis CO.

[12] See art. 3 and 24 FISA.

[13] For intermediated securities and custodians as intermediaries, see art. 4 FISA.

[14] Dispatch DLT (n. 8) 244.

[15] See art. 242a LDEB.

[16] Dispatch DLT (n. 8) 292; *Wyss*, Digitale Vermögenswerte (n. 3) 73; *Corinne Zellweger-Gutknecht/Rolf H. Weber*, Private Zahlungsmittel und Zahlungssysteme, Jusletter 11 January 2021, no. 17.

regulation.[17] Further, the legislator has created a separate type of financial market infrastructure for DLT securities, the so-called DLT trading venue.[18]

However, the most decisive legal adjustment for the transfer of digital assets is the introduction of ledger-based securities.[19] According to article 973d CO, shares, bonds, and all other rights that can be securitized as negotiable securities in the traditional sense can also be structured and transferred as ledger-based securities.[20]

There are no specific rules under Swiss private law for pure crypto-based assets such as cryptocurrencies (e.g. Bitcoin). These assets do not represent a claim nor are they considered to be tangible objects that can be owned. Therefore, these assets can be factually controlled but not legally "owned". The remainder of this article focuses on ledger-based securities and does not treat pure crypto-based assets.

3. *Transfer of Digital Assets*

Under Swiss law, assets can be transferred to third parties on the basis of various transfer rules. Which set of rules is applicable depends on the asset being transferred and its legal nature. Like many legal systems, Swiss law makes a fundamental distinction between the rules governing the transfer of ownership in tangible property and those governing the transfer of other rights, e.g., receivables.[21] While ownership of tangible property is transferred to a third party by means of a valid causa and transfer of possession,[22] receivables are generally transferred to third parties by means of a written assignment.[23]

---

[17] See art. 1a lit. b Federal Act on Banks and Savings Banks (Banking Act, BA), SR 952; art. 1b para. 1 lit. a BA, art. 4^{sexies} BA, art. 16 para. 1bis BA, art. 5a Ordinance on Banks and Savings Banks (Banking Ordinance, BO), SR 952.02; cf. *Wyss*, Digitale Vermögenswerte (n. 3) 73.

[18] See art. 73a Federal Act on Financial Market Infrastructures and Market Conduct in Securities and Derivatives Trading (Financial Market Infrastructure Act, FinMIA); cf. *Mirjam Eggen/Christian Sillaber*, DLT-Handelssysteme, Jusletter 11 May 2020, no. 14; *Benedikt Maurenbercher/Benjamin Leisinger*, Decentralized Finance (Teil 2), SJZ 2022, 704–718, 711; *Rolf H. Weber*, Zivilrechtliche Aspekte von Geschäftsabwicklungen auf DLT-Handelsplattformen, SZW 2021, 450–460, 452 s.

[19] For the term see art. 973d CO, according to which a "ledger-based security is a right which, in accordance with an agreement between the parties: 1. is registered in a securities ledger in accordance with paragraph 2; and 2. may be exercised and transferred to others only via this securities ledger".

[20] For the rights that can be structured as ledger-based securities, see Dispatch DLT (n. 8) 276 s.

[21] *Wyss*, Digitale Vermögenswerte (n. 3) 74.

[22] See *Arnold F. Rusch/Ivo Schwander*, in: Basler Kommentar zum Zivilgesetzbuch II, Art. 457–977 ZGB, Art. 1–61 SchlT ZGB, ed. by Thomas Geiser/Stephan Wolf (2023) art. 714 CC no. 7.

[23] See *Daniel Girsberger/Johannes Lukas Hermann*, in: Basler Kommentar zum Obligationenenrecht I, Art. 1–529 OR, ed. by Corinne Widmer Lüchinger/David Oser (2020) art. 164 CO no. 15.

The transfer of digital assets can follow either of these traditional rules for transferring assets. Much more frequently, however, the special rules created for the trading of securitized assets are applied. Essentially, these are the rules for intermediated securities (art. 24 ss. FISA) and ledger-based securities (art. 973f CO[24]).

For a digital peer-to-peer transfer of digital assets, only the new ledger-based securities come into question. This legal form was introduced by the Swiss legislator in response to the emergence of DLT technology.[25] The advantage of this newly introduced form of securitization is that assets can be transferred digitally without the need for an intermediary.[26]

III. Key concepts

This chapter explains the key concepts behind ledger-based securities. First, it discusses securitization under Swiss law in general. Ledger-based securities are based on the traditional concept of securitization, which is well-known and understood under Swiss law. Consequently, conclusions can be drawn from this proven concept for the newly introduced ledger-based securities. Second, this chapter presents the properties and requirements of ledger-based securities. The key concepts behind ledger-based securities are key to assessing control and ownership issues. These concepts will, therefore, serve as a basis for the detailed analysis in Chapter IV below.

1. Securitization

Securitization is the foundation of ledger-based securities. This section provides a definition of securitization and discusses the different forms of securitization, including their commonalities and differences.

Under Swiss law, securitization refers to the combination of a subjective right (a legal entitlement; "*subjektives Recht*") with an instrument, such that the right can only be exercised or transferred with the instrument.[27] There are three functions associated with securitization:[28]

- *Legitimization*: Possession of the instrument is required to exercise the right.

[24] Federal Act on the Amendment of the Swiss Civil Code (Part Five: The Code of Obligations, CO) of 30 March 1911, SR 220.

[25] See Dispatch DLT (n. 8) 239.

[26] Dispatch DLT (n. 8) 244.

[27] The traditional concept of "securitization" finds its legal basis in art. 965–1186 CO (negotiable securities, "*Wertpapiere*").

[28] *Mirjam Eggen/Christian Cachin*, Gutachten zur Modernisierung der Formerfordernisse bei der Übertragung von Rechten (Zession und Wertpapierrecht), Teil 1 Wertpapierrecht, 22 December 2020, no. 85; *Yves Mauchle*, Die Registrierungsvereinbarung – insbesondere bei tokenisierten Forderungsrechten, SZW 2023, 683–698, 686 s.; *Dieter Zobl/Claude Lampert*, Zur Entmaterialisierung der Wertpapiere, SZW 1991, 117–139, 131 s.; cf. *Dominic Wyss*, Digitale Übertragung von Vermögenswerten, Eine zivilrechtliche Betrachtung mit Überlegungen

- *Transport*: A change of possession of the instrument is required to transfer the right.
- *Market protection*: Good faith acquisition of the right via the instrument is protected.

Securitization requires *(1)* a specific subjective right, *(2)* an instrument, and *(3)* a procedure that "attaches" the right to the instrument:[29]

- *(1) Right:* Only certain types of rights can be securitized. Typically, claims, certain membership rights in corporations, and certain rights *in rem* are eligible for securitization. There are important exceptions, such as ownership rights in tangible and intangible assets.[30] Intermediated securities, as discussed below, require the right in securitized form as an eligible underlying.[31]
- *(2) Instrument:* Depending on the form of securitization, the instrument must meet specific form requirements (e. g., a paper, a ledger, etc.).
- *(3) Procedure:* The form of securitization defines the procedure to attach the right to the instrument. This can be either specific clauses, agreements, bookings, or a combination of these.

Under Swiss law, different forms of securitization exist. The subjective right can be structured in various forms of securitization during its existence.[32] Even though these forms are all based on securitization, they differ in the instrument and the procedure that attaches the right to the instrument.[33]

- *Negotiable securities* ("*Wertpapiere*"): The instrument is a paper, and the procedure involves clauses on the paper.[34]
- *Intermediated securities* ("*Bucheffekten*"): The instrument is a combination of centralized digital registers, the procedure includes bookings in the regis-

---

zu einer Erweiterung der Übertragungsordnung der Registerwertrechte, Diss. Bern 2025, nos. 661 s. with further references.

[29] *Eggen/Cachin*, Gutachten (n. 28) no. 28; *Peter V. Kunz*, Wirtschaftsrecht (2019) no. 260; *Arthur Meier-Hayoz/Hans Caspar von der Crone*, Wertpapierrecht[3] (2018) nos. 1 s.; cf. *Wyss*, Digitale Übertragung (n. 28) nos. 652 ss. with further references.

[30] *Robert Furter*, in: Basler Kommentar zum Wertpapierrecht, Art. 965–1186 OR, Bucheffektengesetz, Haager Wertpapier-Übereinkommen, Art. 108a–108d IPRG, ed. by Heinrich Honsell/Nedim Peter Vogt/Rolf Watter (2012) introduction art. 965–1155 CO nos. 7 s.; *Kunz*, Wirtschaftsrecht (n. 29) no. 261; *Meier-Hayoz/von der Crone*, Wertpapierrecht (n. 29) no. 16; cf. *Wyss*, Digitale Übertragung (n. 28) nos. 682 ss. with further references.

[31] Art. 6 Federal Act on Financial Services (Financial Services Act, FinSA) of 15 June 2018, SR 950.1, in particular negotiable securities, uncertificated securities or ledger-based securities.

[32] *Stefan Kramer/David Oser/Urs Meier*, Tokenisierung von Finanzinstrumenten de lege ferenda, Jusletter 6 May 2019, no. 8, fn. 19 ("*Aggregatszustand*").

[33] Cf. *Wyss*, Digitale Übertragung (n. 28) nos. 648 ss. with further references.

[34] *Robert Furter*, in: Basler Kommentar zum Wertpapierrecht, Art. 965–1186 OR, Bucheffektengesetz, Haager Wertpapier-Übereinkommen, Art. 108a–108d IPRG, ed. by Heinrich Honsell/Nedim Peter Vogt/Rolf Watter (2012) art. 965 CO no. 10; *Meier-Hayoz/von der Crone*, Wertpapierrecht (n. 29) no. 1315; cf. *Wyss*, Digitale Übertragung (n. 28) nos. 680 ss. with further references.

ters.[35] Intermediated securities are created when a custodian accepts negotiable securities, a global certificate, ledger-based securities or so-called uncertificated securities and credits them to one or more securities accounts. Uncertificated securities are created on entry in a book. Although commonly referred to in this context, uncertificated securities do not fulfill the three functions of securitization mentioned above.
- Ledger-based securities ("*Registerwertrechte*"): The instrument is a decentralized digital ledger. The procedure requires a combination of an agreement and bookings in the ledger.[36]

The forms of securitization prevent certain technologies from being used as instruments.[37] Historically, lawmakers have enacted new forms of securitization to allow new technologies to be used as instruments of securitization.[38] The most recent example is ledger-based securities, which we will further discuss below.

2. *Ledger-based Securities*

Ledger-based securities feature new legal properties and requirements despite being based on the traditional concept of securitization.[39] So far, ledger-based securities have been the subject of limited research, and to our knowledge, no case law exists. This section discusses the fundamental properties and requirements of ledger-based securities.

a) Term and Legal Nature

A ledger-based security is a right which, in accordance with an agreement between the parties ("registration agreement"; "*Registrierungsvereinbarung*"), is registered in a qualified securities ledger ("*Wertrechteregister*") and may be exercised and transferred only via this securities ledger.[40]

---

[35] BGE 138 III 137 E. 5.2.1; *Claude Lambert/Luca Dalla Torre*, in: Kommentar zum Bucheffektengesetz (BEG), ed. by Dieter Zobl/Martin Hess/Ansgar Schott (2013) art. 6 FISA no. 5; *Karim Maizar*, Rechtsnatur und Herausgabe von Bucheffekten, GesKR 2012, 445–454, 448; *Hans Caspar von der Crone*, Aktienrecht[2] (2020) no. 288; cf. *Wyss*, Digitale Übertragung (n. 28) nos. 867 ss. with further references.

[36] *Eggen/Cachin*, Gutachten (n. 28) no. 120; *Kramer/Meier*, Tokenisierung (n. 9) 62; *Kramer/Oser/Meier*, Tokenisierung (n. 32) no. 6; cf. *Wyss*, Digitale Übertragung (n. 28) nos. 771 ss. with further references.

[37] E.g., the instrument of intermediated securities is centralized and is difficult to align with decentralized technologies such as Blockchain and Distributed Ledger Technology.

[38] Dispatch on the Federal Act on Intermediated Securities and on the Hague Securities Convention of 15 November 2006, BBl 2006, 9315–9420, 9324 s., 9331 s.; *Sonja Maire/Arie Gerszt*, DLT-Vorlage des Bundesrates: Zivil- und finanzmarktrechtliche Aspekte, in: Kapitalmarkt – Recht und Transaktionen XV, ed. by Thomas U. Reutter/Thomas Werlen (2020) 121–150, 122 ss.; cf. *Wyss*, Digitale Übertragung (n. 28) nos. 664 ss. with further references.

[39] Cf. section 1. above.

[40] Legal definition of a ledger-based security according to art. 973d para. 1 CO.

The legal nature of ledger-based securities has not been specifically defined by the legislator.[41] In our view, ledger-based securities are a specific form of a subjective right. This form affects certain aspects of the right, including its exercise and transfer.[42]

b) Establishment

The legal requirements according to art. 973d CO to establish a right as a ledger-based security are *(1)* a registration agreement and *(2)* a qualified securities ledger:

- *(1) Registration agreement:* In the registration agreement, the debtor and the first creditor agree that a subjective right can only be exercised and transferred through the securities ledger.[43]
- *(2) Securities ledger:* The securities ledger must fulfill four requirements,[44] i. e.
  - *Control:* Technological processes provide the creditors with the power of disposal over their rights.
  - *Integrity:* Technical and organizational measures secure the integrity of the ledger to protect it from unathorised modifications.
  - *Publicity:* The ledger or accompanying data records the content of the rights, the functioning of the ledger, and the registration agreement.
  - *Transparency:* Information and ledger entries are transparent for the creditors.

These legal requirements also specify how ledger-based securities can be exercised and transferred. We will discuss this further below.

c) Exercise and Transfer

Once a ledger-based security has been established, it can be (1) exercised and (2) transferred only via the securities ledger. These legal properties of ledger-based securities are governed by art. 973e and 973f CO and are specified by the legal requirements of the qualified securities ledger mentioned above.

---

[41] *Kramer/Meier*, Tokenisierung (n. 9) 60 s.; *Hans Kuhn*, Digitale Aktiven im schweizerischen Privatrecht, in: Entwicklungen im Schweizer Blockchain-Recht, ed. by Rolf H. Weber/Hans Kuhn (2021) 51–129, nos. 6, 37; *Hans Kuhn/Cornelia Stengel/Luzius Meisser/Rolf H. Weber*, Wertrechte als Rechtsrahmen für die Token-Wirtschaft, Jusletter IT 23 May 2019, no. 23; *Corinne Zellweger-Gutknecht/Lucien Monnerat*, Internationaler Kontext: schweizerische Registerwertrechte, in: Elektronische Wertpapiere, Tagungsband, ed. by Sebastian Omlor/Florian Möslein/Stefan Grundmann (2021) 7–32, 8 ss.; cf. *Cyrill A. H. Chevalley*, The Legal Nature of Bitcoin under Swiss Private International Law, recht 2023, 93–107, 99; *Wyss*, Digitale Übertragung (n. 28) nos. 773 ss. with further references.

[42] Cf. *Kramer/Oser/Meier*, Tokenisierung (n. 32) fn. 19; cf. section IV. 3. below regarding ownership in ledger-based securities.

[43] Art. 973d para. 1 CO; for further information see *Mauchle*, Registrierungsvereinbarung (n. 28) 683–698.

[44] Art. 973d para. 2 CO; *Wyss*, Digitale Übertragung (n. 28) nos. 777 s.

- *(1) Exercise:* The form of a ledger-based security limits how a right can be exercised (art. 973e CO). The obligor of the ledger-based security is only entitled and obliged to perform to the creditor shown in the securities ledger. The obligor is discharged from her obligations upon performance to the creditor shown in the securities ledger.[45] This follows from the publicity and transparency requirements of the ledger.[46]
- *(2) Transfer:* According to art. 973f para. 1 CO, the transfer of ledger-based securities is governed by the registration agreement. This gives the parties flexibility to adapt to specific technologies. However, there are minimum requirements that a transfer must meet. It must:[47]
  - be triggered by the technical procedures (this follows from the control requirement of the ledger),
  - be validated (this follows from the integrity requirement of the ledger), and
  - result in a transfer in the ledger (this follows from the publicity and transparency requirements of the ledger).[48]

A person may acquire a ledger-based security in good faith according to art. 973e para. 3 CO.

d) Termination and Cancellation

The parties have the choice to establish and terminate a right as a ledger-based security. The termination of the ledger-based security is not at the free discretion of the parties but is governed by the registration agreement.

In the event of the loss of the power of disposal, the cancellation of the ledger-based security is subject to a procedure in accordance with art. 973h CO.

The termination and cancellation of the ledger-based security only affects the form of the right but not the right itself. The existence of the right is independent of its form.[49]

3. Analysis

The previous sections established the concepts behind ledger-based securities. This section analyzes the concepts and develops two principles of how securiti-

---

[45] Even if the indicated creditor is not the actual creditor, unless the obligor acts in malice or gross negligence.

[46] Cf. section b) above.

[47] Cf. *Mirjam Eggen*, Die rechtliche Ausgestaltung von Retail CBDC, GesKR 2022, 147–159, 154; *Ronald Kogens/Oliver Blum*, Herausforderung bei der Übertragung von als Registerwertrechte ausgegebenen nicht börsenkotierten vinkulierten Namenaktien, GesKR 2023, 372–380, 375; *Wyss*, Digitale Übertragung (n. 28) nos. 789 ss.; different view: *Mauchle*, Registrierungsvereinbarung (n. 28) 686.

[48] Cf. *Wyss*, Digitale Übertragung (n. 28) nos. 789 ss.

[49] BGE 83 II 445 E. 4; for example: if a claim is constructed as a ledger-based security and the ledger-based security is cancelled then the claim still exists.

zation affects the transfer and exercise of the right. This is important because understanding the transfer and exercise of a right helps to understand the right itself. The principles will, therefore, help to address ownership and control issues in the following chapter.

- (1) Securitization changes the status of a right and modifies how it is exercised and transferred.
- (2) The form of securitization and its underlying instrument, whether physical, digital, centralized, or decentralized, determine the requirements for exercise and transfer:[50]
  - For negotiable securities, the right is transferred by transferring the possession of the physical instrument. For some types of negotiable securities, such as instruments to order ("*Ordrepapiere*"), additional written documentation ("*Indossament*") is required. The properties of the instrument (physical) and its limitations (information about the owner) determine the legal requirements for the transfer (change of possession and written documentation).[51]
  - The same principle applies to ledger-based securities. As shown above, the properties of the ledger determine the requirements of the transfer.

4. Functional equivalence

With the introduction of ledger-based securities, the legislator has also introduced the principle of functional equivalence into Swiss law. Art. 145a PILA[52] stipulates that the question of whether a claim can be securitized in a document or in an equivalent form is determined by the law specified in the instrument. The parties are, therefore, free to subject the securitization of digital assets to a law other than Swiss law. This choice of law is recognized by Swiss private international law as long as the principle of functional equivalence is respected. The parties may also agree that the substance and form are governed by different laws, e.g. by choosing Swiss law for the form of securitization only. In the absence of a choice of law in the instrument, the law of the issuer's country of incorporation or habitual residence shall apply.

IV. Control and Ownership

Possession and ownership are two fundamental concepts of Swiss property law. Possession is a factual concept but legally protected. Ownership is a legal concept.[53] In what follows, we examine whether ledger-based securities are based

---

[50] *Mauchle*, Registrierungsvereinbarung (n. 28) 686 s.; cf. *Wyss*, Digitale Übertragung (n. 28) nos. 648 ss.

[51] Cf. *Wyss*, Digitale Übertragung (n. 28) nos. 648 ss.

[52] Federal Act on Private International Law of 18 December 1987 (PILA), SR 291.

[53] Art. 641 CC; for further information see *Barbara Graham-Siegenthaler*, Berner Kom-

on these concepts. In particular, we consider whether the concept of control is equivalent to that of possession. We start with an overview of the topic, then control and ownership are discussed. The chapter concludes with a discussion of use cases and a summary of the main findings.

1. Overview

Ledger-based securities are rooted in property law and negotiable securities law.[54] The Dispatch on the DLT Mantle Act states that there are similarities between "tokens" and tangible objects.[55]

However, the blueprint for ledger-based securities is not a tangible object but an instrument to order ("*Ordrepapier*").[56] An instrument to order is a paper to which a certain right is attached.[57] From a legal perspective, three elements must be distinguished:[58]

- (1) the right that is attached to the paper.
- (2) the possession of the paper.
- (3) the ownership right in the paper.

Translated to the ledger-based securities, the following applies:

- (1) the right changes its status to a ledger-based security.[59]
- (2) the ledger provides control to the creditors.[60]
- (3) the ledger serves as a substitute for the paper.[61]

mentar, Kommentar zum schweizerischen Privarecht, Zivilgesetzbuch, Das Sachenrecht, Das Eigentum, Allgemeine Bestimmungen, Art. 641–654a ZGB (2022) nos. 466, 485; *Stephan Wolf/Wolfgang Wiegand*, in: Basler Kommentar zum Zivilgesetzbuch II, Art. 457–977 ZGB, Art. 1–61 SchlT ZGB, ed. by Thomas Geiser/Stephan Wolf[7] (2023) art. 641 CC nos. 1 ss.

[54] Dispatch DLT (n. 8) 243, 285; *Eggen/Cachin*, Gutachten (n. 28) no. 121; *Daniel Flühmann/Sarah Vettiger*, Shares in the Form of Ledger-Based Securities, GesKR 2022, 102–105, 104; cf. *Wyss*, Digitale Übertragung (n. 28) no. 803.

[55] Dispatch DLT (n. 8) 243, 285; *Lukas Beeler*, Bucheffekten, Übertragung, Stornierung und gutgläubiger Erwerb, in: SSHW – Schweizer Schriften zum Handels- und Wirtschaftsrecht, ed. by Peter Forstmoster (2013) no. 49, n. 103; *Wyss*, Digitale Übertragung (n. 28) no. 803; cf. *Rolf H. Weber*, Neue Blockchain-Gesetzgebung in der Schweiz, RDi 2021, 186–195, no. 22.

[56] Dispatch DLT (n. 8) 243, 2854 s.; *Kuhn*, Digitale Aktiven (n. 41) nos. 24 ss.; *Mauchle*, Registrierungsvereinbarung (n. 28) 685; cf. *Wyss*, Digitale Übertragung (n. 28) nos. 803, 854.

[57] Cf. section III. 1. above.

[58] *Zobl/Lampert*, Entmaterialisierung (n. 28) 131; see critically: *Rolf Bär*, Entwicklungen der wertpapierrechtlichen Dogmatik, in: Das Obligationenrecht, 1883–1893, Berner Ringvorlesung zum Jubiläum des schwezerischen Obligationenrechts, ed. by Pio Caroni (1984) 177–207, 192; *Eggen/Cachin*, Gutachten (n. 28) no. 82; *Markus Vischer*, Aktien als individualisierte Rechte und die dadurch in der Trias Mitgliedschaft – Wertpapier/Wertrecht – Bucheffekte verursachten Probleme, SZW 2022, 213–228, 218 s. with further references on the prevailing doctrine; cf. *Wyss*, Digitale Übertragung (n. 28) nos. 673 s.

[59] Cf. section III. 2. a. above.

[60] Cf. section III. 2. c. above.

[61] Dispatch DLT (n. 8) 259; cf. *Wyss*, Digitale Übertragung (n. 28) no. 852.

Regarding (2), the question is whether control is the equivalent of possession.

Regarding (3), the question is whether there is an equivalent to the ownership right in the paper.

We discuss both questions in what follows.

2. Control

According to art. 973d para. 2 sec. 1 CO, the ledger must use technological processes to give the creditors, but not the obligor, power of disposal over their rights.

This "control requirement" has two purposes:

- Analogy to concepts of negotiable securities: The Dispatch on the DLT Mantle Act draws an analogy between the control requirement and the possession of tangible objects. This analogy is based on the combination of *(1)* private keys that provide factual control and *(2)* the validation mechanism that excludes double transfers. Based on this analogy, the concepts of negotiable securities can be applied to ledger-based securities.[62]
- Distinction from intermediated securities: The control requirement allows to distinguish ledger-based securities from intermediated securities that are governed by the Federal Act on Intermediated Securities.[63]

Considering these purposes, the control requirement has the following elements that together form the content of the control requirement:

- The control requirement replaces the possession of traditional negotiable securities.[64] The control is technical and of a factual nature (technical element).[65] It is based on private keys or other technological processes that provide factual control and validation mechanisms that prevent double transfers. This technical element of control refers to the transfer of ledger-based securities and requires the ability of the creditors to initiate a transfer.
- In addition, the control requirement allows a distinction from intermediated securities (functional element). According to the Dispatch of the DLT Mantle Act, control requires that the transfer of ledger-based securities must, in principle, be initiated by the creditor without the involvement of a trusted central authority that exclusively manages the ledger and must be carried out accord-

---

[62] Cf. Dispatch DLT (n. 8) 278; *Eggen/Cachin*, Gutachten (n. 28) no. 121; *Thomas Jutzi/ Andri Abbühl*, Fintech und DLT (2023) no. 218; *Zellweger-Gutknecht/Monnerat*, Registerwertrechte (n. 41) 18; for the german eWpG see *Sebastian Omlor*, Verfügungen über elektronische Wertpapiere, in: Elektronische Wertpapiere, ed. by Sebastian Omlor, Florian Möslein, *Stefan Grundmann*, in: Schriften zum Recht der Digitalisierung 8, ed. by Florian Möslein/ Sebastian Omlor/Martin Will (2021) 137–156, 140.

[63] Cf. Dispatch DLT (n. 8) 278 s.

[64] Cf. Dispatch DLT (n. 8) 278 s.

[65] Art. 973d para. 2 sec. 1 CO: "It uses technological processes […]"; *Jutzi/Abbühl*. Fintech (n. 62) no. 218; *Kuhn*, Digitale Aktiven (n. 41) no. 56.

ing to the rules of the securities ledger.[66] This functional element of control requires, in principle, a decentralized transfer without the involvement of central authorities.

The control requirement differs from possession in the following two ways:

- *Degree of control:* The Dispatch on the DLT Mantle Act refers to cryptographic processes as one possible method to provide control to creditors.[67] But this control can be limited by several layers of a distributed ledger, such as the smart contract as well as the validation mechanism. Therefore, the control cannot be of absolute nature as opposed to the possession of tangible objects. In particular, the degree of the control requirement, i. e., to what degree control must exist, is not fully clarified by the law.
- *Dogmatic concept:* According to art. 973d para. 2 sec. 1 CO, the power of disposal refers to the creditor's rights. This is different from possession, which refers to a tangible object and not to ownership rights. In addition, the role of the control requirement as a distinguishing feature, as discussed above, is new and cannot be found in the context of possession. Therefore, the dogmatic concept of the control requirement is new and differs significantly from the established legal concept of possession.[68]

Because of the interplay between the two elements of control (technical and functional), it is difficult to determine the dogmatic concept and the content of the control requirement. In individual cases, it can even be difficult to decide whether a right is to be securitized as an intermediated security or a ledger-based security.[69]

Considering the above, control and possession appear to be factually and conceptually too different to draw meaningful legal analogies. The concept of possession has been established with respect to tangible objects and is of very limited use to better understand the control of purely digital ledger-based securities. This is apparent also from the UNIDROIT Principles that state: "Moreover, because a digital asset is intangible, this functional equivalence to possession involves only the dominion and power over a digital asset but does not involve the physical situs dimension applicable to possession of movables."[70]

From the above principles, it follows that securitization changes the status of a right and determines the requirements for exercise and transfer. Therefore, the content of control must be found in the concept of ledger-based securities and not in analogies from possession that is stripped away of its central characteris-

---

[66] Dispatch DLT (n. 8) 279.

[67] Dispatch DLT (n. 8) 278 s.; cf. *Wyss*, Digitale Übertragung (n. 28) no. 850.

[68] *Wyss*, Digitale Übertragung (n. 28) nos. 850 ss.

[69] *Eggen/Cachin*, Gutachten (n. 28) nos. 274 ss.

[70] Cf. *Unidroit*, UNIDROIT Principles on Digital Assets and Private Law: Draft for Consultation (2023) no. 6.2.

tic (physicality).[71] The control requirement features a technical and a functional element, and *(1)* refers to the initiation of a decentralized transfer of the ledger-based securities *(2)* that allows the distinction from intermediated securities.

3. Ownership

As shown above, securitization changes the status of the right and determines the requirements of its exercise and transfer:

- For instruments to order, the right attached to the paper is transferred by a contractual agreement between the parties and a transfer of the possession of a physical instrument and an additional written documentation ("Indossament"). From a legal perspective, the right attached to the paper follows the ownership right in the paper.[72]
- For ledger-based securities, we concluded that the right changes its status to ledger-based securities, and the law sets forth the requirements of its exercise and transfer.

This means that for ledger-based securities, a distinction between a right in the ledger-based security and a right attached to the ledger-based security is not possible. This is a logical consequence of replacing a tangible instrument (i.e., the paper) with a ledger as the instrument of the securitization. The ledger replaces the paper but cannot be owned in the sense of property law because it is not a tangible object. Therefore, there is no "ownership right" in the ledger-based security distinct from the right in the form of a ledger-based security.[73] There are not two distinct assets, only the right in the form of a ledger-based security.[74]

The right in the form of a ledger-based security is part of the estate of the person entitled to it.[75] The entitlement to a ledger-based security can be acquired either originally or derivatively. But, the control requirement of art. 973d

---

[71] Cf. *Sebastian Omlor*, Rechtspolitik der Blockchain, in: Blockchain und Recht, ed. by Sebastian Omlor/Florian Möslein, in: Schriften zum Recht der Digitalisierung 26, ed. by Florian Möslein/Sebastian Omlor/Martin Will (2024) 3–26, 4: "Dennoch fehlt es weiterhin an einem allgemeinen Privatrecht der Blockchain-Token, das in sich geschlossen und kohärent ist."; *Dominik Skauradszun/Thi Minh Ngoc Nguyen*, MiCAR, UNIDROIT Principles on Digital Assets and Private Law, and their Insolvency Principles, ZVglRWiss 2024, 261–288, 277; *Wyss*, Digitale Übertragung (n. 28) nos. 856 ss., 1146 s.

[72] *Wyss*, Digitale Übertragung (n. 28) no. 673; *Zobl/Lampert*, Entmaterialisierung (n. 28) 131; see critically *Vischer*, Aktien (n. 58) 218 s., with further references on the prevailing doctrine.

[73] Dispatch DLT (n. 8) 259; *Vischer*, Aktien (n. 58) 218 s.; *Wyss*, Digitale Übertragung (n. 28) nos. 775, 781, 852.

[74] *Omlor*, Rechtspolitik der Blockchain (n. 71) 12: "Der Kryptowert, die Verbindung/Tokenisierung und der externe Vermögenswert können unterschiedlichen Regelungen unterliegen."; different view: *Rolf H. Weber*, Non-Fungible Tokens – A New (Legal) Phenomenon in the Crypto Universe, sic! 2022, 487–496, 494 s.

[75] *Wyss*, Digitale Übertragung (n. 28) nos. 64 ss.

para. 2 sec. 1 CO does not indicate "ownership" of the ledger-based security in the sense of property law. Unlike in the case of possession under art. 930 CC, there is no legal presumption that the person controlling the ledger-based security is entitled to it.[76] Instead, the control requirement is solely related to initiating the transfer of a ledger-based security.

4. Use Cases

From a technical perspective, there are different degrees of control in a DLT network, such as private keys, which can be shared between multiple parties.[77] Shared technical control differs from custody arrangements where a third party holds control of ledger-based securities on behalf of the creditor.

In this chapter, we discuss shared control and custody arrangements and assess bankruptcy questions that arise from these use cases.

a) Shared control

Shared control refers to technical arrangements that distribute control among more than one person. This may be achieved, for example, by sharing the private key, multi-signature set-ups or by shrading a key in various parts.

The control requirement features a technical and a functional element, and *(1)* refers to the initiation of a decentralized transfer of the ledger-based securities *(2)* that allows the distinction from intermediated securities.[78] Therefore, it must be assessed whether the control requirement of art. 973d para. 2 sec. 1 CO allows for shared technical control:

The transfer of a ledger-based security can be initiated even if control is technically shared between multiple parties.[79] Shared technical control is feasible under the control requirement as long as control factually exists, even if distributed between various parties. It follows from the functional element of the control requirement that it must be possible, at least in principle, for the creditor to initiate the transfer without a central authority. This prevents technical set-ups that irrevocably vest the ability to initiate the transfer with a central authority that cannot be freely exchanged.[80]

Ledger-based securities are based on a decentralized concept, which is reflected in the functional element of the control requirement. In principle, not only must the transfer of the ledger-based security be initiated without a central

---

[76] It is the indication in the ledger that benefits from such presumption (art. 973e para 3 CO).

[77] *Stefan Kramer/Dominic Wyss*, Verwahrung von digitalen Aktiven, in: Entwicklungen im Schweizer Blockchain-Recht, ed. by Rolf H. Weber/Hans Kuhn (2021) 145–163, nos. 6 ss.

[78] Cf. section 2. above.

[79] *Wyss*, Digitale Übertragung (n. 28) no. 799.

[80] *Eggen/Cachin*, Gutachten (n. 28) no. 146.

authority, but such an authority must also not exclusively maintain the ledger. Therefore, under the functional element of the control requirement, shared control is not an issue.

In summary, ledger-based securities can be held in wallets separately or mutually controlled by different persons.

Shared control does not inherently determine ownership or establish co-ownership. Instead, the underlying legal arrangements between the persons with shared control and, if relevant, the provisions of the registration agreement determine ownership. For example, a wallet under shared control may reflect that the owner of the ledger-based securities has granted powers of attorney for transfers, while retaining sole ownership. Alternatively, shared control may reflect that multiple individuals are entitled to the ledger-based securities by virtue of co-ownership under a legal arrangement. Not all possible scenarios are clear-cut. Whether a legal arrangement can be reflected in a particular shared control scenario needs to be assessed on a case-by-case basis.

b) Custody

Custody refers to arrangements where control of the ledger-based securities is held by a third party on behalf of the creditors under an agreement between the parties.[81]

The control requirement permits custody arrangements provided that control is not irrevocably vested in the custodian and the custodian does not exclusively maintain the ledger.[82]

Therefore, control of the ledger-based securities can be transferred to a custodian. The custodian's main obligation under the custody agreement is to safeguard the technical processes that provide the power of disposal and to maintain records of the client holdings.[83]

The clients remain entitled in the ledger-based securities even when the control is transferred to the custodian.[84] As discussed above, there is no distinction between an ownership right in the ledger-based security and the right it represents. Ownership simply means the client's entitlement to the right, represented in the form of ledger-based security.[85]

There are specific requirements to ensure the bankruptcy remoteness of the client holdings of ledger-based securities. We discuss these requirements in the following chapter.

---

[81] *Wyss*, Digitale Vermögenswerte (n. 3) 82 ss.

[82] Cf. section 2. above.

[83] *Wyss*, Digitale Vermögenswerte (n. 3) 85 with further references.

[84] *Wyss*, Digitale Vermögenswerte (n. 3) 89 with further references.

[85] Cf. section 3. above.

c) Bankruptcy

In bankruptcy, property that does not belong to the bankrupt entity may be separated from the bankruptcy estate and given to the owner.[86] Digital assets are not physical and, therefore, do not constitute property under Swiss law.[87] If they are held by third parties on behalf of the owner, special rules must be complied with to ensure that they can be recovered by the entitled persons in the event of the bankruptcy of the third party. In particular, for assets deposited with banks, there is a special provision in the Banking Act.[88] The segregation of intermediated securities in the event of the bankruptcy of the custodian is governed by art. 17 of the Intermediated Securities Act.[89] In general, if digital assets represent a substantive legal position of the holder, such as a membership right in a company, bankruptcy law will protect that position.[90]

Assets held and traded on a DLT are not necessarily intermediated securities. Furthermore, they are held in so-called wallets and are typically not held by banks. As a result, the segregation solutions discussed above may not apply. Based on this circumstance, the legislator introduced a special provision for the segregation of crypto-based assets: Pursuant to art. 242a of the Federal Law on Debt Enforcement and Bankruptcy (LDEB[91]), the bankruptcy administration shall decide on the allocation of crypto-based assets over which the debtor has sole control at the time of the opening of bankruptcy proceedings and which are claimed by a third party. In order for the third party's claim to be protected, one of the following two conditions must be met:

- The crypto-based assets are individually assigned to a third party. Such an individualized assignment exists if the crypto-based assets are held in a special account.[92] This requirement can be met if the allocation is shown in an internal register of the debtor. However, an individual assignment on the

---

[86] *Marc Russenberger/Marc Wolgemuth*, in: Basler Kommentar zum Bundesgesetz über Schuldbetreibung und Konkurs, ed. by Daniel Staehelin/Thomas Bauer/Franco Lorandi (2021) art. 242 LDEB no. 6.

[87] On the property term see BSK ZGB-*Wolf/Wiegand* (n. 22) introduction art. 641 ss. CC nos. 6 s.

[88] Art. 37d BA; *Martin Hess/Andrea Zbinden*, in: Basler Kommentar zum Bankengesetz, ed. by Rolf Watter/Nedim Peter Vogt/Thomas Bauer/Christoph Winzeler (2013) art. 37d BA no. 1; *Renate Schwob/Thomas S. Müller*, in: Kommentar zum Bundesgesetz über die Banken und Sparkassen vom 8. November 1934, ed. by Dieter Zobl/Renate Schwob/Christoph Winzeler/Christine Kaufmann/Rolf H. Weber/Stefan Kramer (2015) art. 37d BA nos. 3 s.

[89] *Lukas Bopp/Daniel Staehelin*, in: Basler Kommentar zum Wertpapierrecht, Art. 965–1186 OR, Bucheffektengesetz, Haager Wertpapier-Übereinkommen, Art. 108a–108d IPRG, ed. by Heinrich Honsell/Nedim Peter Vogt/Rolf Watter (2012) art. 17 FISA nos. 1 s.

[90] *Kramer/Wyss*, Verwahrung (n. 77) no. 42; *Wyss*, Digitale Vermögenswerte (n. 3) 87 s. with further references.

[91] Federal Law on Debt Enforcement and Bankruptcy of 11 April 1989 (LDEB), SR 281.1.

[92] Dispatch DLT (n. 8) 293; BSK SchKG-*Russenberger/Wohlgemuth* (n. 86) art. 242a LDEB no. 19.

ledger is not required. If the crypto-based assets are technically individualized, it is also sufficient for an individual assignment that each asset can be assigned to a specific holder on the basis of a number or similar.[93]

- The crypto-based assets are assigned to a community, and it is clear what share of the community assets the third party is entitled to. This second variant addresses the case where crypto-based assets of a number of customers are held in a collective account.[94] In this constellation, it should also be possible to segregate the crypto-based assets in the event of bankruptcy.

Bankruptcy protection under Article 242a LDEB does not create a substantive ownership right in crypto-based assets as the provision applies solely in bankruptcy scenarios. Typically, this does not affect ledger-based securities, as they generally represent a substantive legal right of the holder that is protected independently of art. 242a LDEB.[95]

If the requirements of art. 242a LDEB are not met, the application of art. 242b LDEB must be examined on a subsidiary basis.[96] According to this provision, third parties can demand access to data to which they can prove a legal or contractual entitlement.[97]

V. Conclusion

Switzerland recognized at an early stage that the transfer of digital assets from peer to peer would need to be legally possible. This goal was accomplished by creating ledger-based securities. The central element of the new regulation is the control requirement. The creditor must be able to initiate the transfer of the right on the ledger to a third party. However, the intensity of this control is not fully clarified by the legislator, which may lead to legal uncertainty in some cases. On the other hand, shared control over the rights or their custody by third parties is fully compatible with the control concept of ledger-based securities. It remains to be seen whether this new form of securitization will become widely established.

---

93 Dispatch DLT (n. 8) 293; BSK SchKG-*Russenberger/Wohlgemuth* (n. 86) art. 242a LDEB no. 19.

94 Dispatch DLT (n. 8) 293; BSK SchKG-*Russenberger/Wohlgemuth* (n. 86) art. 242a LDEB no. 21.

95 Cf. section 3. above.

96 BSK SchKG-*Russenberger/Wohlgemuth* (n. 86) art. 242a LDEB no. 14; BSK SchKG-*Russenberger/Wohlgemuth* (n. 86) art. 242b LDEB nos. 1 ss., 9.

97 BSK SchKG-*Russenberger/Wohlgemuth* (n. 86) art. 242b LDEB no. 12.

Taiwan

Yueh-Ping (Alex) Yang and Meng-Shiang (Ryan) Lin

I. Introduction

Taiwan has a vibrant virtual asset market and has launched a series of virtual asset regulations since 2018.[1] Following the amendment of Taiwan's Money Laundering Act in July 2024, which introduced a registration requirement for

[1] For a brief of the development of virtual asset regulations in Taiwan, particularly the bottom-up process, see, e.g., *Meng-Shiang (Ryan) Lin* (林盟翔), Digital Marathon in the Regulatory Arena: Ensuring Financial Stability and Protecting Investment and Consumer Rights (監管舞台上的數位馬拉松：確保金融穩定、保護投資、消費者權益), 168 The Taiwan Banker (台灣銀行家雜誌) 28, 30=31 (2024).

virtual asset service providers ("VASPs"), 9 virtual asset service providers were permitted to operate their businesses as of September 2025.[2] Taiwan's Financial Supervisory Commission ("FSC"), the financial regulator, is proposing the Virtual Asset Services Act bill to provide a more comprehensive set of regulations for virtual assets, aiming to establish a licensing regime.[3] It is foreseeable that Taiwan will characterize virtual assets as quasi-financial instruments and regulate VASPs as financial institutions.

That said, Taiwan is a civil law country, whose private laws are generally governed by its Civil Code. Therefore, limited by its mandate, Taiwan's FSC focuses more on the financial regulation aspect of virtual assets in this bill. This leaves the private law aspect related to virtual assets unattended. Currently, no government authorities or legislators have initiated legislative initiatives to clarify the private law issues related to virtual assets, such as their legal characterization, ownership, possession, assignment, and transfer. Furthermore, not many Taiwanese courts have addressed these private law issues as well. Without special laws explicitly addressing these legal issues, exploring whether Taiwan's general private laws are sufficient to address them is necessary.

In this chapter, we attempt to clarify the private law issues related to virtual assets in Taiwan. In Part II, we introduce the current landscape of Taiwan's virtual asset private laws, which focuses on the statutory laws and regulations related to virtual assets. In Part III, we review the development of private law related to virtual assets in Taiwan, focusing on the Taiwanese courts' characterization of virtual assets and the associated interpretations. In Part IV, we reflect on the current Taiwanese court practices and propose different characterizations and rules for virtual assets. We conclude this chapter in Part V.

Throughout this chapter, we define "virtual assets" and VASPs by the legal definition under relevant Taiwanese laws.[4] Virtual assets refer to values that can be digitally stored, exchanged, and transferred using cryptography, distributed ledger technology, and other similar technologies, and are used for payment or investment purposes.[5] VASPs, in turn, refer to enterprises or individuals pro-

---

[2] Securities and Futures Bureau of the Financial Supervisory Commission, Virtual Asset Service Providers, <https://www.sfb.gov.tw/ch/home.jsp?id=1053&parentpath=0,8> (October 16, 2025).

[3] Virtual Asset Services Act bill, <https://join.gov.tw/policies/detail/e90af56a-ad3d-4aad-ad7a-d45eb88161a6> (September 19, 2025).

[4] Regulations for the Money Laundering Control Registration for Enterprises or Persons Providing Virtual Asset Services (提供虛擬資產服務之事業或人員洗錢防制登記辦法) (the "VASPs Registration Regulation").

[5] VASPs Registration Regulation, art. 2(1)(I) (Taiwan). However, digital NTDs and foreign currencies, securities, and other financial assets issued in accordance with other financial laws are excluded from this definition. Under this definition, Bitcoin, for instance, is a virtual asset governed by this Regulation. It is an encrypted digital asset based on decentralization, using a peer-to-peer network and consensus initiative, open source, and blockchain as the underlying technology. Moreover, while Bitcoin may be used to purchase goods or services as

viding virtual asset exchange, transfer, custody, and underwriting services for others within Taiwan's territory as part of their business.[6] These definitions generally align with those of virtual assets and VASPs under the Recommendations of the Financial Action Task Force ("FATF").[7]

II. The Current Landscape of Taiwan's Virtual Asset Private Laws

In this Part, we will provide an overview of the laws and regulations related to virtual assets in Taiwan, focusing on private law aspects.

1. The Overview of Taiwan's Current Regulatory Landscape

Taiwan's regulation of virtual assets stemmed from the Money Laundering Control Act.[8] In November 2018, to align with the FATF Recommendations for the upcoming evaluations of the Asia/Pacific Group on Money Laundering ("APG Evaluations"), Taiwan's Legislative Yuan (i.e., Taiwan's Congress), passed the amendment to the Money Laundering Control Act, which requires enterprises handling virtual currency platforms or transactions to undertake anti-money-laundering obligations in the same manner with financial institutions.[9] Based on this mandate, Taiwan's FSC promulgated the Regulation for Governing Anti-Money Laundering and Countering the Financing of Terrorism for Enterprises Handling Virtual Currency Platforms or Transactions in June 2021, marking the commencement of virtual asset regulation in Taiwan.

As the virtual asset market has continued to boom in Taiwan, virtual assets have become a widespread tool for criminals to launder their illicit proceeds, posing significant investigative challenges to law enforcement. Investment fraud in the name of virtual asset investment also came to widespread attention. In the 2021 National Money Laundering, Terrorist Financing, and Proliferation Financing Risk Assessment Report, Taiwan's Anti-Money Laundering Office

---

the consideration, which bears some exchange value and payment function, it differs from legal tender issued by a sovereign state and, thus, does not fall within the above exclusion.

6 *Id.* art. 2(1)(II).

7 FATF, International Standards on Combating Money Laundering and the Financing of Terrorism and Proliferation: The FATF Recommendations 137 – 38 (2023).

8 Besides money laundering control, Taiwan also introduced a series of rules for virtual assets with the character of securities (the so-called securities tokens) in 2020 for the purpose of protecting investors in securities tokens, which is based on the existing securities regulation in Taiwan. Taipei Stock Exchange, "Rules for Administering Securities Firms' Operating Businesses in Dealing Securities Virtual Assets", (2020) https://www.tpex.org.tw/en-us/service/securities-firm/sto/regulation.html (September 19, 2025). However, this paper will not focus on this aspect because these rules merely govern virtual assets with the nature of securities, which do not extend to mainstream virtual assets such as Bitcoin, Ether, etc.

9 Money Laundering Control Act, art. 5(2) (Taiwan).

identified virtual asset enterprises as a sector with "Very High Vulnerability" to money laundering abuse.[10] In the meantime, scandals in the global virtual asset market, such as the UST and FTX bankruptcies, further alerted Taiwanese financial regulators to the potential risks associated with virtual assets.

To address the above issues and better align with the FATF's Updated Guidance for a Risk-Based Approach to virtual assets and VASPs, issued in October 2021, Taiwan's Legislative Yuan passed an amendment to the Money Laundering Control Act in July 2024, subjecting all VASPs to a registration requirement.[11] This amendment also mandates Taiwan's FSC to regulate and supervise VASPs more comprehensively, including their onboarding evaluations, prevention of market abuses, customer asset segregation, information system security, and wallet management.[12] Based on this mandate, Taiwan's FSC issued the Regulations for the Money Laundering Control Registration for Enterprises or Persons Providing Virtual Asset Services (hereinafter referred to as the "VASPs Registration Regulation") to govern VASPs, often referred to as the "VASPs Registration Regime."

Taiwan's FSC does not plan to stop here. It has recently proposed the Virtual Asset Services Act bill to introduce a more comprehensive regulatory regime for the virtual asset market. Among other provisions, the bill includes a licensing regime for VASPs, laws governing stablecoin issuers, and criminal penalties for virtual asset fraud and manipulation. Taiwan's FSC has finalized the bill and submitted it to the Executive Yuan (i. e., Taiwan's Cabinet) in June 2025 for further deliberation. However, the timeline for its final adoption and promulgation by the Legislative Yuan remains unsettled.

2. *Private Laws for Virtual Assets under the Existing Regulations*

The existing virtual asset regulations issued by Taiwan's FSC stipulate little about the private law aspects of virtual assets due to Taiwan's legal system and the FSC's limited mandates. To begin with, Taiwan is a civil law jurisdiction with a codified Civil Code as the general law governing private law issues in Taiwan. The Ministry of Justice ("MoJ") is in charge of the Civil Code. Following the Ministry of Digital Affairs (MODA)'s incorporation in August 2022, the MODA assumed responsibility for several private law statutes related to digital affairs, including the Electronic Signatures Act. By far, however, neither the MoJ nor the MODA has any initiative in drafting a special law to govern the private law issues related to virtual assets.

---

[10] Anti-Money Laundering Office, Executive Yuan, 2021 National Money Laundering, Terrorist Financing and Proliferation Financing Risk Assessment Report, 66 – 71 (2021).

[11] Money Laundering Control Act, art. 6(1).

[12] *Id.* art. 6(2).

In contrast, Taiwan's FSC's mandate primarily focuses on financial regulation. Specifically, its mandates are for the "development, supervision, regulation, and examination of financial markets and financial service enterprises,"[13] so it is unclear whether FSC's mandate could extend to specific private law issues. This unclear legal mandate somehow prevents Taiwan's FSC from stipulating the private law issues related to virtual assets.

The only provision related to private laws under the VASPs Registration Regulation addresses the ownership of virtual assets between virtual asset custodians and their customers. Specifically, it stipulates that virtual asset custodians shall not agree with a customer to transfer the ownership of their virtual assets in the custodian's custody to the custodian itself.[14] To that extent, it clarifies that when virtual asset investors retain custodians to safeguard their virtual assets, the ownership of those assets belongs to the investors, not the custodians. Except for this provision, the Regulation remains silent on how to create and assign ownership of virtual assets.

3. Summary

In summary, while Taiwan has promulgated several statutory laws governing virtual assets in recent years, these laws do not sufficiently address the aspects of private law. This creates legal uncertainty regarding the legal relationship associated with virtual assets. This uncertainty is particularly problematic, given that Taiwan is a civil law jurisdiction where courts heavily rely on interpreting statutes to resolve private disputes.

Notably, virtual assets involve innovative instruments, markets, and industries with which courts are unfamiliar. Without clear statutory laws, courts may struggle to formulate private laws for virtual assets in their initiatives. This also explains why court cases clarifying the private laws of virtual assets are relatively under-developed in Taiwan, which will be elaborated on in Part III below.

III. Private Law Development Related to Virtual Assets in Taiwan

In the legal vacuum created by statutory laws governing the private law aspects related to virtual assets, Taiwanese courts have issued several decisions that clarify the private law for virtual assets. Notably, Taiwanese courts have clarified that virtual assets are considered personal property, specifically movable things, in Taiwan. The relationship between virtual asset custodians and their customers is characterized as a deposit relationship. In this part, we elaborate on these legal developments among Taiwanese courts.

[13] Organic Act Governing the Establishment of the FSC, art. 2(1).

[14] VASPs Registration Regulation, art. 24(1).

1. Virtual Asset as Movable Things

The private law character of virtual assets provokes numerous discussions in various jurisdictions, particularly regarding whether virtual assets possess the property character.[15] Unlike these jurisdictions, Taiwanese courts have settled on this legal issue and characterized virtual assets as movable things under Taiwanese law.

a) The Primer of Taiwan's Private Law System

To provide a brief overview of Taiwan's private law system. Taiwan is a civil law jurisdiction whose private law system is modeled after and highly influenced by German and Japanese private law. In Taiwan, property rights may be classified into three categories: (1) claims of obligations, (2) rights of things, and (3) intangible property rights. Claims of obligations are governed by Part II Obligations of the Civil Code. In contrast, rights to things are governed by Part III, "Things," of the Civil Code, while intangible property rights are typically governed by special laws.[16] By their nature, claims of obligations are rights *in personae*, while the last two categories are rights *in rem*.

Under Taiwanese laws, the distinction between things and intangible properties is less clear than anticipated. Notably, things under Taiwanese civil laws need not be tangible. For instance, some powers of nature, such as electricity or solar power, which lack physical forms, are widely perceived as movable things under Taiwanese laws.[17] This understanding of things inevitably blurs the line between intangible things and intangible properties. Under Taiwanese law, classic examples of intangible properties include intellectual property rights, such as patents, copyrights, and trademarks.

Electronic records, for instance, are a controversial case. Several Taiwanese district courts have characterized electronic records as intangible properties, rather than intangible things.[18] For example, a district court highlighted that electronic records are not tangible, but are merely stored in a computer system, and are not specific things like movable things that can be directly delivered.[19] Another district court further elaborated that electronic records possess repro-

---

[15] *Andrea Tosato/Christopher K. Odinet*, Crypto and the Property Question, Fla. L. Rev. in: forthcoming, 2026; *Peter G. Watts/Kelvin F.K. Low*, The Case for Cryptoassets as Property, in: Law at the Cutting Edge 281 (Sinéad Agnew/Sir Marcus Smith eds., 2024); *Kelvin F.K. Low/Ernie G. S. Teo*, Bitcoins and Other Cryptocurrencies as Property?, 9(2) L., Innovation/Tech. 235 (2017).

[16] *Tsay-Chuan Hsieh (謝在全)*, Rights of Things of Civil Code (民法物權論) 2 (8th ed., 2023).

[17] *Tze-Chien Wang (王澤鑑)*, General Principles of Civil Code (民法總則) 243 (2021); and Supreme Court 112, Tai-Shang No. 2760, Civil Decision (2024); Supreme Court,112, Tai-Shang No. 2851 Civil Decision (2024).

[18] Taiwan New Taipei District Court 111, Su No. 2170, Civil Decision (2023); Taiwan Shilin District Court 101 Su No. 84 Civil Decision (2012).

[19] Taiwan New Taipei District Court 113, Si-Zhi No. 13837, Civil Ruling (2024).

ducibility, which means people can copy, without harming, the contents of electronic records during repeated reading and transmission. In the court's view, this reproducibility is the defining distinction between electronic records and movable things.[20] Notably, the fact that Taiwan has not promulgated special laws for electronic records does not prevent courts from characterizing electronic records as intangible properties distinct from movable things.

The merits of distinguishing between intangible things and intangible properties lie in the governing laws. As mentioned above, intangible things are movable things governed by Part III of the Civil Code. In contrast, intangible properties are not things and are instead governed by their respective special laws. That said, to the extent that no special laws govern the intangible properties at issue, Part III of the Civil Code may be applied by analogy to these intangible properties.[21] In this sense, the Civil Code may still play a supplementary role in resolving disputes related to intangible properties.

b) The Private Law Character of Virtual Assets

Possibly due to the trichotomy of properties under Taiwanese laws, Taiwanese courts and academics do not characterize virtual assets as claims of obligations simply because they are intangible. Instead, the debate primarily centers on whether to characterize virtual assets as things, particularly movable things, or intangible properties.

In 2018, a Taiwanese district court first addressed the private law character of Bitcoin under Taiwanese law. The dispute involved a Bitcoin lending agreement, in which the lender requested that the borrower repay the borrowed Bitcoin. In ruling that the borrower was obligated to repay the borrowed Bitcoin to the lender, the district court stated, "Bitcoin, by its nature, is a fungible thing."[22] By characterizing Bitcoin as a "thing," Taiwanese courts recognized virtual assets as subjects of *in rem* rights.

A year later, a Taiwanese high court further elaborated on this characterization. In a dispute involving the compulsory enforcement of the debtor's obligation to repay Bitcoin, the high court clarified that "Bitcoin's nature is distinct from the currency in circulation issued by specific governmental organizations. In the court's view, Bitcoin relies on itself to reflect a certain value, enabling Bitcoin holders to exchange equivalent things or currencies. Thus, Bitcoin is an object to which certain rights attach, whose nature shall be 'things,' particularly 'fungible things.'" The Taiwanese high court reiterated this position in a subse-

---

20 Taiwan Taichung District Court 110, Su No. 722, Civil Decision (2021). This decision drew reference from an authoritative criminal court decision, *see* Supreme Court 107, Tai-Shang No. 1096, Criminal Decision (2018).

21 *Tze-Chien Wang* (王澤鑑), Rights of Things of Civil Code (民法物權) 82–83 (4th ed., 2023).

22 Taiwan Tainan District Court, 106 Su-No. 1907, Civil Decision (2018). The decision was not appealed and was final and binding.

quent ruling dealing with the same dispute. These high court decisions affirmed that virtual assets are 'things' under Taiwanese law.

As of 2024, Taiwan's Supreme Court has not opined on the legal character of virtual assets. However, to the extent that some lower-level courts followed suit in adopting the above court opinion while no other courts held differing opinions, it can be said that Taiwanese courts have consistently regarded virtual assets as things that are subjects of *in rem* rights under Taiwanese law.

Characterizing virtual assets as things, particularly movable things, receives some support from Taiwan's academia.[23] However, some disagreements or cautions remain. Some raised the concern that Taiwan's existing laws on things, particularly movable things, can hardly apply to virtual assets because virtual assets are intangible. Therefore, they proposed avoiding applying or analogizing existing laws on movable things to virtual assets. Instead, they proposed characterizing virtual assets as intangible properties rather than things, and legislators should promulgate a special law to govern the private law of these intangible properties.[24]

Others cautioned about the rigidity of Taiwan's laws regarding things. For instance, Part III of the Civil Code upholds the doctrine of *numerus clausus*, which precludes the recognition of certain rights for virtual assets if they are considered things. Therefore, they proposed characterizing virtual assets as intangible properties under Taiwanese law to maintain the legal flexibility to create tailor-made rules for virtual assets. While they agreed to apply some laws on movable things by analogy to virtual assets when appropriate, they also highlighted the need to consider customary rules or practices in the virtual asset market to construct private laws for virtual assets.[25]

For the introductory purpose, in the remainder of Part III, we will first introduce the private laws governing virtual assets in Taiwan, based on the court's characterization of virtual assets as movable things. We will revisit the appropriateness of the court's characterization in Part IV.

---

[23] *Chung-Wei Liao* (*廖崇崴*), The Civil Compulsory Enforcement of Bitcoin (初探比特幣之民事強制執行), 67 Hwa Kang L. Rev. (華岡法粹), 141, 164 (2019); *Jung-Chin Kuo* (*郭戎晉*), The Characterization of Non-Fungible Tokens under Civil Laws (論非同質化代幣（NFT）在民事法下之定性), 5 Taiwan Sci./Tech. L.J. (臺灣科技法學叢刊) 29, 68–70 (2023); *Chia-Wei Ho* (*何家瑋*), Perspectives of Legal Problems on Digital Assets Transactions (數位資產交易之法律問題初探), 6(1) Fin. L. Rev. (財金法學研究) 51, 60–61 (2023).

[24] *Rong-Chwan Chen* (*陳榮傳*), Agreed Currency: What is Bitcoin? (約定貨幣：問比特幣為何物), 67 Cross-Strait L. Rev. (月旦民商法雜誌) 5, 17–20 (2020); *Wen-Chung Cheng* (*鄭文中*), Cybercrime with Virtual Currencies, Their Tracking and Prevention: German Laws as an Example (虛擬貨幣相關網路犯罪及其訴追與預防——以德國法為例), 4(2) Fin. L. Rev. (財金法學研究) 57, 78 (2021).

[25] *Yueh-Ping (Alex) Yang* (*楊岳平*), The Legal Characterization of Virtual Assets: Focusing on Private Laws and Financial Laws (論虛擬通貨之法律定性——以民事法與金融法為中心), 301 Taiwan L. Rev. (月旦法學雜誌) 43, 54 (2020). *Wang*, Rights of Things of Civil Code (民法物權) (n. 19), at 82–83.

2. *The Ownership and Possession of Virtual Assets in Taiwan*

Under Taiwan's Civil Code, "possession" is crucial in movable things. Notably, under Taiwanese laws, the concept of "possession" is a factual status, representing the control over things. It differs from the concept of "ownership," representing a legal right over things. That said, the delivery of movable things (i. e., the transfer of possession) is a prerequisite for transferring rights *in rem* of movable things, including transferring their ownership.[26] Possessors are further presumed to have the legal right, including the ownership, to exercise over the things they possess.[27] Therefore, buyers of virtual assets must obtain possession of the virtual assets to obtain ownership.

Under Taiwan's Civil Code, "possession" refers to having "a *de facto* controlling power over a thing."[28] In the case of virtual assets, while Taiwanese courts have not yet clearly defined how to determine control over virtual assets, they have consistently emphasized the importance of "wallets" and the associated "private keys" or "seed phrases" over time.

In a series of criminal decisions, several Taiwanese courts highlighted the crucial function of wallets in possessing virtual assets. For instance, a Taiwanese high court emphasized that for transactions involving virtual assets, "wallets are the most important thing, serving as the digital medium for storing, transmitting, and receiving virtual assets. In other words, it is very difficult for virtual assets to be sent and received without using wallets. Therefore, to invest in virtual assets, the first step is to possess a wallet, whether a hot wallet, a cold wallet, or a hardware wallet."[29] This finding highlights the importance of wallet possession in determining the possession of virtual assets.

In determining the possession of wallets, some Taiwanese courts further highlighted the possession of private keys and/or seed phrases. For instance, a district court found that "regarding electronic wallets for virtual assets, only the person who possesses the 'key' of the wallet may *de facto* dominate and use the virtual assets stored in the wallet. Furthermore, due to the difficulty in memorizing keys, people often store private keys on specific flash drives or storage devices disconnected from the web, or transform keys into 'seed phrases' that are easier to memorize."[30] [31]

---

[26] Taiwan Civil Code, art. 761(1).

[27] Taiwan Civil Code, art. 943(1).

[28] Taiwan Civil Code, art. 940.

[29] Taiwan High Court Taichung Branch 113, Jin-Shang-Su No. 457, Criminal Decision (2024); Taiwan Kaoshiung District Court 111, Jin-Su No. 401, Criminal Decision (2024); Taiwan Pingtung District Court 111, Jin-Su No. 246, Criminal Decision (2024).

[30] Taiwan Ciaotou District Court 113, Yi-No. 58, Criminal Decision (2024).

[31] Anthony Allen, How to Memorize a Seed Phrase: Building Narratives from Nonsense (2020), https://blog.trezor.io/how-to-memorize-a-seed-phrase-building-narratives-from-nonsense-a306e48dfb39 (September 19, 2025).

Another district court adopted an expert witness's opinion and held that "in normal virtual asset transactions, users of electronic wallets should possess the seed phrases or private keys, which are exclusive, and may thus independently control and dominate their electronic wallets."[32] Therefore, Taiwanese courts are likely to determine possession of virtual assets based on the possession of wallets that store the said virtual assets. In addition, the crucial test might be whether a person possesses the private key or seed phrase for the said wallet.

In summary, while Taiwanese courts have not established a clear and consistent measure for determining the ownership and possession of virtual assets, it can be inferred that they are likely to focus on the possession of wallets through the possession of associated private keys and/or seed phrases. This position also aligns with the methods outlined in the UNIDROIT Principles on Digital Assets and Private Law, which appear to determine control over virtual assets based on knowledge of private keys.[33]

3. The Ownership and Possession of Virtual Assets in Cases Involving Virtual Asset Custodians

In real-world practice, many people invest in virtual assets without holding them in their own self-custodied wallets. Instead, they invest in virtual assets through so-called "centralized trading platforms," which offer custodian services and hold customers' virtual assets in their wallets on their behalf. The ownership relationship in such cases requires separate inquiries.

a) Virtual Asset Custodians as Depositaries

Taiwanese courts generally characterize the legal relationship between virtual asset custodians and their customers as "deposits." For instance, in a dispute between Bito, one of Taiwan's largest virtual asset trading platforms, and its customers, a district court found that Bito provides "virtual asset trading platforms[...] and deposit, withdrawal, and custody services for New Taiwanese Dollars and virtual assets. To the extent that users may deposit New Taiwanese Dollars into their accounts, transfer them to Bito's account to trade in virtual assets, and deposit the virtual assets into Bito's account, the legal relationship between Bito and users is a *deposit relationship* [emphasis added], where users are depositors while Bito is the depositary."[34]

That said, characterizing virtual asset custodians as depositaries does not resolve the ownership issue automatically. This is because Taiwan's Civil Code permits parties to agree upon the ownership of deposited things when the things

---

32 Taiwan Keelung District Court 113, Su-No. 379, Civil Decision (2024).

33 UNIDROIT Principles on Digital Assets and Private Law, 6.16 (2023).

34 Taiwan Taipei District Court 111, Su-No. 634, Civil Decision (2023); Taiwan Taipei District Court 110, Chung-Su No. 922 Civil Decision (2022).

are fungible. Specifically, suppose parties agree that the ownership of the deposited things is transferred to the depositary and that the depositary shall return things of the same kind, quality, and quantity. In that case, the legal relationship between depositaries and depositors is a consumption deposit relationship, where the provisions governing consumption loans are applied *mutatis mutandis*.[35] However, parties may also choose not to agree that the ownership of deposited things is transferred to the depository.[36]

This is when the VASPs Registration Regulation mentioned above resolves the problem. The said Regulation stipulates clearly that virtual asset custodians shall not agree with a customer that the ownership of the customer's virtual assets in the custodian's custody be transferred to the virtual asset custodian.[37] Without such agreements, the ownership of the virtual assets in question rests with the customers.

Moreover, to avoid confusion, the VASPs Registration Regulation prohibits virtual asset custodians from mixing their virtual assets with those deposited by customers. Specifically, it requires virtual asset custodians to keep customers' virtual assets in segregated custody from their proprietary virtual assets and prohibits them from agreeing with customers to commingle customers' virtual assets with their own.[38] This requirement helps clarify the ownership between the custodian and its customers' virtual assets.

Notably, the VASPs Registration Regulation does not prohibit virtual asset custodians from commingling different customers' virtual assets. Therefore, according to Taiwan's Civil Code, virtual asset custodians may keep the same kind and quality of virtual assets belonging to different customers together, provided that they obtain the customers' consent.[39] For instance, they may store all customers' virtual assets in a wallet and their proprietary virtual assets in a separate wallet. In that case, each customer owns the virtual assets in custody in proportion to their share of the combined virtual assets.[40] Upon receiving a withdrawal request, virtual asset custodians may fulfill their duties by returning the virtual assets of the same kind and quality to the requesting customer.[41]

b) The Transfer of Virtual Assets Ownership and Possession

While Taiwanese laws address the ownership relationship between virtual asset custodians and their customers, further inquiries are needed to clarify the relationship when customers buy and acquire virtual assets in the custody of virtu-

[35] Taiwan Civil Code, art. 602(1).
[36] Taiwan Civil Code, art. 603-1(1).
[37] VASPs Registration Regulation, art. 24(1).
[38] VASPs Registration Regulation, art. 24(2) .
[39] Taiwan Civil Code, art. 603-1(1).
[40] *Id.*
[41] Taiwan Civil Code, art. 603-1(2).

al asset custodians. A potential concern may arise if we consider that transferred virtual assets remain in the custodian's physical possession both before and after the transaction.

Two provisions under Taiwan's Civil Code are relevant to this issue. First, Taiwan's Civil Code introduces the concept of "indirect possession" as separate from "direct possession." Specifically, it stipulates that in the case of a deposit relationship, where a depositary possesses a thing owned by another, i.e., the depositor, the depositor is an indirect possessor.[42] Therefore, although customers do not possess the private keys or seed words of the custodian's wallets and, thus, do not directly possess their virtual assets, they are considered the indirect possessors of their virtual assets.

Second, Taiwan's Civil Code provides a flexible method for transferring possession of things. Specifically, in transferring the ownership right of a movable thing, if the thing is in the possession of a third party, the transferor may transfer the claim against such third party for the return of the thing to the transferee in place of its delivery.[43] Therefore, to complete the delivery requirement for the transfer of virtual asset ownership, customers may transfer their claim against virtual asset custodians for the return of their virtual assets to the buyer. In that way, the buyer becomes the depositor against the custodian and the indirect possessor of the transferred virtual asset.

c) Summary

In sum, Taiwan's Civil Code on deposit contracts, supplemented by the VASPs Registration Regulation, stipulates clear rules for addressing the virtual asset ownership issue in cases involving virtual asset custodians. The ownership of virtual assets remains with the customers, while custodians act as depositaries, taking direct possession of the customers' virtual assets on their behalf.

To be sure, there could be other ways to characterize the relationship between virtual asset custodians and their customers. For instance, one may instead understand this relationship as a trust relationship, under which virtual asset custodians, as trustees, hold the virtual assets as trust estates. In contrast, customers' rights over the virtual assets are beneficial interests. However, Taiwanese legislators, regulators, and courts do not adopt this approach.[44]

---

[42] Taiwan Civil Code, art. 941.

[43] Taiwan Civil Code, art. 761(3).

[44] For a more detailed discussion of why Taiwan prefers not to characterize this relationship as a trust relationship: *Yueh-Ping (Alex) Yang*, Trust in a Trustless World: Crypto-Asset Custodians, Trusts and Trust Regulations in Taiwan, in "Asia-Pacific Trust Laws", Volume 2: Adaptation in Context 111 (Ying Khai Liew/Ying-Chieh Wu eds., 2022).

4. Summary

In summary, compared to some jurisdictions that struggle to characterize the private law nature of virtual assets, Taiwanese laws and court decisions have generally settled this issue. Virtual assets are treated as movable things, subject to the Civil Code's provisions governing the ownership and possession of movable things. Specifically, Taiwanese courts tend to find possession of virtual assets based on the possession of private keys and/or seed phrases, which generally aligns with the UNIDROIT Principles.

Taiwanese courts and regulators have further settled on the private law relationship involving virtual asset custodians. It is generally agreed that virtual asset custodians act as depositories and do not own the virtual assets they possess. Instead, customers own and indirectly possess the said virtual assets. Moreover, to the extent that virtual asset custodians comingle different customers' virtual assets, customers co-own the virtual assets in the custodians' custody.

IV. The Way Forward for Private Laws of Virtual Assets in Taiwan

In this part, we discuss several potential issues underlying Taiwan's private laws on virtual assets. Specifically, we revisit the appropriateness of characterizing virtual assets as movable things and applying the laws governing movable things to virtual assets. We conclude this part by proposing a ledger-based approach for identifying the ownership and control of virtual assets in Taiwan.

1. The Pitfalls of Characterizing Virtual Assets as Movable Things

Like most jurisdictions, Taiwan's Civil Code contains comprehensive provisions for movable things, including their ownership, possession, and transfer. Therefore, once courts characterize virtual assets as movable, they find abundant Civil Code provisions that may serve as the basis for their decisions. This explains why Taiwan has developed relatively straightforward private laws for the ownership and custodian relationship of virtual assets.

But perhaps Taiwanese courts erroneously characterize virtual assets as movable things in the first place. As mentioned, some Taiwanese scholars disagreed with the court's characterization of virtual assets as movable things. Their reasons are conceptual and pragmatic, including the following.

a) Conceptual Reasons: Movable Things Do Not Include Intangible Property

Some scholars disagree that virtual assets are movable things for conceptual reasons. To them, the concept of movable things under Taiwanese laws only includes tangible things and powers of nature. Therefore, movable things should not extend to other intangible properties, such as electronic records. To that extent, virtual assets shall not be characterized as movable things because they are more like a special type of electronic record and are intangible.[45]

The legislative evolution of Taiwan's Criminal Code regarding electromagnetic records is also enlightening. To address computer-related crimes, Taiwan amended the Criminal Code in 1997. It introduced the term "electromagnetic recording" to refer to records for computer processing made through the use of electronic, magnetic, optical, or other similar means. To extend the criminal offenses of larceny to the theft of electromagnetic recording, Taiwan further introduced Article 323 to acknowledge that "electricity, thermo-energy, and other energies or electromagnetic recording shall be considered movable things within the meaning of this Chapter." However, academics and practitioners raised the concern that electromagnetic records are reproducible, which is different from the characteristics of electricity, heat, or other energy that are consumed after use. Specifically, when a perpetrator "steals" an electromagnetic record and establishes their possession, they do not destroy the owner's possession of the electromagnetic record. Therefore, characterizing electromagnetic record thefts as larceny is inconsistent with the conventional understanding of larceny under the Criminal Code. To cope with the reproducibility of electromagnetic records and to improve the regulation of computer-related crime, Taiwan deleted electromagnetic records from Article 323. It added a separate Chapter 36 to stipulate the offenses against computer security.

Since virtual assets are also electromagnetic records,[46] the above legal evolution in Taiwan is relevant to the characterization of virtual assets under Taiwanese private laws. The concept of possession under laws for movable things emphasizes the possessor's control over the thing at their free will. However, in the case of virtual assets, such control or domination is not equivalent to the physical control of tangible things. Moreover, considering the position of Taiwan's Criminal Code, it is inappropriate to characterize virtual assets, which are electromagnetic records in nature, as movable things under the Civil Code while treating them differently under the Criminal Code. Therefore, thinking outside the conventional classification and legislating tailor-made rules for virtual assets might be more desirable.

---

[45] *See, e.g.*, Hsieh, *supra* note 14, at 24–25; Wang, *supra* note 19, at 82–83; Chen, *supra* note 22, at 25–26.

[46] In fact, some Taiwanese criminal courts have characterized virtual assets as electromagnetic records under the Criminal Code. *See, e.g.*, Taiwan High Court 110 Jin-Shang-No. 30 Criminal Decision (2023); Taiwan High Court 109 Jin-Shang-No. 59 Criminal Decision (2022); Taiwan High Court 109 Jin-Shang-Zhong-Su-No. 27, Criminal Decision (2022).

b) Pragmatic Reasons: Possession of Virtual Assets is not Publicly Observable

There could be further pragmatic reasons against characterizing virtual assets as movable things. Specifically, certain provisions governing movable things may not be compatible with the nature of virtual assets.

For instance, under Taiwan's Civil Code, possession serves a vital function, known as the "public notice" function. In a nutshell, as mentioned above, the possessor of a movable thing is presumed to have the legal capacity to exercise their rights over the possessed thing,[47] including the capacity to transfer the thing's ownership to a *bona fide* third party.[48] Possession of a movable thing has this public notice function because possession is a fact or status observable by the public. Therefore, *bona fide* third parties have justifications to believe that the possessor of a movable thing has the legal capacity to dispose of the movable thing and transact with the possessor based on such belief. Taiwan's Civil Code, therefore, follows suit and honors the public notice function of possession in the case of movable things.

If virtual assets are movable things, their possession should have the same public notice function mentioned above. However, virtual assets are intangible, rendering their possession status less observable. As mentioned above, their possession is determined by the possession of the wallet's private keys or seed phrases, which are merely pieces of information. Therefore, by their natures, they are not "possessed" but "known" by people. This explains why the UNIDROIT Principles more precisely determine the possession or control of virtual assets based on the "knowledge" of private keys.[49]

However, whether a person "knows" the private key or seed phrase associated with the given virtual assets is not a fact or status observable by the public. Therefore, the possession of virtual assets, determined by knowledge of associated private keys, lacks a public appearance and is, thus, unsuitable for vesting with the public notice function of possession. In other words, *bona fide* third parties have no basis for determining who knows the private key and thus possesses the given virtual asset, which increases the legal uncertainty underlying transactions involving virtual assets.

2. *Proposing a Ledger-Based Approach for the Public Notice of Virtual Assets*

Perhaps there is a more straightforward approach to designing public notices for virtual assets. While virtual assets operate differently from conventional electronic records, their operations remain based on ledgers. They differ merely in that they are based on "distributed" rather than "centralized" ledgers. Moreover,

[47] Taiwan Civil Code, art. 943(1).

[48] Taiwan Civil Code, art. 948(1).

[49] UNIDROIT Principles on Digital Assets and Private Law, 6.16 (2023).

the distributed ledgers on which virtual assets are based are often made public. Therefore, compared to the knowledge of private keys or seed phrases, which are less accessible to the public, records on distributed ledgers might be a more effective public notice approach.

Using trustworthy ledgers to serve the public notice function is not unfamiliar to Taiwan. Intangible securities, such as intangible stocks or bonds, are good examples. Companies intending to issue intangible instead of tangible securities may register their issued securities with the designated centralized securities depository enterprise,[50] which is now the Taiwan Depository and Clearing Corporation ("TDCC"). After registration, these intangible securities may be transferred or pledged through TDCC's book-entry system. In practice, TDCC maintains a consolidated ledger that documents the securities holdings of each investor and updates these records as necessary when a transaction occurs. TDCC's ledger is a classic use case of centralized ledger technology.

Taiwan's Company Act and Securities Exchange Act further acknowledge the public notice function of TDCC's centralized ledger by explicitly stipulating the ledger's authority. Traditionally, for tangible stocks or bonds, holders transfer them by endorsing the documents and transferring physical possession.[51] However, for intangible stocks or bonds registered at TDCC, Taiwan's Company Act and Securities Exchange Act explicitly stipulate that holders must transfer them, including the issuance of new ones, through TDCC's book-entry system.[52] Based on these regulations, TDCC's book entry, instead of the transfer of physical possession, becomes the prerequisite for transferring TDCC-registered intangible securities. TDCC's book entry becomes the authoritative record for identifying the holder of a given intangible security.

Perhaps virtual assets may follow the same suit. Similar to intangible securities, virtual assets' transfer and holding records are also recorded on their underlying distributed ledgers. Furthermore, these distributed ledgers, particularly those based on permissionless blockchain, could arguably be as trustworthy as the ledger centrally managed by the TDCC. More importantly, these ledgers, at least the public ones, are publicly accessible and observable. Therefore, determining or at least presuming ownership and control based on the records of a virtual asset's underlying distributed ledger may have the advantage of reducing legal uncertainty in virtual asset transactions.

To be sure, the proposed ledger-based approach is not a panacea. A key unresolved issue underlying this approach is the pseudonymous nature of distributed ledger technology. Specifically, distributed ledgers merely record the addresses used by virtual asset holders to store their virtual assets, rather than the

50 Taiwan Company Act, art. 161-2(2) and 257-2(1).

51 Taiwan Company Act, art. 164 and 260.

52 Taiwan Company Act, art. 161-2(3) and 257-2(2) ; Taiwan Securities Exchange Act, art. 43(2) and (3).

real names and identities of these holders. Therefore, if one reviews distributed ledgers, virtual asset holders are merely identifiable, not identified. To determine the actual holder, one must further investigate who controls the associated address of the given virtual assets. To that extent, the ledger-based approach may operate similarly to the current possession-based approach.[53]

That said, distributed ledger records are undeniably more available to and observable by the public than the individual knowledge of private keys or seed phrases. Therefore, distributed ledgers remain a more effective approach for public notice in identifying the rightholder of virtual assets.

3. Envisaging Future Legal Adjustments

To introduce the above ledger-based approach, Taiwan will need to reconsider whether to recharacterize virtual assets as intangible property rather than movable things. After all, under Taiwanese law, possession is the designated method of public notice for movable things, rendering the transfer of possession a prerequisite for the transfer of movable things. Characterizing virtual assets as intangible property, rather than movable things, can avoid this interpretative result and create room to introduce the ledger-based approach for the public notice function.

Moreover, Taiwan needs to enact legislation to introduce a ledger-based approach for virtual assets. After all, Taiwan is a civil law jurisdiction where courts rely heavily on statutory laws. Therefore, legislation similar to the provisions above under the Company Act or Securities Exchange Act, governing the public notice method for intangible securities, needs to be in place. Besides, virtual assets, as a new category of intangible property, also require a governing special law; otherwise, Taiwanese courts would tend to apply the existing Civil Code provisions governing movable things to virtual assets by analogy. Therefore, a special law is needed to govern the private law relationship for virtual assets.

The proposed Virtual Asset Services Act bill may serve as a starting point. Currently, the bill does not contain provisions that comprehensively govern the private law issues of virtual assets. However, the bill notably uses "property right" instead of "ownership" to refer to customers' rights over virtual assets.[54] This terminology may pave the way for re-characterizing virtual assets as intangible properties instead of movable things in Taiwan. The Virtual Asset Services Act may also lay the foundation for introducing private law provisions for

[53] In these cases, we might still need to determine the actual holder on a case-by-case basis, considering the following factors for instance: whether a person knows the private key to the virtual asset wallet, the mnemonics or the account password of the relevant account or vehicle, possesses the hardware wallet, holds or has access to the wallet records, has a virtual asset platform verification code, etc.

[54] Virtual Asset Services Act bill, art. 26.

virtual assets in the future, similar to the provisions in the Company Act and Securities Exchange Act for intangible securities.

To be sure, incorporating private law provisions into the Virtual Asset Services Act might be easier said than done. As mentioned above, the competent authority in charge of the said Act is the FSC, which tends to refrain from engaging in private law issues that are typically beyond its mandate. That said, the FSC is also the competent authority responsible for the Securities Exchange Act and the TDCC. Therefore, it is not prohibitive for the FSC to engage in private law issues when necessary. Perhaps when more private law disputes arise in Taiwan, the FSC will reconsider stipulating private law provisions in this Act.

V. Conclusion

Compared to other jurisdictions, Taiwanese courts appear to settle on characterizing virtual assets as movable things. Based on this characterization, Taiwanese courts emphasize the importance of the possession, i.e., control, of virtual assets, which plays a central role under Taiwan's movable things laws, and find control based on the possession of private keys and/or seed phrases. This understanding somewhat echoes the UNIDROIT Principles, which find the control of virtual assets based on the knowledge of private keys.

Contrary to the Taiwanese courts' understanding, this paper offers a different perspective. We argue that, as manifested by the UNIDROIT Principles, possessing private keys and/or seed phrases inherently implies knowledge of the said information. Such knowledge, however, is not available to or observable by the public, which is incompatible with the public notice function of possession under Taiwan's movable things laws.

Drawing on Taiwan's experience in legislating private law provisions for intangible securities, we propose that the public notice approach for virtual assets should be based on records of their underlying distributed ledgers. Specifically, the book entry of these ledgers shall be the prerequisite for transferring the property rights of virtual assets. In this direction, we propose that Taiwanese courts characterize virtual assets as intangible properties instead of movable things. Taiwanese legislators may further consider stipulating this ledger-based approach in the upcoming Virtual Asset Services Act. We believe that, compared to the possession of virtual assets, a somewhat illusory concept, distributed ledger records offer a more reliable public notice approach due to their enhanced objectivity, accessibility, and observability.

Furthermore, given the different characteristics between virtual assets and movable things and the experience of Taiwan's Criminal Code, we propose that virtual assets should be better characterized as intangible properties instead of movable things. On the other hand, given the ever-changing nature of emerging technologies, legislating a special law to govern the private law issues related to virtual assets could be challenging. Therefore, court interpretation is crucial for developing rules for virtual assets to form the basis for future legal amendments or enactments.

UNIDROIT*

Kadir Berk Kapancı

I. Introduction

UNIDROIT's DAPL Principles, providing soft law rules on the topic of digital assets from a contract and property law perspective were adopted in 2023, as the result of a significant three-year effort by its working group, composed of eminent scholars and practitioners.[1]

In total, the DAPL Principles consist of seven different sections (I. – Scope and Definitions, II. – Private International Law, III. – Control and Transfer, IV. – Custody, V. – Secured Transactions, VI. – Procedural Law including Enforcement, VII. – Insolvency) and nineteen principles.[2] They aim to bring legal

* This paper was completed during my research stay at UNIDROIT, between June 2024 and February 2025, supported by a long-term research leave granted by MEF University and a scholarship granted by UNIDROIT's Asian Transnational Law Centre (ATLC). In this context, I would like to express my deepest gratitude to MEF University and UNIDROIT for their valuable support. Another special thank also goes to dear Prof. Dr. Matthias Lehmann, who put me in touch with the editors.

[1] For detailed information, see *UNIDROIT,* Digital Assets and Private Law, Study LXXXII – Digital Assets and Private Law Project, <https://www.unidroit.org/work-in-progress/digital-%20assets-and-private-law/> (16 September 2025); *Asian Development Bank (ABD),* Key Aspects of UNIDROIT Principles on Digital Assets and Private Law, Cross-Border Settlement Infrastructure Forum Brief No. 4 of August 2024, <https://www.adb.org/publications/unidroit-principles-digital-assets> (16 September 2025) 3; *Teresa Rodríguez de las Heras Ballell,* Tracing the Path of the Role of Technology in UNIDROIT instruments, in: The Elgar Companion to UNIDROIT, ed. by Ben Köhler/Rishi Gulati/Thomas John (2024) 80–95, 94.

[2] For the text and commentary of the UNIDROIT Principles on Digital Assets and Pri-

certainty and provide guidance for legal transactions involving digital assets.[3] As can be seen from the section titles, the DAPL Principles only cover a specific area of private law, more precisely contracts and property law, but of course with a limited scope.[4]

On the whole, among other aspects, the "control" (of digital assets), creating a remarkable red thread between the different topics treated, is a key component under the DAPL Principles. Admittedly, it plays a major role especially in defining digital assets, attributing proprietary rights to digital assets, accepting innocent acquisition of digital assets, concluding custody greements regarding digital assets, and finally creating security rights with an erga omnes effect in digital assets. Moreover, control may also play a role in the transfer of right with the proprietary effect in the digital assets, however the DAPL Principles has not chosen to develop a clear principle on this issue, leaving it to national (domestic) legislators.[5]

The DAPL Principles generally describe the concept of control in relation to the person exercising it.[6] According to Principle 6 of the DAPL:

> "A person has 'control' of a digital asset if: / (a) subject to paragraphs (2) and (3), the digital asset, or the relevant protocol or system, confers on that person: / (i) the exclusive ability to prevent others from obtaining substantially all of the benefit from the digital asset; / (ii) the ability to obtain substantially all of the benefit from the digital asset; and / (iii) the exclusive ability to transfer the abilities in sub-paragraphs (a)(i), (a)(ii) and (a)(iii) to another person; / and (b) the digital asset, or the relevant protocols or system, allows that person to identify itself as having the abilities set out in sub-paragraph (a)."

In addition, the identification requirement is further elaborated in Principle 7 of the DAPL:

> "(1) In any proceeding in which a person's control of a digital asset is at issue: / (a) it is sufficient for that person to demonstrate that the identification requirement in Principle 6(1)(b) is satisfied in respect of the abilities specified in Principle 6(1)(a); / (b) if that person demonstrates that it has the abilities specified in Principles 6(1)(a)(i) and 6(1)(a)(iii), those abilities are presumed to be exclusive. / (2) The identification mentioned in Principle 6(1)(b) may be by a reasonable means, including (but not limited to) an identifying number,

---

vate Law, see <https://www.unidroit.org/wp-content/uploads/2024/01/Principles-on-Digital-Assets-and-Private-Law-linked-1.pdf> (16 September 2025).

[3] *UNIDROIT*, Principles on Digital Assets and Private Law: Draft for Consultation (2023) i s.; *ABD*, Key Aspects (n. 1) 4 s.

[4] See also *UNIDROIT*, Principles (n. 3) no. 1.2; *Rodrìguez de las Heras Ballell*, Role of Technology (n. 1) 94.

[5] See furthermore *UNIDROIT*, Principles (n. 3) no. 0.15; *ABD*, Key Aspects (n. 1) 7, 10; *Teresa Rodríguez de las Heras Ballell*, The Emergence of Principles and Best Practices on Digital Assets: Proprietary Rights and Enforcement, European Journal of Risk Regulation of 4 October 2024, 1–12, 6; *Frederick Rieländer*, Eigentum an digitalen Vermögenswerten – Auf dem Weg zu einem sachenrechtlichen Zuordnungsregime für Krypto-Assets, ZeuP 2024, 769–804, 789, 791.

[6] *Angelika K. Layr*, Funktionale Äquivalenz digitaler Rechtgeschäfte (2024) 188.

a cryptographic key, an office, or an account number, even if the means of identification does not indicate the name or identity of the person to be identified."

This concept of control was previously developed and used – albeit in a somewhat similar form – in the UNCITRAL's Model Law on Electronic Transferable Records (MLETR[7]), which applies to electronic transferable records.[8] Under the MLETR, an electronic transferable record may be considered equivalent to a physical document when the information contained in the latter is included in the former and a reliable method is used for identification, control and ensuring data integrity.[9]

For comparison, Article ("art.") 11 of the MLETR titled as "Control" provides:

"Where the law requires or permits the possession of a transferable document of instrument, that requirement is met with respect to an electronic transferable record if a reliable method is used: / a) to establish exclusive control of that electronic transferable record by a person; and / b) to identify that person in control. / 2. Where the law requires or permits transfer of possession of a transferable document or instrument, that requirement is met with respect to an electronic transferable record through the transfer of control over the electronic transferable record."

It should also be noted that while the MLETR focuses on the digitalization of physical documents, the DAPL Principles go one step further by applying the concept of control to digital assets that exist in purely digital form.[10]

At its core, control of digital assets under the DAPL Principles can be understood as the functional equivalent of possession of movable (tangible) objects.[11] However, it should not be regarded as entirely identical, since the legal interpretation of this concept may vary across jurisdictions.[12,13] Nevertheless, it may serve as a good starting point.

[7] For the text and commentary of the MLETR see *United Nations Commission on International Trade Law (UNCITRAL)*, UNCITRAL Model Law on Electronic Transferable Records (2018) <https://uncitral.un.org/sites/uncitral.un.org/files/media-documents/uncitral/en/mletr_ebook_e.pdf> (16 September 2025). For general information on the MLETR, see *Henry Deeb Gabriel*, The UNCITRAL Model Law on Electronic Transferable Records, Uniform Law Review 24 (2019) 261–280, 261 ss.

[8] See also *Rodrìguez de las Heras*, The Emergence of Principles (n. 5) 6; *Gabriel*, Model Law (n. 7) 273.

[9] *UNCITRAL*, Model Law (n. 7) art. 10 no. 86–88; *Rodrìguez de las Heras Ballell*, The Emergence of Principles (n. 5) 5; *Gabriel*, Model Law (n. 7) 263 s.

[10] See also *Rodrìguez de las Heras Ballell*, The Emergence of Principles (n. 5) 6; *Layr*, Funktionale Äquivalenz (n. 6) 189; *Henry Deeb Gabriel*, The Concept and Necessity of 'Control' in the Use of Emerging Technologies in Commercial Transactions, Uniform Law Review 28 (2023) 257–268, 258.

[11] For an earlier similar interpretation of the concept of possession in the context of data, under the alternative label of "*Datenbesitz*" (data possession), see *Thomas Hoeren*, Datenbesitz statt Dateneigentum?, Jusletter 11 May 2020, nos. 1 ss.

[12] *UNIDROIT*, Principles (n. 3) no. 6.2 s.; *ABD*, Key Aspects (n. 1) 10.

[13] For an interesting view asserting that "control" is a broader concept than "possession",

Let us take a general look at the concept of possession from the perspectives of Turkish[14,15] and Swiss[16] law to further compare it with the concept of control.

including the latter in its own scope, see *Gabriel,* The Concept (n. 10) 262 s. This idea seems quite convincing at its core, since in the definition of "possession" (in this regard, see the following explanations provided in the main text) it is spoken of a dominion over tangible items through "physical control".

[14] It should be noted here that Turkish Civil Law and Law of Obligations are highly influenced by Swiss Law – with minor nuances – as the Republic of Türkiye took Swiss Civil Code ("SCC") and Code of Obligations ("SCO") as a model in the beginning of 20th century, enacting its own codes. Despite the fact that the Turkish Civil Code (which entered into force in 2002; "TCC") and the Turkish Code of Obligations (which entered into force in 2012; "TCO") that are currently in force are reformed in the beginning of 21st century, the effect of Swiss law has continued to a large extent, especially in the fields of contract law and property law, thus most of the articles (of TCC and TCO) have their exact equivalents in the Swiss Law (in SCC and SCO). As a result, it can be said that Swiss Law's general principles, conceptions, doctrinal views and high court decisions have also – in a way – shaped (and continue to have an effect on) Turkish law.

[15] Under Turkish Law, there are two main legal instruments that are directly related to crypto assets, as a sub-set of digital assets within the framework of UNIDROIT DAPL Principles. These are more of public law related instruments, meaning that they have effect on the market participants, regulating mostly the qualities that they must have in order to operate and the correct behavior to be displayed. The first one (2021) is a by-law, prohibiting the usage of crypto assets in payments in exchange of provision of goods and services, that is to say that these items cannot be used to buy goods or to order services, rather they can only be bought and sold in exchange of fiat money (see <https://resmigazete.gov.tr/eskiler/2021/04/20210416-4.htm> (16 September 2025)). Of course, this by-law is related to Turkish Banking Law, and has mainly a regulatory character which foresees an administrative fine in case of any infringement. An interpretation which argues that the infringement of such a regulation will bring invalidity, taken into consideration the Turkish Constitution which is protecting freedom of contract and seeing it as a general principle that can only be restricted through the enactment of a law (statute), and not a by-law. The second one (2024) is newer, a specific law introducing additional regulations to the Turkish Capital Markets Law (see <https://resmigazete.gov.tr/eskiler/2024/07/20240702-1.htm> (16 September 2025)). Various issues such as trading platforms (exchanges), custodians, issuance of capital market instruments as crypto assets, the activities and liability regime of crypto assets service providers are regulated under its scope. Turkish Capital Markets Board, which is the relevant authority in the implementation of the said law issued two communiqués (2025) as secondary regulation, detailing the application of the additional provisions (see *Sermaye Piyasası Kurulu*, Sermaye Kripto Varlık Hizmet Sağlayıcılarına İlişkin İki Tebliğ Yayımlandı of 13 March 2025, <https://spk.gov.tr/duyurular/basin-duyurulari/2025/kripto-varlik-hizmet-saglayicilarina-iliskin-iki-teblig-yayimlandi> (16 September 2025)). As indicated, these amendments are mostly regulatory in their nature. In both of the said instruments, crypto assets are defined. However, these instruments do no bring any specific norm with regard the legal characterization of a crypto asset, or any specific rule that is related to property law.

[16] It should be noted that on 1 February 2021, the Swiss Federal Council enacted the Federal Act on the Adaptation of Federal Law to Developments in Distributed Ledger Technology. The enacted amendments concern the Swiss Code of Obligations, the Federal Intermediated Securities Act and the Federal Act on Private International Law, affecting only DLT based investment tokens, as a sub-set of "digital assets" in terms of the UNIDROIT DAPL Principles. With the said amendments, a new category of securities under the label of "ledger-based securities" (*"Registerwertrechte"/"Droits-valeurs inscrits"*), creating the possibility of issuing shares in the form of cryptographic tokens. In that sense, Swiss Law did not ap-

Under Turkish and Swiss legal systems (see art. 973 ss. TCC and art. 919 ss. SCC), possession is understood as a purely factual concept that nevertheless gives rise to certain legal consequences.[17] It essentially refers to physical control over movable or immovable (tangible/corporeal) objects and consists of two main components: *animus possidendi* (intention to possess the object) and *corpus possidendi* (physical control over the object, so that the object can be accessed, used and disposed).[18]

Both Turkish and Swiss Laws recognize collective possession, which may involve multiple possessors at the same level. These can be either *simple co-possession*, where each possessor enjoys the possession independently or *qualified co-possession*, where they can only enjoy the possession altogether at once.[19] Moreover, the law provides for *tiered/layered* possession which may involve multiple possessors in different levels, the first being called *direct possessor* who has the actual physical control but also recognize the indirect control of the second, and the second, *indirect possessor*, see art. 975 TCC).[20,21] In contrast, it is

---

proach the issue from the perspective of rights in rem. Nevertheless, within the context of this paper, in order to create a possible ground of comparison with the UNIDROIT DAPL Principles' approach, references are only given to the existing provisions of Swiss property law, which also serves a basis to the Turkish property law. (see *Federal Council of Switzerland*, Federal Council brings part of DLT bill into force, 11 December 2020, <https://www.news.admin.ch/en/nsb?id=81563> (16 September 2025)).

17 For Turkish Law see *Kemal Oğuzman/Özer Seliçi/Saibe Oktay-Özdemir,* Eşya Hukuku[22] (2020) no. 275a; *Rona Serozan,* Eşya Hukuku I[3] (2014) no. 406; *Lâle Sirmen,* Eşya Hukuku[5] (2017) 39; *Halûk Nami Nomer/Mehmet Serkan Ergüne,* Eşya Hukuku[7] (2019) nos. 67, 85; *Selâhattin Sulhi Tekinay/Sermet Akman/Halûk Burcuoğlu/Atilla Altop,* Tekinay Eşya Hukuku, Cilt I[5] (1989) 37. For Swiss Law, see *Paul Henri Steinauer,* Les droits réels – Tome I[6] (2019) nos. 176 ss.; *Jörg Schmid/Bettina Hürlimann-Kaup,* Sachenrecht[6] (2022) nos. 89 ss.; *Stephanie Hrubesch-Millauer/Barbara Graham-Siegenhalter/Vito Roberto,* Sachenrecht[5] (2017) no. 02.03.

18 For Turkish Law see *Oğuzman/Seliçi/Oktay-Özdemir,* Eşya Hukuku (n. 17) nos. 281–284; *Serozan,* Eşya Hukuku (n. 17) nos. 409–422; *Sirmen,* Eşya Hukuku (n. 17) 41 s.; *Nomer/Ergüne,* Eşya Hukuku (n. 17) no. 74; *Tekinay/Akman/Burcuoğlu/Altop,* Eşya Hukuku (n. 17) 39. For Swiss Law, see *Steinauer,* Les droits réels – Tome I (n. 17) nos. 188, 197; *Schmid/Hürlimann-Kaup,* Sachenrecht (n. 17) nos. 96 ss.; *Hrubesch-Millauer/Graham-Siegenhalter/Roberto,* Sachenrecht (n. 17) nos. 02.05, 02.14.

19 For Turkish Law see *Oğuzman/Seliçi/Oktay-Özdemir,* Eşya Hukuku (n. 17) nos. 324–328; *Serozan,* Eşya Hukuku (n. 17) nos. 467 s.; *Sirmen,* Eşya Hukuku (n. 17) 50; *Nomer/Ergüne,* Eşya Hukuku (n. 17) nos. 109 s.; *Tekinay/Akman/Burcuoğlu/Altop,* Eşya Hukuku (n. 17) 57 s. For Swiss Law, see *Steinauer,* Les droits réels – Tome I (n. 17) nos. 256–262; *Schmid/Hürlimann-Kaup,* Sachenrecht (n. 17) no. 116; *Hrubesch-Millauer/Graham-Siegenhalter/Roberto,* Sachenrecht (n. 17) no. 02.50.

20 For Turkish Law see *Oğuzman/Seliçi/Oktay-Özdemir,* Eşya Hukuku (n. 17) no. 319; *Serozan,* Eşya Hukuku (n. 17) nos. 438–442; *Sirmen,* Eşya Hukuku (n. 17) 50; *Nomer/Ergüne,* Eşya Hukuku (n. 17) nos. 100–103; *Tekinay/Akman/Burcuoğlu/Altop,* Eşya Hukuku (n. 17) 55 s. For Swiss Law, see *Steinauer,* Les droits réels – Tome I (n. 17) nos. 234–237; *Schmid/Hürlimann-Kaup,* Sachenrecht (n. 17) nos. 113 s.; *Hrubesch-Millauer/Graham-Siegenhalter/Roberto,* Sachenrecht (n. 17) nos. 02.40–02.44.

21 In terms of tiered/layered possession another existing classification is the one with re-

important to highlight the concept of *agent in possession* : This person (someone who has no possibility to take initiative on how to exercise physical control but has to follow the instructions of someone else (possessor), like in the case of an employee) is not considered as a possessor but it exercises factual control over the object on behalf of the possessor.[22] Therefore, although there are more than one person (possessor and agent in possession) when an agent in possession comes into play, it should be pointed out that there is no tiered/layered structure (of possession) in the technical sense.

Besides, the concept of possession has *different functions* in the Turkish/Swiss property law systems (some of which only applicable to movable objects):[23]

- *Publicity function* (only movables): Since rights in rem on the movable objects produce an absolute (*erga omnes*) effect against third parties, they must be apparent with the components that are perceptible from the outside, in order to be respected by them. In that regard, possession generally fulfills the publicity requirement for movables. This function is also concretely reflected in the so-called "ownership presumption" (the possessor is presumed to be the owner or the holder of the claimed (limited) right *in rem*) and in the good

gard to "originary (independent) and derivative (dependent) possession", which specifically considers the very source and background of possession attaching importance to legal situation (rights in the object of possession and their interrelation) that has given rise to such a tiered/layered scheme (see art. 974 TCC/art. 920 SCC). In that regard, this classification differs from the one of "direct and indirect possession" which is mostly concentrating on the level of intensity of the physical control on the object rather than the rights. Moreover, it should be also noted that there is an ongoing debate in the legal literature on what to be exactly understood from "originary (independent) and derivative (dependent) possession". The prevailing view asserts the following idea: In a concrete example where there is an owner, holder of a usufruct right and a lessee (who has a lease contract with the holder of the usufruct right); the owner is the originary (independent) possessor in its relation with the holder of usufruct right, while the latter is the derivative (dependent) possessor. However, in the relation of the holder of a usufruct right and lessee, the holder of a usufruct right is the originary (independent) and the lessee, the derivative (dependent) possessor. For more details in terms of Turkish Law, see *Oğuzman/Seliçi/Oktay-Özdemir,* Eşya Hukuku (n. 17) nos. 312–318; *Serozan,* Eşya Hukuku (n. 17) nos. 443–448; *Sirmen,* Eşya Hukuku (n. 17) 49 s.; *Nomer/Ergüne,* Eşya Hukuku (n. 17) nos. 91–99; *Tekinay/Akman/Burcuoğlu/Altop,* Eşya Hukuku (n. 17) 52–55. For more details in terms of Swiss Law, see *Steinauer,* Les droits réels – Tome I (n. 17) nos. 238 s.; *Schmid/Hürlimann-Kaup,* Sachenrecht (n. 17) nos. 110 s.; *Hrubesch-Millauer/Graham-Siegenhalter/Roberto,* Sachenrecht (n. 17) nos. 02.36–02.39.

[22] For Turkish Law see *Oğuzman/Seliçi/Oktay-Özdemir,* Eşya Hukuku (n. 17) no. 318; *Serozan,* Eşya Hukuku (n. 17) no. 462; *Sirmen,* Eşya Hukuku (n. 17) 51 ss.; *Nomer/Ergüne,* Eşya Hukuku (n. 17) no. 116; *Tekinay/Akman/Burcuoğlu/Altop,* Eşya Hukuku (n. 17) 61–65. For Swiss Law, see *Steinauer,* Les droits réels - Tome I (n. 17) no. 219; *Schmid/Hürlimann-Kaup,* Sachenrecht (n. 17) no. 105; *Hrubesch-Millauer/Graham-Siegenhalter/Roberto,* Sachenrecht (n. 17) no. 02.23.

[23] For Turkish Law, see *Oğuzman/Seliçi/Oktay-Özdemir,* Eşya Hukuku (n. 17) nos. 300a–300d; *Serozan,* Eşya Hukuku (n. 17) nos. 423–433; *Sirmen,* Eşya Hukuku (n. 17) 39–40; *Nomer/Ergüne,* Eşya Hukuku (n. 17) no. 64; *Tekinay/Akman/Burcuoğlu/Altop,* Eşya Hukuku (n. 17) 48–51. For Swiss Law, see *Layr,* Funktionale Äquivalenz (n. 6) 138 ss.; *Hrubesch-Millauer/Graham-Siegenhalter/Roberto,* Sachenrecht (n. 17) nos. 02.63 ss.

faith acquisitions from the possessor without the ownership (ordinarily from an entrusted possessor, in case of money and bearer instruments from any type of possessor).

- *Transfer function* (only movables): Transfer of possession of the object is considered as a tool and also a condition precedent for the transfer (more technically, as a *condicio iuris* (a requirement imposed by law for the validity) of the act of disposal/dispositive transaction) of the underlying right *in rem*.
- *Protection (offensive/defensive) function* (movables and immovables): The bare possession, even without the cover of an underlying right, provides itself the necessary legal tools, which are *(i)* direct self-protection (meaning self-defense against an attack and to some extent usage of force as a form of self-help) and *(ii)* possessory legal actions against the possible unlawful interferences of third parties. This function is also related with the aim of social peacekeeping and maintaining the stability of the existing state of legal relations *(status quo)* until the intervention of competent public authorities. To illustrate, the legitimate (real) right holder cannot seek justice on its own, on the basis of its absolute right, against a thief (wrongful possessor) who has the possession of a movable property item that it has already stolen from the right holder. Otherwise, it would be considered as an unlawful attack, as even a thief's possession is protected. The right holder should request the help of public authorities to recover the (lost) possession.
- *Right-conferring function* (movables and immovables): Gaining possession may also function as a prerequisite in the acquisition of rights *in rem*, such as in the cases of acquisition through innocent (good faith) acquisition, appropriation and acquisitive prescription.

When it comes (back) to the concept of control under the DAPL Principles, it is worth pointing out that control is also a pure factual[24] concept (it does not de-

[24] The ELI Principles on the Use of Digital Assets as Security, which also work with the concept of control, rather define it – slightly differently – in its scope as "control' in respect of a digital asset means the legal power or factual capability of any natural or legal person to deal in and/or extinguish such assets, as the case may be;". As can be seen, in these principles' conception, control may also be a legal power; apparently, they rather opt for a hybrid concept (See particularly the part of the definition where emphasis added). Nevertheless, for security interest perfection and some other purposes like in the creation of security interests (see ELI Principle 3(5)), for third party effectiveness (see ELI Principle 4(6)) and moreover to protect the interests of bona fide credit providers), it is still specifically required factual control. See furthermore *European Law Institute (ELI)*, ELI Principles on the Use of Digital Assets as Security, Report of the European Law Institute (2022) 20; *Christiane Wendehorst*, Proprietary Rights in Digital Assets and The Conflict of Laws, in: Blockchain and Private International Law, International and Comparative Business Law and Public Policy, ed. by Andrea Bonomi/Matthias Lehmann/Shaheeza Lalani (2023) 101–127, 103, fn. 7. For the ELI Principles' text and commentary see <https://www.europeanlawinstitute.eu/fileadmin/user_upload/p_eli/Publications/ELI_Principles_on_the_Use_of_Digital_Assets_as_Security.pdf> (16 September 2025).

pend to a legal conclusion)[25] and it is separate from the (possible) proprietary right in the digital asset.[26] It is also clear that control only involves a digital dominion, and not a physical one given the very nature of the digital asset.[27] As for the main components, control consists of an exclusive ability to obtain all of the substantial benefits from a digital asset and to prevent others to do the same, and it should also comprise the ability to transfer the said abilities to another person (change of control).[28] The exclusivity requirement is relaxed if the digital asset itself or the relevant protocol or the system creates restrictions or makes changes on its own,[29] in accordance with Principle 6(3) DAPL:

"(3) An ability for the purposes of sub-paragraph (1)(a) need not be exclusive if and to the extent that: (a) the digital asset, or the relevant protocol or system, limits the use of, or is programmed to make changes to, the digital asset, including change or loss of control of the digital asset; or [...]"

In addition to the said components, the person in control must be also identifiable. As mentioned above, the implication of this last requirement is further elaborated in Principle 7 DAPL. For the sake of clarification, this requirement can be fulfilled through a (asymmetric) cryptographic key[30] (such as in the case of crypto assets on a blockchain) or an account number.[31]

Furthermore, the DAPL Principles are open to a collective control structure (at the same level).[32] Indeed, according to Principle 6 (3) (b) DAPL:

"An ability for the purposes of sub-paragraph (1)(a) need not be exclusive if and to the extent that: [...]/(b) the person in control has agreed, consented to, or acquiesced in sharing that ability with one or more other persons."

So, based on the manner of benefiting from the abilities, there may be different schemes of co-control (simple/qualified).[33]

On the other hand, unlike the concept of possession under Turkish and Swiss Law, the DAPL Principles' system is closed to a tiered/layered control structure, control may only exist in a single layer (only one person in control at a time).[34]

---

[25] *Rodrìguez de las Heras Ballell,* The Emergence of Principles (n. 5) 6.

[26] See also *UNIDROIT,* Principles (n. 3) nos. 6.5, 6.9.

[27] *UNIDROIT,* Principles (n. 3) nos. 6.2.

[28] *UNIDROIT,* Principles (n. 3) no. 0.11; *ABD,* Key Aspects (n. 1) 10; *Rodrìguez de las Heras Ballell,* Role of Technology (n. 1) 94.

[29] See also *UNIDROIT,* Principles (n. 3) no. 6.11.

[30] In such an encryption scheme, it is used a pair of keys that work together: public and private keys. While public key can be shared openly like an account address, private key must be kept secret and confidential, like an account password. In the main text associated with this footnote, it is specifically referred to the public key.

[31] *Layr,* Funktionale Äquivalenz (n. 6) 188.

[32] *Rodrìguez de las Heras Ballell,* The Emergence of Principles (n. 5) 7; *Rieländer,* Eigentum an digitalen Vermögenswerten (n. 5) 791.

[33] For a specific example of shared control, see *UNIDROIT,* Principles (n. 3) no. 6.13.

[34] *ABD,* Key Aspects (n. 1) 10.

Nevertheless, there is still a place for an agent in control who is exercising the relative abilities on behalf of the actual person in control, following its instructions, similar to an agent in possession under Turkish and Swiss Law that we explained above.[35]

Moreover, under the DAPL Principles, although the exact functions of the concept of control are not clearly cited, upon careful examination, it can be said that control has – to some extent – a publicity function, since Principle 6 DAPL deems necessary the identifiability of the person in control. In addition, Principle 8 DAPL adopts the innocent acquisition rule (see also the section IV. below), which further indicates that control has a publicity function. Other than that, although it would not be contradictory or inconsistent with their entirety, there is no rule under the DAPL Principles specifically addressing a "proprietary right presumption" over control. The adoption of such a presumption may be further taken into consideration when the DAPL Principles are implemented in national (domestic) laws. However, for the sake of coherence, this point is mainly dependent on how the matter is regulated in relation to possession of movable property items in the related national (domestic) law system.

Coming to the transfer (of the right) function, there is obviously room for that, but the DAPL Principles explicitly left this issue to be regulated by national (domestic) laws.[36] This approach is fully understandable given the divergent technicalities of different law systems. It is solely indicated under the DAPL Principles' Commentary that the change of control is different than the transfer of the (possible) proprietary right over the digital asset (see also the section VII. below).[37]

Other than these, there is no mention of a possible protection function of control under the DAPL Principles, since no such protective mechanisms are directly provided by the instrument. One may open to discussion in the first place the need of deployment of protective tools related to control for digital assets. It is quite obvious that self-protection schemes would not be necessary; however, there may be room for legal actions based on the "bare" control.

Finally, (bare) control may have a right-conferring function over innocent acquisition. This function reflects only to Principe 8 DAPL on innocent acquisition (see also the section IV. below). Briefly, gaining/obtaining the (bare) control of a digital asset in the belief of acquiring the proprietary right from a transferee who is not the right holder, in good faith (which will be determined in accordance with the requirements of the relevant national (domestic) law), may result in the valid acquisition of the proprietary right in the asset.[38] The DAPL Principles do not deal with neither appropriation nor acquisitive prescription.

---

[35] *UNIDROIT,* Principles (n. 3) no. 6.6.

[36] *Layr,* Funktionale Äquivalenz (n. 6) 189.

[37] *UNIDROIT,* Principles (n. 3) nos. 2.26, 6.5.

[38] *UNIDROIT,* Principles (n. 3) no. 8.1.

As we see it, while the reason behind not considering the former – although it may be rarely the case – is easily conceivable even without any clear regulation, the latter is not even entirely apt and useful for the case of digital assets. Let us delve into more details: Appropriation may not come into play in the case of digital assets in contrast to tangible objects, as it can be imagined, possible examples would be far contrived. And for the case of acquisitive prescription, if the door to instant acquisition of the proprietary right is directly left open to the innocent acquirer without making differentiation from whom it has obtained it (which seems to be the most suitable solution, see also the section IV. below), obviously there will be no need to further deploy this – other – scheme based on good faith, which would have come into play when the first one failed and the acquirer still continues to be in good faith.

II. Control and definition of digital asset

So far, despite various attempts, there has been no unique and universally agreed-upon definition of "digital asset" in the legal realm.[39,40] It must also be acknowledged that this concept includes different sub-categories in accordance with the use, the characteristics and holding methods.[41]

The DAPL Principles, for their part, operate with their own narrower definition focusing rather on the digital assets that can be subject of control,[42] without developing a specific taxonomy, which may be challenging, if not problematic.[43] However, to fully grasp the significance of the concept of control in the definition outlined by the DAPL Principles and also to understand the reasoning behind such a choice (of a narrower definition), it is essential to first consider the digital asset in its broad sense.

Hence in the following explanations, we will firstly address digital asset in its broad sense and then proceed to its narrower sense as adopted by the DAPL Principles.[44]

In the broad sense, digital asset can be defined as identifiable data representing information with an economic value.[45] In order to further understand this

[39] In the same vein see also *Rodrìguez de las Heras Ballell,* The Emergence of Principles (n. 5) 5; *Wendehorst,* Proprietary Rights (n. 24) 102; *Asian Development Bank (ABD),* An Introduction to Digital Assets, Cross-Border Settlement Infrastructure Forum Brief No. 3 of August 2024, <https://www.adb.org/publications/introduction-digital-assets> (1 June 2025) 2.

[40] For an overview of different definition attempts, see *ABD,* An Introduction to Digital Assets (n. 39) 3 ss.

[41] See also *Rodrìguez de las Heras Ballell,* The Emergence of Principles (n. 5) 5; *ABD,* An Introduction to Digital Assets (n. 39) 10 s.

[42] *ABD,* Key Aspects (n. 1) 10.

[43] See also *ABD,* An Introduction to Digital Assets (n. 39) 5.

[44] For a similar approach see also *Layr,* Funktionale Äquivalenz (n. 6) 183 ss.

[45] *Layr,* Funktionale Äquivalenz (n. 6) 186.

definition, it is important to comprehend the sub-concepts of data and information.

If we begin with the concept of data; at its core, data may consist of a text, a picture, a video footage etc.[46] Besides data can also be the object of computer operations, that is to say, it can be digitally processed, stored and transferred.[47] Instead of a myriad of growing number of definitions which are given considering different components,[48] a far more simple one according to media theory states that data may be seen as a digital representation of information.[49] In the end, all of the definitions of data involve with the concept of information to some extent, in connection to its different levels that will be explained in the next paragraph.

If we move on to the concept of information, this can be defined in three different levels that are well interrelated: The first level is the *semantic* level, in which the focus is on the knowledge content, differently said in the meaning embedded therein. The second level pertains to the *syntactic* level, in which information is rather understood as a set of signs or symbols (like letters, words, numbers or codes) and the inter-relation of these with each other. The third and last level is the *structural* level which is directly oriented to the physical or digital embodiment of (semantic) information.[50] In my view, with relation to the definition of data, despite the existence of different views, all of the said information layers should be taken into consideration altogether, as they cannot be fully – and practically – separated from each other.

It should be further noted that, data representing information must also be identifiable and have an economic value in order to be considered as digital asset in its broad sense.[51]

If we shift our focus to the DAPL Principles' narrower definition, Principle 2(2) DAPL sets forth the subsequent one:

"'Digital asset' means an electronic record which is capable of being subject to control."[52]

---

[46] *Layr,* Funktionale Äquivalenz (n. 6) 183, 186; *Marc Amstutz,* Datenigentum, AcP 218 (2018) 439–551, 469.

[47] *Layr,* Funktionale Äquivalenz (n. 6) 183; *Amstutz,* Dateneigentum (n. 46) 469.

[48] For instance, see *Herbert Zech,* Information als Schutzgegenstand (2012) 56; *Amstutz,* Dateneigentum (n. 46) 452; *Mario Martini/Michael Kolain/Katja Neumann/Tobias Rehorst/David Wagner,* Datenhoheit, MMR-Beil 2021, 3–23, 3 s.; *Pascal Pichonnaz,* Le concept de maîtrise exclusive des données numériques: Quelques réflexions discursives, RDS/ZSR 2021, 427–451, 435 s.

[49] See also *Layr,* Funktionale Äquivalenz (n. 6) 183; *Amstutz,* Dateneigentum (n. 46) 469.

[50] *Layr,* Funktionale Äquivalenz (n. 6) 184 s.; *Martini/Kolain/Neumann/Rehorst/Wagner,* Datenhoheit (n. 48) 3; *Pichonnaz,* Le concept de maîtrise (n. 48) 435 s.

[51] *Layr,* Funktionale Äquivalenz (n. 6) 186.

[52] See and compare with the definition of the ELI Principles on the Use of Digital Assets as Security: "b. 'digital asset' means any record or representation of value that fulfils the following criteria: / (i) it is exclusively stored, displayed and administered electronically, on or through a virtual platform or database, including where it is a record or representation of a real-world, tradeable asset, and whether or not the digital asset itself is held directly or through

From this definition two key components are identified: *Electronic record* and *control.*[53] Control and its requirements under DAPL Principles are already defined above under the section I., so reference is made to this section here in order to avoid unnecessary repetitions. As for the electronic record, Principle 2(1) DAPL provides the following definition:

"'Electronic record' means information which is (i) stored in an electronic medium and (ii) capable of being retrieved."

In this definition, while electronic medium comprises any type of digital technology (for instance those that depend on electrons, hard disks utilizing magnetic fields, DVDs using physical changes in the material and so forth), it is also critical that the information stored in the medium is retrievable in a form that can be perceived. Oral communications which are not stored/preserved in a medium or information that is retained only through the human memory do not clearly enter in the related scope.[54] To sum up, not all electronic records but only the ones that are capable of being subject to control amount to digital asset in the sense of the DAPL Principles.[55]

If the definitions of digital asset in the broad sense and in the narrower sense of the DAPL Principles are compared, the following observations can be easily made: In both of the definitions, the sub-concept of information convergently recurs. Moreover, although they are not directly defined in a similar fashion, through identical components, the concepts of data and electronic record largely overlap.[56]

---

an account with an intermediary; / (ii) it is capable of being subject to a right of control, enjoyment or use, regardless of whether such rights are legally characterised as being of a proprietary, obligational or other nature; and / (iii) it is capable of being transferred from one party to another, including by way of voluntary disposition." Briefly examined, this definition is focused on three different components: *(i)* intangible nature of the asset, *(ii)* subsistence of control on the asset and *(iii)* transferability of the asset. See *ELI,* Principles (n. 24) 18 s.

[53] These components are also present in the United States of America' ("USA") Uniform Commercial Code's ("UCC") definition of "Controllable electronic records (CERs)", which is introduced as a new concept to address legal aspects of a sub-category of digital assets, with the last amendments brought in 2022. Briefly, CERs are defined under § 12 UCC, as records stored in an electronic medium that can be subjected to control (it should be further noted that control is also defined in a similar manner in the UCC, comparing with the DAPL Principles' requirements). For further details regarding these amendments on the subject of digital assets in the model code of the USA (UCC), which provide legislative guidance to state laws, see *Uniform Law Commission*, Uniform Commercial Code (UCC) 2022 Amendments to, <https://www.uniformlaws.org/viewdocument/final-act-164?CommunityKey=1457c422-ddb7-40b0-8c76-39a1991651ac> (16 September 2025). See also *ABD,* An Introduction to Digital Assets (n. 39) 6; *Spyridon V. Bazinas,* Digital Assets and Private law: Is There A Need For A Uniform Law?, Uniform Law Review 28 (2023) 381–389, 382 s.

[54] *UNIDROIT,* Principles (n. 3) no. 2.1.

[55] *UNIDROIT,* Principles (n. 3) no. 2.3.

[56] In the same vein, see also *Layr,* Funktionale Äquivalenz (n. 6) 187.

The component that is distinguishing and forming the subset of digital assets under the DAPL Principles is clearly the control. A digital asset must be controllable to fall within the scope of the DAPL Principles.[57]

It may be asked why the DAPL Principles narrowed its scope focusing only on this subset of digital assets. The answer is twofold: The (exclusive) control as a component confers to digital assets both the characteristics of rivalrousness (although not explicitly stated)[58] and exclusivity.[59,60] Upon closer examination, it is spoken of rivalrousness, when the use or consumption of a good or a resource by one person reduces its availability for others. In contrast, exclusivity concentrates on the restricted/limited access to a good or a resource only by someone or a group of individual. With the component of (exclusive) control added in the equation, this specific subset of digital assets gains a feature that makes them similar to movable property items which are making part of the objects of proprietary rights, assertable against third parties.[61] Further explanations on this matter will be given under the following section III.

To illustrate and render the subject more concrete, the DAPL Principles' digital asset definition comprises first and foremost distributed ledger technology based crypto assets (more precisely coins, fungible tokens, non-fungible tokens (NFTs)) and central bank digital currencies (CBDCs).[62] However the definition is not – certainly – only limited thereto, with its highly abstract character and the DAPL Principles' technology neutral[63] approach. In each and every inspection of a particular digital item, the existence of components must be carefully checked.

In the DAPL Principles Commentary, the social media or social networking platform individual accounts with password protection are directly left outside

---

[57] *Rieländer,* Eigentum an digitalen Vermögenswerten (n. 5) 790; *ABD,* An Introduction to Digital Assets (n. 39) 5.

[58] See also *Rieländer,* Eigentum an digitalen Vermögenswerten (n. 5) 790.

[59] With regard to exclusivity, see furthermore *UNIDROIT,* Principles (n. 3) no. 6.10.

[60] Digital assets can further be categorized in detail, in accordance with their relative degrees of rivalrousness and exclusivity: *(i)* in the first category, replication of the asset is possible (both from legal and technical perspectives) for anyone, *(ii)* in the second category, replication is still possible for anyone but the right holder's consent is further required, *(iii)* in the third, replication of the asset is only possible for right holder or the system owner, *(iv)* in the fourth, duplication is again only possible for the system owner, however there is a legally binding promise made by this one not to do it, *(v)* finally in the fifth and last category, duplication is technically out of question for anyone including the system owner. In this categorization, crypto assets on a (public and permissionless) blockchain belong the last one and provides a perfect example of digital asset in the conception of the DAPL Principles. For more details see *Wendehorst,* Proprietary Rights in Digital Assets (n. 24), 103 s.

[61] See also *Rieländer,* Eigentum an digitalen Vermögenswerten (n. 5) 790.

[62] *Rieländer,* Eigentum an digitalen Vermögenswerten (n. 5) 790; *UNIDROIT,* Principles (n. 3) nos. 2.8–2.13.

[63] On the technology neutral character of the DAPL Principles see *UNIDROIT,* Principles (n. 3) no. 0.5; *ABD,* Key Aspects (n. 1) 5.

of the definition's scope. As justification, the Commentary states that these types of platforms usually deploy licensing arrangements in their relation with users, in which they straightforwardly indicate that it is not permitted to acquire proprietary rights of these accounts. Moreover, they do not confer to their users the abilities which may possibly amount to control. Thus, these accounts cannot be treated as digital assets in the conception of the DAPL Principles.[64] The same holds also true for individual e-mail accounts which can be reached through passwords.[65]

Another – yet problematic – example presented by the Commentary that is worthy of discussion, is the case of an Excel or Word file with password protection. Insofar as the key components of the definition (electronic records that are capable of being subject to control) can be found in these password-protected files, they seem to be fitting in the scope.[66] However it should be further noted that, again as also indicated in the Commentary, the DAPL Principles are not likely to create an impact nor to have always a utility for the said type of digital assets. On the top of that, it may also lead to difficulties of application. For instance, when a such password protected file is electronically sent (through an e-mail attachment) to another person, the received file (as an electronic record) will be another new one (a copy), despite the fact that it carries the same information to which one may have access with the password created for the initial one. So, while it is still possible to argue that both of these – sent and received – files (as controllable electronic records) will enjoy the protection of proprietary rights (but also, from another point of view, these reproducible type of files do not perfectly fit in the conception of such rights, given that they are not rivalrous); it is not a case where there is an occurrence of change of control (on the initial sent file) under the conception of the DAPL Principles, because there are two different files involved in the related process. Anyways, given these problematic issues, one cannot clearly claim that the DAPL Principles are exactly designed for this type of digital assets.[67]

---

[64] *UNIDROIT,* Principles (n. 3) no. 2.16.

[65] *Rieländer,* Eigentum an digitalen Vermögenswerten (n. 5) 791.

[66] Actually, from the point of view of the categorization of digital assets (mentioned in fn. 60 above with relation to their degrees rivalrousness and exclusivity, though still controllable, this asset type can be categorized in the third category, that is the reason why there are suspicions in their inclusion in the scope of the DAPL Principles. For more details regarding this categorization, see again *Wendehorst,* Proprietary Rights in Digital Assets (n. 24) 103 s.

[67] See furthermore *UNIDROIT,* Principles (n. 3) no. 2.17.

III. Control and proprietary rights in digital assets

Principle 3 (1) DAPL states that:

"A digital asset can be subject of proprietary rights."

With this initial premise, on which all the DAPL Principles are built, it is aimed to bring legal certainty with regard to the issue whether or not digital assets can be the objects of proprietary[68] rights.[69]

The DAPL Principles base this approach on the main idea of functional equivalence.[70] As known, functional equivalence refers to the point that different concepts may be considered equivalent if they achieve the same function or outcome. Such a resemblance justifies treating the concepts equally and applying similar legal rules, despite their apparent differences.[71]

Let us embark on a demonstration activity from scratch, in order to fully comprehend the DAPL Principles' approach on the issue, which will also help us to grasp the key significance of the concept of control in that regard.

Well, so as to accept the main idea that proprietary rights can also be created in digital assets, the starting point may be the comparison of these with the classical objects of this type of rights. However, since the subject is highly controversial and is likely to show significant differences from one legal system to another, we will use as a reference point, the example of the movable property items and the rights *in rem* (with their *erga omnes* effect) that are attributed thereto under Turkish/Swiss civil law systems. This will also help us to render the explanations more concrete.

According to Turkish and Swiss Law, movable property items are subject to rights *in rem* that have absolute (*erga omnes)* effects, assertable against third parties.[72] Although the Turkish/Swiss Civil Codes do not give an explicit defi-

---

[68] The term "proprietary right" is used in a broad sense under the DAPL Principles. Its meaning comprises both *(i)* proprietary interests (*which is composed of real rights (rights in rem) to control property, good or things (direct); and the rights to control property, good or things, attributed to third parties (indirect)*), and *(ii)* rights with proprietary effects (*rights with exclusive controllable effects, whether legal or illegal, or in other words, with or without the involvement of ownership*). This way, the DAPL Principles are designed to be fit for purpose for different jurisdictions throughout the World. In this regard, see particularly *ABD,* Key Aspects (n. 1) 9. Within the context of this paper, unless stated otherwise, we mainly (and only) refer to "proprietary rights" in the meaning direct "proprietary interests".

[69] *Rodrìguez de las Heras Ballell,* The Emergence of Principles (n. 5) 7.

[70] *UNIDROIT,* Principles (n. 3) nos. 0.5, 2.20.

[71] More on this principle, see *Andreas Furrer/Luka Müller,* «Funktionale Äquivalenz» digitaler Rechtsgeschäfte – Ein tragendes Grundprinzip für die Beurteilung der Rechtsgültigkeit von Rechtsinstituten und Rechtgeshäften im schweizerischen Recht, Jusletter 18 June 2018, nos. 8–13; *Anne Veerpalu,* Functional Equivalence: An Exploration Through Shortcomings to Solutions, Baltic Journal of Law & Politics 12/2 (2019) 134–162, 139 ss.; *Layr,* Funktionale Äquivalenz (n. 6) 118.

[72] For Turkish Law, see *Oğuzman/Seliçi/Oktay-Özdemir,* Eşya Hukuku (n. 17) no. 88;

nition of a movable property item, the legal literature unanimously agree on the main characteristics thereof. In brief, save for the exceptions (see art. 762 TCC/ art. 713 SCC),[73] an object in order to be considered as a movable property must possess the characteristics of *(i)* tangibility (physical existence), *(ii)* exclusivity, *(iii)* determinability, *(iv)* limitability, *(v)* having an economic value and finally *(vi)* an independent character from personality values.[74] Moreover, although it is not clearly indicated as a separate characteristic, it can be added there that by their nature, movable property items are also rivalrous, their usage or consumption by one (or by a group) persons will inevitably lead to the unavailability for the others.

So, in order to assert that digital assets as intangibles are functional equivalents of movable (tangible) property items, it must be shown that their intrinsic characteristics, despite their differences at first sight, satisfy these requirements.

At that point, it is obvious that only the digital asset type (that we labeled in the scope of this paper as the digital assets in the narrower sense) defined under the DAPL Principles seems fit to comply therewith. After all, digital assets in the broad sense (apart from the qualified subset of the DAPL Principles) are generally non-exclusive and non-rivalrous,[75] and therefore they fall far short of satisfying the said requirements.

To render the issue even more concrete and easier to understand, a good and simple analogy (that we borrowed from *Layr*[76]) may be deployed: In this analogy, digital assets in the broad sense (apart from the qualified subset of the DAPL Principles) can be deemed similar to the flowing (drinkable) water of a certain river. Many people can benefit from the water of the river in order to relieve their thirst without any limit (for the sake of the analogy), it has also an economic value for the ones who are benefiting from it. However, the flowing water

---

Serozan, Eşya Hukuku (n. 17) no. 42; *Sirmen,* Eşya Hukuku (n. 17) no. 1; *Nomer/Ergüne,* Eşya Hukuku (n. 17) no. 4; *Tekinay/Akman/Burcuoğlu/Altop,* Eşya Hukuku (n. 17) 12. For Swiss Law, see *Steinauer,* Les droits réels – Tome I (n. 17) no. 8; *Schmid/Hürlimann-Kaup,* Sachenrecht (n. 17) no. 17; *Hrubesch-Millauer/Graham-Siegenhalter/Roberto,* Sachenrecht (n. 17) no. 01.37.

[73] For Turkish Law, see *Oğuzman/Seliçi/Oktay-Özdemir,* Eşya Hukuku (n. 17) no. 34; *Serozan,* Eşya Hukuku (n. 17) no. 280; *Sirmen,* Eşya Hukuku (n. 17) 12; *Nomer/Ergüne,* Eşya Hukuku (n. 17) no. 8; *Tekinay/Akman/Burcuoğlu/Altop,* Eşya Hukuku (n. 17) 21 s. For Swiss Law, see *Steinauer,* Les droits réels – Tome I (n. 17) nos. 119 ss.; *Schmid/Hürlimann-Kaup,* Sachenrecht (n. 17) no. 7; *Hrubesch-Millauer/Graham-Siegenhalter/Roberto,* Sachenrecht (n. 17) no. 01.12.

[74] For Turkish Law, see *Oğuzman/Seliçi/Oktay-Özdemir,* Eşya Hukuku (n. 17) no. 19; *Serozan,* Eşya Hukuku (n. 17) no. 273; *Sirmen,* Eşya Hukuku (n. 17) 4–11; *Nomer/Ergüne,* Eşya Hukuku (n. 17) nos. 28 s.; *Tekinay/Akman/Burcuoğlu/Altop,* Eşya Hukuku (n. 17) 19 ss. For Swiss Law, see *Steinauer,* Les droits réels – Tome I (n. 17) nos. 62–71; *Schmid/Hürlimann-Kaup,* Sachenrecht (n. 17) nos. 4–9; *Hrubesch-Millauer/Graham-Siegenhalter/Roberto,* Sachenrecht (n. 17) nos. 01.06 ss.

[75] In this regard see also *Pichonnaz,* Le concept de maîtrise (n. 48) 438.

[76] See also *Layr,* Funktionale Äquivalenz (n. 6) 188, 190.

of the river – as it is – cannot be seen suitable to be the possible object of a right *in rem,* since it does not generally exhibit the main characteristics of a movable property item. So is the case for the digital assets in the broad sense (apart from the qualified subset of the DAPL Principles). That being said, the situation drastically changes when the flowing water is filled up in a physical container (bottle) by a person. This time, the water inside the bottle is exclusive to this person, its content is limited/restricted (by the very contours of the container) and rivalrous (once it is consumed by this person, it will not be available for others), such as in the case of digital assets in the narrower sense of the DAPL Principles. This type of assets are suitable to be the object of proprietary rights, with their similar characteristics satisfying the said requirements.

All in all, since the main component that imparts the quality required for digital assets to be part of the qualified subset of the DAPL Principles is the concept of control, it is fair to say that this concept plays also a key role in the recognition of proprietary rights in digital assets.

IV. Control and innocent (*bona fide*) acquisition of proprietary rights in digital assets

In terms of the transfer of proprietary rights over the digital assets, the DAPL Principles essentially work with the general principle of *"Nemo dat quod non habet"* (No one can give what it does not have) or *"Nemo plus iuris ad alium transferre potest quam ipso habet"* (No one can transfer more rights to another than it already has).[77] The implication of this general principle is crystallized in Principle 9(1) DAPL:

> "Subject to Principle 8, a person can transfer only the proprietary rights that it has in a digital asset, if any, and no greater proprietary rights."

However, as directly and clearly indicated therein, the application of this principle is subject to the exception of innocent (*bona fide*) acquisition rule, conditions and effects of which are set out in Principle 8 DAPL.[78] At that point, it should be stated that here again, the concept of control has a primary role.

According to Principle 8(1) DAPL:

> "In order to qualify as an innocent acquirer, a transferee must: / (a) obtain control of a digital asset; and / (b) comply with requirements equivalent to those found in the relevant good faith acquisition and take-free rules as specified by the relevant State."

As can be seen, in the framework established by the DAPL Principles, obtaining of the control of the relevant digital asset from a transferor who is not the legit-

---

[77] *UNIDROIT,* Principles (n. 3) nos. 8.1, 9.1.

[78] *UNIDROIT,* Principles (n. 3) no. 8.1.

imate (real) right holder is a first condition, which will be added to the transferee's good faith (second condition) who is in the belief to have rightfully and validly acquired the proprietary right. The evaluation of whether the requirement of good faith is fulfilled is an issue left to national (domestic) laws, as stated in the relative principle.

The effects of innocent acquisition are further stated under Principle 8(2 and 3) DAPL:

> "(2) An innocent acquirer takes a digital asset free of conflicting proprietary rights ('proprietary claims'). / (3) No rights based on a proprietary claim relating to a digital asset can be successfully asserted against an innocent acquirer of that digital asset."

According to these rules, innocent acquirer will become the right holder on the digital assets in question at the end of the related process. Additionally, as could be anticipated, the negatively affected person (previous right holder) who has lost its digital assets cannot assert a proprietary claim against the innocent acquirer. This person will have to deal with the wrongfully acting transferor who caused this loss.[79]

To evaluate the issue from the standing point of Turkish and Swiss Law, the rules related to the *bona fide* (good faith) acquisition of rights *in rem* over movable property items through the acquisition of their possession should firstly be taken into consideration as a possible frame of comparison.

There are specific rules governing *bona fide* (good faith) acquisition for the related scheme under Turkish and Swiss Law. The general rule being *"Nemo plus iuris ad alium transferre potest quam ipso habet"*, these rules are of exceptional nature, and come into play in order the protect the reliance on appearance in legal transactions.[80] They may be divided into two different types from a temporal perspective.

- The first type of protection ("immediate/instant good faith protection") delivers immediate/instant outcomes and requires good faith only and specifically at the time of the dispositive legal transaction. Following this moment onward, subsequent bad faith does not prejudice anymore the acquired right *in rem* (*Mala fides superveniens non nocet*).[81] There are two different appearances of this type of protection:

---

[79] *UNIDROIT*, Principles (n. 3) no. 8.3.

[80] For Turkish Law, see *Serozan*, Eşya Hukuku (n. 17) no. 1132; *Sirmen*, Eşya Hukuku (n. 17) 90. For Swiss Law, see *Steinauer*, Les droits réels – Tome I (n. 17) no. 531; *Schmid/Hürlimann-Kaup*, Sachenrecht (n. 17) no. 69; *Hrubesch-Millauer/Graham-Siegenhalter/Roberto*, Sachenrecht (n. 17) no. 01.57.

[81] For Turkish Law, see *Oğuzman/Seliçi/Oktay-Özdemir*, Eşya Hukuku (n. 17) no. 517; *Serozan*, Eşya Hukuku (n. 17) no. 1137; *Sirmen*, Eşya Hukuku (n. 17) 93; *Nomer/Ergüne*, Eşya Hukuku (n. 17) no. 237. For Swiss Law, see *Steinauer*, Les droits réels – Tome I (n. 17) no. 558; *Schmid/Hürlimann-Kaup*, Sachenrecht (n. 17) no. 291.

(i) In the first one, the transferor must be an entrusted (direct) possessor to which the legitimate (real) right holder conferred the possession. To speak of an entrusted possession, the possessor must have obtained it with the consent of the right holder. If the legitimate (real) right holder intentionally leaves the possession of the movable property item to another person while it has its capacity of discernment, this person will be qualified as an entrusted possessor. A transferee in good faith (relying on the appearance created by the possession, at the time of the dispositive transaction) can acquire the ownership (or other rights *in rem)* of the movable property item from an entrusted possessor.[82] This rule generally applies to all movable property items except the ones that are subject to the second appearance (see art. 988 paragraph ("para.") 1 TCC/art. 933 para. 1 SCC).

(ii) In the second one, which applies only to bearer instruments and money, there is even no need that the transferor's possession is an entrusted one. In other words, as long as the transferee is in good faith at the time of the dispositive transaction, it does not differ how the transferor obtained (before) the possession (with or without the intention of the right holder) of the said asset, the transferee can acquire the ownership (or other rights *in rem*) in any case (see art. 990 TCC/art. 935 SCC).[83]

– The second type of protection ("protection of good faith that is spread over time") can only produce results over time and the good faith possession of the transferee who acquired the direct possession of the movable property item (for its own) in the belief to become a right holder must last without being interrupted or subjected to a lawsuit for the duration of so-called acquisitive prescription period of five years (see art. 777 para. 1 TCC/art. 728 para. 1 SCC).[84]

---

[82] For Turkish Law, see *Oğuzman/Seliçi/Oktay-Özdemir,* Eşya Hukuku (n. 17) nos. 520–527; *Serozan,* Eşya Hukuku (n. 17) no. 1135; *Sirmen,* Eşya Hukuku (n. 17) 91–94; *Nomer/Ergüne,* Eşya Hukuku (n. 17) nos. 238–248; *Tekinay/Akman/Burcuoğlu/Altop,* Eşya Hukuku (n. 17) 165 ss. For Swiss Law, see *Steinauer,* Les droits réels – Tome I (n. 17) nos. 539 ss.; *Schmid/Hürlimann-Kaup,* Sachenrecht (n. 17) nos. 297 ss.; *Hrubesch-Millauer/Graham-Siegenhalter/Roberto,* Sachenrecht (n. 17) nos. 02.217 ss.

[83] For Turkish Law, see *Oğuzman/Seliçi/Oktay-Özdemir,* Eşya Hukuku (n. 17) nos. 528 s.; *Serozan,* Eşya Hukuku (n. 17) no. 1136; *Sirmen,* Eşya Hukuku (n. 17) nos. 94 s.; *Nomer/Ergüne,* Eşya Hukuku (n. 17) nos. 249 ss.; *Tekinay/Akman/Burcuoğlu/Altop,* Eşya Hukuku (n. 17) 184 s. For Swiss Law, see *Steinauer,* Les droits réels – Tome I (n. 17) nos. 570 ss.; *Schmid/Hürlimann-Kaup,* Sachenrecht (n. 17) no. 310; *Hrubesch-Millauer/Graham-Siegenhalter/Roberto,* Sachenrecht (n. 17) nos. 02.267 ss.

[84] For Turkish Law, see *Oğuzman/Seliçi/Oktay-Özdemir,* Eşya Hukuku (n. 17) nos. 2660–2669; *Serozan,* Eşya Hukuku (n. 17) no. 1281; *Sirmen,* Eşya Hukuku (n. 17) nos. 500 s.; *Nomer/Ergüne,* Eşya Hukuku (n. 17) nos. 922–932; *Tekinay/Akman/Burcuoğlu/Altop,* Eşya Hukuku (n. 17) 184. For Swiss Law, see *Paul Henri Steinauer,* Les droits réels – Tome II[6] (2020) nos. 3142 ss.; *Schmid/Hürlimann-Kaup,* Sachenrecht (n. 17) nos. 1131 ss.; *Hrubesch-Millauer/Graham-Siegenhalter/Roberto,* Sachenrecht (n. 17) nos. 05.165 ss.

In my opinion, generally speaking in terms of Turkish and Swiss Law, among these said schemes the one with regard the instant protection of good faith in the case of bearer instruments and money seems to be the most correct and appropriate point of reference for the case of innocent acquisition of digital assets, given their similar nature to the said tangible assets.[85] That is to say, ordinarily there should be no further need to add the "entrusted" control (of the transferor) component to the relevant equation. After all, digital assets are often put into trade in distributed ledgers or other electronic networks that permit instantaneous transactions and where the actors are pseudonymous.[86] Therefore the reasonable trust of transferees must be fully protected without being subject to other restrictions.

As a matter of fact, such an approach would also be in line with the idea followed by the DAPL Principles, which becomes more or less apparent in Principle 8(4) DAPL:

"An innocent acquirer can acquire a proprietary right in a digital asset even if control of that digital asset is changed by a transferor who is acting wrongfully and has no proprietary right in the digital asset."

The Commentary of the DAPL Principles further clarifies the meaning of this part, indicating that even if the innocent acquirer may have received the digital asset in question from a thief or a hacker (that is to say, the control is obtained by this person without the will of the right holder), its qualification of being an "innocent acquirer" will not change.[87]

V. Control and custody agreements regarding digital assets

Considering that the digital assets under the scope of the DAPL Principles will often be maintained by custodians,[88] the DAPL Principles allocate an entire section consisting of four different principles (10–13) to custody agreements,[89] which holds a more particular meaning within its context.

As a matter of fact, the DAPL Principles identify specific indispensable features for these agreements which are clearly indicated under Principle 10(3 and 4) DAPL:[90]

"(3) Subject to paragraph (4), an agreement for services to a client in relation to a digital asset is a 'custody agreement' if: / (a) the service is provided in the ordinary course of the

[85] See also *UNIDROIT,* Principles (n. 3) no. 8.2.
[86] See also *UNIDROIT,* Principles (n. 3) no. 8.4.
[87] *UNIDROIT,* Principles (n. 3) no. 8.9.
[88] See explicitly *UNIDROIT,* Principles (n. 3) no. 0.17.
[89] *UNIDROIT,* Principles (n. 3) no. 10.1.
[90] See moreover *UNIDROIT,* Principles (n. 3) nos. 10.6 s.

service provider's business; / (b) the service provider is obliged to obtain (if this is not yet the case) and to maintain the digital asset for the client; and / (c) the client does not have the exclusive ability to change the control of the digital asset within the meaning of Principle 6(2). / (4) An agreement to which paragraph (3) applies is not a custody agreement if it is clear from the agreement that, if the service provider enters into an insolvency-related proceeding, the digital asset would be part of the service provider's assets available for distribution to its creditors."

In the light of these principles, the following observations can be made:

- A custody agreement is concluded between a client (to whom the service is provided) and the custodian (who provides the service). A sub-custody agreement establishes essentially a similar framework, with the only difference being that, in this structure, the "client of the sub-custodian" is the custodian who already entered into a custody agreement with its (own) client.[91]
- The custodian is required to obtain (if it is not yet obtained) and maintain digital assets as part of its regular business operations. At that point, it should also be noted that under the DAPL Principles a specific narrow meaning has also been given to the term "maintain".[92] In accordance with Principle 10(2) DAPL:

"A custodian 'maintains' a digital asset for a client if: / (a) that custodian has control of the digital asset; or / (b) that custodian enters into a custody agreement, as defined in paragraph (3), with a sub-custodian with respect to the digital asset in the circumstances set out in Principle 11(4)."

- Another point to be emphasized in this qualification is the requirement according to which, the client should not have control over the digital assets for which the custody service is provided.[93]
- Finally, there is a negative condition that must be met. Accordingly, an agreement falls outside the scope of the DAPL Principles' custody agreement qualification, if it explicitly states that in the event of service provider's insolvency, the maintained digital assets will be treated as a part of its own assets.[94]

As can be inferred from what we have outlined, the concept of control plays a key role for custody agreements.[95] In particular, it clearly manifests itself in two different ways: The first appearance is within the concept of maintaining the digital assets since in this framework either the custodian or the sub-custodian (if any) must hold the control of the digital assets. The second appearance involves, on the other hand, the requirement according to which, the client should not have control over the digital assets.

[91] *UNIDROIT,* Principles (n. 3) no. 10.3; *ABD,* Key Aspects (n. 1) 11.
[92] *UNIDROIT,* Principles (n. 3) no. 10.4.
[93] *UNIDROIT,* Principles (n. 3) no. 10.3.
[94] *UNIDROIT,* Principles (n. 3) no. 10.7.
[95] *ABD,* Key Aspects (n. 1) 11.

From the perspective of Turkish and Swiss Law, as mentioned above, the DAPL Principles stipulate specific requirements for custody agreements. No such specific requirements are provided by the existing[96] rules of Turkish Code of Obligations/Swiss Code of Obligations with regard the "contract of deposit" (a similar type of contract to the custody agreement of the DAPL Principles) which aims the safekeeping of movable property items of the depositor by the depository (see art. 561 ss. TCO/art. 472 ss. SCO). In such a contractual relationship, the depository (as the service provider) receives the direct possession of the contractual object (to be safely kept) and the depositor (as the client) continues to remain an indirect possessor (as for the meaning of "direct/indirect possession", see the section I. above).[97] Besides, under the general principle of freedom of contract, parties may conclude any type of contract (nominate or innominate) at their own discretion, respecting the limits determined by the mandatory legal provisions (see art. 26 TCO/art. 19 para. 1 SCO). Thus, in the absence of the precise rules of the DAPL Principles, under the current state of Turkish and Swiss Law, custody agreements regarding digital assets will be governed by parties' designated contractual rules, if these are not partly/fully available, by the optional provisions of the TCO/SCO with regard the contract of deposit (along with the ones regarding the mandate contracts (see art. 502 ss. TCO/art. 394 ss. SCO), which will be applied by analogy. However, there is no particular objection to be raised to such specific requirements foreseen by the DAPL Principles regarding the custody agreements, given the inherent characteristics of digital assets and the technicalities that may come to play with relation to their management by persons other than the proprietary right holder. They are perfectly adoptable by Turkish and Swiss Law. Moreover, once the concept of control and proprietary rights in digital assets are recognized and adopted by Turkish and Swiss Law, the rules of the DAPL Principles with regard to the custody agreements will perfectly and aptly complement them.

VI. Control and security rights in digital assets

The DAPL Principles devote a whole section with four different principles (14–17) to secured transactions (more specifically security rights that have the character of proprietary rights in terms of Principle 2(2) DAPL).[98] Two of these prin-

[96] Custody agreements with regard to crypto assets are partly addressed from a regulatory perspective, along with the duties and liabilities of custodians, as crypto asset service providers- under the Turkish Capital Markets Law and its secondary regulations. However, there is no clear indication as to the provisions to be applied to these agreements.

[97] For Turkish Law, see *Fikret Eren*, Borçlar Hukuku Özel Hükümler[7] (2019) 745 ss. For Swiss Law, see *Jörg Schmid/Hubert Stöckli/Frédéric Krauskopf*, OR BT Schweizerisches Obligationenrecht Besonderer Teil[3] (2021) nos. 2152 ss.

[98] See also *UNIDROIT*, Principles (n. 3) no. 14.1.

ciples are directly related to the concept of control. In a nutshell, while Principle 15 DAPL takes into consideration as a method for achieving third-party effectiveness, Principle 16 DAPL is related to the priority of security rights where control plays an important role. It should be noted that the DAPL Principles do not directly deal with the domestic conceptions of security rights, rather they just intend to provide adequate protection to secured creditors. In that regard, rules regarding third party effectiveness and priority of security rights in digital assets are particularly recognized.[99]

If we go further into the details of the subject, Principle 15 DAPL stipulates as follows:

"A security right in a digital asset can be made effective against third parties by control of the digital asset if one of the following requirements is fulfilled: / (a) the secured creditor has control of the digital asset as defined in Principle 6; or / (b) a custodian maintains the digital asset for the secured creditor as set out in Principle 10(2)."

Under this principle, control is recognized as one the methods for third-party effectiveness, along with other possible alternative methods, such as the registration in a specific registry established for the secured transactions under the relevant national (domestic) law.[100] In order to achieve this effect, either the control must be conferred to the secured creditor for whom the security is provided or the digital asset must be maintained by a custodian *(that is to say, either it will directly hold the control of the digital or the control will be held by a sub-custodian on its behalf in accordance with the Principle 10(2) DAPL)* for the secured creditor.[101] In the first option where the control is conferred to secured creditor, it is further worth mentioning that the secured creditor may be the sole person holding the control or it may constitute a party of a "shared control" scheme.[102] Either way, the security provider will be excluded from control. Of course, if the security provider is one of the parties of the shared control scheme, then this scheme must foresee a qualified co-control structure (see also the section I. above), in a way to ensure that it cannot enjoy control solely by itself.

The use of control as a third-party effectiveness method has ties with and closely resembles to the legal situation of the so-called "possessory pledge" of movable property items under Turkish and Swiss Law (see art. 939 ss. TCC/ art. 884 ss. SCC).[103] Possessory pledge provides the secured creditor with a lim-

---

[99] See also *UNIDROIT,* Principles (n. 3) no. 15.3.

[100] *UNIDROIT,* Principles (n. 3) no. 15.1.

[101] *UNIDROIT,* Principles (n. 3) no. 15.6.

[102] *UNIDROIT,* Principles (n. 3) no. 15.6.

[103] For Turkish Law, see *Oğuzman/Seliçi/Oktay-Özdemir,* Eşya Hukuku (n. 17) nos. 3657 ss.; *Serozan,* Eşya Hukuku (n. 17) nos. 1458 ss.; *Sirmen,* Eşya Hukuku (n. 17) 659 ss.; *Nomer/Ergüne,* Eşya Hukuku (n. 17) nos. 1218 ss. For Swiss Law, see *Paul Henri Steinauer,* Les droits réels – Tome III[4] (2012) nos. 3125 ss.; *Schmid/Hürlimann-Kaup,* Sachenrecht (n. 17) nos. 1884 ss.; *Hrubesch-Millauer/Graham-Siegenhalter/Roberto,* Sachenrecht (n. 17) nos. 10.40 ss.

ited right *in rem* securing its claim towards a debtor and grants it the authority to liquidate the pledged movable property item if its claim is not fulfilled by the debtor. In its structure, the pledge is strictly possessory which allows its publicity as a right *in rem,* and avoids possible false impressions by third parties regarding the actual creditworthiness of the pledgor (which may be the debtor or a third party).[104] In order to establish this right, it must be made certain the pledgor is not the sole and direct possessor of the pledged movable.[105] This is ordinarily carried out by the transfer of the (direct) possession to the pledgee (secured creditor), but it can also be handled through its transfer to a third party or through the creation of a qualified co-possession scheme (in particular, if the pledgor remains in the co-possession structure).[106] However, since this strictly possessory establishment structure has strong impracticability and disadvantages (especially for the debtor/third party security provider who cannot use the pledged property item and sometimes also for the secured creditor who keeps the item in its possession), it is not perceived as a popular or ideal type of security in the legal practice, other movable security schemes involving the entry (registration) to a specific registry instead of the transfer of the possession are more favored.[107] Nevertheless, from the perspective of digital assets, the situation is entirely different. Unlike the (possessory) pledge of movables, the transfer of control does not involve such impracticability and disadvantages, given the very abstract/intangible nature of the digital assets. Therefore, this method of creating third party effectiveness through the transfer of control is more likely to demonstrate popularity in comparison to its "old cousin", which provides the said effectiveness through the transfer of possession.

[104] For Turkish Law, see *Oğuzman/Seliçi/Oktay-Özdemir,* Eşya Hukuku (n. 17) no. 3669; *Serozan,* Eşya Hukuku (n. 17) no. 1459; *Sirmen,* Eşya Hukuku (n. 17) 660; *Nomer/Ergüne,* Eşya Hukuku (n. 17) no. 1220. For Swiss Law, see *Steinauer,* Les droits réels – Tome III (n. 103) no. 3150; *Schmid/Hürlimann-Kaup,* Sachenrecht (n. 17) no. 1874; *Hrubesch-Millauer/Graham-Siegenhalter/Roberto,* Sachenrecht (n. 17) no. 10.58.

[105] For Turkish Law, see *Oğuzman/Seliçi/Oktay-Özdemir,* Eşya Hukuku (n. 17) no. 3669; *Serozan,* Eşya Hukuku (n. 17) no. 1462; *Sirmen,* Eşya Hukuku (n. 17) 660. For Swiss Law, see *Steinauer,* Les droits réels – Tome III (n. 103) no. 3150; *Schmid/Hürlimann-Kaup,* Sachenrecht (n. 17) no. 1890; *Hrubesch-Millauer/Graham-Siegenhalter/Roberto,* Sachenrecht (n. 17) no. 10.55, 10.57.

[106] For Turkish Law, see *Oğuzman/Seliçi/Oktay-Özdemir,* Eşya Hukuku (n. 17) no. 3670; *Serozan,* Eşya Hukuku (n. 17) nos. 1459 ss.; *Sirmen,* Eşya Hukuku (n. 17) 660 s.; *Nomer/Ergüne,* Eşya Hukuku (n. 17) no. 1221. For Swiss Law, see *Steinauer,* Les droits réels – Tome III (n. 103) no. 3151; *Schmid/Hürlimann-Kaup,* Sachenrecht (n. 17) no. 1890; *Hrubesch-Millauer/Graham-Siegenhalter/Roberto,* Sachenrecht (n. 17) no. 10.55.

[107] As a result, non-possessory (subject to registration to a certain registry) pledge is also accepted under Turkish/Swiss Laws for certain movable property items. For Turkish Law, see *Oğuzman/Seliçi/Oktay-Özdemir,* Eşya Hukuku (n. 17) nos. 3588 ss.; *Serozan,* Eşya Hukuku (n. 17) nos. 1467 ss.; *Sirmen,* Eşya Hukuku (n. 17) 649 ss.; *Nomer/Ergüne,* Eşya Hukuku (n. 17) nos. 1178 ss. For Swiss Law, see *Steinauer,* Les droits réels – Tome III (n. 103) nos. 3200 ss.; *Schmid/Hürlimann-Kaup,* Sachenrecht (n. 17) no. 1869a; *Hrubesch-Millauer/Graham-Siegenhalter/Roberto,* Sachenrecht (n. 17) nos. 10.15 s.

Continuing on, if Principle 16 DAPL is closely looked at, it will be seen that it states the following:

"A security right in a digital asset that is made effective against third parties by control in accordance with Principle 15 has priority over a security right in the digital asset that is made effective against third parties only by a method other than control."

This principle addresses a particular situation in which there is a plurality of secured creditors and in the provision of the said security rights other methods of establishment are also deployed, apart the one related to control. It suggests that the security right established by way of control must have priority over the competing others whether or not they are established earlier in time.[108]

From the perspective of Turkish and Swiss Law, the approach of Principle 16 DAPL clearly conflicts with the general principle of "*Prior in tempore, potior in iure*" (Earlier in time, stronger in right) indicating that priority of rights *in rem* are generally determined in accordance with their date of establishment (see also art. 948 TCC/art. 893 SCC).[109] Of course, its acceptance as an exceptional rule of priority for the case of digital assets will be a pure legal policy preference but it is highly likely to create confusion with its possible controversial consequences affecting the related – other – parties' (stakeholders') interests. Therefore, such an acceptance in these law systems is open to discussion and requires strong justification.

On its own, Principle 16 DAPL's Commentary presents different reasons for the justification of this preference:[110]

- First of all, a secured creditor who takes extra steps for the establishment of a security right demonstrates more reliance on the encumbered asset, therefore priority must be given to such a creditor. Under some national (domestic) laws, there are similar situations, such as the case where a secured creditor takes possession of a negotiable instrument have priority over a security rights established through registration.
- Secondly, if such a priority principle is not accepted, a creditor which would like to obtain a security right established through control would be indirectly forced to conduct an exhausting investigation in different registries and this will be quite impracticable.
- Thirdly, this principle aligns with the so-called "margin-lending" practice where creditors may extend to their clients to acquire assets and expect to have a priority over rights earlier established through registration.

---

108 *UNIDROIT,* Principles (n. 3) no. 16.1.

109 For Turkish Law, see *Oğuzman/Seliçi/Oktay-Özdemir,* Eşya Hukuku (n. 17) no. 2709; *Serozan,* Eşya Hukuku (n. 17) no. 268; *Sirmen,* Eşya Hukuku (n. 17) 509; *Nomer/Ergüne,* Eşya Hukuku (n. 17) no. 1212. For Swiss Law, see *Steinauer,* Les droits réels – Tome III (n. 103) no. 3172; *Schmid/Hürlimann-Kaup,* Sachenrecht (n. 17) no. 77; *Hrubesch-Millauer/Graham-Siegenhalter/Roberto,* Sachenrecht (n. 17) nos. 01.80, 07.34.

110 For more details, see *UNIDROIT,* Principles (n. 3) no. 16.2.

- Fourthly, this principle is aligning the priority position with the position on default and thus creating an incentive for the secured creditors.
- Finally, the implication of this principle is also in line with international instruments such as UNCITRAL Model Law on Secured Transactions and UNIDROIT Convention on Substantive Rules for Intermediated Securities (Geneva Securities Convention).

These justifications may constitute a basis for the implementation of this principle in national (domestic) laws, however their persuasiveness is debatable and to be further evaluated in accordance with the existing legal principles in the relevant national (domestic) law.

In my opinion, from the Turkish and Swiss Laws' perspective, the implementation of such a principle would be quite challenging, since it is blatantly in conflict with the general understanding of the priority relations of rights *in rem* between themselves, which based in the above mentioned *prior in tempore* general principle. Besides, the reasons for its justification enumerated in the DAPL Principles' Commentary do not seem fully convincing from the standing point of Turkish and Swiss Law, though maybe the situation in other national (domestic) laws would differ. This DAPL principle is of course raising concerns for the situation of the secured creditor who obtained a security right through control in relation to others, however doing that, it creates an imbalance undermining the interests of the other secured creditors which are worthy of protection as well. My simple recommendation on the issue for Turkish and Swiss Law would be the following: Instead of adopting such an approach, the legal framework may be designed to exclude from the outset the availability of any method of establishing a security right in a digital asset other than control. In that way, the problem of priority between the established security rights would be resolved in advance even before it even arises.[111]

VII. Change of control and its relation with the transfer of proprietary rights in digital assets

Change of control and transfer of proprietary rights in digital assets are separately defined under different parts of the DAPL Principles (6(2) and 1(5)). Other than that, there is no clear indication of to what extent the control must be conferred along with the transfer of the right as required under the DAPL Principles, the choice is directly left to national (domestic) laws.[112]

[111] See and compare Turkish Capital Markets Law's (Art. 35/B para. 10) approach to the issue in domestic matters. This provision stipulates that security rights in digital assets cannot be established in accordance with the Law on Movable Pledge in Commercial Transactions, that is to say through an entry that will be made to the relevant register.

[112] *UNIDROIT,* Principles (n. 3) no. 2.23.

To begin with, on change of control, Principle 6(2) DAPL states the following:

"A 'change of control' means a transfer of the abilities in sub-paragraph (1)(a) to another person, and includes the replacement, modification, destruction, cancellation, or elimination of a digital asset, and the resulting and corresponding derivative creation of a new digital asset (a 'resulting digital asset') which is subject to the control of another person."

Clearly this definition comprises different factual situations which may affect the control of the digital asset such as: *(i)* replacement, *(ii)* modification, *(iii)* destruction, *(iv)* cancellation, *(v)* elimination of digital assets and furthermore *(vi)* resulting and corresponding derivative creation of new ones.[113]

Moving forward, transfer of proprietary rights is referred to in Principle 1(5) DAPL:

"In relation to a transfer of a digital asset: / (a) 'transfer' of a digital asset means the change of a proprietary right in the digital asset from one person to another person; / (b) the term 'transfer' includes the acquisition of a proprietary right in a resulting digital asset; / (c) 'transferor' means a person that initiates a transfer, and 'transferee' means a person to which a proprietary right is transferred; / (d) the term 'transfer' includes the grant of a security right in favour of a secured creditor, and 'transferee' includes a secured creditor."

Once again, it must be said that under the DAPL Principles, most probably out of practical reasons, transfer of digital assets may also carry different meanings beyond *(i)* the usual situation of the change of proprietary right from one person to another, such as: *(ii)* the acquisition of proprietary right in a resulting digital asset, and *(iii)* the granting of a security right in a digital asset.[114]

If we compare these two occurrences (*change of control v. transfer of proprietary right*): the first one involves certain changing circumstances that are purely factual in their nature, whereas the second one pertains to right-based changes that are of legal nature. Apparently, they may be eventually combined but it is not always necessary. That is to say, to the contrary there may be cases in which they are not associated at all. For instance, one may obtain control but not the proprietary right in the digital asset, such as in the case of the custodian in custody agreements (under the DAPL Principles).[115] In such a setting (see also the section V. above), although the control must be passed – ordinarily – to the custodian (custody service provider), the proprietary right in the digital assets stays with the client (to whom the custody service is provided).

At that point, it will not be incorrect to mention that there is a significant parallelism with the "other couple" of transfer of possession and ownership (as

[113] For specific examples of change of control, see *UNIDROIT*, Principles (n. 3) nos. 6.14–6.16.

[114] *UNIDROIT*, Principles (n. 3) nos. 2.24 s.

[115] *UNIDROIT*, Principles (n. 3) no. 2.23.

a right *in rem*) of movables under Turkish and Swiss Law. This is the ordinary consequence of the understanding of the DAPL Principles, according to which the control is seen as a functional equivalent of the possession. Within this framework, in both of these legal systems, transfer of possession does not necessarily result in the transfer of ownership, it may happen on its own, like in the case of the lessee to whom the (direct) possession of the leased item is conferred by the lessor as a usual consequence of the lease agreement. However, in order that the second one (transfer of ownership) occurs, the first one (transfer of possession) is a general requirement, as it is the indispensable/inseparable component of the act of disposal (dispositive transaction) which conveys the right *in rem*. To further clarify, in order to effectuate the transfer of the ownership of a movable property item, the transfer of its possession must accompany the related (dispositive) transaction (see art. 763 para. 1 TCC/art. 714 para. 1 SCC).[116] The logic behind such a setting is that since the ownership as a right *in rem* is assertable to third parties, a possible transfer thereof must be recognizable from the outside by them, under the light of the well-respected publicity principle.[117]

VIII. Conclusion

In the last decade, digital assets, as a new class of assets have gained increasing popularity and triggered an important transformation in the global financial landscape. With the value they create, digital assets are more and more stored for investment purposes and used in transactional exchanges. While traditional markets are trying to adapt themselves to the ongoing rapid transition, there is also a growing perception of risk which is mostly due to the existing legal uncertainty, particularly with regard to the legal characterization of this type of asset from the perspective of property law.

In this regard, the UNIDROIT DAPL Principles as a soft law instrument for international harmonization, have provided an important guidance on some issues with regard to contract and property laws. Briefly, the DAPL Principles

---

[116] For Turkish Law, see *Oğuzman/Seliçi/Oktay-Özdemir*, Eşya Hukuku (n. 17) no. 2581; *Serozan*, Eşya Hukuku (n. 17) no. 95; *Sirmen*, Eşya Hukuku (n. 17) 34, 39; *Nomer/Ergüne*, Eşya Hukuku (n. 17) no. 41; *Tekinay/Akman/Burcuoğlu/Altop*, Eşya Hukuku (n. 17) 49. For Swiss Law, see *Steinauer*, Les droits réels – Tome II (n. 84) no. 2965; *Schmid/Hürlimann-Kaup*, Sachenrecht (n. 17) no. 65; *Hrubesch-Millauer/Graham-Siegenhalter/Roberto*, Sachenrecht (n. 17) no. 02.66.

[117] For Turkish Law, see *Oğuzman/Seliçi/Oktay-Özdemir*, Eşya Hukuku (n. 17) no. 268; *Serozan*, Eşya Hukuku (n. 17) nos. 231, 478; *Sirmen*, Eşya Hukuku (n. 17) 34; *Nomer/Ergüne*, Eşya Hukuku (n. 17) no. 41; *Tekinay/Akman/Burcuoğlu/Altop*, Eşya Hukuku (n. 17) 24. For Swiss Law, see *Steinauer*, Les droits réels – Tome II (n. 84) no. 2965; *Schmid/Hürlimann-Kaup*, Sachenrecht (n. 17) no. 65; *Hrubesch-Millauer/Graham-Siegenhalter/Roberto*, Sachenrecht (n. 17) no. 02.63.

suggest that digital assets with certain intrinsic characteristics can be subject to proprietary rights, used as security, held by custodians and acquired by innocent acquisition.

This is exactly where the concept of control comes into play. As a pure factual concept and a functional equivalent of the classic property law concept of possession, it gives the digital assets the characteristics of rivalrousness and exclusivity, enabling the possibility of equating digital assets with the classical items of property. In various respects, this concept has a key role within the scope of the DAPL Principles, therefore its correct and proper understanding is of utmost importance. Accordingly, this paper aims to provide that, placing the concept of control at its center.

Nevertheless, it must also be kept in mind that as a soft law instrument, the DAPL Principles offer only a good starting point, and the rest of the burden of creating legal certainty is left on the shoulders of the national (domestic) legislators. After all, it can only be the national (domestic) legislators who can create the expected harmonization effect by aptly adopting these principles, without of course compromising the technicalities of their own legal systems.

United Kingdom

Marcus Bagnall and Benjamin Towell

I. Introduction

English law's distinctive methodology – one that combines precedent, analogy, and incremental judicial development – equips it well to address novel forms of wealth and commerce. Distributed ledger technology (DLT) based digital assets, including crypto-tokens and non-fungible tokens (NFTs), test that methodology in a contemporary setting. The question is whether these *digital objects* can be integrated into the classical taxonomy of personal property, which has been historically divided into tangible property being *things in possession*, while intangible property (such as debts, shares or intellectual property) are *things in action*.[1]

Crypto-tokens typically exist in distributed, digital forms with no physical manifestation and function through consensus mechanisms operating across a network of participants.[2] English courts have shown a growing willingness to

[1] *Colonial Bank v. Whinney* [1886] 11 App Cas 426 (HL) 440, per Lord Blackburn; see also *Frederick Pollock/Robert Samuel Wright*, An Essay on Possession in the Common Law (1888) 1.

[2] *UK Jurisdiction Taskforce*, in: Legal Statement on Cryptoassets and Smart Contracts of November 2019, <https://technation.io/wp-content/uploads/2019/11/6.6056_JO_Cryptocurrencies_Statement_FINAL_WEB_111119-1.pdf> (16 September 2025) nos. 27–32; *United*

treat such crypto-tokens as property – although neither strictly *choses in possession* nor *in action* – owing to the tokens' distinct "rivalrousness", definability, and the practical possibility of exercising control.[3] Judges have granted proprietary and freezing injunctions to restrain misappropriated crypto-tokens on the basis that they are indeed property.[4] However, lingering uncertainty remains over the precise conceptual underpinnings: are these tokens best subsumed under an expanded conception of *choses in action*, or should they stand as a discrete *tertium quid* of personal property?[5]

Against this backdrop, the Law Commission has proposed clarifying that certain intangible, data-based assets or rather *data objects* – particularly crypto-tokens – should be recognised as a novel category of property. The Commission's recent *Digital Assets* reports[6] and subsequent draft legislation proposed by the UK Government[7] aim to confirm (without exhaustively defining) that such data objects can indeed be the subject of property rights.

II. Traditional categories of personal property and the advent of crypto-tokens

English law has long distinguished between *things in possession* and *things in action*; the former encompassing corporeal movables susceptible to direct physical control,[8] while the latter describing intangible property enforceable by legal action[9] such as debts, shares, and other intangible claims involving enforceable rights against specific legally recognised obligors.[10]

Yet digital objects manifesting from modern DLTs have enabled crypto-tokens (e.g. Bitcoin and ETH) that are rivalrous and do not rely on a central

---

Kingdom Law Commission, Digital Assets: Final Report of 27 June 2023, Law Com No. 412, no. 1.19.

[3] *AA v. Persons Unknown* [2019] EWHC 3556 (Comm) 55–61; *Ion Science Ltd v. Persons Unknown* (28 January 2022, unreported, High Court); Fetch.ai *Ltd v. Persons Unknown* [2021] EWHC 2254 (Comm) 12.

[4] *Ion Science Ltd v. Persons Unknown* (n. 3); Fetch.ai *Ltd v. Persons Unknown* (n. 3); see also *Piroozzadeh v. Persons Unknown* [2023] EWHC 1024 (Ch) (granting freezing relief).

[5] See *United Kingdom Law Commission,* Digital Assets (n. 2) ch. 3, on debate regarding crypto-tokens and property categorisation.

[6] *United Kingdom Law Commission,* Digital Assets (n. 2); *United Kingdom Law Commission*, Digital Assets as personal property: Supplemental report and draft Bill of 29 July 2024, Law Com No. 416.

[7] *United Kingdom Law Commission,* Digital Assets as personal property (n. 6).

[8] *Michael Bridge/Louise Gullifer/Kelvin Low/Gerard McMeel,* The Law of Personal Property[3] (2021) nos. 1-003–1-005; see also *Colonial Bank v. Whinney* (n. 1).

[9] *Hugh Beale,* Chitty on Contracts[33] (2018) no. 32–013.

[10] *Pollock/Wright,* An Essay (n. 1) 3. Pure information historically fell outside property rights altogether: *Your Response Ltd v. Datateam Business Media Ltd* [2014] EWCA Civ 281 [2015] QB 41, 33.

obligor or a conventional contract right[11] and challenge the traditional paradigm: crypto-tokens neither neatly fit into a tangible *thing in possession* nor are they a simple *in personam* claim akin to a debt.[12]

In its 2019 Legal Statement on Cryptoassets and Smart Contracts, the UK Jurisdiction Taskforce concluded that cryptoassets can exhibit the "proprietary" hallmarks (definability, exclusivity, control) necessary for recognition as property under English law.[13]

Armstrong DLW GmbH v. Winnington Networks Ltd – although dealing with intangible carbon emission allowances rather than crypto-tokens – was the first English decision recognising that intangible items not readily classified as *choses in action* could attract proprietary remedies.[14] *AA v. Persons Unknown* confirmed that Bitcoin could be classified as property even though it lacks tangibility and does not conform neatly to *choses in action*.[15] The High Court has issued freezing and disclosure orders over misappropriated tokens, such as in *Ion Science Ltd v. Persons Unknown* and Fetch.ai *Ltd v. Persons Unknown*.[16] In *Tulip Trading Ltd v. Van der Laan*, the Court of Appeal accepted that Bitcoin can be "property" under English law, though it left unresolved whether open-source protocol developers might owe fiduciary or tortious duties to owners who lose private keys.[17]

Nevertheless, courts have not comprehensively articulated whether crypto-tokens should simply be *things in action* or if they are *tertium quid*, rather noting that crypto-tokens can be treated as property without definitively resolving the deeper question of *how*.[18] *OBG Ltd v. Allan* makes clear that intangible property is ordinarily not protected by the tort of conversion,[19] creating potential gaps where crypto-tokens are destroyed rather than misappropriated.

---

[11] *Satoshi Nakamoto*, Bitcoin: A Peer-to-Peer Electronic Cash System (2008), <https://bitcoin.org/bitcoin.pdf> (16 September 2025).

[12] *United Kingdom Law Commission*, Digital Assets (n. 2) no. 1.19; *David Fox*, It's Virtually Money, in: Cryptocurrencies in Public and Private Law, ed. by David Fox/Sarah Green (2019).

[13] *UK Jurisdiction Taskforce*, Legal Statement (n. 2) nos. 27–32.

[14] *Armstrong DLW GmbH v. Winnington Networks Ltd* [2012] EWHC 10 (Ch), [2013] Ch 156, 86, 93.

[15] *AA v. Persons Unknown* (n. 3).

[16] *Ion Science Ltd v. Persons Unknown* (n. 3); Fetch.ai *Ltd v. Persons Unknown* (n. 3).

[17] *Tulip Trading v. Van der Laan* [2023] EWCA Civ 83.

[18] "Cryptoassets are [...] to be treated in principle as property": *UK Jurisdiction Taskforce*, Legal Statement (n. 2) no. 15. See, for example, *AA v. Persons Unknown* (n. 3); *Ion Science Ltd v. Persons Unknown* (n. 3); Fetch.ai *Ltd v. Persons Unknown* (n. 3) endorsing the UKJT's approach.

[19] *OBG Ltd v. Allan* [2007] UKHL 21, [2008] 1 AC 1, 11–13.

III. A *tertium quid*: data objects

The Law Commission's Digital Assets reports recommend recognising certain "data objects" as a third category of personal property – neither physically possessable nor co-extensive with purely *in personam* rights. "Data objects" can be defined by four main criteria:[20]

- *Independence from persons* – The object's existence does not depend solely on a person's legal right or on centralised control.
- *Rivalrousness* – One party's use or control necessarily excludes another's concurrent use.
- *Definability or identifiability* – The object can be discerned and identified.
- *Excludability* – The holder can exclude others from using or benefiting from it.

Crypto-tokens often exemplify these traits: they cannot be "double-spent," they are individually identifiable on a ledger, and the ability to transfer or "spend" them depends on cryptographic keys rather than any state-based obligor.[21] The defining characteristic is rivalrousness without a central obligor in which *control* is the practical lynchpin of ownership.[22]

Following consultations,[23] the UK Government introduced the Property *(Digital Assets etc) Bill* (the "Bill"), which seeks to confirm that "things" (including those of a digital or electronic nature) are not disqualified from being objects of personal property rights simply because they fail the *Colonial Bank v. Whinney* categories.[24] The Bill is intended to address uncertainties regarding whether digital assets are property without perfectly fitting within the *choses in action* category,[25] leaving courts free to elaborate on criteria for recognising them as a *tertium quid* and to make any adjustments to existing frameworks to better accommodate them.[26]

Historically, English law has demonstrated flexibility in assimilating novel asset classes via incremental judicial development.[27] Accordingly, and under the banner of "technology neutralism" and preserving flexibility, the proposed Bill does not prescribe what "things" will be considered *tertium quid*, nor does it address any surrounding complexities.[28] Instead, it places continued reliance

---

[20] *United Kingdom Law Commission*, Digital Assets (n. 2) ch. 3.

[21] *United Kingdom Law Commission*, Digital Assets (n. 2) nos. 3.56–3.70.

[22] *United Kingdom Law Commission*, Digital Assets (n. 2) nos. 3.56–3.70; *Tulip Trading v. Van der Laan* (n. 17) 24.

[23] *United Kingdom Law Commission*, Digital Assets as personal property (n. 6).

[24] *Colonial Bank v. Whinney* (n. 1).

[25] *United Kingdom Law Commission*, Digital Assets (n. 2) nos. 1.46–1.48.

[26] *United Kingdom Law Commission*, Digital Assets (n. 2) nos. 8.80–8.161.

[27] *Armstrong DLW GmbH v. Winnington Networks Ltd* (n. 14) 84; see also *Michael Howard/John Knott/John Kimbell*, Foreign Currency: Claims, Judgments and Damages (2016) 40.

[28] *United Kingdom Law Commission*, Digital Assets as personal property (n. 6) ch. 3.

upon judicial adaptation of established doctrines as new fact patterns emerge,[29] and while the adaptability of the common law is often lauded, it can present real commercial risks – particularly when potential litigants face years of uncertainty pending an appellate decision.

The need for the Bill is far from settled. At a basic level, the Bill leaves open the very question of defining the bounds of *tertium quid*, which many expected would be the clarity that the Bill needed to bring. While it may be helpful to know that market leading crypto-tokens such as Bitcoin and ETH are likely *tertium quid*, this challenge is magnified by the sheer diversity of blockchain consensus protocols governing crypto-tokens, each of which may have different methods for recording or validating ownership or transactions on-chain. Without explicit statutory guidance, businesses and investors may hesitate to engage with digital assets under English law, fearing unpredictable outcomes.

The complexity of crypto-token involving offerings also mean complex legal implications considering the many areas they intersect with – property, contract, trusts, insolvency, conflict of laws, to name a few – meaning that mere piecemeal reform risks inconsistencies.[30] Moreover, such a short confirmatory Bill leaves unresolved crucial areas such as negotiability, good-faith acquisition, and conversion-like tortious liability for interference with cryptoassets,[31] enforceability of security over tokens, or cross-border conflicts.[32] These remain unsettled, and deeper statutory guidance may eventually be necessary. Meanwhile, the inevitable gradual, and no doubt necessarily significant, extension of existing legal doctrines to *tertium quid* will likely give rise to parallel discussions about whether (and how) existing statutory regimes and legal principles can (or should) be adapted to a property category that did not exist when those regimes were developed. Cross-border enforceability inherent in non-centralised networks would also render any purely domestic solution necessarily incomplete.[33] For instance, a UK investor's crypto-tokens hacked and transferred offshore raises immediate questions about which jurisdiction's property laws or enforcement mechanisms apply, for which the Bill's minimal framework offers no direct guidance on cross-border conflict rules or asset recovery.

On a practical level, while common law solutions may often prove robust, the pace of DLT innovation may also unfortunately outstrip the courts' judicial capacity to provide comprehensive and timely guidance. This view supports the creation of a single, comprehensive "Digital Assets Code" which could instead

[29] *United Kingdom Law Commission*, Digital Assets (n. 2) nos. 1.48, 3.82–3.83.

[30] *United Kingdom Law Commission*, Digital Assets (n. 2) nos. 1.46–1.48.

[31] *United Kingdom Law Commission*, Digital Assets (n. 2) nos. 3.81–3.83; *Crypto Council for Innovation*, Response to the Law Commission's Digital Assets Consultation Paper of 3 February 2023, <https://media.cryptoforinnovation.org/2023/02/UK-Law-Commission-CCI-digital-assets-letter-final.pdf> (16 September 2025) 2.

[32] *Crypto Council for Innovation*, Response (n. 31) 2, 6–7.

[33] *United Kingdom Law Commission*, Digital Assets (n. 2) nos. 3.25–3.30.

provide greater commercial certainty[34] and unify rules on issues such as transfer, security, finality, and good-faith purchase and enhance commercial predictability.[35] On the other hand, an overly detailed code might "freeze" the law around the technology as it currently stands, and have a stifling effect on adaptation.

From a law reform perspective, it is also noteworthy to consider why amongst all the observed harms and challenges posed by crypto-tokens (such as fraud, intangibles destruction, tortious lacunae or other systemic risks) that the focus of the Law Commission and advocacy in the UK has been on the somewhat more academic debate regarding personal property classification. While this clarification should in theory underpin better legal tools for addressing wrongdoing, the Bill itself leaves unaddressed core concerns such as consumer protections, custodial obligations, cross-border enforcement, and fraud-prevention measures. For instance, the Bill does not propose statutory rules on how exchanges must segregate customer assets – one of the key flashpoints particularly in more recent high-profile exchange insolvencies. Nor does it introduce explicit frameworks for good-faith purchasers or for finality in on-chain transactions. There is an apparent disconnect between public announcements about the Bill spurring "responsible innovation" against the Bill's narrow focus on categorising assets, leaving legislative inertia in precisely those areas where real-world harms seem more acute.

IV. Key challenges: Control, transfer, security, torts, and regulatory arbitrage

1. Factual control and title

a) Crypto-key control as ownership

Blockchain-driven non-centralisation and distributed networks illustrate how cryptographic control can redefine property ownership. In a genuinely distributed network with no central authority (e.g., a distributed ride-hailing or content platform), possession of private keys may be the primary mode of asserting ownership. Yet, the 'non-centralised' nature also complicates recourse for lost or compromised keys, raising novel questions about whether any entity (e.g.,

[34] See, for example, the revised § 12 UCC in the United States of America: *Uniform Law Commission*, Uniform Commercial Code (UCC) 2022 Amendments to, <https://www.uniformlaws.org/viewdocument/final-act-164?CommunityKey=1457c422-ddb7-40b0-8c76-39a1991651ac> (16 September 2025).

[35] It could, for instance, designate "controllable electronic records" or their English-law equivalent, define how they transfer, and confer holder-in-due-course protections for payment-type tokens, akin to revised § 12 UCC: *Crypto Council for Innovation*, Response (n. 31) 6–9.

developers or node operators) can or should alter the ledger to restore an owner's access. This echoes the analysis in blockchain-driven network contexts, where disaggregation and distribution often outpace established legal frameworks for asserting or restoring ownership rights.

As DLTs typically make transfer contingent on cryptographic authority, it can be argued that the party holding the private key effectively "owns" the token, merging factual control with legal ownership. Crypto-tokens subsist and operate within a distributed ledger, validated by a consensus mechanism rather than state action.[36] In contrast, a chose in action typically requires a state-based remedy to exist at all (for instance, a debt obligor's duty to pay) and arises from legally cognisable rights, not mere cryptographic capabilities.[37] For example, in-game items on centralised servers are unlikely to satisfy the 'independence from persons or systems' criteria as their existence depends entirely on the developer's ongoing platform control.

However, even if a person controls a token by possessing the private key, from a practical standpoint, if that person has irretrievably lost their key, retaining legal "title" in name only may offer scant utility unless a court can order ledger alterations (as *Tulip Trading* argued could be required of developers).[38] The legal uncertainty surrounding distributed control models further complicates ownership claims, especially where multi-signature arrangements or smart contract-based governance structures are involved.

b) "Extinguishment/re-creation" vs. persistent transfer

Another flashpoint is whether an on-chain transfer truly "destroys" one token entry and "creates" a new token, or whether the transferred token remains the "same" property from one owner to the next. Some technology-based analyses suggest that, on-chain, the ledger extinguishes one token and creates a new entry upon every transfer.[39] Crypto-tokens could be better viewed as "the right to have the ledger updated" (i.e., a persistent claim that travels across each on-chain transfer) instead of discrete intangible items that might be "destroyed and re-created" with every ledger update.[40] In jurisdictions like New Zealand, courts have likewise characterised tokens as intangible property that can be the subject of a trust, focusing on the ledger's functional reality; the data strings themselves (for instance, a ledger entry) do not alone define the property, rather,

---

[36] *United Kingdom Law Commission,* Digital Assets (n. 2) nos. 3.60–3.62.

[37] *Alastair Hudson*, Equity and Trusts[9] (2022) 95–99.

[38] *Tulip Trading v. Van der Laan* (n. 17) 71–72.

[39] *United Kingdom Law Commission,* Digital Assets (n. 2) nos. 9.25–9.30, on the "extinguishment" or "persistence" debate.

[40] *Crypto Council for Innovation*, Response (n. 31) 5–6.

it is the combination of data with the system's active operation and consensus acceptance that yields a discrete, digitally manifested object of property.[41]

If courts adopt the "extinguishment and re-creation" theory, proprietary remedies like proprietary restitution or following/tracing of the "old" token may be imperilled.[42] It may come down to a case-by-case examination of how a particular ledger's consensus mechanism functions rather than reflexively assuming each transaction destroys the "old" token,[43] noting that treating the crypto-token as persisting (albeit under new control) may better align with conventional ideas of title continuity.

Decentralised finance (DeFi), which broadly replicates lending, swaps, and other complex financial arrangements through processes involving self-executing smart contracts, provides ample examples of these challenges. Code-based "flash loans" or multi-signature escrow structures do not neatly map onto conventional definitions of mortgages or charges.[44] Similarly, bridging protocols that "lock and mint" crypto-tokens across chains raise questions about whether the user's property right to the original tokens persists or is replaced by a new token on the secondary chain.[45] While courts have begun grappling with these matters, no authoritative framework yet exists in English law.[46]

2. *Crypto-tokens as secured assets and negotiable instruments*

As crypto-tokens become more widely used and important in the economy, then so too will be the need for commercial parties to take or grant security over them. Traditional instruments (such as mortgages, charges, assignments) presuppose that intangible property is either a chose in action or "documentary intangibles" that can be pledged by physical delivery (e.g. bills of exchange).[47] Crypto-tokens do not fit neatly into this description. Certain crypto-tokens (particularly stablecoins) might also qualify as "cash" or "financial instruments" for purposes of the Financial Collateral Arrangements (No. 2) Regulations 2003 ("FCARs"[48]), but the broader question of how to perfect security over intangible data objects remains unresolved.[49]

---

[41] *Ruscoe v. Cryptopia Ltd (in liquidation)* [2020] NZHC 728, 47.

[42] *United Kingdom Law Commission,* Digital Assets (n. 2) no. 9.25.

[43] *United Kingdom Law Commission,* Digital Assets (n. 2), nos. 9.32–9.34.

[44] *Fabian Schär,* Decentralized Finance: On Blockchain- and Smart Contract-Based Financial Markets of 4 February 2021, <https://ssrn.com/abstract=3571335> (16 September 2025) 5.

[45] *United Kingdom Law Commission,* Digital Assets (n. 2) ch. 7; *Tai Mo Shan Ltd v. Oazo Apps Ltd* (6 March 2023, unreported, EWHC).

[46] *United Kingdom Law Commission,* Digital Assets (n. 2) no. 5.33.

[47] *Bridge/Gullifer/Low/McMeel,* Personal Property (n. 8) nos. 2-012–2-018.

[48] Financial Collateral Arrangements (No. 2) Regulations 2003 (SI 2003/3226) (FCARs).

[49] *United Kingdom Law Commission,* Digital Assets (n. 2) nos. 8.80–8.161.

The FCARs permit streamlined enforcement for collateral over "financial instruments" in the possession or control of the secured party,[50] yet intangible crypto-tokens can be held through multi-signature or smart-contract arrangements where no single party has unilateral negative control.[51] Courts have stated that intangible collateral must be under a legally cognisable power to exclude the grantor (e.g. the lender's enforceable right), which pure factual "control" of cryptographic keys may or may not satisfy.[52] Not only does this hamper mainstream banks or other lenders from securing their risk with on-chain tokens, it also reveals deeper structural misalignment between intangible data-coded "ownership" and intangible property law's existing frameworks. It is difficult to see a way through without a broader statutory scheme allowing security to attach where crypto-tokens are "provided" as collateral, recognising the diverse ways in which crypto-lending and DeFi structures operate.[53]

Another analogy can be seen in the Bills of Exchange Act 1882 and dematerialised securities regimes, under which bills of exchange and bearer shares can be treated like physical chattels for the purpose of transfer and *nemo dat* exceptions.[54] Intangible property in principle cannot be pledged by physical delivery, but commercial demands for swift, final transactions prompt calls for something like "negotiability", ensuring good-faith acquirers take free from prior defects of title (subject to possible fraud). A question arises whether this approach should apply to certain crypto-tokens functioning like money (e.g. payment tokens) to enjoy "negotiable instrument" status, enabling good-faith acquirers to take free from prior defects.[55]

Adopting such a blanket displacement of *nemo dat quod non habet* however may be problematic as many tokens (e.g. NFTs, utility access tokens, etc) are not primarily used as money or payment and instead serve non-monetary functions, making a single "negotiability" regime potentially overbroad.[56] Such a rule may also inadvertently enable fraudulent transfers, given the pseudonymous nature of many crypto-token holdings.

3. *Tort of wrongful interference for crypto-assets?*

Even though English courts recognise crypto-tokens as 'property,' the unavailability of a property-based tort remedy underscores that mere classification is

[50] Regs. 3–4 FCARs 2003.

[51] *Re Lehman Brothers International (Europe) (in administration)* [2012] EWHC 2997 (Ch) 131–136.

[52] *Re Lehman Brothers International (Europe) (in administration)* [2012] EWHC 2997 (Ch) 131–136; *Private Equity Insurance Group SIA v. Swedbank AS* [2017] EWHC 115 (Comm) 55.

[53] *United Kingdom Law Commission,* Digital Assets (n. 2) nos. 8.94–8.95.

[54] Bills of Exchange Act (BoEA) 1882 (c. 61).

[55] ss. 29–30 BoEA 1882.

[56] *United Kingdom Law Commission,* Digital Assets (n. 2) nos. 6.113–6.134.

only half the battle. In what is arguably the most pressing lacuna for digital objects, the tort of conversion under English law applies only to tangible chattels (and certain documentary intangibles), not to intangible assets.[57] Hence, if a defendant "burns" or irretrievably destroys a crypto-token so that it no longer exists or cannot be traced, the victim may lack a direct property-based remedy, as proprietary restitution or unjust enrichment cannot apply if the defendant is not enriched or does not retain the token or a traceable substitute.[58] *OBG Ltd v. Allan* underscores that intangible property is excluded from conversion, forcing victims to rely on personal or equitable claims, which may be inadequate if the defendant was never enriched.[59]

To address this lacuna, courts might need to develop a new *wrongful interference* tort for intangible data objects by analogy with conversion.[60] Alternatively, a statutory extension of the Torts (Interference with Goods) Act 1977 could expressly include intangible digital assets, or a standalone statutory framework introduced, to address burning or permanently lost crypto-tokens.[61] While the common law could be left to develop solutions on a case-by-case basis, further widespread hacking and "token-burning" might move up demands to create an enforceable remedy requiring statutory intervention, where absent such a cause of action claimants may be left with only personal claims in fraud or other equitable recourse which will likely be inadequate in the circumstances.

For example, consider a situation where a hacker gains access to a decentralised wallet and uses a smart contract "burn" function to irreversibly destroy a supply of NFTs or fungible tokens. The hacker neither retains the tokens nor enriches themself; they simply obliterate them on-chain. Under current law, the victim would struggle to bring a claim in conversion (which is limited to tangible goods) or in unjust enrichment (as the defendant has not gained). If no new wrongful interference tort or statutory extension of the Torts (Interference with Goods) Act exists, the owner's only recourse might be a personal claim in fraud or trespass to goods by analogy – both of which are ill-fitting and might fail to capture the specific harm of digital asset destruction.

A new statutory or common law cause of action would allow owners to sue specifically for the intangible property right that was violated by the act of burning, thereby ensuring a direct remedy for the destruction (and not merely misappropriation) of tokens. Such a development could be analogous to how the law historically evolved to protect certain categories of intangible property

57 *OBG Ltd v. Allan* (n. 19).

58 *United Kingdom Law Commission,* Digital Assets (n. 2) nos. 9.64–9.79; and see *OBG Ltd v. Allan* (n. 19).

59 *United Kingdom Law Commission,* Digital Assets (n. 2) no. 9.63.

60 *United Kingdom Law Commission,* Digital Assets (n. 2) nos. 9.64–9.83.

61 See, for example, § 12 UCC which could offer a model that can be adapted into English law.

(e.g., documentary intangibles) via extended forms of conversion. In the absence of legislative guidance, however, any recognition of this new tort would likely rely on judicial willingness to draw creative analogies, a process that may prove uncertain and time-consuming given the limited case law to date.

Indeed, a further complication arises from the anonymity or pseudonymity that often characterises cryptotoken transactions. Even if a new tort of wrongful interference were recognised, identifying and serving the defendant can prove challenging when the misappropriator employs sophisticated obfuscation tools or transacts across multiple jurisdictions.[62] In such scenarios, victims might be forced to rely on novel investigative orders (e.g. Norwich Pharmacal[63] orders against exchanges or node operators) simply to discover the defendant's identity.[64] While courts have shown a willingness to grant interim relief in these contexts, the lack of a clear legislative framework on intangible conversion or a wrongful interference tort can leave victims with no straightforward cause of action when the token is irretrievably destroyed rather than merely transferred or retained.

4. Custody, intermediation, and trusts

Many practical scenarios involve "custody," where an exchange or custodian holds private crypto-keys on behalf of users. The question then arises whether the customer retains a proprietary interest (e.g. via a trust) or merely an unsecured contractual claim in respect of those crypto-tokens or a personal claim to an account balance.[65] Custodial arrangements for crypto-tokens in the context of DeFi introduce particular complexities, as unlike traditional custody arrangements where a single custodian may hold assets on behalf of a client, DeFi platforms rely on smart contracts to manage user assets. These arrangements raise questions about the extent to which smart contracts can replicate fiduciary duties traditionally associated with trustees.[66]

In Ruscoe v. Cryptopia Ltd (in liquidation) and *Re Gatecoin Ltd (in liquidation)*, courts in New Zealand and Hong Kong respectively held that where the exchange held crypto-token keys, absent a trust or an established proprietary mechanism, users are treated as unsecured creditors, however provided little

---

[62] *UNIDROIT*, UNIDROIT Principles on Digital Assets and Private Law: Draft for Consultation (2023), no. 8.4, noting the complexities of multijurisdictional claims.

[63] *Norwich Pharmacal Co. & Others v. Customs and Excise Commissioners* [1974] AC 133 (HL).

[64] *Bloomsbury Publishing Group Plc v. News Group Newspapers Ltd* [2003] EWHC 1205 (Ch).

[65] *United Kingdom Law Commission,* Digital Assets (n. 2) ch. 7; *Quoine Pte Ltd v. B2C2 Ltd* [2020] SGCA(I) 02.

[66] *United Kingdom Law Commission,* Digital Assets (n. 2) nos. 3.70–3.85.

guidance on whether smart contracts can similarly establish trust relationships.[67]

English law is similarly capable of recognising a trust in intangible assets, provided the necessary intention and subject matter exist. However, given the pseudonymous, distributed nature of many crypto-tokens, it may be difficult for beneficiaries to identify their crypto-tokens on-chain during an insolvency.[68] Statutory rules may be needed to clarify custody relationships to ensure that client tokens remain ring-fenced from the custodian's estate.[69]

5. Regulatory arbitrage

The English approach, while respecting the open-ended and fast-evolving nature of digital technologies, might inadvertently shift market participants to more prescriptive – but more certain – regimes abroad. As industry waits for test cases and appeals in order to establish authoritative guidance, large-scale investment commitments are likely to be put on hold until fundamental issues are clarified.[70] By contrast, other common law jurisdictions such as Singapore, Australia, and New Zealand have not adopted specific legislation to create new property classifications but appear content to extend existing classifications to accommodate crypto-tokens.[71]

An explicit statutory acknowledgment of data objects as tertium quid would reinforce market confidence and spur investment in blockchainbased enterprises. Codifying only the broad – as is the case with the Bill – may generate uneven litigation outcomes, allow harms to continue in the meantime and encourage forum shopping. Major crypto-market participants – seeking predictability in areas like finality of settlement or the legal validity of on-chain security arrangements – may simply choose jurisdictions with detailed statutory schemes. Singapore and Switzerland for example have either enacted or proposed (relatively) more detailed frameworks for certain forms of tokenisation, which may prove more attractive for large institutional actors who value certainty.[72] An English parallel in a different domain is the (historically) piecemeal approach to netting and set-off, where lack of early comprehensive legislation led some fi-

---

[67] *Ruscoe v. Cryptopia Ltd (in liquidation)* [2020] NZHC 728, 43–47; *Re Gatecoin Ltd (in liquidation)* [2023] HKCFI 914.

[68] *United Kingdom Law Commission,* Digital Assets (n. 2) nos. 7.54, 7.115.

[69] *Crypto Council for Innovation*, Response (n. 31) 10–13.

[70] *United Kingdom Law Commission,* Digital Assets (n. 2) nos. 6.77–6.89.

[71] See, for example, *B2C2 Ltd v. Quoine Pte Ltd* [2020] SGCA(I) 2; *Ruscoe v. Cryptopia Ltd* (n. 41); see also *Re Blockchain Tech Pty Ltd* [2024] VSC 690.

[72] See, for example, the Swiss Federal Act on the Adaptation of Federal Law to Developments in Distributed Ledger Technology of 25 September 2020, BBl 2020, 7801–7820; Singaporean Payment Services Act (No. 2) 2019. Switzerland, via its Federal Act on the Adaptation of Federal Law to Developments in Distributed Ledger Technology, offers bespoke rules on ledger-based securities and clear procedures for enforcement.

nancial actors to prefer jurisdictions that provided explicit statutory frameworks, forcing Parliament eventually to codify netting provisions in the Companies Act reforms and in industry-specific regulations. A modern parallel can be seen in telecom infrastructure, where operators experiment with open RAN solutions or DLT-based identity management to reduce costs and enhance coverage. Disaggregated architectures introduce cross-border challenges in securing hardware and software from multiple vendors, each subject to different regulatory requirements. Without clear property or governance framework for these on-chain components, operators will move highly valuable R&D or deployment to other jurisdictions with more predictable rules.

6. *Other challenges*

Protocol-level events (e.g. forks or protocol upgrades) can copy or alter token states, complicating continuity of ownership. *Tulip Trading* also raised the (still undecided) possibility that protocol developers might owe duties to token owners if they alone can modify the underlying software.[73] Although that case was discontinued, such arguments illustrate how recognising crypto-tokens as property leads to broader questions about the responsibilities of those with power over the ledger. Forks and protocol upgrades also raise issues of ownership continuity and governance, particularly in distributed networks where liability and accountability are often unclear. These challenges may indicate a need for further legal clarity to address such complexities.

Another emerging concern is "governance token" models, where individuals holding certain tokens possess the right to vote on or otherwise influence fundamental protocol changes. These models blur the line between property rights and participatory rights akin to corporate shareholding. In a hard fork scenario, rival factions may each claim legitimacy for their chain, spawning parallel governance tokens. From a legal standpoint, it remains unsettled which faction holds the "authentic" version of the original token, particularly when both blockchains continue to operate concurrently and claim wide user adoption, raising questions regarding continuity of ownership and the enforceability of rights across forks.[74] Courts may need to address whether property rights extend to tokens on both chains or whether a statutory framework is required to define the parameters of ownership during such events.[75] Decentralised govern-

[73] *Tulip Trading v. Van der Laan* (n. 17) 71–72.

[74] *Zellweger-Gutknecht,* Developing the Right Regulatory Regime for Cryptocurrencies and other Value Data, in: Cryptocurrencies in Public and Private Law, ed. by David Fox/Sarah Green (2019) ch. 4, discussing forkrelated complexities and potential solutions; compare *Self v. Self* [1962] 1 WLR 1711, where identity of an entity hinged on continuity of membership.

[75] *Tulip Trading v. Van der Laan* (n. 17), raising questions about developer obligations during protocol changes; *Kelvin F. K. Low*, Cryptoassets and the Renaissance of the *tertium*

ance tokens, particularly in content or infrastructure projects, also risk creating an environment where no single actor is accountable. This could prove fatal for consumer protection or transaction certainty if regulatory frameworks do not evolve accordingly.

It is also important to note the emerging body of "soft law" guidance being produced by international organisations. The UNIDROIT Working Group on Digital Assets, for instance, has tabled several principles intended to promote global harmonisation in areas such as custody, secured transactions, and conflict of laws.[76] Although not binding, these transnational standards may influence how English courts and legislators view the Bill's adequacy and whether further reforms are necessary to keep England and Wales competitive as a governing law hub. Similarly, the Financial Stability Board (FSB) has suggested that digitalasset systems may require heightened coordination among regulators, adding a supranational dimension to questions of property classification and enforceability.[77]

The Law Commission's focus on acknowledging digital objects as *tertium quid*, while in theory providing conceptual clarity, falls short of offering practical solutions to pressing real-world questions regarding crypto-tokens – such as how forks, governance tokens, and developer duties should be governed. For example, DLT-based ride-hailing or music streaming platforms illustrate the complexities of crypto-token governance. Such platforms rely on distributed participants who collectively validate transactions and set usage terms via smart contracts. The absence of a single control authority means that proprietary or governance tokens could shift ownership entitlements purely through on-chain mechanics. In practice, this can blur lines between property, licensing, and contractual rights, especially if local regulations or consumer protection laws demand a central actor responsible for disputes. These real-world use cases underscore how a purely distributed system tests the adequacy of existing property constructs and highlights the tension between efficiency gains from non-centralisation and the potential legal vacuum that arises when central control is entirely absent.

By leaving these complexities to judicial development, there is a risk of significant delay before the courts can articulate consistent rules on key obligations, rights, and even on the parameters of what digital object qualify as *tertium quid*.

---

quid?, in: Research *Handbook* on Property Law and Theory, ed. by Chris Bevan (2024) 463–478.

[76] See the Principles contained in *UNIDROIT*, Principles (n. 62) reflecting a thorough cross-jurisdictional analysis of proprietary interests in digital assets while specifically emphasising crossborder uniformity.

[77] *FSB*, Regulation, Supervision and Oversight of CryptoAsset Activities and Markets, Consultative document of 11 October 2022, <https://www.fsb.org/uploads/P111022-3.pdf> (16 September 2025) recs. 2–4 and in particular rec. 3, recognising the risk of regulatory fragmentation and conflicts of law.

This incremental approach may, in the interim, undermine commercial certainty and impede more robust adoption of cryptoassets under English law.

V. Conclusion

English law has, to date, pragmatically recognised crypto-tokens as property capable of attracting proprietary relief, with first-instance courts granting interim remedies on the basis that these intangible, ledger-based crypto-tokens exhibit rivalrousness without a central obligor. This ongoing recognition tracks the Law Commission's proposals for a third category of personal property – "data objects" – within which crypto-tokens would sit.

Although the proposed Bill would confirm that digital objects are not excluded from property status merely because they do not neatly fit traditional categories, it stops short of creating a comprehensive digital assets code. Its underlying premise is that English courts can and should adapt existing principles incrementally through real-world disputes, preserving flexibility. Whether a more detailed statutory code is needed remains an open question, with pressing issues remaining outside the Bill's scope. While the English approach aligns with centuries of common law evolution, digital assets clearly push the boundaries more than many past innovations. If Parliament enacts only the current minimalist Bill, the courts must continue to lead; nonetheless, the adequacy of judge-made law – without tailored legislative support – could be tested as crypto-tokens become ever more pervasive.

Hence, the English position remains a double-edged sword. By relying on the adaptability of common law, the UK risks ceding their current advantage to more forward-thinking regimes that offer more prescriptive and therefore more predictable frameworks. As blockchain-driven non-centralisation spreads into more parts of the economy – finance, marketplaces, content distribution, and infrastructure – the need for clear statutory guidance on property and control of digital assets intensifies.

United States

Lewis Cohen, Linda Jeng, and Rebecca Simmons[1]

I. Introduction

In the 16 years since the invention of bitcoin in 2008, the market value of blockchain-based digital assets, or "crypto assets," has grown exponentially.[2] By Sep-

[1] Disclaimer: All views and conclusions expressed in this chapter are those of the authors alone. The authors are grateful for the generous insights shared by several industry experts during the preparation of this chapter. In particular, we thank Thomas (TJ) Connolly, Andreas Freund, Jayasudha Jayakumaran, Jameson Lopp, John McCarthy, and Tatyana Vinogradova, for taking the time to share their technical expertise. Their perspectives greatly enriched our understanding of technical practices and industry approaches to crypto wallet security, key management and control of crypto assets. The authors also thank Edwin Smith and Charles Mooney, Jr. for their valuable comments provided during the peer review of this chapter. Lastly, we thank K. Patricia Ramirez Sanchez, Amil Sumaiya Malik, and Patrick M. Gaughan for their research and editorial support.

[2] *CoinmarketCap*, Cryptocurrency Historical Data Snapshot, <https://coinmarketcap.com/currencies/bitcoin/> (September 19, 2025).

tember 19, 2025, the market for bitcoin alone reached US$2.2 trillion[3]. However, in light of the novel nature of crypto assets, their status under US private commercial law has been uncertain. Acknowledging this legal gap and the growing market in crypto assets, the American Law Institute and the Uniform Law Commission began work in 2019 to amend the Uniform Commercial Code ("UCC") to more clearly define property rights in crypto assets.[4] This work led to a public consultation in 2021, and to the publication of the "2022 Amendments to the Uniform Commercial Code-Emerging Technologies" (the "2022 Amendments")[5]. The 2022 Amendments are now going through the process of being adopted into law by individual states.[6]

The 2022 Amendments added a new article, Article 12, to the UCC, defining a new type of property – "controllable electronic records" ("CERs").[7] This category would be expected to cover most of what are commonly referred to as, "crypto assets". Article 12 adapts concepts used in other articles of the UCC – particularly Article 3, relating to negotiable instruments, and Article 8, relating to investment securities – to electronic records that meet the specified criteria.

As the new term suggests, the ability to "control" an electronic record, such as a crypto asset, is a key element in distinguishing electronic records that are subject to Article 12 from those that simply serve to record information or that fall under other commercial law regimes. Article 12 establishes a particular meaning of the term "control" for this purpose: a person has control of a CER if the person has (1) the power to avail itself of the benefits of the electronic record, the exclusive power to prevent others from enjoying those benefits, and the exclusive power to transfer control of the electronic record, and (2) the abil-

---

[3] *CoinmarketCap*, Crypto Market Overview, <https://coinmarketcap.com/charts/> (September 19, 2025).

[4] The UCC is a "uniform" code that establishes a consistent framework for commercial law across the United States. The UCC is drafted by the American Law Institute and the Uniform Law Commission. Each state can choose whether to adopt the UCC or any amendment to the UCC in the form proposed by Uniform Law Commission/American Law Institute or make changes specifically relevant to that state. In some cases, states elect not to enact model statutes and continue to rely upon pre-existing law. The American Law Institute and Uniform Law Commission periodically revise the UCC to account for developments in commercial law. Currently, all 50 states, the District of Columbia, Puerto Rico and the U.S. Virgin Islands have adopted the UCC, with some variants.

[5] *Uniform Law Commission (ULC),* Uniform Commercial Code Amendments (2022), <https://www.uniformlaws.org/committees/community-home?CommunityKey=1457c422-ddb7-40b0-8c76-39a1991651ac> (September 19, 2025).

[6] As of August 2025, thirty-two states have enacted the 2022 Amendments. *ULC*, 2022 Amendments (n. 5).

[7] Article 12 governs not only crypto assets like cryptocurrencies and non-fungible tokens, but also "controllable accounts" and "controllable payment intangibles," which are subject to many of the same rules under Article 12. However, given the focus of this volume, this chapter will focus only on assets that are "controllable electronic records" as defined under UCC Article 12.

ity to identify itself as having those powers and rights.[8] Article 12 does not seek to define what the benefits of a CER may be, how the power to enjoy those benefits may be exercised, or the technological means used to identify oneself or to transfer control of the CER.[9] (See Part II for a discussion of Article 12).

As this definition of "control" indicates, Article 12 was drafted in functional terms, in a manner intended to be technology neutral, adaptable as the mechanisms for holding and transferring digital assets evolve over time. However, Article 12 was drafted when "wallets" (that is, software or hardware that stores the cryptographic information used to control transfers of crypto assets) that are associated with network addresses referred to on some blockchain networks as "externally owned accounts" (commonly known as "EOA wallets") were the most common type of wallet used on blockchain networks.[10] EOA wallets are self-custodial[11] with a single private key and require the user to know this private key to have access to and control of the crypto assets in the EOA wallet.[12] If another party gains knowledge of the user's private key (whether intentionally on the part of the user or otherwise), the other party would gain control of the user's crypto assets, subject only to any agreement the user has made with the third party. Hence, the mantra in crypto: "not your keys, not [really] your crypto."

This dependency on never misplacing or losing unique control over one's private key for EOA wallets created the potential for a single point of failure, leading to a less than ideal experience for users.[13] This security risk for users has

---

[8] UCC § 12-105. For more discussion about the definition of "control", see Part II.

[9] Prefatory note 1 to UCC Article 12: "Article 12 creates a legal regime that is meant to apply more broadly than to electronic (intangible) assets that are created using existing technologies such as distributed ledger technology (DLT), including blockchain technology, which records transactions in bitcoin and other crypto assets. It also aspires to apply to electronic assets that may be created using technologies that have yet to be developed or even imagined."

[10] Note that EOA wallets initially generate a "seed phrase", which is a sequence of 12 or 24 random words. The seed phrase acts the ultimate "master key" for that wallet and is used to generate the public-private key pair associated with the EOA. Loss of a private key itself does not result in loss of the assets held at the EOA so long as the user maintains knowledge of the associated "seed phrase".

[11] This paper focuses on "self-custodial" (also known as "non-custodial" or "unhosted") wallets that store cryptographic information applicable to crypto assets maintained on the Ethereum blockchain network, although similar terminology is commonly used with respect to other blockchain networks as well. When a third party maintains control over crypto assets stored in a wallet on behalf of a customer that is intended to be the beneficial owner of the relevant crypto asset, the technology is the same, but the arrangement raises additional legal issues, which are discussed in Part III. *See Ethereum*, Ethereum Accounts <https://ethereum.org/en/developers/docs/accounts/> (September 19, 2025).

[12] *Ismael Darwish*, Ethereum wallets today and tomorrow – EIP-3074 vs. ERC-4337, <https://medium.com/nethermind-eth/ethereum-wallets-today-and-tomorrow-eip-3074-vs-erc-4337-a7732b81efc8> (September 19, 2025).

[13] Unsophisticated users have not always recorded their seed phrases, and even sophisticat-

incentivized the development of other types of more user-friendly and secure wallets, such as multi-signature (Multi-sig) and multi-party computation-threshold signature scheme (MPC-TSS)[14] wallets.

Multi-sig and MPC-TSS wallets both involve distributing the power to control the digital assets across more than one party. The technologies for these two types of wallets differ, but the principle of distributing control across multiple parties is the same. For Multi-sig wallets, multiple separate keys are required to control the digital assets. For MPC-TSS wallets, a process of distributed computation is used to create separate key ‚shares' held by different parties. To authorize a transaction, these parties use their shares in a cryptographic process that generates a valid signature without ever combining the shares to form a complete private key. This ensures the private key is never exposed on any single device. Depending on how the MPC-TSS wallet is set up, a certain number of key shares may be required to generate a valid signature.[15][16]

---

ed users have lost them. Moreover, private keys could be compromised by bad actors to steal crypto assets (including, at times, by force – a concept known as "wrench attacks." For more reading on wrench attacks, see *TRM Labs*, The Rise of Wrench Attacks and Crypto-related Violent Crime (2025), <https://www.trmlabs.com/resources/blog/the-rise-of-wrench-attacks-and-crypto-related-violent-crime> (September 19, 2025). One of the most notorious cases of such a theft was the Ronin Bridge Hack in 2022, in which hackers used stolen private keys to steal approximately US$600 million of Ethereum (ETH) and USD Coin (USDC).

[14] MPC protocols allow for multiple parties to share and transact with each other without anyone revealing any data. *See IEEE*, What Is Multiparty Computation?, <https://digitalprivacy.ieee.org/publications/topics/what-is-multiparty-computation> (September 19, 2025); *Intu Official*, Learning from the Past: MPC Vulnerabilities & How INTU remains unscathed, <https://medium.com/@intuofficial/learning-from-the-past-mpc-vulnerabilities-how-intu-remains-unscathed-7a871e2bd249#167b> (September 19, 2025). For further information on the development of MPC, see also *Andrew C. Yao*, Protocols for Secure Computations, University of California Berkley <https://research.cs.wisc.edu/areas/sec/yao1982-ocr.pdf> (September 19, 2025); *Andrew C. Yao*, "How to generate and exchange secrets" <https://ieeexplore.ieee.org/document/4568207> (September 19, 2025).

[15] For example, two of three, three of three, or three of five key shards. Each key shard gives the holder the power to partially sign. When a sufficient number of partial signatures are provided, the blockchain transaction is digitally signed. The MPC-TSS wallets discussed in this wallet are a type of EOA wallet. (Note: MPC-TSS can also be applied to smart contract wallets, which are managed by code and can execute any logic without requiring a seed phrase. However, adoption has been limited. See *Ethereum*, Ethereum Wallets – Holding the keys to your digital future, <https://ethereum.org/en/wallets/> (September 19, 2025).

[16] There have been efforts underway to make account abstraction more widely adopted, including the Ethereum Foundation's EIP 3074 and now its recent release of EIP 7702 which allows for the temporary delegation of an EOA to a smart contract and control of assets without exposing the private key. *See* EIP-7702 (2025), https://eip7702.io/ (September 19, 2025). See *BuildBear Team*, EIP-3074 and EIP-7702: A New Era to Account Abstraction (2024), <https://medium.com/buildbear/eip-3074-and-eip-7702-a-new-era-to-account-abstraction-80bf2c177cd9> (September 19, 2025); and *Darwish*, Ethereum wallets today and tomorrow. EIP-3074 vs. ERC-4337 (n. 12) above, which describes the different wallet technologies under development and in the process of being adopted by the Ethereum Foundation at the time of writing.

Both Multi-sig and MPC-TSS wallets (for purposes of convenience of reference in this article only, "multi-control wallets") distribute control across multiple parties, such as family members, friends or employees.[17] Any transaction involving the relevant assets would require one or more of these chosen parties to participate (in the case of Multi-sig wallets). Or, if the user loses their private key, the user can call on their assigned parties, which usually includes the wallet provider, to generate a valid signature to authorize a transaction using the key shares of the assigned parties (in the case of MPC-TSS wallets). However, there are governance and operational risks inherent in these distributed arrangements. A family member could decide not to participate, or some team members may decide to collude against others or against their employer. Thus, users need to be mindful about selecting the parties to whom they assign key responsibilities. As a general matter, best practice in these cases is to utilize a standard legal agreement (with appropriate consideration to be binding) so that there is a clear and enforceable obligation on each party to cooperate in a pre-agreed manner.

Although Article 12 does anticipate the existence of CERs in respect to which control is "shared with another person,"[18] the question must be asked whether Article 12's definition of "control" is broad enough, or flexible enough, to contemplate all the new wallet permutations that have developed. The distribution of control – in the practical sense – across multiple parties in the manner contemplated by these new technologies, and the continued evolution toward decentralization, raise interesting legal questions regarding how the test for "control" – in the legal sense – established by Article 12 applies to this new generation of wallets. With recent developments in account abstraction like EIP 7702, the temporary delegation of EOA wallets to smart contracts, which may not be controlled by any party, also raises interesting questions outside the scope of this paper.

This paper discusses the issue of "control" under the UCC in Part II. Part III discusses "custody" and the UCC, followed by policy suggestions in Part IV. Part V provides the authors' concluding thoughts.

II. Discussion of "Control" and the UCC

Article 12 was intended to reduce the legal risks arising from the increasing use of CERs by "providing legal rules governing the transfer – both outright and for

[17] Please note while both technologies distribute control, they do so differently: Multi-sig wallets enforce rules through on-chain smart contracts, while MPC-TSS wallets use off-chain cryptography to produce a standard transaction.

[18] *See, e.g.*, UCC 12-102(b) ("Subject to subsection (c), a power [to exclude another from enjoying the benefits of an asset or to transfer it] is exclusive … , even if: … (2) the power is shared with another person."

security – of interests in some, but not all, electronic records."[19] In short, Article 12 addresses "property rights" relating to such assets. The principal "problem" solved by the 2022 Amendments was to establish negotiability for crypto assets by creating rules to determine when a transfer of a crypto asset is complete. What follows first discusses the concept of "control" and the crypto assets that are within the scope of this chapter, followed by a discussion of how Article 12 addresses these issues.

1. Scope of Article 12 and Control

As noted above, Article 12 applies to "controllable electronic records," which are a subset of digital assets. The definition of a "controllable electronic record" under the UCC is reflected in the term's constituent words. A "record" is information that is retrievable in perceivable form.[20] An electronic record is a record that is stored in an electronic medium.[21] "Controllable" means that the record can be subjected to "control," as defined in Section 12-102(a)(1). An electronic record that is not capable of being subjected to control under Section 12-105 is outside the scope of Article 12.[22]

The UCC includes different definitions of "control" tailored to the types of property to which they relate and the purposes for which "control" is to be established.[23] For those CERs commonly referred to as "crypto assets", Article 12 provides that a person has "control" over the crypto asset if the crypto asset itself, a related record, or the system in which the crypto asset is recorded:

(1) gives the person the power to enjoy "substantially all the benefit" from the crypto asset;

(2) gives the person the exclusive power to:

  (a) prevent others from enjoying "substantially all the benefit" from the crypto asset; *and*

[19] Prefatory Note 1 to UCC Article 12.

[20] UCC § 1-201(b)(31) (defining "record").

[21] UCC § 1-201(b)(16A) (defining "electronic").

[22] Controllable electronic records also do not include: (1) controllable "accounts" (which are governed by other provisions of Article 12); (2) controllable payment intangibles (governed by other provisions of Article 12); (3) deposit accounts (governed by UCC Article 4); (4) electronic copies of records evidencing chattel paper (*i. e.*, electronic documents of title) (governed by UCC Article 7); (5) electronic money (governed by other provisions of Article 9); (6) investment property (governed by Article 8); (7) transferable electronic records (governed by the federal Electronic Signatures in Global and National Commerce Act or, in states that have enacted it, the Uniform Electronic Transactions Act ("UETA"), also published by the Uniform Law Commission).

[23] *See, e. g.*, UCC § 7-106 ("control" of electronic documents of title); § 8-106 ("control" of securities and security entitlements); § 9-104 ("control" of deposit accounts); § 9-105 ("control" of chattel paper); § 9-105A ("control" of electronic money); § 9-106 ("control" of "investment property"). The meaning of "control" in the UCC depends on the type of property involved.

(b) transfer control or to cause another person to obtain control; *and*
(3) enables the person "readily to identify itself" as having these powers.[24]

"Exclusivity" may exist even if the powers described above are shared with another person (*e. g.*, assets in a Multi-sig or MPC-TSS wallet (subject to the discussion below)), or the crypto asset (or related record or system) limits the use of the crypto asset or has a protocol programmed that may cause a change in the person's powers with respect to the use of the crypto asset. However, a person (Person A) is not deemed to "share" control (so exclusivity does not exist) with another person (Person B) if:
(I) Person A can exercise a power only if Person B also exercises the power, *and*
(II) Person B *either* can exercise the power without Person A, *or* Person B is the person that transferred control over the record to Person A.[25]

We will refer to this test as the "*exclusivity carve-out*".

To illustrate and underscore this definition of "control," three hypothetical examples follow:

- *Example 1*: Wallet X is a Multi-sig wallet with three keys. All three of the keys are needed to sign the transfer of CERs held within Wallet X. Persons A, B and C each hold a key. None of these persons A, B or C transferred the CER to each other (*e.* g., A or B did not transfer to C; B or C did not transfer to A; and A and C did not transfer to B).[26] Do any of the persons A, B and C have "control"? Do A, B and C have control collectively?
  - Each of A, B, and C has control.
    - Because *each* of the keys held by A, B and C are needed to sign the transfer of the CER, holding the CER in Wallet X gives each of A, B, and C the power to enjoy "substantially all the benefit" from the crypto asset, allows each of A, B and C to prevent anyone else from prevent others from doing so, and enables each of them "readily to identify themselves" as having these powers. Thus, prongs (1), (2)(a) and (3) of the definition of "control" are satisfied with respect to each of A, B and C.
    - A, B and C collectively may transfer control of the tokens to another person. Under Section 12-105, A, B and C "share" the power to transfer

[24] Importantly, the definition refers to the power to exercise these powers and authorities, not the legal right to do so. In other words, the definition is functional and whether control exists or not depends on what the purported holder is capable of doing with the crypto asset. The legal implications of control are determined by other provisions of Article 9 and Article 12 and other applicable law.

[25] UCC § 12-105(a).

[26] The official comments to Article 12 indicate that if one of the persons transferred the CER to the other two, and the other two are capable of transferring the CER without the participation of that transferor, those other two would nonetheless have "exclusive control" over the CER. (*See* Official Comment 5 to UCC § 12-207, Example 3).

the tokens in the wallet because none of the persons A, B or C can exercise the power to transfer without both of the other persons. This means that the first prong of the exclusivity carve-out is satisfied ("the person can exercise the power only if the power also is exercised by the other person") but the second prong is not satisfied for two reasons: (1) no "other person ... can exercise the power without exercise of the power by the person"), and (2) none of the persons A, B and C is the transferor of the interest in the tokens to any of the others. This means that the exclusive power is "shared" by all three of A, B and C and that the exclusivity carve-out does not apply. As a result, prong 2(b) of the definition of "control" is satisfied with respect to each of A, B and C as well.

- Thus, each of A, B, and C meets all three of Article 12's criteria for control.

- *Example 2*: Persons A, B and C enter into a multi-signature arrangement where A can exercise the power to transfer crypto assets only with the consent of either B or C, but each person B and C may exercise the power to transfer crypto assets unilaterally. Who has control?
  - B and C have control. A does not.
  - Holding the CER in Wallet X gives A, B, and C the power to enjoy "substantially all the benefit" from the crypto asset, allows no other person to do so, and enables each of them to "readily identify themselves" as having these powers. Thus, prongs (1), (2)(a) and (3) of the definition of "control" are satisfied.
  - B and C have the power to transfer unilaterally. Therefore, each person B and C has the exclusive power to transfer control or to cause another person to obtain control. Thus, prong (2)(b) is satisfied with respect to B and C.
  - Accordingly, B and C meet all three of Article 12's criteria for control.
  - A, however, cannot transfer without consent of either B or C. Under the exclusivity carve-out, A does not have exclusive control over transfers of the CERs. Therefore, A does not meet prong (2)(b) of Article 12's definition of control.

- *Example 3*: Wallet X is a Multi-sig wallet with three keys. Persons A, B and C each hold a key. Two of the three keys are needed to sign the transfer of CERs held within Wallet X to another wallet. None of the persons A, B and C acting alone has the power to transfer the CER. None of the persons A, B and C was the person that transferred the CER to any of the others. Do A, B and C have "control"? Does A, B and C collectively have "control"?
  - Each person A, B, and C has control.
  - Holding the CER in Wallet X gives each person A, B, and C the power to enjoy "substantially all the benefit" from the crypto asset, and allows no

other person other than A, B or C to do so. It also enables each of them to "readily to ... identify themselves" as having these powers. Thus, prongs (1), (2)(a) and (3) of the definition of "control" are satisfied.

- Do any of A, B and C have the "exclusive" power to transfer tokens in the wallet? The commonsense answer would be no, because none of the persons A, B and C can exercise the power to transfer without at least one of the others. This means that the first prong of the exclusivity carve-out is satisfied ("the person can exercise the power only if the power also is exercised by the other person").
- However, this also means that the second prong of the exclusivity carve-out is not satisfied ("the other person ... can exercise the power without exercise of the power by the person").
- This means that the exclusive power is "shared" by all three – and all three have "exclusive" control.

- Thus, each of A, B, and C meets all three of Article 12's criteria for control.[27]
- Example 4: Person A holds a CER in a wallet that is programmed to sell the CER if the price goes above a predetermined price. Does A have the exclusive power to transfer his bitcoin?
  - Yes, assuming that the other criteria in the definition of "control" are satisfied, A has exclusive power to prevent others from availing themselves of the benefits of the CER or to transfer the CER because exclusivity exists even if the CER (or a related record or system) limits the use of the CER or has a protocol programmed that may cause a change in the person's rights, including a transfer.

2. Article 12's Roots in UCC Article 3

As noted above, the drafters of the 2022 Amendments sought to establish negotiability for crypto assets by creating rules to determine when a transfer of a crypto asset is complete. The 2022 Amendments pursued their stated goals by,

---

[27] Recognizing that this result might be confusing, the drafters of Article 12 included the following official comment:

"Example 2: Pursuant to a multi-sig arrangement, control of propofols ... is shared by Campbell, Elizabeth, Mia, and Natasha. Under the multi-sig arrangement, the exercise of powers over the propofols requires action by three of the four persons having control. None of the participants acting alone has the power to exercise the relevant powers. Subsection (b)(2) makes clear that all four participants have control over the propofols and exclusivity is not impaired by the shared control under the multi-sig arrangement.

Although all four persons in Example 2 have control, *that may leave many questions as to the rights of the four as among themselves*. For example, if more than one of the four were secured parties, it would be important for them to settle by agreement issues such as relative priorities and enforcement rights. Similar situations can arise in other contexts and with respect to other types of collateral."

Official Comment 5 to UCC § 12-207, Example 2 (emphasis added).

among other things, drawing on three concepts from UCC Article 3, which governs negotiable instruments such as notes and checks.[28] These concepts are: (1) the holder in due course; (2) the take-free rule; and (3) the shelter rule.[29]

A holder in due course of a negotiable instrument, under Article 3, is a person who took the instrument (1) for value, (2) in good faith, and (3) without notice of defects, claims or defenses.[30] A negotiable instrument is transferred "for value" when it is transferred in exchange for completed performance, the granting of a security interest or lien, in satisfaction of an antecedent claim, in exchange for another instrument, or for the incurrence of an irrevocable obligation consideration.[31] "Good faith" means ... means honesty in fact and the observance of reasonable commercial standards of fair dealing.[32] And a person has "notice" of a fact if the person: (1) has actual knowledge of it; (2) has received a notice or notification of it; or (3) from all the facts and circumstances known to the person at the time in question, has reason to know that it exists.[33]

Taking these elements together, a holder in due course of a negotiable instrument is a person who receives a negotiable instrument in exchange for qualifying consideration, honestly in the observance of reasonable commercial standards of fair dealing, and without knowledge of or reasons to know of any defects, claims or defenses with respect to the negotiable instrument.

Being a holder in due course of a negotiable instrument allows the holder to avail itself of the "take-free rule," which provides that a holder in due course of a negotiable instrument takes the instrument free of claims of third parties and most defenses.[34] The take-free rule is intended to reduce the risk, created by accepting a negotiable instrument from someone other than its maker, that the maker of the negotiable instrument will have legal ground for refusing to pay

[28] UCC § 3-201(a) (defining "negotiation" as "a transfer of possession, whether voluntary or involuntary, of an instrument by a person other than the issuer to a person who thereby becomes a holder").

[29] Note that this does not mean that crypto assets are necessarily similar in their terms, purpose or content to negotiable instruments; rather, Article 12 draws upon the recognition that the use of digital signatures to transfer crypto assets is a mechanism similar to the traditional use of signatures to transfer paper instruments.

[30] More specifically, the transferee must take the instrument (i) without notice that the instrument is overdue or has been dishonored or that there is an uncured default with respect to payment of another instrument issued as part of the same series, (ii) without notice that the instrument contains an unauthorized signature or has been altered, (iii) without notice of any claim to the instrument described in UCC Section 3-306, and (iv) without notice that any party has a defense or claim in recoupment. UCC § 3-302. In addition, the instrument, when issued or negotiated to the holder, must not bear apparent evidence of forgery or alteration nor otherwise be so irregular or incomplete as to call into question its authenticity. *Id.*

[31] UCC § 3-303. In other words, the instrument must be exchanged for something of value.

[32] UCC § 1-201(b)(20).

[33] UCC § 1-202(a). Note that there is no affirmative duty to look for a competing claim (*e.g.*, no duty to search for UCC filings).

[34] UCC § 3-305.

and that someone else will claim ownership of the negotiable instrument. By protecting the holder in due course from third-party claims and defenses, the take-free rule largely eliminates the need for holders in due course to research the origin of the negotiable instrument and the possibility of third-party claims.[35] One court has stated that:

"The purpose of conferring HDC [*i. e.*, holder in due course] status is to encourage and facilitate the circulation of commercial paper. It is sometimes said that the holder in due course doctrine is like oil in the wheels of commerce and that those wheels would grind to a quick halt without such lubrication. [...] It permits a specified class of holders to receive negotiable instruments free of the risks of claims or defenses which might be valid against the original recipient. These risks are twofold. First, the HDC is assured that he will not lose any action brought to enforce the instrument due to such claims or defenses. This is the substantive effect of the rule. Second, and perhaps just as important, the holder is assured that should he acquire HDC status he will not incur high transaction costs in the form of protracted litigation when seeking to enforce the contract. This is the procedural effect of the rule."[36]

The take-free rule distinguishes "negotiable" instruments from property such as goods, as to which a buyer from a thief normally obtains no rights.[37] By doing so, it facilitates a liquid market in these instruments.

The shelter rule provides that, subject to the transferee's own wrongdoing, a transferor of an instrument vests in the transferee such rights as the transferor had in the instrument or had the right to transfer.[38] Accordingly, a holder in due course that transfers an instrument transfers those rights as a holder in due course to the purchaser.[39] Like the take-free rule, the policy motivating the shelter rule is to assure the holder in due course a free market for the instrument.[40]

---

[35] *Gregory E. Maggs*, The Holder in Due Course Doctrine as a Default Rule, 32 Ga. L. Rev. 783, 10 (1998) <https://scholarship.law.gwu.edu/cgi/viewcontent.cgi?article=1823&context=faculty_publications> p.793 (September 19, 2025).

[36] *Western State Bank v. First Union Bank & Trust Co.*, 360 N.E.2d 254 (Ind. Ct. App. 1977) (citations omitted).

[37] 2022 Amendments at 231.

[38] UCC § 3-203. With respect to most types of property, the transferee's rights in the property are derivative of the transferor's rights. As a result, the transferor cannot transfer more rights than it has in the property to the transferee – *i. e.*, the transferee of a stolen necklace does not receive good "title" to the necklace. In the context of negotiable instruments (and certain other financial instruments, as discussed below), a holder in due course is not only protected from defenses and claims, but can convey the same protections to a transferee – even if the transferee would not independently qualify as a holder in due course.

[39] UCC § 3-203.

[40] UCC § 3-203, cmt. 2.

3. *Article 12: Substantive Provisions and Negotiability of Virtual (Non-Fiat) Currencies*

The drafters of the 2022 Amendments believed that the ability to take a controllable electronic record free of third-party property claims would be necessary for a controllable electronic record to have commercial utility. The drafters argued that "as is the case with Articles 2, 3, 7, and 9, Article 12 would facilitate commerce by affording to certain good-faith purchasers for value (buyers as well as secured parties) greater rights than their transferors had or had power to transfer."[41]

Analogous to Article 3's holders in due course, Article 12 created a subset of purchasers called "qualifying purchasers." Qualifying purchasers are purchasers that obtain control of a controllable electronic record for value, in good faith, and without notice of any claim of a property interest in the controllable electronic record.[42] Like a holder in due course of a negotiable instrument, a qualifying purchaser of a controllable electronic record takes the controllable electronic record free of third-party property claims.[43]

4. *Article 12: Distinction Between the CER and Rights Evidenced by CERs*

A controllable electronic record is, at its core, a record (*i. e.*, information). Some records have value simply because the market treats such records as having value. Bitcoin, for example, is such a record because the market is willing to exchange valuable goods and services in exchange for the ability to control some number of bitcoin as recorded in the records maintained by the computers comprising the bitcoin network at any given time.

Some CERs, however, are used to evidence, or effect the transfer of, legal rights of the parties created under a separate (traditionally documented) agreement, such as a debt or equity security. For example, a contract reduced to writing creates valuable rights and obligations of the parties to the contract. The paper on which the contract is written is a *record* of the contract, but gaining possession or ownership of the paper record does not cause the holder to become a party to the contract. With respect to such records, there is a fundamental difference between ownership of the record and ownership of the legal rights that are evidenced by the record.

In some cases, a physical record may serve as evidence of title to tangible property. For example, title to a car may be proof of ownership of the car; signing and handing over the paper title may (subject to the satisfaction of other conditions) have the legal effect of transferring title to the car to the recipient of

---

[41] 2022 Amendments, at 232.
[42] UCC § 12-102(a)(2).
[43] UCC § 12-104(e).

the paper title. A stock certificate may evidence ownership of a share of a company; endorsement and delivery of the certificate may (subject to the satisfaction of other conditions) result in transfer of ownership of the share.

There are numerous examples of using CERs to evidence, or facilitate transfers of, securities and rights to or in other kinds of financial or physical "real world" assets. The idea that the transfer of ownership of property could be facilitated by means of a transfer of a digital asset is very appealing, particularly with respect to asset types that are currently subject to burdensome, time consuming or expensive procedures and requirements. However, although Article 12 would govern the question of whether the control over an electronic record in the form of a CER is effectively transferred from one person to another, it expressly does not determine whether the transfer of a CER that purports to represent title to a real world asset will effectively transfer title.[44]

For example, if the CER claims to be "tethered" to an interest in real estate, intellectual property or other property where ownership is reflected on a centralized government register, Article 12 does not determine whether the "tethering" is effective or whether a transfer of control over the CER effects a transfer of the "tethered" asset.[45] Typically, the person obtaining control over a controllable electronic record would not acquire ownership of the property tethered to the CER *merely* by obtaining control over the CER – compliance with the legal requirements applicable to the relevant type of property would be necessary to achieve that change in title.[46]

There is, however, an exception to the above rule in Article 12 for controllable accounts and controllable payment intangibles. The exception relates to rights to payment (*i. e.*, accounts and payment intangibles) that are evidenced by a controllable electronic record and as to which the obligor (account debtor) under-

---

[44] UCC § 12-104(f). Please note that there may be other bodies of law that determine whether someone other than the qualifying purchaser has property rights in the asset. For example, a car could be titled to Mr. X who then passes away. Mr. X's daughter validly inherits the car but has not had the opportunity to re-register title. The daughter would be the *owner* of the car notwithstanding the title is still in the name of the deceased father. There could be other types of valid transfers of ownership that do not involve re-titling. The title certificate may be evidence of ownership but neither the name on the title certificate nor the holding of the title certificate is dispositive as to who the "rightful" *owner* of the car is.

[45] Please note that this distinction may not exist in other jurisdictions.

[46] Parties may seek to achieve a transfer of ownership indirectly by, for example, titling an asset in the name of a trustee or similar party, issuing CERs representing beneficial interests in the trust, and establishing a system under which the parties agree that the party holding a CER may exercise the rights with respect to the asset created by the trust arrangement. Others may credit the relevant assets to securities accounts maintained by securities intermediaries and record the security entitlements relating to such assets on a distributed ledger, using digital assets to reflect those security entitlements or to make changes to the ledger. Such efforts require careful consideration of the property law applicable to the relevant asset, the laws governing the establishment of the related trust or account, and the interaction between ownership of the CERs and ownership of the underlying assets, among other issues.

takes to pay the person that has control of the controllable electronic record. In other words, an "account" or "payment intangible" may be effectively "tethered" to the related CER if the account debtor agrees to pay the person that has control of the CER. These rights to payment are referred to as "controllable accounts" and "controllable payment intangibles."[47] A qualifying purchaser of a controllable account or controllable payment intangible takes free of property claims and is protected from certain actions.[48] [49]

5. Security Interests in CERs

Security interests in CERs (including controllable accounts and controllable payment intangibles) may be perfected by the secured party obtaining "control" of the pledged CERs or by filing a financing statement with the applicable state filing office.[50] For example, a custodian holding the keys to a wallet that contains a CER will have a perfected security interest in the CER by virtue of its "control" of the CER (assuming the arrangement satisfies the definition of control discussed above). As with negotiable instruments and investment property, filing of a financing statement in and of itself is not notice of a property claim to the CER – meaning that a party that obtains control over the asset will not be deemed to have notice of the security interest of the party who has perfected its security interest only by filing a financing statement. Further, perfection by control takes priority over perfection by filing.

---

[47] UCC § 9-102(a)(27A) (defining "controllable account") and (27B) (defining "controllable payment intangible").

[48] Note that payment intangibles do not include deposit accounts, instruments, investment property (such as securities) or letter of credit rights. In each of these cases, either there is a separate framework already in place governing the relevant instruments (such as the framework for uncertificated securities established by Article 8 of the UCC) or a regulatory framework governing the asset that may require further elaboration before the UCC is amended to address them (such as deposit accounts). There have been efforts to utilize distributed ledgers and related CERs for many of these assets, but the legal analysis of these arrangements is continuing.

[49] It was also observed that there is not a perfect parallel between a holder in due course of a negotiable instrument and a qualifying purchaser of a CER evidencing a controllable account or controllable payment intangible. The account debtor on such a controllable account or controllable payment intangible may still assert claims or defenses against a qualifying purchaser unless those claims and defenses have been waived pursuant to UCC § 9-403.

[50] Under the UCC, many types of security interests may be perfected by filing UCC-1 financing statements with the relevant filing office in the appropriate jurisdiction. The filing must include an indication of the relevant collateral. Parties to existing agreements under which CERs serve as collateral will not necessarily have to be updated if the relevant state enacts Article 12. For purposes of Article 9 terminology, a CER is a "general intangible," a controllable account is an "account", and a controllable payment intangible is a "payment intangible." Existing financing statements would likely have used this terminology, which will continue to encompass CERs after Article 12 takes effect.

6. *Crypto Assets as "Money" Under the UCC*

In 2021, El Salvador adopted bitcoin as legal currency, alongside the U.S. dollar.[51] Although this decision was recently reversed, at least in part,[52] the possibility that crypto assets could be adopted as legal tender led to inclusion of an amendment to Article 1 of the UCC to provide that an "money" does not include "an electronic record that is a medium of exchange recorded and transferable in a system that existed and operated for the medium of exchange *before* the medium of exchange was authorized or adopted by the government."[53] As a result, bitcoin, for example, would not be considered "money" under the UCC even while El Salvador accepted it as legal tender, because bitcoin was recorded and transferable in a system that existed and operated before the electronic record was adopted by El Salvador.

At the same time, a definition of "electronic money" was added to Article 9. "Electronic money" means, simply, "money in electronic form."[54] Electronic money is not necessarily issued in the same manner as a CER, but some crypto assets, such as a central bank digital currency ("CBDC") would constitute electronic money. Security interests in electronic money can be perfected only by "control," which is defined specifically for this purpose in a manner similar to the definition of "control" for CERs described above.[55] Although crypto assets that are "electronic money" are not CERs subject to Article 12,[56] if a CBDC comes into general use, parties could perfect security interests in the CBDC by obtaining control in the manner described with respect to CERs above.[57]

7. *Choice of Law*

A challenging problem with respect to crypto assets created on decentralized ledgers used globally is determining what laws governs the matters discussed in this chapter. If the governing law question is raised in a jurisdiction that has

---

51 *Taylor Watson*, In a global first, El Salvador adopts bitcoin as legal currency, *The Week* (June 9, 2021) <https://theweek.com/news/1001342/in-a-global-first-el-salvador-adopts-bitcoin-as-legal-currency> (September 19, 2025).

52 *Harriet Marsden*, The collapse of El Salvador's bitcoin dream, *The Week* (Mar. 2025), <https://theweek.com/business/economy/el-salvador-bitcoin-cryptocurrency-collapse> (September 19, 2025).

53 UCC § 1-201(24) (emphasis added).

54 UCC § 9-102(a)(31A). Subject to the limitation described in the prior paragraph, "money" means a medium of exchange that is currently authorized or adopted by a domestic or foreign government. The term includes a monetary unit of account established by an intergovernmental organization, or pursuant to an agreement between two or more countries. *Id.* § 1-201(24).

55 UCC § 9-105A.

56 UCC § 12-102(a)(1).

57 To the extent that electronic money is held in a securities account, security interests in the electronic money will likely be governed by the Article 8 provisions relating to investment property, as discussed in Section III.

enacted Article 12, UCC Section 12-107 will determine which jurisdiction's law will govern the matters that are addressed by Article 12. The result of this provision will be not only to provide a clear rule as to which law will govern these matters, both in practice and in disputes, but also to simplify the provision of legal opinions that are often required in the context of commercial transactions.

The general rule established by Article 12 is that the local law of a "controllable electronic record's jurisdiction" governs the matters covered by Article 12.[58] If the CER or the system in which the CER is recorded expressly specifies what the controllable electronic record's jurisdiction is, then the law specified will govern. If the CER and the system in which it is recorded do not specify the controllable electronic record's jurisdiction, then the governing law will be determined based on the designation of the law governing the CER or the system generally. Several other options are provided for determining the controllable electronic record's jurisdiction, but if no other option is applicable (e.g., where an open and permissionless system like the Ethereum network which does not purport to be governed by any particular system of law is used), the governing law will be deemed to be that of the District of Columbia.[59] Whether such a deemed choice will be respected in a dispute outside of the United States or in a state that has yet to adopt § 12-107 is of course a separate matter.

The law of the controllable electronic record's jurisdiction governs the perfection and priority of security interests in CERs, controllable accounts, and controllable payment intangibles. Perfection by filing, however, is governed by the law of the location of the debtor.[60]

---

[58] There is an exception to this general rule in connection with controllable accounts and controllable payment intangibles. If there is an effective agreement between the account debtor (*i. e.*, the person who owes money under the item) and the person assigning the record (the pledgee), the agreement may specify a different law to govern the rights and duties of the account debtor in respect of the debtor's discharge under the item. UCC § 12-107(b).

[59] The amendments seek to provide an answer to the question of which law governs which state's law will apply to the matters addressed by the amendments:

- Similar to Article 8 and Article 9, the "law of the CER's jurisdiction" will govern these issues
- If the CER itself, or a related record that is "readily available for review", specifies the "law of the CER's jurisdiction", that law will be the law of the CER's jurisdiction
- If not, but the rules of a system on which the CER is recorded, specifies the law of the CER's jurisdiction, that law will be the law of the CER's jurisdiction
- If the CER itself, or a related record that is "readily available for review", specifies the governing law, that law will be the law of the CER's jurisdiction
- If not, but the rules of a system on which the CER is recorded, specifies the governing law, that law will be the law of the CER's jurisdiction
- If not, but the laws of the District of Columbia will be the law of the CER's jurisdiction (subject to transition provisions until the District of Columbia adopts the amendments).

The relevant jurisdiction may have no relation to the location of the purchaser.

[60] UCC § 9-306B.

III. Crypto Assets Held by Custodians

1. What Does "Custody" Mean with Respect to Crypto Assets?

Although one of the hallmarks of crypto assets is the ability of owners to hold and control their own assets, custodians have come to play an important role for owners and users of crypto assets. One reason for their importance is the same risk of key loss or theft that has given rise to "multi-control" wallets as discussed in Section I above. Other reasons relate to the desire to hold assets in a manner that facilitates trading; the ability to rely upon the technological and operational sophistication of professional custodians; the desire to utilize related services, such as staking; or the desire to obtain financing or other benefits from the custodian.

Custody generally refers to the safekeeping and servicing of an investor's assets by a financial institution or other entity that often provides related services, such as receiving any payments or distributions made in respect of the asset, alerting the investor of votes or other actions the investor needs to take with respect to the asset and, if the investor wishes to sell the asset or purchase another asset, processing the transaction on the investor's behalf.[61] In the context of crypto assets, "custody" refers principally to controlling, managing, and safeguarding these assets on behalf of their owner. At its core, custody of crypto assets centers on the capability of the custodian to issue instructions that determine the movement or use of the asset. For crypto assets, providing these services generally necessitates having control (in both a practical and legal sense) over the private keys associated with the blockchain address of the relevant assets.[62]

Custodians can range from start-ups managing private keys for customers in multi-control wallets to institutional custodians offering sophisticated services to investors and entities. Institutional custody services often offer additional security measures, such as utilizing MPC-TSS wallets or advanced authentication mechanisms, to ensure that control over the assets is exercised responsibly and securely. These risks have been heightened, in some respects, as compared to the risks faced by custodians for traditional financial assets, by the lack of a legal framework for the ownership and transfer of crypto assets. The legal framework governing the ownership and transfer of funds and securities, the responsibilities and liabilities of custodians for those assets, the "default" rules

[61] The Clearing House, The Custody Services of Banks (July 2016), at 2, <https://bpi.com/wp-content/uploads/2018/07/20160728_tch_white_paper_the_custody_services_of_banks.pdf.> (September 19, 2025).

[62] As discussed in Part I above, keys are the cryptographic credentials required to authorize transactions, and whoever possesses these keys has the practical authority to direct the asset.

that apply when fraud, errors or operational failures result in loss of assets, and the tools for tracing and recovering lost assets have developed for financial assets over centuries, through industry practice, judicial decisions and statutes. For crypto assets, the body of experience, judicial interpretation and statute, is simply much smaller. Article 12 is intended to fill a part of that gap.

2. *Regulation of Crypto Asset Custodians*

Custodians for traditional financial assets are generally regulated on the basis of the nature of the assets for which they provide custody. In the United States, only banks may accept deposits.[63] In most states, only banks and broker-dealers may provide custodial services to the public,[64] and the Securities and Exchange Commission (the "SEC") regulates parties providing securities custodial services to and by broker-dealers and investment advisers and their customers, as well as to registered investment companies. The Commodity Futures Trading Commission regulates the provision of custodial services to futures commission merchants, commodity pool operators, commodity trading advisers and their customers.

Until recently, most federally regulated banks, broker-dealers and commodity brokers were effectively precluded from providing custodial services for crypto assets. Instead, most custodians for crypto assets have been either state-chartered trust companies or digital asset service providers regulated by state regulators under regulatory frameworks established to regulate the digital asset industry. Many of their customers have been broker dealers, investment advisors and, more recently, registered investment companies subject to the requirements established by the SEC and other regulators.

3. *Article 12 and the Financial Asset Election Under Article 8*

Although the regulatory framework applicable to the custodial services for crypto assets may vary, depending upon the type of entity for whom the custodian is acting and the regulatory classification given to the crypto assets, the commercial law framework under which most custodians currently offer this service derives principally from Article 8 of the UCC. In most cases, the custodian holds the assets in custody under agreements in which the custodian is acting as a "securities intermediary"[65] under Article 8 of the UCC, the assets are

---

[63] Glass-Steagall Act § 21(a)(2), 12 U.S.C. § 378(a)(2).

[64] Securities Exchange Act of 1934 § 15(c)(3), 15 U.S.C. § 78o(c)(3); 17 C.F.R. § 240.15c3-3; and *SEC*, Custody of Funds or Securities of Clients by Investment Advisers, Investment Adviser Act Release No. 2968 (2009), <https://www.sec.gov/rules/final/2009/ia-2968.pdf> (September 19, 2025).

[65] UCC § 8-102(a)(14).

credited to a "securities account",[66] and the parties have made a "financial asset election" with respect to the crypto assets.[67]

Article 8 of the UCC was designed principally to address the commercial law relating to investment securities, and covers two broad areas: (1) the law governing the issuance and transfer of securities, and (2) the law governing the operation of securities accounts and the treatment of financial assets credited to those accounts. This second area may have been intended, initially, to address the holding of securities by banks and broker-dealers for their customers, but the drafters of Article 8 provided for other types of financial assets – including those not yet created when the statute was drafted – to be included in custodial accounts and held for customers.

Under Article 8 of the UCC "any ... asset" that a securities intermediary and its customer agree to treat as a financial asset is considered a financial asset under Article 8 and therefore becomes subject to the provisions of Part 5 of Article 8 relating to the establishment of "security entitlements" by custodians for their customers. Customers often make such a "financial asset election" in their account agreements with their securities intermediaries.

If the customer has made a financial asset election and the securities intermediary has credited the financial asset to the customer's "securities account" at the securities intermediary, the customer (referred to in Article 8 as the "entitlement holder") obtains a proprietary interest in, and contractual and statutory rights against the securities intermediary with respect to, the financial asset. That proprietary interest and contractual right are, together, referred to in Article 8 as a "security entitlement." The security entitlement consists of the rights of the customer, and the duties of the custodian, contained in Part 5 of Article 8, and include (among other things) the duty of the custodian to obtain and maintain a sufficient amount of the relevant asset to cover all the security entitlements it has created;[68] the duty to deliver to the holder all payments or distributions made by the issuer of the financial asset (if any);[69] the duty to exercise rights arising from the financial asset as directed by the holder;[70] and the duty to transfer the financial asset as directed by the holder.[71]

The financial assets to which the customers of a securities intermediary have security entitlements are not property of the securities intermediary,[72] and are not subject to the claims of the securities intermediary's creditors under Article 8, with very limited exceptions.

---

[66] UCC § 8-501.
[67] UCC § 8-102(a)(9)(iii).
[68] UCC § 8-503.
[69] UCC § 8-505.
[70] UCC § 8-506.
[71] UCC § 8-507.
[72] UCC § 8-503(a).

As is evident, Article 8 addresses the question of the property rights of customers in assets that have been credited to their securities accounts. It does not address, for assets other than investment securities, the commercial law under which the custodian gains legal rights to the assets that it holds for its customers. Until Article 12 is enacted in all U.S. jurisdictions, custodians and their customers may continue to rely upon the combination of operational control and broader principles of property law to assure that they have gained legal ownership of the assets that they have credited to customer accounts. However, once enacted, Article 12 is intended to provide the same level of certainty as to the custodian's ownership of digital assets that Article 8 provides for investment securities. As a result, it will enhance the legal framework under which custodial assets are held for both the custodians who hold the assets and for their customers whose entitlements relate to those assets.

Article 8 has also facilitated the granting of security interests in crypto assets prior to the enactment of Article 12. This is because Article 8 creates a framework for perfecting security interests in financial assets credited to securities accounts that does not depend on the nature of those assets. This is because, as noted above, once a financial asset has been credited to the customer's account, the customer's property is a "security entitlement", not the underlying financial asset itself.[73] In general, a security interest in a security entitlement may be perfected by means of an agreement by the securities intermediary that it will comply with instructions originated by the secured party without further consent by the entitlement holder.[74] The practice of entering into "securities account control agreements" for this purpose has become common in the securities industry, and has been utilized by many seeking to perfect security interests in crypto assets (*i. e.*, certain CERs) as well.[75] Nevertheless, it is important to distinguish a CER in which a person may have property rights (such as bitcoin) that may be subject to a "financial asset election" as discussed above, from a CER that is used as a means of providing an *instruction* to a securities intermediary by their customer and which is not intended to create an asset or property interest that is separate from the related securities entitlement itself.

---

[73] To be more precise, the customer that holds a security entitlement has a pro rata property interest in all interests in that financial asset held by the securities intermediary, without regard to the time the entitlement holder acquired the security entitlement or the time the securities intermediary acquired the interest in that financial asset. U.C.C. § 8-503(b).

[74] U.C.C. §§ 9-314, 9-106, 8-106. Security interests in security entitlements may also be perfected by filing a financing statement, U.C.C. § 9-312(a), but this approach is taken less frequently because a security interest perfected by control will take priority over a security interest perfected by filing. U.C.C. § 9-328(1).

[75] *Jason Finger and Steven O. Weise*, Part II: NFT Lending – Legal Issues Involving Secured Transactions under the UCC, Pre- and Post-Article 9 and 12 Amendments (2023), <https://www.blockchainandthelaw.com/2023/11/part-ii-nft-lending-legal-issues-involving-secured-transactions-under-the-ucc-pre-and-post-article-9-and-12-amendments/> (September 19, 2025).

The drafters of Article 12 have emphasized that the amendments made to the UCC by the 2022 Amendments do not affect the ability of securities intermediaries and their customers to make a financial asset election under Article 8 for crypto assets, nor will it disturb any financial asset election made under existing agreements. This is important because a valid financial asset election with respect to CERs under Article 8 both facilitates the customer's ability to take such actions as pledging the CERs as collateral, and entitles the customer to significant protection from the failure of its custodian.[76] However, as noted above, whether a financial asset election is made or not, Article 12, will help to complete the legal framework governing the rights of customers of custodians.

IV. Policy Recommendations

1. The Distributed Ledger May Be More Important Than the CERs

As blockchain technology has matured and its usefulness in various use cases has become better understood, it is becoming clear that there may be some contexts in which the ability to utilize a permissioned distributed ledger may have value independent of crypto assets of the type maintained on public permissionless blockchain networks. Some promising applications of blockchain technology rely primarily on the distributed ledger and use "tokens" only as a technological means to an end (maintaining the currency of the ledger). In those cases, Article 12's focus on the CERs themselves, and the mandatory application of Article 12 to CERs that meet its definition, may create some challenges in the application of Article 12 to these use cases.

Mandatorily subjecting such CERs to Article 12 may create more challenges than it solves by raising questions of property rights in contexts where the tokens should not be viewed as having any property-like characteristics at all. Consider a permissioned blockchain for tracking pharmaceuticals. A ‚token' representing a batch of medicine has no market value and is not intended to create separate property rights; its purpose is to serve as an unforgeable entry on a ledger shared between the manufacturer, distributor, and pharmacy. The value is in preventing counterfeiting and ensuring an accurate chain of custody. Subjecting this ‚data token' to the same property law as bitcoin could unnecessarily complicate its function. It may be appropriate to make the application of Article 12 optional, at least for private permissioned blockchain-based systems

[76] *Carl S. Bjerre et al.* Missing an Opportunity: Cryptocurrency Exchanges and Their Customers Should Consider Using UCC Article 8, ABA (April 3, 2023), <https://www.americanbar.org/groups/business_law/resources/business-law-today/2023-april/missing-opportunity-cryptocurrency-exchanges-their-customers/#:~:text=Once%20the%20financial%20asset%20election,statutory%20rights%20against%20the%20securities.> (September 19, 2025)

where the participants in the system can agree to an alternate framework to govern their rights and obligations.[77]

2. Situations in which No One Controls

As the crypto asset industry has developed, smart contract-based decentralized applications (known as "dApps") have arisen, particularly in the "DeFi" or "decentralized finance" context, in which it could be argued that no one "controls" a crypto asset held at the address of the related smart contract, either practically or under the definition of control provided in Article 12. DeFi dApps handle control through a variety of different mechanisms. Some allow DeFi project sponsors to retain administrative keys that provide control over the smart contracts and the crypto assets held at the smart contract address of the dApp, while others distribute control over these administrative keys to a community of governance token holders. In some cases, the administrative keys are "burned" (or destroyed). In the latter case, "control" is embedded in the immutable code of the smart contract, and the assets at the smart contract address are accessible only to those who can meet the smart contract's predefined conditions. The legal challenge lies in mapping these forms of automated or distributed governance to the definition of "control" under Article 12. Control in DeFi is not absent; it is simply transformed. We can distinguish between:

1. *Administrative Control:* Many smart contracts have „admin keys" that allow a developer or company to upgrade the contract or pause its functions. In this case, someone *does* have control.
2. *Governance Control:* In decentralized protocols, control is often devolved to a community of governance token holders. This community can vote on changes to the protocol. This is a form of distributed, collective control.
3. *Control by Code ("Code is Law"):* For truly immutable, non-upgradable smart contracts, control is ceded to the logic of the code itself. The assets are not in an uncontrolled void; they are in a transparent, automated vault whose rules are unchangeable and publicly auditable. A user „controls" their assets by being the only one who can satisfy the conditions of the code to release them (*e.* g., repaying a loan to unlock collateral).

The third category is of greatest interest here. For example, a user can send one crypto asset (as "collateral") to the address of an immutable, non-upgradeable smart contract and receive back (or "borrow") another crypto asset from a separate pool maintained at that smart contract address. In this case, one can argue

[77] Note that the key issue in certain permissioned blockchain use cases may not be whether Article 12 "applies" or is "optional," but whether a property interest in the CER is relevant to the CER's role in that context. Even if Article 12 gives a CER property-like characteristics, ownership of the CER may be incidental where its sole function is as a record within a ledger or registry, similar to a paper record in a title book.

that the smart contract address that holds the relevant crypto assets is not controlled by any single company or person. But one can also argue that the user "controls" their asset (or, more correctly, an equivalent amount of the asset they initially sent to the smart contract – not the exact same assets) by satisfying the conditions of the code to release them. The official comments to the UCC may suggest that there may be circumstances of this kind – acknowledging that the system in which a CER is recorded may limit the benefits of the CER that are available to those who interact with the system:

"In determining whether a person has the power to avail itself of substantially all the benefit from a controllable electronic record ..., or to prevent others from availing themselves of substantially all the benefit from a controllable electronic record ..., only the benefit that the system makes available (subject to the system's inherent limitations) should be considered."[78]

It is not clear that this discussion is focused on circumstances such as those described above – or that it goes far enough to address circumstances in which crypto assets cannot be released until certain conditions are met. What is clear is that only a legal person can enjoy the benefits of a crypto asset, and it will be necessary to determine what constitutes "control" when a crypto asset is bound up in a framework that ensures that no legal person can do so until certain conditions are met.

3. Considering Whether Article 12's Approach to Choice of Law is Consistent with the Respective Roles of Wallets and the Blockchain Protocol Itself

The official comments to Article 12 repeatedly caution that the terms of the statute should not be read too literally. One place in which this admonition may have particular relevance is in the interpretation of what technology is attached to or logically associated with a crypto asset. This concept is important in several places, including in the definition of control[79] and provisions relating to the determination of governing law.[80] Urging that the language not be interpreted too literally, the official comment notes:

"The statutory language must be adapted and applied in a functional manner to technology, systems, and infrastructure that may be developed and employed in the future. The goal is to embrace records and systems that are connected to a particular electronic record in such a manner that the information contained in or the functions performed by those "attached" or "associated" records are appropriately and reasonably attributable to and identifiable as connected with the electronic record itself. See also, e.g., Sections 7-106, 9-105, 9-105A, 9-306A, 9-605, 9-628, and 12-107."[81]

---

[78] U.C.C. § 12-105 off. cmt. 3.
[79] U.C.C. § 12-105(a), (b)(1).
[80] U.C.C. § 12-107.
[81] U.C.C. § 12-105 off. cmt. 2.

The discussion of the evolution of wallets and smart contracts in the text above indicates both the wisdom and the importance of this admonition.

V. Conclusion

Article 12 brings welcome clarity to many aspects of the legal framework governing crypto assets. Not least of its benefits will be the increased ability of lawyers to provide clear answers to some of the most basic questions of parties involved in commercial transactions utilizing these assets. However, the question remains whether the drafters' careful attention to neutrality as to technology and design will be broad enough to encompass the continuing creativity of the crypto asset markets[82].

[82] During the preparation of this chapter, the authors and contributors discussed the importance of continued vigilance in monitoring and updating the Official Comments to the UCC and, where appropriate, issuing new Permanent Editorial Board (PEB) Commentary, to help mitigate interpretive and practical issues as technology and market practices evolve.

List of Contributors

Australia

Scott Farell, Dr. iur., BEc and LLB (Hons); Adjunct Professor of Law, UNSW Sydney, Australia and Strategic Counsel at King & Wood Mallesons Sydney, Australia.

Max Allan, BEc and LLB (Hons); Partner at King & Wood Mallesons Sydney, Australia.

Brazil

Guilherme C. Hellwig, Dr. iur. (Federal University of Rio Grande do Sul); Legal Counsel, Central Bank of Brazil (BCB); Co-chair of the Legal Subgroup, Tokenization Working Group, BCB; Visiting lecturer in postgraduate law programs at the Advanced School of the Office of the Attorney General of Brazil (ESAGU) and at the University of Vale do Rio dos Sinos (UNISINOS).

Marcus Paulus de O. Rosa, Dr. iur. candidate (State University of Rio de Janeiro); Legal Counsel, Central Bank of Brazil (BCB); Co-chair of the Legal Subgroup, Tokenization Working Group, BCB; Visiting lecturer in the course "Fintechs, Regulation and Competition in Digital Markets" in the LL.M. in Law, Innovation and Technology at Fundação Getulio Vargas (FGV) Rio de Janeiro Law School.

France

Etienne Farnoux, Dr. iur.; Professor of Law, Strasbourg University, France, seconded to Saint Joseph University of Beirut, Lebanon.

Germany

Sebastian Omlor, Dr. iur., LL.M. (NYU), LL.M. Eur.; Professor of Law, Director of the Institute for Law and Regulation of Digitalization (IRDi), Marburg University, Germany.

Hong Kong

Urszula McCormack; Partner, King & Wood Mallesons, Hong Kong.

Mexico

Miguel Gallardo Guerra, LL.M. (NYU), C.J.; Professor of Law, Universidad Iberoamericana, Mexico; Partner, Head of Banking, Finance, FinTech and Compliance Practice, Bello, Gallardo, Bonequi y García, S.C. ("bgbg"), Mexico City, Mexico.

Javier Pérez Moreno; Partner, Head of FinTech, Crypto, Insurance and Compliance Practice, Bello, Gallardo, Bonequi y García, S.C. ("bgbg"), Mexico City, Mexico.

Gustavo Salaiz Gabriel; Professor of Blockchain, Instituto Tecnologico Autonomo de Mexico; Partner, Web23 Advisors, Mexico City, Mexico.

Singapore

Christian Hofmann, Dr. iur. habil., LL.M. (NYU); Associate Professor at the Faculty of Law of the National University of Singapore and the Deputy Director of the Centre for Banking & Finance Law.

Ryan Chan-Wei, LL.M. (Harvard); Adjunct Research Fellow at the Faculty of Law of the National University of Singapore.

Switzerland

Mirjam Eggen, Dr. iur., LL.M. (UBC); Professor of Civil Law, University of Bern, Switzerland.

Dominic Wyss, Dr. iur., LL.M. (UChicago Law); Legal Counsel, Zurich, Switzerland.

Taiwan

Yueh-Ping (Alex) Yang, S.J.D., LL.M (Harvard), LL.M., LL.B. (Nat'l Taiwan U.); Associate Professor of Law, Deputy Director of the Center for Innovative Enterprise Law, National Taiwan University, Taiwan.

Meng-Shiang (Ryan) Lin, Ph.D. (Nat'l Taipei U.), LL.M. (Nat'l Chung Cheng U.), LL.B. (Soochow U.); Associate Professor of Financial Technology and Law, Director of the Department of Financial Technology Applications, School of Financial Technology, Ming Chuan University, Taiwan.

UNIDROIT

Kadir Berk Kapancı, Dr. iur., LL.M. (BİLGİ); Professor of Civil Law, MEF University Istanbul, Turkey.

United Kingdom

Marcus Bagnall, BLaw and Economics, LL.M. (UNSW); Partner at Wiggin LLP London, England.

Ben Towell, BLaw; Senior Regulatory Advisor at Wiggin LLP London, England.

United States

Linda Jeng, J.D. (Columbia Law School), LL.M. Eur. (University of Toulouse); Visiting Scholar on Financial Technology at the Institute of International Economic Law, Georgetown University Law Center, United States; and CEO of Digital Self Labs.

Lewis Rinaudo Cohen, J.D. (Benjamin N. Cardozo), B.A. (Clark University); Partner, Co-Chair of CahillNXT – Digital Assets & Emerging Technology Practice, Cahill Gordon & Reindel LLP, New York.

Rebecca J. Simmons, J.D. (Columbia), A.B. (Harvard); Partner, Head of Payments Practice and Co-Head of FinTech Practice, Sullivan & Cromwell LLP, New York.